Exam	Prentice Hall Title	MCSE Certification Credit	MCSE + Internet Certification Credit	MCDBA Certification Credit	MCSD Certification Credit	MCP + Site Building Certification Credit	MCP + Internet Certification Credit
70-079	*MCSE: Implementing and Supporting Microsoft Internet Explorer 4 by Using the Microsoft Internet Explorer Administration Kit*, Dell, 1999	1 of 2 Elective Requirements	1 of 7 Core Requirements	NA	NA	NA	NA
70-081	*MCSE: Implementing and Supporting Microsoft Exchange Server 5.5*, Goncalves, 1998	1 of 2 Elective Requirements	1 of 2 Elective Requirements	NA	NA	NA	NA
70-085	*MCSE: Implementing and Supporting Microsoft SNA Server 4*, Mariscal, 1999	1 of 2 Elective Requirements	1 of 2 Elective Requirements	NA	NA	NA	NA
70-086	*MCSE: Systems Management Server 2*, Jewett, 1999	1 of 2 Elective Requirements	NA	NA	NA	NA	NA
70-087	*MCSE: Implementing and Supporting Microsoft Internet Information Server 4*, Dell, 1999	1 of 2 Elective Requirements	1 of 7 Core Requirements	1 of 1 Elective Requirement	NA	NA	1 of 3 Requirements
70-088	*MCSE: Implementing and Supporting Microsoft Proxy Server 2*, Ryvkin, 1999	1 of 2 Elective Requirements	1 of 2 Elective Requirements	NA	NA	NA	NA
70-098	*Core MCSE*, Dell, 1998	1 of 4 Core Requirements	1 of 7 Core Requirements	NA	NA	NA	NA
70-175	*MCSD: Designing and Implementing Distributed Applications with Microsoft Visual Basic 6*, Houlette, 1999	NA	NA	1 of 4 Core Requirements and 1 of 1 Elective Requirement	1 of 1 Elective Requirement	NA	NA
70-176	*MCSD: Designing and Implementing Desktop Applications with Microsoft Visual Basic 6*, Holzner, 1999	NA	NA	NA	1 of 1 Elective Requirement	NA	NA

MICROSOFT® CERTIFIED SYSTEMS ENGINEER SERIES

FRANK JEWETT

MCSE:
Systems Management Server 2

ISBN 0-13-017857-8

90000

Prentice Hall PTR, Upper Saddle River, NJ 07458
www.phptr.com

9 780130 178572

Library of Congress Cataloging-in-Publication Data

Jewett, Frank.
      MCSE: Systems Management Server 2 / Frank Jewett.
          p. cm -- (Microsoft certified systems engineer series)
      Includes bibliographical references and index.
      ISBN 0-13-017857-8
      1. Electronic data processing personnel--Certification. 2. Microsoft
      software--Examinations--Study guides. 3. Microsoft Systems management server.
      I. Title. II. Series.

      QA76.3 .J49 1999
      005.7'1--dc21   99-049135

Editorial/Production Supervision: Nicholas Radhuber
Acquisitions Editor: Jeffrey Pepper
Marketing Manager: Bryan Gambrel
Development Editor: Jim Markham
Manufacturing Manager: Maura Goldstaub
Cover Design Director: Jerry Votta
Cover Design: Anthony Gemmellaro
Series Interior Design: Gail Cocker-Bogusz

© 2000 Prentice Hall PTR
Prentice-Hall, Inc.
Upper Saddle River, NJ 07458

All product names mentioned herein are the property of their respective owners.

Prentice Hall books are widely used by corporations and government agencies for training, marketing, and resale.

The publisher offers discounts on this book when ordered in bulk quantities. For more information, contact the Corporate Sales Department, phone: 800-382-3419; fax: 201-236-7141; email: corpsales@prenhall.com or write Corporate Sales Department, Prentice Hall PTR, One Lake Street, Upper Saddle River, NJ 07458.

Use of the Microsoft Approved Study Guide logo on this product signifies that it has been independently reviewed and approved in complying with the following standards:

- acceptable coverage of all content related to Microsoft exam number 70-086 entitled Implementing and Supporting Microsoft Systems Management Server 2;

- sufficient performance-based exercises that relate closely to all required content; and

- technically accurate content, based on sampling of text.

Printed in the United States of America

10 9 8 7 6 5 4 3 2 1

ISBN 0-13-017857-8

Prentice-Hall International (UK) Limited, *London*
Prentice-Hall of Australia Pty. Limited, *Sydney*
Prentice-Hall Canada Inc., *Toronto*
Prentice-Hall Hispanoamericana, S.A., *Mexico*
Prentice-Hall of India Private Limited, *New Delhi*
Prentice-Hall of Japan, Inc., *Tokyo*
Pearson Education Asia Pte. Ltd.
Editora Prentice-Hall do Brasil, Ltda., *Rio de Janeiro*

To my patient wife, Yvette,
and my adorable daughter, Natasha

CONTENTS

PART ONE

Overview   *1*

1

What Is Systems Management Server?   *3*

2

Using SMS to Monitor an Enterprise   *23*

About the Author

Frank Jewett lives in Miami, Florida with his wife, Yvette, and daughter, Natasha.

He works for MicroDesk Corporation. Frank attended St. Thomas University where he received a Bachelor's degree in Management Information Systems, BBA, and Master's in Business Administration, MBA. His certifications include A+ Certified Technician, Microsoft Certified Systems Engineer (MCSE), Microsoft Certified Trainer (MCT), Hewlett-Packard Star Certification, and Novell CNA. Outside of writing and consulting, Frank is a dynamic instructor who brings years of experience to his upbeat training style. He is a recognized industry expert with years of computer sales, support, and training experience. He welcomes comments from readers; his email address is frankj@pocketmail.com.

Acknowledgments

To begin with, I want to thank Microdesk Corp. for giving me the time and opportunity to complete this great project, especially Henry, Mike, and Sulet. I'd also like to thank the Prentice Hall team, specifically Jim Markham, for his relentless pursuit of perfection. Finally I would like to thank the TwoConnect team (Javier and Carmen Mariscal) for their excellent support throughout the project.

Closer to home, my lovely wife, Yvette, and my darling daughter, Natasha, were always there to let me know when a break was needed. I love you both. And finally to my parents who have always believed in me. Thank you all very much.

#	MCSE Requirement for Exam 70-086: Implementing and Supporting Microsoft Systems Management Server 2.0	Prentice Hall Chapter/ Syllabus No.	Related Question(s)
1	Planning Design a Microsoft Systems Management Server (SMS) site; plan for various elements. *Identify location of resources.*	3/3.2 3/3.1	TRUE/FALSE (T/F) T/FQ #8 Multiple Choice Question (MCQ) #4, 5, 6
2	Planning Design a Microsoft Systems Management Server (SMS) site; plan for various elements. *Identify types of resources, which consist of computers, printers, routers, users, and user groups.*	3/3.1 3/3.2	MCQ #4
3	Planning Design a Microsoft Systems Management Server (SMS) site; plan for various elements. Choose features of SMS to be implemented.	3/3.1 3/3.2	MCQ #7
4	Planning Design a Microsoft Systems Management Server (SMS) site; plan for various elements. Identify hardware and software requirements for site systems.	3/3.1 3/3.2	MCQ #6 MCQ #7
5	Planning Design an SMS site hierarchy. Identify the number of layers needed, based on considerations that include: *number and types of resources.*	3/3.1 3/3.2 4/4.3	MCQ #4, 5 MCQ #6
6	Planning Design an SMS site hierarchy. Identify the number of layers needed, based on considerations that include: *network connectivity.*	4/4.1 4/4.3	T/FQ #5

MCSE Requirements Matrix, continued.

#	MCSE Requirement for Exam 70-086: Implementing and Supporting Microsoft Systems Management Server 2.0	Prentice Hall Chapter/ Syllabus No.	Related Question(s)
7	Planning Design an SMS site hierarchy. Identify the number of layers needed, based on considerations that include: *international issues such as language.*	4/4.3	MCQ #9
8	Planning Plan a security strategy for SMS servers. *Implement appropriate SMS accounts.*	5/5.1 5/5.2 5/5.3	T/FQ #1, 8 MCQ #6
9	Planning Plan a security strategy for SMS servers. *Implement access permissions for varying levels of SMS administration.*	5/5.1 5/5.2 5/5.3	Open Ended Question (OEQ) #1 T/FQ #8 MCQ #6, 7
10	Planning *Plan the interoperability or upgrade for various situations.*	6/6.1 6/6.2 6/6.3	T/FQ #2, 3, 4, 6, 7 MCQ #1, 3, 4, 6 OEQ #1
11	Planning *Plan the interoperability of a mixed SMS 1.2 and SMS 2.0 site.*	6/6.1 6/6.2 6/6.3	T/FQ #2, 3, 4, 6, 7 MCQ #1, 3, 4, 6 OEQ #1
12	Planning *Plan the upgrade of an SMS 1.2 site to an SMS 2.0 site.*	6/6.1 6/6.2 6/6.3	T/FQ #2, 3, 4, 6, 7 MCQ #1, 3, 4, 6 OEQ #1
13	Installation and Configuration Install, configure, and modify a primary site server. *Use Express Setup and Custom Setup.*	7/7.1 7/7.2	T/FQ #5, 20

#	MCSE Requirement for Exam 70-086: Implementing and Supporting Microsoft Systems Management Server 2.0	Prentice Hall Chapter/ Syllabus No.	Related Question(s)
13 A?	Installation and Configuration Install, configure, and modify a primary site server. *Install Microsoft Internet Explorer*	4.017/7.2	T/FQ #20
14	Installation and Configuration Install, configure, and modify a primary site server. Configure the Windows NT Server computer that will be the site server.	7/7.1 7/7.2 7/7.3	OEQ #2 T/FQ #6, 7, 17
15	Installation and Configuration Install, configure, and modify a primary site server. Set up SQL Server during SMS setup.	7/7.1 7/7.2 7/7.3	T/FQ #1, 2, 3, 10, 11, 16, 18 MCQ #1
16	Installation and Configuration Install, configure, and modify a primary site server. Use a remote SQL Server computer.	7/7.2	T/FQ #3, 16
17	Installation and Configuration Install, configure, and modify a primary site server. Shut down, reset, and restart the current installation.	7/7.2	T/FQ #6
18	Installation and Configuration Install, configure, and modify a primary site server. *Modify the SMS service account to a different user name or password.*	7/7.1 7/7.2	T/FQ #3, 7, 8
19	Installation and Configuration Install, configure, and modify a primary site server. *Change the SQL Server information.*	7/7.1 7/7.2 7/7.3	T/FQ #8, 19 OEQ #1
20	Installation and Configuration Install, configure, and modify a primary site server. *Remove SMS.*	8/8.1 8/8.2	T/FQ #6

MCSE Requirements Matrix, continued.

#	MCSE Requirement for Exam 70-086: Implementing and Supporting Microsoft Systems Management Server 2.0	Prentice Hall Chapter/ Syllabus No.	Related Question(s)
21	Installation and Configuration Install, configure, and modify a primary site server. *Install new SMS components.*	8/8.1 8/8.2	T/FQ #6 MCQ #1
22	Installation and Configuration Install a secondary site server. Perform the installation from the CD-ROM.	7/7.1 7/7.2	T/FQ #9
23	Installation and Configuration Install a secondary site server. *Perform installation by using files from the network or the CD-ROM.*	7/7.1 7/7.2 7/7.3	T/FQ #11, 19 OE Q #1
24	Installation and Configuration Configure site system roles. Configure component servers.	7/7.1 7/7.2 7/7.3	T/FQ #4, 5, 10, 12, 18, 20 OEQ #1
25	Installation and Configuration Configure site system roles. Configure logon points.	3/3.2 4/4.1	T/FQ #7 T/FQ #7
26	Installation and Configuration Configure site system roles. Configure distribution points.	7/7.1 7/7.3	M/CQ #2, 3
27	Installation and Configuration Configure site system roles. Configure client access points.	4/4.1	T/FQ #7, 8
28	Installation and Configuration Configure site system roles. Configure software metering servers.	7/7.3	T/FQ #11
29	Installation and Configuration Configure site system roles. *Configure the SMS Administrator console.*	7/7.2 7/7.3	T/FQ #12
30	Installation and Configuration Configure a site hierarchy. *Configure site addresses.*	4/4.1 4/4.2	T/FQ #9

#	MCSE Requirement for Exam 70-086: Implementing and Supporting Microsoft Systems Management Server 2.0	Prentice Hall Chapter/ Syllabus No.	Related Question(s)
31	Installation and Configuration Configure a site hierarchy. *Add and configure senders, which consist of Standard, Courier, and RAS.*	7/7.3	T/FQ #13
32	Installation and Configuration Configure a site hierarchy. *Implement parent-child relationships.*	7/7.1 7/7.3	T/FQ #14
33	Installation and Configuration Configure a site hierarchy. *Remove a site from the site hierarchy.*	7/7.2 7/7.3	T/FQ #15
34	Configuring and Managing Resources Configure software and hardware inventory collection for a site. *Enable and configure hardware inventory collection.*	9/9.1 9/9.3	T/FQ #1, 2, 4, 7, 13 MCQ #1 OEQ #1
35	Configuring and Managing Resources Configure software and hardware inventory collection for a site. *Enable and configure software inventory files to be scanned and collected.*	9/9.1 9/9.2	T/FQ #1, 3, 5, 6, 13 MCQ #2, 3
36	Configuring and Managing Resources Manage inventory. *View inventory data*	9/9.1 9/9.2	T/FQ #7 MCQ #1, 2
37	Configuring and Managing Resources Manage inventory. *Use the SMS Administrator console to manage inventory.*	10/10.1 10/10.2 10/10.3	MCQ #3
38	Configuring and Managing Resources Manage inventory. *Customize inventory data.*	1/1.1	T/FQ #1
39	Configuring and Managing Resources Distribute software. *Use SMS Advertisements or Installer to produce custom installation.*	10/10.2	T/FQ #10

MCSE Requirements Matrix, continued.

#	MCSE Requirement for Exam 70-086: Implementing and Supporting Microsoft Systems Management Server 2.0	Prentice Hall Chapter/ Syllabus No.	Related Question(s)
40	Configuring and Managing Resources Distribute software. *Create a query to locate target computers.*	10/10.2	T/FQ #5, 6 MCQ #3
41	Configuring and Managing Resources Distribute software. *Create a collection of target computers.*	10/10.2	T/FQ #6
42	Configuring and Managing Resources Distribute software. *Create a package, program, and advertisement to distribute software.*	10/10.1 10/10.2 10/10.3	T/FQ #7, 8, 9, 10 MCQ #1, 3, 4
43	Configuring and Managing Resources Distribute software. Monitor the software distribution process by using status messages.	10/10.2	T/FQ #8
44	Configuring and Managing Resources Distribute software. Use the SMS client software to run or install a program on a client computer.	10/10.1 10/10.2	OEQ #2 T/FQ #1, 2, 3, 4
45	Configuring and Managing Resources Distribute software. *Remove advertised software from distribution points.*	10/10.2	MCQ #4 T/FQ #9
46	Configuring and Managing Resources Create database reports. *Use Info Crystal Reports to view data and create reports.*	10/10.1 10/10.3	MCQ #2
47	Configuring and Managing Resources Configure and use software metering. *Configure software metering server and client components.*	9/9.2 9/9.1	MCQ #4 T/FQ #8, 9, 10
48	Configuring and Managing Resources Configure and use software metering. *Add products to be licensed.*	9/9.2 9/9.3	T/FQ #8, 9, 10
49	Configuring and Managing Resources Configure and use software metering. Configure licensing options.	9/9.2	T/FQ #9

#	MCSE Requirement for Exam 70-086: Implementing and Supporting Microsoft Systems Management Server 2.0	Prentice Hall Chapter/ Syllabus No.	Related Question(s)
50	Configuring and Managing Resources Configure and use software metering. Exclude products from being metered.	9/9.2	T/FQ #8
51	Configuring and Managing Resources Configure and use software metering. Meter software.	9/9.2	T/FQ #8, 9, 10 MCQ #4
52	Configuring and Managing Resources Configure and use software metering. Manage software metering data.	9/9.2	T/FQ #10
53	Configuring and Managing Resources Configure and use software metering. *Generate reports and graphs.*	9/9.1 9/9.2 9/9.3	T/FQ #10, 13 OEQ #1
54	Integration and Interoperability Install and configure an SMS client computer. Discover clients.	2/2.1 2/2.2	T/FQ #1, 7, 8 MCQ #6
55	Integration and Interoperability Install and configure an SMS client computer. *Configure client setup methods.*	2/2.2	T/FQ #7
56	Integration and Interoperability Install and configure an SMS client computer. Run the client installation.	1/1.1	T/FQ #2
57	Integration and Interoperability Install and configure an SMS client computer. Identify changes made to client.	6/6.1 6/6.3	T/FQ #2, 3, 5, 8 MCQ #1, 2, 3
58	Integration and Interoperability Install and configure remote utilities on clients. Configure Remote Control Agent at the site server.	11/11.1 11/11.2 11/11.4	T/FQ #4
59	Integration and Interoperability Install and configure remote utilities on clients. Configure remote control settings at the client.	11/11.2 11/11.4	T/FQ #1

MCSE Requirements Matrix, continued.

#	MCSE Requirement for Exam 70-086: Implementing and Supporting Microsoft Systems Management Server 2.0	Prentice Hall Chapter/ Syllabus No.	Related Question(s)
60	Integration and Interoperability Install and configure remote utilities on clients. Configure protocols on clients.	1/1.1 11/11.2 11/11.3	T/FQ #3 T/FQ #7
61	Integration and Interoperability Install and configure remote utilities on clients. *Use diagnostic utilities for clients.*	11/11.2 11/11.4	T/FQ #2, 3, 4
62	Integration and Interoperability Install and configure remote utilities on clients. *Use remote tools.*	11/11.1 11/11.2 11/11.4	MCQ #4
63	Integration and Interoperability *Install and configure Windows NT Event to SNMP Trap translator.*	1/1.1 11/11.3	T/FQ #4 T/FQ #8
64	Integration and Interoperability *Install and configure Health Monitor to monitor Windows NT Server computers.*	11/11.4	T/FQ #5, 6 OEQ #1
65	Monitoring and Optimization Identify changes to a site server after SMS installation. Types of site servers: domain controllers.	1/1.1 12/12.3	MCQ #4 T/FQ #9 T/FQ #3, 4
66	Monitoring and Optimization Identify changes to a site server after SMS installation. Types of site servers: nondomain controllers.	12/12.3	T/FQ #4
67	Monitoring and Optimization Identify changes to a site server after SMS installation. Types of site servers are: secondary site servers.	2/2.1 2/2.2 12/12.3	T/FQ #8 T/FQ #5
68	Monitoring and Optimization Monitor SMS status messages. Configure status messages.	1/1.1 12/12.4	T/FQ #2 MCQ #1, 2, 3 T/FQ #6

#	MCSE Requirement for Exam 70-086: Implementing and Supporting Microsoft Systems Management Server 2.0	Prentice Hall Chapter/ Syllabus No.	Related Question(s)
69	Monitoring and Optimization Monitor SMS status messages. *Configure and use SMS Status Message Viewer.*	7/7.1	T/FQ #12, 18
70	Monitoring and Optimization Monitor SMS status messages. *Configure and use SMS logs to monitor SMS process activity.*	7/7.2	T/FQ #16
71	Monitoring and Optimization Monitor the progress of SMS functions. *Monitor the progress of client installation.*	3/3.1 3/3.2 12/12.4 12/12.5	T/FQ #1, 4, 7, 8 MCQ #3, 5, 6 T/FQ #6, 7
72	Monitoring and Optimization Monitor the progress of SMS functions. *Monitor the progress of inventory collection.*	1/1.1 12/12.5	T/FQ #5 T/FQ #8
73	Monitoring and Optimization Monitor the progress of SMS functions. Monitor the progress of software distribution.	1/1.1 12/12.5	T/FQ #6 T/FQ #7
74	Monitoring and Optimization Monitor the progress of SMS functions. Monitor the progress of remote control.	7/7.2 7/7.3 12/12.3 12/12.5	MCQ #1 T/FQ #9
75	Monitoring and Optimization Monitor the progress of SMS functions. Monitor the progress of software metering.	4/4.1	T/FQ #9
76	Monitoring and Optimization Use SMS utilities to monitor SMS functions. Use the Windows NT Event Viewer to view SMS error messages.	7/7.2	T/FQ #12, 17
77	Monitoring and Optimization Use SMS utilities to monitor SMS functions. Use the Status Message Viewer to monitor SMS components and processes.	7/7.1 7/7.2 7/7.3	T/FQ #4, 5, 10, 12, 18, 20 OEQ #1

MCSE Requirements Matrix, continued.

#	MCSE Requirement for Exam 70-086: Implementing and Supporting Microsoft Systems Management Server 2.0	Prentice Hall Chapter/ Syllabus No.	Related Question(s)
78	Monitoring and Optimization Use SMS utilities to monitor SMS functions. Use Network Monitor to view and filter network traffic.	12/12.1	T/FQ #2 MCQ #3, 4, 8
79	Monitoring and Optimization Use SMS utilities to monitor SMS functions. Use Network Trace to trace the SMS network.	7/7.3	T/FQ #11, 19
80	Monitoring and Optimization Use SMS utilities to monitor SMS functions. Use SMS Trace to track and view log files.	14/14.1 14/14.2	T/FQ #3, 6
81	Monitoring and Optimization Optimize SQL Server for SMS.	1/1.1 13/13.5	T/FQ #8 MCQ #4
82	Monitoring and Optimization Optimize sender network utilization.	2/2.2 4/4.1 4/4.2 4/4.3	T/FQ #9 MCQ #1, 8
83	Monitoring and Optimization Monitor the SMS database. Configure SMS database maintenance tasks.	1/1.1 12/12.6	T/FQ #7 T/FQ #10
84	Monitoring and Optimization Monitor the SMS database. Back up and restore the site database.	14/14.1 14/14.2	T/FQ #2, 4
85	Monitoring and Optimization Back up an SMS site.	14/14.1 14/14.2	T T/FQ #2, 4, 5, 6 MCQ #5 OEQ #1

#	MCSE Requirement for Exam 70-086: Implementing and Supporting Microsoft Systems Management Server 2.0	Prentice Hall Chapter/ Syllabus No.	Related Question(s)
86	Troubleshooting *Choose the appropriate diagnostic tool.*	13 /13.3	T/FQ #11, 12, 13, 14, 15, 16, 17, 18, 19 MCQ #3 OEQ #1
87	Troubleshooting Diagnose and resolve installation problems in SMS site systems. *Diagnose and resolve installation problems involving the primary site server.*	14/14.1 14/14.2	T/FQ #6 MCQ #3
88	Troubleshooting Diagnose and resolve installation problems in SMS site systems. *Diagnose and resolve installation problems involving the secondary site server.*	9/9.1 9/9.3 13/13.1 13/13.3 13/13.4	T/FQ #7, 12 T/FQ #7, 8, 9, 10, 11 MCQ #3 OEQ #1
89	Troubleshooting Diagnose and resolve installation problems in SMS site systems. Diagnose and resolve installation problems involving client access points.	9/9.1	OEQ #1
90	Troubleshooting Diagnose and resolve installation problems in SMS site systems. Diagnose and resolve installation problems involving distribution points.	13/13.1 13/13.3 13/13.5	T/FQ #7, 8
91	Troubleshooting Diagnose and resolve installation problems in SMS site systems. Diagnose and resolve installation problems involving logon points.	13/13.4	T/FQ #8

#	MCSE Requirement for Exam 70-086: Implementing and Supporting Microsoft Systems Management Server 2.0	Prentice Hall Chapter/ Syllabus No.	Related Question(s)
92	Troubleshooting Diagnose and resolve installation problems in SMS site systems. Diagnose and resolve installation problems involving: component servers.	13/13.3 13/13.4	T/FQ #9, 15, 16
93	Troubleshooting *Diagnose and resolve installation problems involving clients.*	13/13.1 13/13.2 13/13.3 13/13.4	T/FQ #1, 2, 3, 4, 5, 6 MCQ #1, 2 OEQ #1, 2
94	Troubleshooting *Diagnose and resolve problems involving software distribution.*	11/11.1 11/11.4	T/FQ #6
95	Troubleshooting *Diagnose and resolve problems involving inventory collection.*	9/9.1 9/9.3	T/FQ #1, 2, 3, 4, 5, 6, 7, 12, 13 MCQ #1, 2, 3 OEQ #1
96	Troubleshooting *Diagnose and resolve problems involving remote control.*	13/13.1 13/13.2 13/13.3 13/13.4	T/FQ #5 MCQ #1, 2, 4
97	Troubleshooting *Diagnose and resolve problems involving software metering.*	9/9.2	T/FQ # 8, 9, 10 MCQ #4
98	Troubleshooting *Diagnose and resolve problems involving SNMP integration.*	9/9.1	T/FQ #14
99	Troubleshooting Restore an SMS site: *Restore a SQL Server.*	14/14.1	T/FQ #1, 2, 3 MCQ# 1, 2, 3, 4, 5 OEQ #1

#	MCSE Requirement for Exam 70-086: Implementing and Supporting Microsoft Systems Management Server 2.0	Prentice Hall Chapter/ Syllabus No.	Related Question(s)
100	Troubleshooting Restore an SMS site: *Restore a site server.*	14/14.2	T/FQ # 5, 6 MCQ # 5 OEQ #2
101	Troubleshooting Restore an SMS site: Restore logon points.	14/14.1 14/14.2	T/FQ #7
102	Troubleshooting Restore an SMS site: Restore client access points.	14/14.1 14/14.2	T/FQ # 8
103	Troubleshooting Restore an SMS site: Restore distribution points.	14/14.1 14/14.2	T/FQ #9
104	Troubleshooting *Diagnose and resolve problems involving site-to-site communication.*	13/13.1 13/13.2 13/13.3 13/13.4	T/FQ #8, 10

So, you want to be a Microsoft Certified Systems Engineer? You've come to the right place, or book I should say! Greetings, and welcome to *MCSE: Systems Management Server 2.*

This book is a step-by-step study guide to prepare for Microsoft Certified Professional Exam 70-086. It provides system administrators and engineers with the knowledge and skills required to effectively plan, install, configure, administer, integrate, monitor, troubleshoot, and use Microsoft System Management Server (SMS), version 2.0 within your enterprise environment. The book gives an in-depth description of how to use SMS to monitor the enterprise; design SMS sites; create an SMS site hierarchy; develop an SMS security strategy plan; choose the right interoperability/upgrade plan; establish the primary SMS site; configure and modify the SMS site; configure, audit, and control network clients with SMS; manage the SMS system model; install and configure the SMS network; integrate the SMS network; monitor SMS; optimize SMS; diagnose and resolve SMS problems; and restore SMS sites. It also covers various management functions such as remote diagnostics, metering, inventory, and software distribution. More importantly, this book prepares you to meet the certification requirements to become a Microsoft Certified Systems Engineer.

Each chapter in the book concludes with a summary and a set of review questions that test your knowledge of MCSE exam-specific issues. A combination of true/false, multiple-choice and open-ended questions are used. The book includes two appendices that contain answers to chapter review questions and a glossary.

Who This Book Is For

This book is primarily targeted toward domestic and international system managers, network administrators, system and network integrators, system engineers, and support personnel who need to optimize and maintain enterprise networks using SMS. Basically, the book is targeted to all types of professionals and organizations around the globe who have the responsibility of supporting and implementing SMS in local and wide area network environments. More importantly, this book was developed for those who plan to take the related MCSE exam 70-086, "Implementing and Supporting Microsoft Systems Management Server 2.0."

You will come away from this book with an in-depth knowledge of the following MCSE exam-specific main components of what SMS provides to allow it to grow with any size enterprise:

- Year 2000 compliance checking
- Server health monitoring
- Software program removal
- Introduction of new wizards, status tools, canned reports, query tools, and security configurations
- Support of more environments like: Windows NT 4.0, Windows 2000, Novell Netware, Alpha platform, and SMS 2.0
- Remotely controlling and troubleshooting client computers
- Monitoring enterprise computers and network traffic
- Performing software management and distribution
- Collecting custom inventory information
- Querying the SMS database
- Exploring SMS Utilities and creating SMS alerts
- Configuring SQL Server for optimum SMS results
- Using Performance Monitor and Event Viewer monitoring tools

Furthermore, you will come away with extensive experience provided by hands-on exercises (in addition to your hands-on training experience with SMS) that provide the practical experience needed to install and configure SMS. This intermediate-to-advanced comprehensive MCSE SMS 2.0 study guide helps you install and use SMS to create enterprise solutions like:

- Practical tips on how to utilize SMS as a help desk tool, install Windows NT 4.0 system services, and monitor performance.
- How to execute SQL queries against SMS inventory for strategic business planning and plan and administer distributed SMS sites.
- How to use SMS to control an enterprise network using client auditing, software distribution, and remote troubleshooting.
- How to use latest SMS 2.0 features in preparation for the exam.

What You'll Need

This book provides the core foundation for supporting Microsoft Windows NT Primary/Backup Domain Controller, Windows NT Member Server (must be a member of a domain), Windows NT Server, LAN Manager, Novell Netware 3.x Bindery, and Novell 4.x Netware Directory Services. Therefore, you should have a working knowledge and have taken related courses pertaining to operating systems, such as Microsoft Windows NT 3.51, 4.0, and 2000; Windows 95 and Windows 98; Windows 3.1 or higher; and Windows for Workgroups 3.11 or higher.

Hardware Requirements for Exam

As a prerequisite for the exam, you should also have a working knowledge of the following SMS 2.0 hardware requirements:

- 133MHz Pentium processor
- 64 MB of RAM minimum (128 MB recommended)
- 1 GB of free disk space on an NTFS partition
- 100 MB of free space on the system drive
- Access to any CD-ROM drive supported by Windows NT Server 4.0 Service Pack 4

Software Requirements for Exam

You should also a have a working knowledge of the following software requirements:

- Fresh install (recommended) of Windows NT 4.0, Service Pack 4
- Internet Explorer 4.01

The following software is on the Systems Management Server 2.0 CD-ROM:

- Microsoft Internet Explorer 4.01
- Windows NT 4.0 Service Pack 4
- SQL Server 6.5 / Service Pack 4 or SQL Server 7.0
- Microsoft Management Console
- Systems Management Server 2.0
- SMS 2.0 Service Pack 1 (recommended)

How This Book Is Organized

This self-paced study guide combines hands-on training, notes, and review questions to instruct the reader on how to implement and support SMS 2.0 on Windows NT 4.0 and Windows 2000. The book is organized into seven parts and includes two appendices, one of which is a glossary of SMS terms and acronyms. It also has an MCSE Exam 70-086 Requirements Matrix in the front of the book that cross-references all the MCSE requirements to the chapter syllabus numbers and related questions at the end of each chapter.

The book provides a step-by-step approach to everything you need to know about SMS 2.0 as well as information about many topics relevant to the planning, design, and implementation. The book gives an in-depth overview of the latest SMS 2.0 features. It discusses what background work needs to be done, such as developing an SMS 2.0 installation plan, and shows how to develop these plans for all types of organizations. More importantly, this book shows how to install primary and secondary sites, along with the techniques used to test them. It covers many of the common troubleshooting maintenance issues as well as the ongoing ones. The book concludes with a discussion about how to restore an SQL Server, a site server, logon points, client access points, distribution points, and diagnose and resolve problems involving site-to-site communications.

Descriptions of the different sections of the book follow.

Part 1: Overview

The introductory part of the book is a discussion about what SMS provides. The discussion centers around such MCSE exam-specific issues as ease of use, integrated and centralized management, its scalable solution, support for heterogeneous environments, and its open architecture. The part concludes with a discussion of SMS sites by examining the following components: considerations for implementation hierarchies and sites, domains, servers, clients, and SMS server services.

Part 2: Site Planning

Part 2 begins with an overview of site planning by performing the following tasks: configuring your environment to provide additional computer support; checking client and server system requirements; creating user accounts and login IDs; configuring SQL Server on a remote computer if it is not installed on the site server; and configuring clients. Next, it discusses the various elements of the design of an SMS site, such as site system resources; location of resources; types of resources, which consist of computers, printers, routers, users, and user groups; and features of SMS to be implemented. Furthermore, Part 2 clarifies which MCSE exam-specific design components are needed to upgrade client operating systems at an SMS site; design the SMS site hierarchy model prior to installation for the enterprise; design the SMS security strategy plan prior to installation for the organization; upgrade an SMS site to a newer version; and plan the interoperability of a mixed SMS 1.2 and 2.0 site.

Part 3: Installing and Configuring SMS Server

Part 3 covers how to install SMS and how to add clients to the database in your SMS system. It also describes the client's view of configuring, modifying, and navigating the SMS, as well as the administrator's, site.

Part 4: Configuring and Managing Resources

This part begins by taking a look at how to test for Year 2000 compliance and how to automatically collect information on personal computer configurations. It concludes by taking a close look at how to use Crystal Reports to view data and create reports.

Part 5: Interoperability of an SMS Network

This part examines numerous areas, including the use of diagnostic utilities for clients, client experience during remote control, and how to configure a remote control agent at the site server.

Part 6: Monitoring and Optimization

This part of the book examines the essentials of administering a distributed network. It also shows how to configure SMS database maintenance tasks.

Part 7: Troubleshooting

Finally, Part 7 shows how to directly monitor and control your inventoried computers by taking you through the SMS 2.0 Diagnostic and Help Desk utilities. The book concludes by taking a peek at how to use the Internet to perform a number of management tasks with SMS.

Appendices

Two appendices provide the additional information. Appendix A contains the chapter review answers. In Appendix B, you find a glossary of SMS-related terms and acronyms.

Conventions Used In This Book

This book uses different features to help highlight key information.

Chapter Syllabus

The primary focus of this series is to address those topics that are to be tested in each exam. Therefore, each chapter opens with a syllabus that lists the topics to be covered. Each topic directly corresponds to the level-1 headings in the chapter. So, if there are six level-1 headings in a chapter, there will be six topics listed under the chapter syllabus. There may be instances when the topics are not exam specific. In these cases, the chapter syllabus area is empty, and level-1 heads do not correspond to exam topics.

Icons

Icons represent called-out material that is of significance, either as additional information or as important warnings. Icons include:

MCSE

`MCSE  xx.xx` MCSE Title Here

This layout is used to identify MCSE-specific chapter syllabus topics and appropriate MCSE sections in each chapter.

NOTE

This icon is used to call out information that deserves special attention; one that the reader may otherwise run a highlight marker through.

TIP

This icon is used to flag particularly useful information that will save the reader time, highlight a valuable technique, or offer specific advice.

WARNING

 This icon flags information that may cause unexpected results or serious frustration.

Study Break Sidebars

These sidebars are used to highlight related information, give an example, discuss an item in greater detail, or help you make sense of the swirl of terms, acronyms, and abbreviations so prevalent in this field. The sidebars are meant to supplement each chapter's topic. If you're in a hurry on a cover-to-cover read, skip the sidebars. If you're quickly flipping through the book looking for juicy information, read only the sidebars.

Chapter Review Questions

Each chapter ends with a series of review questions. These questions are designed to simulate a part of an actual exam and to reinforce what you have just learned. The number of questions will vary depending on the length of the subject matter of the individual chapter. All the questions are taken directly from the material covered in the chapter, and the author's answers can be found in the Appendix.

About the Companion Web Site

There's a companion Web site with this book. The Prentice Hall Companion Web site is located at http://www.phptr.com/phptrinteractive. The Companion Web Site contains some of the following information.

Practice Questions

This critical area contains at least ten multiple choice questions per chapter with hints and coaching comments to aid you in your learning. These questions are *not* the same ones found in the book. A *hint* provides a reference to where in the book the answer is, and *coaching comments* are utilized as a way to connect the book with the site. For hints or coaching comments, chapters and sections are referred to as the source for information about the question.

Message Board

This is a place where you can post information relating to the content of the book. The Message Board can provide usable feedback about the challenges you have utilizing the workbook and companion Web site. It is a place for open dialog (unmoderated) and is a viable way to gauge the nature of conversations among the users of the workbook series.

Scholars.com

This is a page that can be accessed from the home page. On this page, scholars.com courses that relate to this book are listed.

Overview

Part One discusses what SMS provides, such as: integrated and centralized management; a scalable solution; support for heterogeneous environments; an open architecture; and ease of use. This first part of the book also provides a snapshot of the following SMS advantages: a comprehensive solution to manage your networked PCs; integration with your existing systems; and an open scalable foundation that can be extended easily.

Next, there is a discussion of the main components of SMS: software and hardware inventory collection; distribution of software; sharing software applications; troubleshooting remotely; and working with mixes of networks of various sizes. This section also instructs you on what you will need to work with SMS.

Finally, this part focuses on viewing the software inventory, which is the baseline on which all other SMS features are built to monitor the enterprise.

This concludes by discussing SMS and examining the following components: hierarchies and sites; domains; servers; clients; SMS server services; and considerations for implementation.

What Is Systems Management Server?

As organizations move to distributed client/server systems, one of the biggest challenges is managing these types of systems. Thousands of desktop PCs in numerous locations worldwide must be maintained by large businesses; IT resources must be stretched to the limit by medium-sized organizations; and small businesses can't afford outside services, let alone in-house resources.

All of these needs are addressed by Microsoft® Systems Management Server (SMS), version 2.0. It is a comprehensive solution for centrally managing personal computers on a network of any size. It enables network administrators to send key information back to a central database, detect every machine on the network, and inventory software and hardware configurations.

This MCSE study guide is intended to help you prepare for Microsoft's certification Exam 70-086, "Implementing and Supporting Microsoft Systems Management Server 2.0." In doing so, it should also serve as an easy reference for discovering how SMS functions, how it is implemented or installed, and how it can help you improve the management of your desktop computers. Working from a business perspective so that you may see how it applies to your environment, step-by-step instructions, and user scenarios will give you insight and an introduction to the main components and capabilities of SMS 2.0.

To complete the MCSE exam-specific requirements in this book, if you're already using SMS 2.0, go straight to "What's New in System Management Server 2.0?" found at http://www.microsoft.com/smsmgmt/guide/. If you're not already using SMS, look at "System Requirements for 2.0" at the same URL.

URLs, as well as requirements, features, and components, are subject to change without notice.

Overview of Systems Management Server

A lot of money is being spent today by businesses to upgrade, maintain, and support software on desktop computers. As previously mentioned, large businesses are burdened with trying to maintain thousands of desktop PCs that may be located all over the world. Medium-sized businesses have a variety of systems that are often distributed over several locations. These medium-sized businesses usually have limited Information Technology (IT) expertise. While small businesses are recognizing the value of desktop PCs, they don't have the money or the knowledge to maintain them, and hiring outside consultants is often too expensive.

Data collected by the GartnerGroup indicates that the capital cost of acquiring personal computers for a networked environment is approximately 21% of the total cost of ownership over the five-year life cycle of the computers.[1] The typical cost of ownership for a Windows®-based personal computer over five years is shown in Figure 1.1.

The vast majority of the cost is for support, administration, and operations. According to Microsoft, SMS should allow you to start to reduce dra-

---

1. *Total Cost of Ownership; Reducing PC/LAN Costs in the Enterprise.* GartnerGroup corporate headquarters, 56 Top Gallant Road, Stamford, Connecticut, 06904, February 1996.

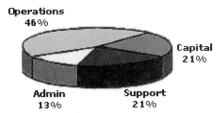

Figure 1.1   *Total Cost of Ownership—Reducing PC LAN Costs in the Enterprise.*

matically the cost of managing your distributed desktop PCs. In short, SMS provides centralized management tools for effective management of your computing resources.

According to Microsoft, whether you are migrating to Windows NT 4.0 or upgrading other system features, you can also save time and cost on remote administration and installation (see Figure 1.2).[2] For example, you can simply click an icon at your central console to find out the software

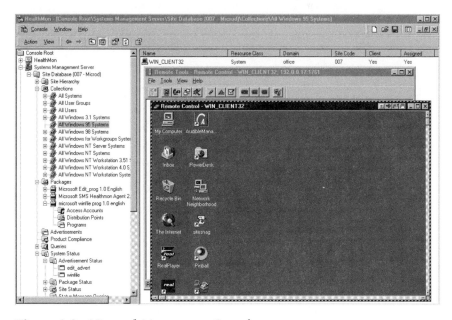

Figure 1.2   *Microsoft Management Console.*

---

2. Copyright © 1998 Microsoft and/or its suppliers, One Microsoft Way, Redmond, Washington 98052-6399 U.S.A. All rights reserved.

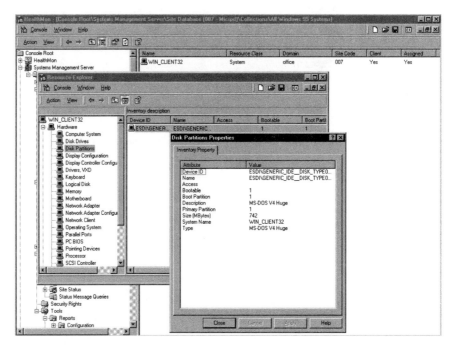

Figure 1.3   *Remote Tools / Remote Control Utility.*

inventory and configuration of a particular machine. You can perform remote troubleshooting by taking over a user's workstation screen, mouse, and keyboard to get configuration information, execute applications, or help the user through the proper use of new software (see Figure 1.3).

Network Monitor can detect bottlenecks and reroute traffic as shown in Figure 1.4. As a result, you can increase network efficiency and reliability.

Is SMS Unique?

A number of servers on the market today perform some of the services that IT professionals require to manage their desktop PCs. These work only in specific environments, however, and tend to have limited functionality. SMS provides:

- Integrated and centralized management
- A scalable solution
- Support for heterogeneous environments
- An open architecture
- Ease of use

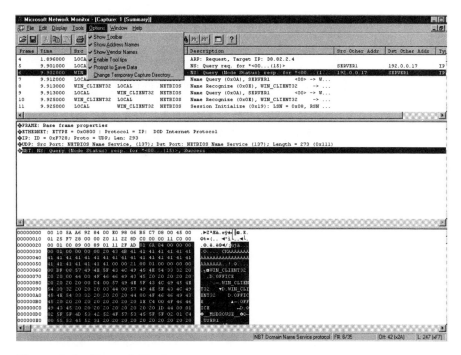

Figure 1.4 *Network Monitor.*

CENTRALIZED AND INTEGRATED MANAGEMENT

SMS utilizes a resource discovery process to find devices within its site boundary, including every PC on the network. SMS performs software and hardware inventory, software distribution, remote controlled diagnostics, and troubleshooting. All of this is accomplished from one central location (Primary Site) and with one package.

SCALABLE SERVER

Utilizing SMS's distributed design to balance many management functions, it's no surprise that it works with ease on small or large networks. Also, the ability for you can change the structure of your network without having to reinstall your management solution is what makes SMS so flexible.

HETEROGENEOUS ENVIRONMENTS SUPPORT

Since SMS supports leading client and server operating systems, it can work in most existing environments. Also, you can now manage your operating systems from any location on the network, because SMS supports these systems across most popular wide area network (WAN) and local area network (LAN) protocols.

OPEN ARCHITECTURE

So that you can easily extend the inventory information stored in the SQL Server database, SMS uses Management Information Format (MIF) files. This allows easy access by any Open Database Connectivity (ODBC) program that can communicate with the database. In addition, to extend the provided information, you can write to the Application Program Interface (API) of SMS. Windows NT/2000 event log records (system, security, application) can be converted to industry standard Simple Network Management Protocol (SNMP) traps, SMS can even integrate with any SNMP network management product.

EASE OF USE

By installing management servers at one central location (site) and periodically checking on the status of the network, SMS makes life easier for an administrator. SMS *system status node can monitor* and warn the administrator if a process is not running correctly. In addition, SMS can automatically identify different types of resources, including every PC on the network, collect inventory, and install the client (client installation) management agents. All of this is done from one central location (site) or various locations (sites).

Resolving Problems with SMS

Systems management on mainframe computers has been available for quite some time now. It consists of managing operating systems (like OS/2, DOS, Windows, or UNIX®), managing the data, and managing applications. It also performs other tasks, such as scheduling system events, making sure there is enough capacity, and charging different departments for computer time. Systems management typically means local management in this environment. In other words, everything is inside one computer room or, in the case of a large company, two or three computer rooms around the world. Thus, fully automated or *lights out* management has been achieved with this approach.

Nevertheless, systems management has lagged behind as businesses have deployed more and more personal computers. Managing distributed environments that are spread throughout many locations has created new problems, even though some basic issues have remained the same. For instance, an administrator is concerned with version control of many different systems, including user administration and automation of repetitive tasks for a large number of systems. Furthermore, the management of configuration files may be different on every computer. Also well known is the problem of simply locating all the PCs within an enterprise. Even more difficult is determining the hardware and software within each computer. Usually this is done during nonworking hours to not disrupt the user. In a large distributed enterprise, these procedures can take months to accomplish. In addition, installing and upgrading software on all desktops has its own associated problems. For example, such problems involve making sure that the versions are correct and that the computers are capable of running the new software.

As you know, things can go wrong with even the most comprehensive plan. To ensure that a computer is not unavailable for any length of time, you need tools to locate and diagnose problems. Equally important is the diagnosis and resolution of problems from a central location, thereby reducing the cost of managing your systems. In other words, in your existing environment, all these problems need to be resolved today and in the future as your business requirements change.

Let's take a look at what types of businesses can benefit from the problem-solving solutions of SMS.

Turning Problems into Benefits

SMS can help any company that has the need to manage networked desktop PCs, especially those running Windows. From the very small to the very large, SMS has been designed to integrate easily with a wide range of businesses. The following are some typical environments for which SMS can provide a complete solution to most system administration problems.

SMALL BUSINESSES

Often, small businesses have no skilled IT professionals on staff. Usually a staff member who is computer literate helps out the other staff members. The company calls its local service provider to come onsite when upgrades are needed or troubleshooting is required. This is an ideal environment for SMS. Normally a single site system can be installed and managed by the service provider, providing dial-up remote access to diagnose and resolve various computer problems and to perform routine maintenance.

MEDIUM BUSINESSES

Medium-sized businesses often consist of a central office with a number of remote offices. The IT staff is usually responsible for supporting all locations and is based at the central office. The deployment of a central SMS site is an ideal management solution in this type of environment. The site would manage both the central office and all the remote offices. It would be linked by existing telecommunication lines or by simple asynchronous dial-up link— the universally familiar analog public telephone system in which dial-up connections are established to provide voice communication links. This network is still of major significance as a platform for data transmissions via modem or facsimile. Therefore, without sending someone to each office to troubleshoot and perform maintenance tasks, the communications link allows the central office to manage all remote sites.

In some cases various primary sites can be linked to the central site if remote location WAN link is a slow connection with many clients on the remote side.

DOMAIN CONTROLLERS

Primary domain controllers (PDC) are (first-tier site servers) that are used by a specific set of sites for logon authentication. The name and size of these master user domains are many times determined by geographic limitations, network topology, and the number of accounts to be supported by the medium-sized business. For example, the PDC for the master user domains for Europe, North America, and South America could be located in Europe. Others could be located near the constituent user population where local data centers provide administrator resources. A backup domain controller (BDC) for the master user domain is located at each respective remote site for authentication of accounts at that site. For instance, the European master user domain PDCs could be physically located in England, with a BDC for the appropriate European master user domain located in each respective European site. In addition, a BDC for the global master user domain could also be physically located at each network hub site worldwide.

LARGE BUSINESSES

Large businesses usually have many offices spread throughout a wide geographical area. Each office would have its own IT staff to perform support and maintenance for local users. Deploying SMS primary sites in each office enables IT resources to provide their own centralized functions. All offices report to the central IT group in the main office. This means that there is one centrally located record of all the computers within the enterprise.

Now that we've looked at some of the problems that can be resolved with SMS, let's examine its key components or major features.

Microsoft and Management

Through the Zero Administration Initiative for Windows, Microsoft is committed to making the Windows operating system the best-managed platform and the best environment from which to manage the enterprise. Microsoft has specified four objectives in order to achieve this goal:

1. Build and develop infrastructure for Windows that allows programmatic control of critical components and makes management information available. Infrastructure components include the Web Based Enterprise Management instrumentation and Microsoft Management Console.

2. Provide configuration management and basic data security in the operating system. Today, the basic services that come as part of the Microsoft Windows NT Server 4.0 operating system include security management; user and policy administration; backup and restore; and review of basic performance and operational data. Microsoft IntelliMirror™ configuration management is in Windows NT Server 2000.

3. Make available sophisticated management solutions such as SMS for managing applications and Windows-based systems. Also, many third parties provide management applications for Windows-based systems that complement SMS.

4. By exposing interfaces and services that these applications can use, integrate both management and infrastructure management solutions with enterprise management platforms.

MCSE 1.1 SMS Key Components and Features

SMS 2.0 has a number of new features or components. These provide comprehensive benefits to computer professionals dealing with the cost and complexity of building, maintaining, and managing distributed networks of PCs.

Components and Benefits at a Glance

SMS allows you to perform a variety of management tasks ranging from monitoring the integrity of the network to identifying how many computers you have on your network. The main components of SMS are as follows:

- Software and hardware inventory collection
- Distribution of software
- Troubleshooting remotely
- Working with mixed network environments of various sizes

SOFTWARE AND HARDWARE INVENTORY COLLECTION

SMS allows the administrator to process an inventory collection (resource discovery) to automatically build a master database of computer hardware and software. Once this data is collected, it can be used to perform a number of administrative tasks, such as identifying systems that need bios upgrades or hard drives that are almost full to capacity. Administrators can determine how many computers they have in the organization or figure out how many copies of a software application are installed.

To provide you with specific data requirements SMS has predefined queries or you can build custom queries to your needs using Query Builder Tool. for example, a query can display a list of all PCs with 64 MB of memory and Windows NT 4.0 SP4 installed. These are very powerful tools to collect and analyze resources.

DISTRIBUTION OF SOFTWARE

A major cost to organizations with distributed networks is software maintenance. Often a support engineer must configure, install, and upgrade each computer manually. Using SMS from a single and central location, you can configure, install, and upgrade each computer remotely. Also, at specified times, you can schedule and distribute individual software files or complete software applications to specific computers. SMS even allows you to initiate automated, unattended distribution of software to selected computers. This can be performed during off-hours when the majority of users have gone home.

TROUBLESHOOTING REMOTELY

SMS allows you to remotely control the screen, keyboard, and mouse of a client's desktop. You can also remotely restart a client, run commands at a client (i.e., run the client installation), or even transfer files directly to a client.

The client's parameters can be monitored by the SMS diagnostic capabilities. For example, you can monitor memory use and client environment variables. The Network Monitor tool also allows you to perform general network analysis, perform checks on the integrity of communications links, monitor traffic statistics on remote or local area network (LAN) segments, and capture packets. Network Monitor can now automatically interpret what it finds, making it a valuable tool for administrators, whether or not they have an extensive knowledge of packet decoding. Real-time monitors and postcapture experts have been added to Network Monitor to make it more intelligent in analyzing data. These include monitoring for rogue DHCP servers, duplicate IP addresses, and attempted Internet break-ins.

Your organization can minimize the number of onsite support visits by the use of these remote troubleshooting capabilities. This makes it possible for the same number of technicians to support a growing number of resources.

Working with Mixes of Networks and Various Sizes

By strategically placing Windows NT 4.0-based computers throughout an organization, SMS can be implemented across different sizes of networks. Therefore, it is not necessary to make any actual modification to your organization's physical network.

The leading client and server operating systems are supported by SMS. Support is provided across popular WAN and LAN protocols and through configuring these protocols on clients. This allows you to manage your SMS system from any location on your network.

In every network environment, not every SMS feature is available on all supported clients. For more information on the latest client systems requirements and client features, refer to http://www.microsoft.com /smsmgmt/guide/. Remember, system requirements are always subject to change without notice (see Part 2, "Site Planning," for extensive system requirement considerations).

What's New, at a Glance

The following new features, components, or enhancements are incorporated in the latest release of SMS 2.0:

- Remote control for Windows clients
- CIM-based hardware inventory
- Software metering
- More-specific distribution targeting
- Server health monitoring
- New network topology tracing tool
- New Network Monitor experts

- Support for Novell NetWare Directory Service environments
- Event to Trap Translator
- New network analysis tools
- Crystal Reports 6
- Sender bandwidth controls
- Forced update of package distribution servers
- Added extensibility
- Performance

REMOTE CONTROL FOR WINDOWS CLIENTS

You can now remotely control computers running the Windows Operating system. The same user interface and integration is available for Windows NT 4.0-based computers as it is for other supported clients. Also, all of the Diagnostics and Help Desk options are provided.

The ability to specify a list of administrators who can remotely control a client is an additional feature, although the user at the client ultimately determines whether or not one of the specified administrators can perform remote control. The user also determines the extent of the Help Desk options available.

CIM-BASED HARDWARE INVENTORY

Microsoft is supporting the Common Information Model (CIM) information from multiple sources, such as SNMP, DMI, and the Microsoft Win32 application programming interface. Microsoft has built Windows Management Instrumentation, which is CIM-compliant, into the Microsoft Windows NT version 4.0 operating system and Windows 2000 operating system environments. Microsoft Systems Management Server 2.0 has been designed to collect data in a CIM format. This means that it has access to data from many sources, including Win32, SNMP, and DMI, and administrators have greater collection of inventory information available. Given the large number of inventory objects, filtering options have been added so that an administrator can choose which data is most important.

SOFTWARE METERING

SMS 2.0 provides new tools to analyze, monitor, and control the use of applications on servers and workstations. The administrator has many levels of control, ranging from simple alerts to actively preventing applications from running. This control can be exercised over specific applications with quota limits defined by the administrator, or any application that is not specifically allowed by the administrator. Any application on any client or server can be monitored for compliance. The administrator can predefine a quota for a particular application. As users launch applications, the system checks to see if the quota has been exceeded.

EVENT TO TRAP TRANSLATOR

Support for the Simple Network Management Protocol (SNMP) is now provided by SMS. Windows NT 4.0 events to SNMP traps can now be mapped. To alert administrators of other management systems of the event, these traps can now be forwarded to them, but not necessarily SMS. Also, the Event to Trap Translator can be installed on all SMS clients running Windows NT 3.51/NT4/2000.

MORE SPECIFIC DISTRIBUTION TARGET

Systems Management Server 2.0 provides specific options for targeting software distribution. In addition to targeting machines (as in version 1.2), Systems Management Server 2.0 can now distribute to any combination of the following: Users, User groups, TCP/IP network segments, Machines.

This allows applications to be sent in a more directed manner. For instance, a particular Windows NT based user group could be sent a software patch that was only relevant to that group, or all machines in a network segment could be sent a printer driver pertaining to the printer in that segment.

SERVER HEALTH MONITORING

A server monitoring tool known as HealthMon is a completely new feature in Systems Management Server 2.0. It is designed to provide critical performance information on processes in Windows NT Server and Microsoft BackOffice Server.HealthMon uses information provided by CIM, allowing administrators to set critical or warning thresholds.

NEW NETWORK TOPOLOGY TRACING TOOL

Systems Management Server 2.0 delivers a new network topology tracing tool that makes systems management tasks network aware. This new feature provides a graphical display of the network routes between servers within a site, including the activity of the infrastructure devices (such as routers and hubs) connecting those points. It also displays the status of services on servers between those points. This allows for easy analysis of the potential success or failure of an action such as software distribution to a remote location.

EXTENDED SOFTWARE AUDITING

The customizable audit database that allows you to identify installed software applications has been extended. This database now comes preconfigured to identify more than 8,000 software applications. You simply run a query, and the software applications referenced in the file are detected automatically for you.

SUPPORT FOR NOVELL NETWARE DIRECTORY SERVICE ENVIRONMENTS

Systems Management Server 2.0 adds support for Novell 4.x NetWare Directory Service environments to existing support for Novell 3.x bindery and Windows NT-based server environments.

NEW NETWORK ANALYSIS TOOLS

The Network Monitor tool has been enhanced to provide support for the network driver interface specification (NDIS) 4.0 or later and for a number of new protocol parsers. Network Monitor also includes additional functionality such as the ability to obtain statistical information about who is consuming the most bandwidth on your network (using experts). It also includes the ability to determine what protocols on your network are consuming the most bandwidth and how your network is being used.

IMPROVED DATABASE MAINTENANCE

The Database Manager utility includes additional functionality such as the ability to display a list of duplicate computers that can be deleted from the database. It also includes the ability to view the list of duplicate computers and then delete information for a computer or merge the information of two computers together. The ability to delete by date historical collected files is also included.

CRYSTAL REPORTS 6.0

SMS includes a single-user, runtime version of Crystal Reports 6.0. With this application, you can retrieve and correlate information in the database and present this information in report format. Crystal Reports 6.0 allows you to save data in a number of formats including Microsoft Excel, Rich Text Format, and HyperText Markup Language (HTML). Crystal Reports is a product of Crystal Computer Services, Inc. Microsoft does not provide support services for Crystal Reports. You'll need to contact Crystal Reports Technical

Support for help or choose About Crystal Reports from the Help menu in the Crystal Reports application.

SENDER BANDWIDTH CONTROL

You can control sender and address-based bandwidth use by using the Sender Manager. You can also specify the estimated link speed and the percentage of the link to be used for a selected site server.

FORCED UPDATE OF PACKAGE DISTRIBUTION SERVERS

SMS supports guaranteed updates to packages on distribution servers. Previously, the delivery of the package could potentially fail if any file contained in an SMS package was being used during the delivery of an update to that package. You can now configure the Windows NT 4.0 Server Registry to force disconnection of files in use during package delivery. To do this, you can specify the number of retries before a forced disconnection takes effect and the amount of time to elapse after notification of a disconnection.

ADDED EXTENSIBILITY USING MICROSOFT MANAGEMENT CONSOLE

Now, through the SMS Administrator, you have direct access to third-party applications. Through the SMS Microsoft Management Console, you can also access SMS tools such as the Security Manager and Service Manager, as well as some of the Windows NT 4.0 administrative tools. See the Microsoft BackOffice Software Development Kit for information about extending the SMS Administrator.

PERFORMANCE ENHANCEMENTS

To help you and the client users of SMS, the overall speed and performance of SMS version 2.0 has been improved. In particular, this enhancement provides quicker processing of event and job-related information and faster processing of database information.

■ Summary

Microsoft has recently made available Systems Management Server 2.0 Service Pack 1. SMS 2.0 reduces total cost of ownership by centrally managing Windows operating system-based networks. It delivers the most comprehensive solution for Windows management through software distribution, hardware and software inventory, remote diagnostics, and software metering.

This release delivers key Zero Administration Initiative for Windows features by exploiting new management infrastructure components, providing better ease-of-use facilities, ensuring greater scalability, extending the existing features of SMS 1.2, and adding new functionality for SMS 2.0.

You should come away from this chapter with an in-depth knowledge of the following MCSE exam-specific highlights of what SMS provides:

- Integrated and centralized management
- A scalable solution
- Support for heterogeneous environments
- An open architecture
- Ease of use

You should also now have a general knowledge of how to solve business problems—which is what systems management is all about—with SMS for organizations of any size. SMS provides you with the following advantages:

- A comprehensive solution to manage your networked PCs
- Integration with your existing systems
- An open scalable foundation which can be easily extended

SMS also allows you to perform a variety of management tasks ranging from monitoring the integrity of the network itself to identifying how many computers you have on your network. The main components of SMS are as follows:

- Collection of software and hardware inventory
- Distribution of software
- Troubleshooting remotely
- Integration with different networks of various sizes

You'll need to have specific and detailed knowledge of what you need to work with SMS. The system requirements are not limited to the fact that SMS 2.0 has been designed to collect data in a CIM format. Not only does this help with Windows98 and Windows NT 2000 environments, but SMS is also able to use this architecture to get information out of all 32-bit Windows operating systems. This means that SMS 2.0 has access to data from many sources, including the Microsoft Win32® application programming interface, SNMP, and DMI.

Finally, you need to understand that the system's distributed, balanced design allows changing the structure of the network as you grow without having to reinstall your system management solution. With that in mind, you'll be set for today and for the future.

▲ CHAPTER REVIEW QUESTIONS

▲ True/False

1. *True or False? To provide you with company-specific data, you can extend the inventory database information by creating customized queries. For instance, you can run queries that request type of operating system and bios date. When the inventory is run, this customized information is collected and added to the standard inventory data.*

2. *True or False? By installing management servers from one central location and periodically checking on the status of the network, SMS makes life easier for an administrator. SMS writes an event to warn the administrator if a process is running correctly.*

3. *True or False? The leading client and server operating systems are supported by SMS. Support is provided across popular WAN and LAN protocols and through configuring those protocols on clients. This allows you to configure or manage your SMS system from any location on your network.*

4. *True or False? Support for the Simple Network Management Protocol (SNMP) is now provided by SMS. Windows NT events to SNMP traps can now be mapped. To alert administrators of other management systems of the event, these traps can now be forwarded to them as well as SMS. Also, the Event to Trap Translator can be installed on all SMS clients running the Windows NT operating system, version 3.51 or later.*

5. *True or False? SMS does not allow you to automatically build a master database of computer software and hardware details.*

6. *True or False? A major cost to organizations with distributed networks is software maintenance. Often a support engineer must configure, install, and upgrade each computer manually. Using SMS from a single and central location, you can install, monitor, upgrade, and configure each computer. Also, at specified times, you can distribute individual software files or complete software applications to specific computers, schedule the distribution, and monitor the progress. SMS even allows you to initiate automated, unattended distribution of software to selected computers. This can be performed when the majority of users have gone home during off-hours.*

7. *True or False? SMS installation has been combined with Microsoft SQL Server™ installation to obtain the highest optimization possible to dramatically ease the setup required for SMS. Without removing any of the flexibility*

of choosing where to install SQL Server, the setup options intelligently install and configure SQL Server in preparation for SMS. Further, SMS can now be hosted on any Microsoft Windows NT® operating system-based Member Server, removing the previous PDC/BDC requirement.

8. *True or False? Types of site servers are domain servers.*

▲ Multiple Choice

1. *SMS 2.0 delivers a status system that provides a common reporting mechanism for all components. This results in the following except:*
    A. Messages representing activity flow in the system, such as packages and advertisements
    B. Windows NT 4.0 Event conversion into CIM events
    C. Automated consolidation of status messages
    D. Powerful filtering for storage and forwarding
    E. Windows NT 4.0 Event conversion into SMS events

2. *SMS adds a status system node that provides a common reporting mechanism for all components. This results in the following except:*
    A. Messages representing activity flow in the system, such as packages and advertisements
    B. Automated consolidation of status messages
    C. Complex filtering for storage and forwarding
    D. Windows 98 conversion to SMS events
    E. Windows NT 4.0 Event conversion to SMS events

3. *Persistent Status Summaries are provided in conjunction with Crystal Reports. Summaries are available for the following except:*
    A. Site
    B. Component
    C. Package
    D. Advertisement
    E. Data

4. *Which of the following is a Server Role minimum requirement:*
    A. Windows 2000
    B. Windows NT version 4.0, Service Pack 4
    C. SQL Server 6.5

    D. Windows NT 4.0 Primary/Backup Domain Controller

    E. Windows 95 and 98

5. *The following are clients that are supported by SMS 2.0 except:*

    A. Windows NT Server 4.0

    B. Windows 95 and Windows 98

    C. Windows 3.1

    D. Windows for Workgroups 3.11

    E. Windows NT Workstation 3.51 and 4.0

6. *The following are network operating systems that are supported by SMS 2.0 except:*

    A. Windows NT Server 4.0

    B. LAN Manager

    C. Crystal Reports Server

    D. Novell 4.x NetWare Directory Services

    E. Novell NetWare 3.x Bindery

▲ Open Ended

1. What are the five primary functions of SMS?

Using SMS to Monitor an Enterprise

Working within just about any enterprise, from the smallest to the largest, Systems Management Server (SMS) version 2.0 is designed to be scalable from the ground up. Every component is designed to be multithreaded, modular, and distributed.

Version 2.0 is designed to support even larger environments than version 1.2. A number of improvements have been made to the basic architecture that prevent possible bottlenecks from occurring. This allows SMS to work in enterprises of any size.

Brief instructions on how to use the following SMS components are examined in the second part of this chapter of the study guide: sites, domains, servers, clients, and services. There are many key components that allow SMS to grow with any size enterprise, and those will be covered in Chapter 4, "SMS Site Hierarchy."

Each component plays a specific role in the distribution of software, in sharing software applications, in troubleshooting remotely, in working with mixes of networks with various sizes, and with software and hardware inventory collection. The first part of this chapter will focus on viewing basic resource discovery (Hardware and Software inventory)—the baseline on which all other SMS features are built to monitor the enterprise.

MCSE 2.1   Viewing Software and Hardware Inventory

The basis on which all other features of SMS are built is the resource discovery or inventory. You need to know what resources, computers, software and users you have including the configurations of those resources before you can use the SMS system to manage and support your network.

SMS provides the enterprise with the ability to view inventory for all computers included in the site boundary. As each computer is added to SMS discovery process, hardware inventory is collected automatically (see the Study Break Sidebar, "Collecting Hardware and Software Inventories with SMS 2.0").

Once inventory has been gathered from each client, hardware and software data is placed on the SMS server database. In addition, the SMS service at the primary site server periodically determines (at intervals set by administrator) what hardware and software changes have taken place since the last time the inventory data was collected, especially after the initial hardware and software data has been collected. Any new information that comes in is updated automatically in the database.

Inventory information for the entire SMS system is passed up the site hierarchy to the central site. A primary site database stores the inventory and system information its own site and for all sites beneath it. Secondary sites do not have their own database (use the primary site's database). The inventory for a secondary site is stored at its parent site.

Inventory Tools and Data Use

From the inventory information that has been collected and stored, SMS allows the user to perform a number of common management tasks. Along with the specific SMS inventory feature the user can use to achieve them, Table 2.1 lists the types of tasks that can be performed.

INVENTORY DATA VIEWING

You should have the primary site server and at least one other computer in the database to view the inventory data. When you install SMS, the site server

Table 2.1 *Performing Different Types of Tasks*

Task	Description	Feature
Viewing Inventory Data	Go to the appropriate site using the SMS Administrator. Identify the site, using collection node choose client type. This will enable you to look at the data in the database.	After Resource Discovery then use Resource Explorer
Locating Inventory Data	A number of predefined queries are provided for your convenience. You can query the inventory data to find the data that match criteria you set in order to quickly locate specific information stored in the database.	Collection / Queries / Resource Explorer
Gathering Application Software Details	Go to the appropriate site using the SMS Administrator. Identify the site, using collection node choose client type. Search for specific software from specific clients and look at details for software installed on clients.	Collections / Queries / Resource Explorer

is automatically added. See Chapter 11, "SMS Network Installation and Configuration," for information on how to add clients to the database.

HOW TO VIEW INVENTORY DATA • First bring up the SMS Administrator screen (see Figure 2.1). From the SMS Administrator toolbar, perform the following tasks as shown in Figure 2.1.[1]

1. Select site and expand node
2. Select Collections node and expand node
3. Choose predefined collection or create a new one
4. Once collection is complete, choose client on detail right pane
5. Using mouse, right-click selected client and run Resource Explorer

The Resource Explorer window displays the details for the selected computer (client). You will see several items in the window, each of which display different information related to the selected computer. Also, as new clients are collected their information is added to the SMS database, you can

---

1. Copyright © 1998 Microsoft and/or its suppliers, One Microsoft Way, Redmond, Washington 98052-6399 U.S.A. All rights reserved.

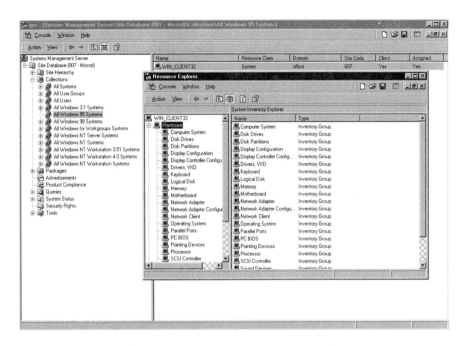

Figure 2.1 *SMS Administrator Screen to View Inventory Data.*

then scroll through various collection to find newly discovered resources on your network.

HOW TO LOCATE SPECIFIC INVENTORY DATA • To locate information in the database, create and run queries. For instance, you can create and run a query so that it finds all the computers in your SMS system with based on a specific criteria. You can also limit the query to find computers in a set of sites or subsites. Additionally, you can identify any property for a resource, computer, users and machines, such as the network address of the network adapter card or the installed software.

WHAT IS AN SMS 2.0 QUERY? • A query allows an administrator, using SMS functions such as collections node, to find information in the site database. All the data stored in the site database can be queried, including specific information pertaining to computer resources, computers (using Windows 16-bit and Windows 32-bit clients), software distribution, sites, users, and groups. A query is made up of an simple expression or multiple expressions conveyed using the new WBEM Query Language (WQL). Queries are executed against a site database in order to retrieve data. Using the WBEM schema, the SMS Provider retrieves all data in the site database tables that meet the criteria defined in the expression. The result of a query run from Query Builder Tool is reported in the SMS Administrator console.

There are many options for configuring queries. For example, you can create a query and save it for later use, or you can create a query that is run immediately. When the queries are run, you can specify that they prompt for information. For instance, before a query is run, you could create a query that prompts for the computer operating system to be entered. The query can also be specified as a target for a Run Command on a Workstation. SMS queries define and store the criteria for sets of database objects that you want to find. When used against an SMS site database, a query is a specific set of instructions that extract information about a defined set of objects. You can create queries and store them in the SMS site database. By running a query, you search the database for information about the objects that match the query criteria.

The results of a query can also be used to trigger SMS alerts (a warning signal). You can use the results to create groups of computers. These computers are then targeted for software distribution such as an operating system upgrade.

The following set of tasks shown in Figure 2.2 describe how to create a query to determine which clients in the SMS system are running Windows NT Workstation as their operating system and have Greater than 32 MB memory installed. To create, edit, save or run this query, you have to perform the following set of tasks from the SMS Administrator:

1. Select site and expand node
2. Select Queries node and expand node
3. Click on predefined Query to edit or create a new one
4. Using Query Builder tool set criteria for client
5. Once completed, Save query and run to get results

The Query Statement Properties dialog box appears as shown in Figure 2.3. The criteria or rules that you set for evaluating the query are displayed by the Query Statements Properties dialog box. Expressions make up the rules. Each expression is an instruction to search for items that have a specified relationship to an attribute and a value. As indicated by the following, you can run, edit predefined queries, or create your own query with an AND operator and two expressions:

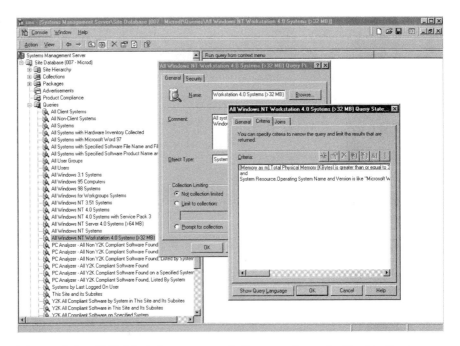

Figure 2.2 *SMS Administrator console Query node can be Used to Create and Save a Query to Locate Computers Running Windows NT Workstation and that Have Greater than 32 MB Memory Installed.*

```
[memory as m].Total Physical Memory[KBytes] is greater than
or equal to 31000
```

AND

```
System Resource.Operating System Name and Version is like
'Microsoft Windows NT Workstation 4.0%'
```

The dialog box has the fields and buttons shown in Table 2.2.

You are now ready to view the following settings shown in Figure 2.3. In the field across from element Query Name is:

```
Windows NT Workstations
```

Now, in the field across from the Comment element is:

```
Query to find Windows NT Workstation
```

Table 2.2 *Query Properties Dialog Box Buttons and Fields*

Element	Description
Query Name	A unique name that identifies the query.
Comment	Text that describes the query. This text is displayed in the Queries window.
Object Type	Before you begin defining a query, you must choose which object type you are looking for. Seven predefined object types exist in the SMS database. In most cases, you will query the System Resource object type, which defines computers, but it is possible to run queries against the other object types as well.
Collection Limitating	Limit the query to a collection, instead of the entire site database

Now, the object type field is:

```
system resources
```

Click on the edit query statement button. The Query Statement Properties dialog box appears (see Figure 2.4). The Query Statement Properties dialog box has three tabs (General, Criteria, and Joins) the General Tab section is described in Table 2.3.

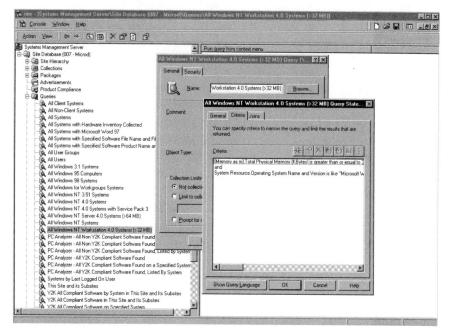

Figure 2.3 *Using Query Node to right click and edit Query Properties.*

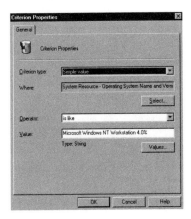

Figure 2.4   *Query Properties Dialog Box.*

Table 2.3   *Query Statement Properties (General tab)*

Element	Description
Find Object Type	Omits duplicate rows
Results	Provides more descriptive detail for the group. The class consists of three elements: the name of the organization that defined the group, a group name that describes the contents of the group, and the version number. For example, the class for disk drives is MICROSOFT|DISK|2.0.
Show Query Language	Provides the property of a group. Each attribute is assigned a value. The set of attribute values for a group comprises the inventory for that group. For example, a Disk group on a computer with an architecture of Personal Computer has attributes such as Disk Index, Serial Number, % Disk Full, and so on.

Select the following record from the Query Criteria Tab dialog box as shown in Figure 2.5.

```
System Resource.Operating System Name and Version is like
'Microsoft Windows NT Workstation 4.0%'
```

Since this query is predefined, double-click on the expression to expand the criterion dialog shown in Figure 2.5.

In the Operator box:

```
'is like.'
```

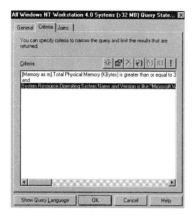

Figure 2.5 *Query Expression Properties Dialog Box.*

Table 2.4 *Query Statement Properties (Criteria tab)*

Element	Description
Criteria Type	The criterion type indicates what you will compare the attribute to. It may be, for example, a simple value or a null value. Your choice of criterion type determines what types of comparison values can be part of the expression. For example, the **Subselected values criterion type allows you to define a query based on the results of another query**
Where	The attribute class and attribute for the expression appears in the "Where" field. Clicking **Select displays the Select Attribute dialog box. From this dialog box, you select the attribute class and attribute. You may also choose to create an alias for the attribute class from the Select Attribute dialog box.**
Operator	When you choose an attribute, the possible relational operators are displayed. The type of relation depends on the type of value to which the attribute is being compared. Simple values are numeric, string, or date/time.
Value	The actual string value

In the Value box:

```
Microsoft Windows NT Workstation 4.0
```

If any changes are made in the criterion dialog they will appear in the Query Criteria Tab dialog box with the results of the expression displayed as shown in Figure 2.5.

Double-click on the second expression to view its criteria.

```
[memory as m].Total Physical Memory[KBytes] is greater than
or equal to 31000
```

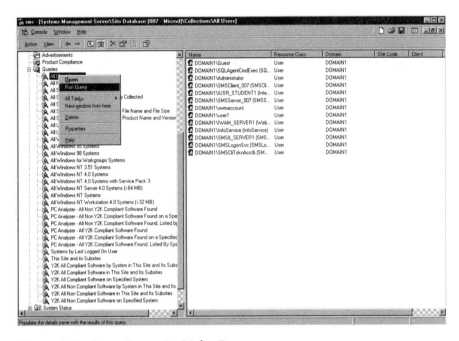

Figure 2.6 *Query Properties Dialog Box.*

Table 2.5 *Query Statement Properties (joins tab)*

Element	Description
Attribute Class Joins	Combine data from two attribute Classes. System resources, etc. . . .
Show Query Language	You can edit the query statements in WQL

Click OK in the criterion dialog and return to the Query Statement Properties dialog box. The query is displayed in the Query window.

This procedure can be used edit or create new queries. As was shown in the simple exercise above queries can be used to create simple or very complicated expression. By combining many expressions together using Add AND and Add OR, you can create very complex queries.

So, how do you run a query using the SMS Administrator Console? Let's take a look.

HOW TO RUN A QUERY USING THE SMS ADMINISTRATOR • To run queries using the SMS Administrator, perform the following tasks.

1. Select site and expand node.
2. Select Queries node and expand node .
3. Click on predefined Query (or one you've created) and right click then run query.
4. On the right pane your results should appear.

The Query Results window appears, listing all the resources that meet the criteria set out in the query. This is shown in Figure 2.7.

APPLICATION SOFTWARE DETAILS: THE COLLECTION

Software inventory provides two inventory services: inventory collection and file collection. Inventory collection writes file information (such as file size, modification date, and manufacturer) to the SMS site database. File collection places inventoried files in a directory on the site server and provides the administrator with access to the file through the SMS Administrator console's Resource Explorer snap-in.

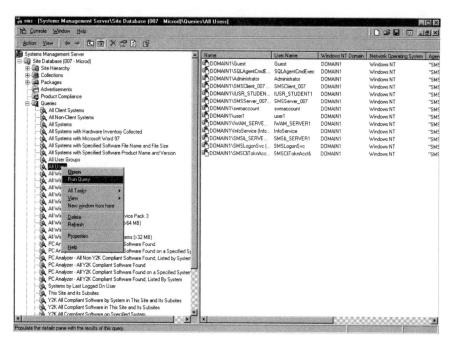

Figure 2.7 *SMS Administrator Screen to View Inventory Data.*

SMS inventory collection is very simple to use and highly configurable. By using the SMS Administrator console, you are not only able to specify what kind of information should be collected, you control how and when inventory should run on the client computer. Hardware and software inventory collection is configured by selecting the Client Agent node (remember client agents must be setup before resource discovery can take place) in the SMS Administrator console, then accessing the properties of the Hardware Inventory Client Agent and the Software Inventory Client Agent.

THE SOFTWARE INVENTORY CLIENT AGENT • The CIM Object Manager running on Windows 32-bit clients is not involved in the software inventory process. So software inventory collection is similar on Windows 16-bit and Windows 32-bit client computers. When the software inventory client agent runs, it attempts to collect the following information from files it has configured, through the SMS Administrator console, to inventory:

- File name, size, description, and time of creation
- Company and product name
- Product version and language

All the software data is sent to site server from the client unlike in hardware collection were Windows 32-bit clients keep data copy on local client system. Some software inventory information cannot be collected if the file doesn't contain the data sought by the inventory client agent. For example, if the file header does not include product version information, this data cannot be collected. Executable files, which are files with EXE or COM extensions, are most likely to contain file header information identifying the characteristics of the file. Therefore, software inventory provides the most information when these files types are read by the Software Inventory Client Agent. By default, once the Software Inventory Client Agent is enabled in the SMS Administrator console, it will inventory all files with EXE extensions. Files with COM extensions are not included because they are less common than files with EXE extensions. Any file or file type can be inventoried by adding the file name or file type to the Inventory Collection tab in the SMS Administrator console. Inventory data collected by the Software Inventory Client Agent is sent to the CAP (Client Access Points). A CAP can be a server running Windows NT/2000, Netware Bindery Server, or a Netware NDS Server in addition to the actual Primary Site. Once the data are collected it is added to the site server database by a thread of the SMS Executive Service.

To instruct the Software Inventory Client Agent to collect files from the client computer, file names or file types are added to the File Collection tab in the SMS Administrator console. The Software Inventory Client Agent collects the files and appends the collected files to software inventory collection data sent to the CAP. The CAP forwards the software inventory to the site server and the site server separates software inventory collection data from collected files. The software inventory collection data are added to the site database and collected files are stored on the site server's hard disk. The site server maintains the five most recent versions of collected files from each client computer. Thus it contains an archive of file changes, which makes it easy to track changes and recover previously saved versions of a collected file. This entire process is automatic and invisible to the end user. Remember a collection and almost all other functions of SMS can be schedule to run at any time.

Table 2.6 *When to Use Inventory Software Data*

Use Inventory Collections to…	Use File Collections to…
Find file size, modification date, and manufacturer	Find inventoried files in a directory on the site server
Look for specific programs that are on client computers	Capture files for later use
Gather software information to do software upgrades	Examine software that can be causing corruption on client side
Check what user has added any additional software (programs, games, etc. . .	

SOFTWARE INVENTORY COLLECTION • The settings under the Software Inventory Client Agent—Inventory Collections tab are used to modify the data retrieval characteristics of software inventory collection. File types (application files, EXE by default) or file names are inventoried based on the settings under this tab. The level of product reporting detail is also configured from the Inventory Collections tab. File reporting details are categorized by known products, files associated with known products, and files not associated with known products.

To gather file reporting details, the Software Inventory Client Agent reads the header of the files you instruct it to collect. Known product information includes company name and product name, product version, and product language. For known products, renaming a file to be inventoried will not conceal the identity of the file. If the Software Inventory Client Agent is configured to report on files associated with known products, it will collect information on files that support the product, such as dynamic link libraries. If product information cannot be determined by inspecting file header data, software inventory can still be collected, but the software will not be categorized by manufacturer in the site database.

The settings under the Software Inventory Client Agent—File Collection tab are used to configure the file names or file types that should be collected and sent to the site server.

File names longer than the 8.3 format can be specified on computers that support long file names (LFN). File names using wildcards other than *.* can be used for file collection. Using wild cards for file collection or collecting large files from client computers is not advisable, since doing so can quickly fill up the site server's hard disk. In most cases, only small files should be collected. However, you can control the maximum amount of data that may be collected on each client computer by file collection.

VIEWING SOFTWARE INVENTORY

You can view software inventory on a per-computer basis through the Collection node. To do so, first use the SMS Administrator console as shown in Figure 2.8:

1. Open Site.
2. Look for Collections node.
3. Click Collections node to expand.

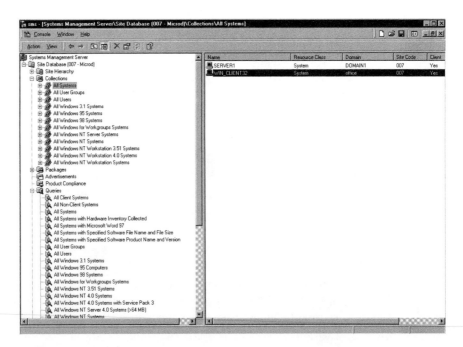

Figure 2.8 *SMS Administrator Console.*

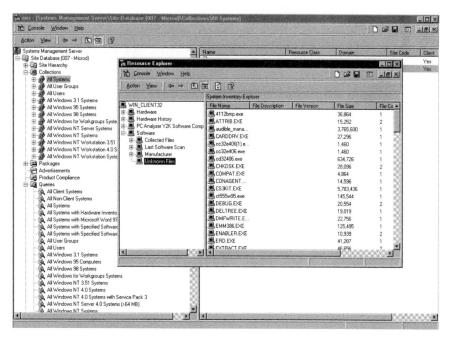

Figure 2.9 *Resource Explorer Window.*

4. Choose the criteria for the collection.
5. Right-click on the computer (right pane) and run Resource Explorer.
6. In the Resource Explorer, choose software node.

The Resource Explorer Properties (Software node) window appears like the one shown in Figure 2.9, displaying information about the selected computer. The right pane displays the software detected for the selected computer. The attributes of this pane are described in Table 2.7.

Table 2.7 *Personal Computer Properties Window Attributes*

Attribute	Description
Software Name	The name of the software found.
Path	The full path to the directory where the first file defined in the package is located.
Size	The size of the first file defined in the package.
Date	The date and time of the first file defined in the package.

SCHEDULE A SOFTWARE COLLECTION

At a time specified by you, discovery of resources allows you to scan for multiple software applications on targeted computers. You typically schedule a collection of specified system then run a query using the collected resources. This could occur at relatively infrequent periods, however—for example, every four months or every seven months.

HOW TO VIEW SOFTWARE DETECTED ON A COMPUTER • View software on a computer from the SMS Administrator console by following the steps shown in Figure 2.8:

1. Choose Site.
2. Choose the Collections node and correct system.
3. From the results right window, choose client.
4. Right-click and run Resource Explorer.

The Resource Explorer Properties (Software node) window appears, displaying information about the selected computer in Figure 2.9.

Study Break

A Deeper Look at Collecting Hardware and Software Inventories with SMS 2.0

CIM-Based Hardware Inventory

As part of the Web-Based Enterprise Management (WBEM) initiative, Microsoft is supporting the Common Information Model (CIM) specification developed by the Desktop Management Task Force. This provides a common way of presenting management information from multiple sources, such as the Microsoft Win32 application programming interface, SNMP, and DMI. Microsoft is building CIM into the WindowsNT2000 and Windows98 operating system environments.

SMS 2.0 has been designed to collect data in a CIM format. Not only does this help with Windows98 and Windows 2000 environments, but SMS also uses a CIM-based agent to get information out of all 32-bit Windows operating systems. This means that SMS 2.0 has access to data from many sources, including Win32, SNMP, and DMI. Administrators have a much richer collection of inventory information available in Figure 2.10.

Filtering options have been added, given the large number of inventory objects. This means that an administrator can choose which data is most important.

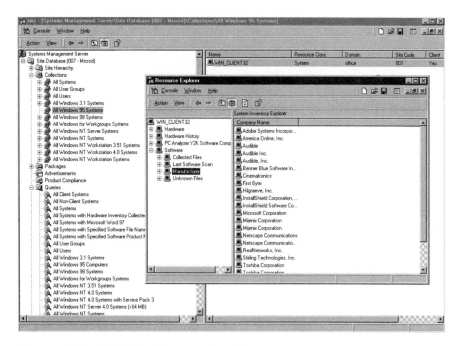

Figure 2.10 *SMS Administrator Console.*

Discovery-Based Software Inventory

Software inventory information is collated centrally. This way the administrator can quickly see which applications from which vendor are installed on which systems.

To provide better software inventory, SMS 2.0 searches for version resource information on every executable on the client machine, rather than checking against a predefined database. This provides a dynamic and efficient way of getting detailed information on every application on every PC.

MCSE 2.2 · Working with SMS Sites

This part of the chapter discusses working SMS sites and examines the following components:

- Site Boundary
- Hierarchies and Sites
- Domains
- Servers
- Clients

- SMS Server Services
- Considerations for Implementation

The first step, is to decide which servers and client computers will make up a site. A site is categorized by resource boundaries based on network segments (IP subnets or IPX networks). A site should never span a low-speed or unreliable network connection. Will the entire network be a single site or have multiple sites? Will the sites be divided based on geographic or logical location? Will all servers and computer resources be part of a site? What site system roles will various computers play in the site design (Secondary site, CAP servers, logon servers or Software Distribution Server?

As data is gathered in the assessment of current environment, list the computers that could be made available to SMS as site systems. A site system is a Windows NT/2000 Server computer, a NetWare NDS Server, or a Net-Ware bindery Server that plays a role in the site. There are nine different site system roles in an SMS site. Each one has different requirements with respect to the microprocessor, RAM, hard disk space, and operating system.

Hierarchies and Sites

Figure 2.11 illustrates a site hierarchy with four sites: the Houston site at the top and three additional sites each representing a group of servers and computers at different geographical locations. Sites take on specific roles—central, primary, or secondary—in an SMS site hierarchy.

To store SMS information for the computers in a primary site, the site must have its own SQL Server. This primary site must also include all the computers in sites beneath it in the hierarchy. To directly manage its own site and all the sites beneath it, the primary site must also have all SMS administrative components installed.

The central site is the primary site at the top of a site hierarchy. The central site is created when you install SMS. The central site stores system-wide information. From this site you can view all sites and computers in your SMS system. After the central site has been created, you create additional primary sites using the SMS Setup program.

SMS lets you organize your existing network structure into logical groupings called sites. Sites can large and complex containing many SMS servers. Typically, a site is used to group computers located in a single geographical area.

Your SMS system can consist of one large single site from which you can manage all computers or you can also reduce network traffic between physical sites, create multiple sites (a site hierarchy) to represent the structure of your organization, or split management duties between sites. Based on your organizational and managerial needs, SMS allows you to build a site hierarchy.

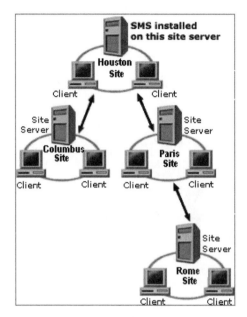

Figure 2.11   *Site Hierarchy.*

A site without an SQL Server of its own is known as a secondary site. For processing and storage, it forwards information to its primary site. A secondary site does not have administrative tools and must be administered through its primary site. In addition, any primary site (including the central site) can have a secondary site connected to it as described in Table 2.8.

Table 2.8 *Description of Sites*

Sites at a Glance	Definition
Central	The primary site at the top of the site hierarchy created when you install SMS. Only one central site exists and must have SQL Server database setup.
Primary	A site that has an SQL Server database and SMS administrative tools for managing the site and its subsites.
Secondary	A site without an SQL Server database. Subsites cannot exist under a secondary site. Any primary site can create a secondary site—including the central site.
Parent	Any site that has a subsite. A primary or a secondary site can be a subsite.
Child	Any site that has a parent site. A secondary site is always a child site. A child site can be a subsite. However, a subsite cannot exist under a child site. When there is another primary site above it, a primary site is a child site.
Subsite	A site beneath another site in the site hierarchy.

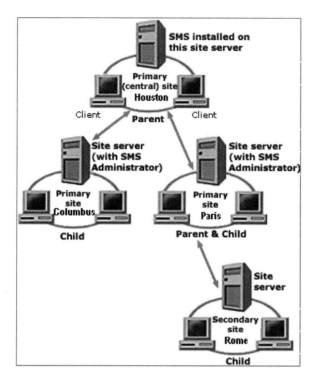

Figure 2.12   *Site Hierarchy Showing Primary and Secondary Sites.*

Figure 2.12 illustrates some of the parent/child relationships of sites.

Any SMS site that has a site beneath it is a parent site. A primary site or a secondary site can be beneath a parent site. Data are passed up through each parent site to the central site. Additionally, any site that has a parent site is also a child site as shown in Figure 2.12.

You must configure one or more senders for each site to enable each site to communicate with the central site, as well as its parent and child sites. To transmit instructions and data from one site to another (such as reporting inventory information or installing software on clients in another site), SMS uses a sender (a Windows NT component). The LAN Sender is available and runs on the site server by default. Other senders, such as the remote access service (RAS) sender and the systems network architecture (SNA) sender, must be added by using the SMS® Administrator. You must also define the address of the receiving site for each sending site. Thus, an address contains specific information used to connect to another site.

Domains

In addition to sites, SMS uses domains as a means of further grouping computers for management purposes. At least one domain is always contained in a site: the domain of the Windows NT Server-based computer. SMS can be installed on a (PDC) Domain server or a member server. Often SMS is installed on a member server for performance since the PDC is busy with logon authentications.

PDC Domain server must be on the same LAN (segment) as the primary site server. You can choose to automatically add all the additional logon servers in the domain to your SMS system to network reduce traffic. The clients that are logged on to the servers in the SMS site boundary are added to the SMS system by resource discovery and later having the setup program run automatically through the client logon script.

Figure 2.13 illustrates how each of the sites shown in Figures 2.11 and 2.12 can further divided to include SMS sites. To perform logon validation for SMS clients, each SMS site must have a network logon server.

Servers

Servers can perform many roles in an SMS site. There are several possible site server roles. All of the roles can be assigned to the primary site server, or they

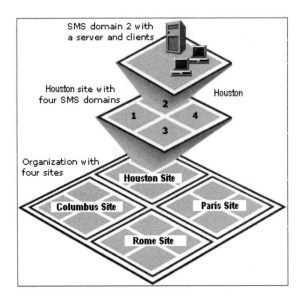

Figure 2.13 *SMS Sites with different geographical locations.*

can be spread out over several different site server systems. Some of the roles are assigned during installation, and others are assigned through the SMS Administrator console.

Site Servers can be classified as *Site system server, CAP (Client Access points) Server, Logon point server,* and *Distribution server.* A computer running Windows NT Server that is configured as a primary or backup domain controller is can also be a site server. For one site of up to 3,000 clients, a single site server running Windows NT Server and SQL Server can perform all SMS-based tasks. Server-based tasks should be divided among the site server and the other types of servers to distribute server load for larger organizations.

 As long as the site server has access to that computer, you can install SQL Server on a separate computer.

An SMS logon server acts as the intermediary between the site server and client computers. It functions as a transfer point between clients and site servers and as an installation source for SMS clients. SMS logon servers is a site system that hosts the logon discovery and logon installation methods. In the site server's SMS domain, the site server is automatically added as an SMS logon server.

An SMS logon server may or may not be a network logon server. The validation of users logging on to a network are supported by network logon servers. All computers configured as domain controllers are network logon servers in a Windows NT Server domain. They can all log users onto the network. All the Windows NT Server network logon servers are also SMS logon servers if you include all the computers configured as domain controllers into an SMS domain in a site. Also, only the included network logon servers are considered to be SMS logon servers, if you include only some of the Windows NT Server logon servers in an SMS site. An SMS logon server can be running a Windows NT/2000 Server computer, a Novell® NetWare NDS Server, or a Novell® NetWare bindery Server. A distribution server is a repository for software. SMS uses distribution servers to install and download software on clients. A distribution server can also be running a Novell® NetWare NDS Server, or a Novell® NetWare bindery Server. An SMS logon server running Windows NT Server must be a site server. SMS various services can also be moved from one primary site server to another primary site server. Therefore, easing the load on the first site server.

Clients

SMS client software is run by computers identified as clients (Windows 16-bit and Windows 32-bit systems). When a computer is discovered by an SMS system, the SMS client software is installed. The client can do the following using the SMS client software:

- Update client information
- Check for advertisements/run applications
- Allow for remote tools/remote control of client for Help Desk Services

An administrator can perform the following operations on a client:

- Collect hardware and software inventory
- Distribute and install software to the client
- Remotely control and troubleshoot the client
- Monitor connectivity between the site server and the client

There is very little that a user has to do once the SMS client software has been installed. The inventory data for the client is collected automatically at logon (the user may experience a slightly longer logon process); software can be installed automatically on the client; and a new icons are added to the clients control panel for initiating if needed client services from site.

SMS SERVICES

The SMS services are started automatically for you when you first install SMS. The SMS services monitor all SMS logon servers for all SMS clients in a site, the database, and the SMS directories and system files on the site server. Here are Some of SMS services are as follows:

- SMS Executive
- SMS Client Service
- SMS Remote Client Service
- SMS Site Component Manager
- SMS NT Logon Discovery Agent
- SNA Receiver (only for sites with the SNA® Sender installed)

You can use SMS without configuring the services. Nevertheless, you want to configure the services as your SMS system grows. For instance, you may want to move a service to a server other than the site server in order to distribute system load or to alter monitoring frequency.

Considerations for Implementation

A successful implementation of SMS is dependent on careful planning of its deployment across your enterprise. Consider the following, at a minimum:

- The design of your SMS system
- Policies and guidelines
- Your resource needs
- Testing
- Deployment

Document your current computing environment before you design your SMS system. During the documentation process, you will need to consider many issues that may affect your SMS system design, such as your network, domain structure, servers, current client software, and so on. You can define your SMS site infrastructure once this has been done. Determine how the sites will fit together into a site hierarchy, how many sites you will need, where you should create site boundaries, and what the types of sites will be.

You need to define policies and guidelines, such as naming conventions, policies for backup, security, and so on, to promote standardization and efficiency during implementation and subsequent use of SMS. Understand your resource needs, and determine whether or not your current hardware and staff can support the proposed design of your SMS system.

Set up a test environment before deployment, and install and run SMS in this test system. Also, in the day-to-day operation of your organization, focus on the important functions and configurations. To meet the minimum recommended configuration for the role it will play, each computer in your test environment should be configured.

Implement SMS in phases, rather than implementing it on your entire network at once. When you are sufficiently prepared to implement SMS across your organization, be aware that users will have questions and concerns that will require attention from your support staff. Deploying SMS in phases will help minimize the impact on your users and support staff, as well as help prevent network traffic bottlenecks.

■ Summary

By offering the administrator access to comprehensive computing information, hardware and software inventory capabilities have been substantially improved in Systems Management Server 2.0. In addition, a new Year 2000 (Y2K) compliance-checking tool has been included that evaluates the inventory data against a compliance database and generates reports on Year 2000 status. See more about the Y2K compliance in Chapter 9, "Configuring, Auditing, and Controlling Network Clients with SMS."

Working in any size enterprise—from the smallest to the largest—SMS is scalable from the ground up. Every component is designed to be modular, distributed, and multithreaded. This allowed SMS 1.2 to scale well beyond 100,000 clients in tests documented at http://www.microsoft.com/smsmgmt/showcase/sms_scale.asp. SMS 2.0 is designed to support even larger enterprise environments. To stop possible bottlenecks from occurring, a number of improvements have been made to the basic architecture. This will allow SMS to work in enterprises of any size.

For the MCSE exam, come away from this chapter with an in-depth knowledge of how these SMS components support any size enterprise:

- Sites
- Domains
- Servers
- Clients
- Services
- Implementation

Each of these components play a specific role in collecting inventory, distributing software, troubleshooting remotely, and working with mixes of networks of various sizes.

▲ CHAPTER REVIEW QUESTIONS

▲ True/False

1. *True or False? When locating inventory data, go to the appropriate site using the SMS Administrator. Next, identify the site/collections that contain the clients for which you wish to view inventory data in order to look at the data in the database.*

2. *True or False? When gathering software details for later analysis, you can use the inventory process to retrieve software files and store them at an appropriate location.*

3. *True or False? You cannot specify the collection frequency on a per site basis.*

4. *True or False? You can collect information from an SMS 1.2 site.*

5. *True or False? An error will appear if no files were collected from the selected computer.*

6. *True or False? SMS site boundary use ip segments and netbeui protocol for setup.*

7. *True or False? A site with an SQL Server of its own is known as a secondary site server. For processing and storage, it forwards information to its primary site. Also, for direct administration of the site, a secondary site server does not have administrative tools. A secondary site server must be administered through its primary site. In addition, any primary site (including the central site) can have a secondary site server connected to it.*

8. *True or False? You must optimize sender network utilization for each site. You must also configure two or more senders for each site to enable each site to communicate with the central site, as well as its parent and child sites. To transmit instructions and data from one site to another (such as reporting inventory information or installing software on clients in another site), SMS uses a sender (Windows NT component). The LAN Sender is available and runs on the site server by default. Other senders, such as the remote access service (RAS) sender and the systems network architecture (SNA) sender, must be deleted by using the SMS Administrator. You must also define the address of the receiving site for each sending site. Thus, an address contains specific information used to connect to another site.*

▲ Multiple Choice

1. *When viewing Collection inventory from the SMS Administrator, perform the following tasks except:*
   A. Choose Site Node.
   B. In the Sites Node, double-click the appropriate site to display SMS subnodes.
   C. Choose Package Node.
   D. Choose Correct Criteria (System type).

2. *During the process of trying to locate inventory data locations, a Query Properties dialog box appears. The Query Properties Dialog box contains many buttons and fields except:*
   A. Query Name
   B. Comments
   C. Object Type
   D. Class
   E. Edit Query Statement

3. *To view software detected on a computer from the SMS Administrator, do the following except:*
   A. Choose Site Node.
   B. In the Sites Node, double-click the appropriate site to display SMS subnodes.
   C. Choose Collections Node.
   D. Choose Correct Criteria (System type).
   E. Choose New.

4. *To view the list of collected files from the SMS Administrator toolbar, do the following except:*
   A. Choose Site Node.
   B. In the Sites Node, double-click the appropriate site to display SMS subnodes.
   C. Choose Collections Node.
   D. Choose Correct Criteria (System type).
   E. Double-click the computer name.

5. *SMS Sites include the following components except:*
   A. Hierarchies and sites
   B. SMS Executive
   C. Domains
   D. Servers
   E. Clients

6. *The user at a client can do the following using the SMS client software except:*
   A. Provide customized information to the database
   B. Install software applications from servers
   C. Run applications from servers
   D. Allow remote control by enabling help desk options
   E. Collect hardware and software inventory.

▲ Open Ended

1. What are the seven SMS services?
2. A successful implementation of SMS is dependent on you carefully planning how it is to be deployed across your enterprise. What should you consider as a minimum?

Site Planning

This part begins with an in-depth look at site planning by performing the following tasks:

- Checking client and server system requirements.

- Creating user accounts and login IDs.

- Configuring SQL Server on a remote computer if it is not installed on the site server.

- Configuring clients.

- Configuring your environment to provide additional computer support.

Next, part two looks at the various elements that are included during the design of an SMS site such as: location of resources; types of resources, which consist of computers, printers, routers, users, and user groups; features of SMS to be implemented; and site system resources. It also examines resource discovery.

The part also clarifies which MCSE exam-specific design components are needed to design the SMS site hierarchy model prior to installation for the enterprise; to design the SMS security strategy plan prior to installation for the organization; and to upgrade an SMS site to a newer version, plan the interoperability of a mixed SMS 1.2 and 2.0 site, and upgrade client operating systems at an SMS site.

SMS Site Design

This chapter begins with an in-depth look at Part 2, "Site Planning." Before installing Systems Management Server, you need to set up your environment by performing the following tasks, which are the focus of the first part of this chapter:

- Check client and server system requirements.
- Create user accounts and login IDs.
- Configure SQL Server on a remote computer, if it is not installed on the site server.
- Configure clients.
- Configure your environment to provide additional computer support.

Next, to design an SMS site you must plan for various elements to be included, such as:

- Location of resources.
- Types of resources, which consist of computers, printers, routers, users, and user groups.
- Features of SMS to be implemented.
- Site system resources.

53

With that in mind, the second part of this chapter examines more closely resource discovery. This is the initial process by which SMS discovers information, installs client agents, and makes data available to an administrator.

MCSE 3.1 Planning an SMS Installation

There are several important tasks to perform before installing SMS 2.0. The following sections examine these preinstallation activities.

Client and Server System Minimum Requirements

At minimum you need a primary site server computer to install SMS. When required, other types of servers can be incorporated into your SMS system. See Chapter 2, "Using SMS to Monitor an Enterprise," for information on the roles of these servers.

SITE SERVER SYSTEM REQUIREMENTS

Microsoft Windows NT Server 4.0 SP4a/2000 can be configured as a primary domain controller or member server (remember SMS requires the site server to be part of domain). The partition on which SMS is to be installed must be formatted as a Windows NT file system (NTFS). Microsoft SQL Server 6.x, 7.0, or higher must be installed on the site server or on a remote computer. The system requirements for the servers you can include in your SMS system are listed in Table 3.1.

Use only SQL Server 6.5 and 7.0 on Windows NT Server 4.0, since SQL Server 6.0 is not supported on Windows NT Server 4.0.

In addition to the minimum system requirements shown in Table 3.1, Table 3.2 outlines system requirements for SMS 2.0. The following are also suggested minimum requirements from Microsoft.

An SMS computer running **Windows NT Server** as a member server must be part of a domain. Also additional servers running **Discovery** resource agents or **Distribution Manager** services must be all part of a domain.

In addition to the minimum system requirements shown in Table 3.1, Table 3.2 outlines system requirements for SMS 2.0. The following are also suggested minimum requirements from Microsoft.

System requirements are subject to change at any time without prior notice at the discretion Microsoft. Please check Microsoft Website **WWW.MICROSOFT.COM /SMS** for any updated material.

Table 3.1 *Site Server System Requirements*

Server Type	Minimum Requirements	Other Requirements and Recommendations
Primary Site Server	Pentium133 processor or higher/Alpha	
	Windows NT Server 4.0 (SP4a)/2000	
	Access to a CD-ROM drive supported by Windows NT Server 4.0/2000	
	NTFS volume with 500 MB of free disk space	1 GB free disk space recommended. Multiple drives or drive (RAID) array for faster disk input/output.
	64–96 MB of random access memory (RAM) minimum	128 MB RAM recommended
	Microsoft SQL Server 6.5, Service Pack 4, or SQL Server version 7.0, local or remote.	

Table 3.1 *Site Server System Requirements (Continued)*

Server Type	Minimum Requirements	Other Requirements and Recommendations
Secondary Site Server	Pentium133 processor or higher, Alpha, Windows NT Server 4.0 or higher configured as a domain controller or member server	Recommended as a member Server for higher performance
	NTFS volume with 500 MB of free disk space.	1 GB free disk space recommended. Multiple drives or drive (RAID) array for faster disk input/output.
	64 MB RAM	128 MB RAM Recommended
SMS Logon Server	50 MB free disk space	100 MB free disk space
	An SMS logon server can run any of the following: • If configured as a domain controller, Windows NT Server 4.0/2000 • NetWare 3.12 • NetWare 4.1 (in NetWare 3. X Bindery Emulation Mode)	Requirements: Windows NT 4.0 Server Gateway Service for NetWare must be installed on the site server to support NetWare clients.
Component Server	NTFS volume. If configured as domain controller, Windows NT Server 4.0 or higher	
Distribution Server	A distribution server can run any of the following: • Windows NT Workstation 3.5 or higher • Windows NT Server 4.0 or higher • NetWare 3.12 or 4.1	Requirements: • The free disk space should exceed the size of the contents of the distribution source directory. • Windows NT 4.0 Server Gateway Services for NetWare must be installed on the site server to support NetWare distribution servers.

Table 3.2 *System Requirements for SMS 2.0*

Server Hardware Requirements	• 133 MHz Pentium processor or higher • 64–96 MB of RAM minimum (128 MB recommended) • 500 MB of free disk space on an NTFS partition and 100 MB on the system drive • Access to any CD-ROM drive supported by Windows NT Server 4.0 SP4a/2000
Server Software Requirements	• Fresh install (recommended) of Windows NT 4.0, Service Pack 4./2000 • Internet Explorer 4.01 SMS 2.0 CD-ROM contains: • Microsoft Internet Explorer 4.01 • Windows NT 4.0, Service Pack 4 • SQL Server 6.5, SP • SQL Server 7.0, Service Pack 3 • Microsoft Management Console • SMS 2.0
Server Role	• Windows NT 4.0 Primary/Backup Domain Controller • Windows NT 4.0 Member Server (must be a member of a domain)
Clients Supported	• Windows NT 3.51 and 4.0 • Windows 95 and Windows 98 • Windows 3.1 • Windows for Workgroups 3.11
Network Operating Systems Supported	• Windows NT 4.0 Server/2000 • Novell NetWare 3.x Bindery • Novell 4.x NetWare NDS Directory Services

The following additional client restrictions are specific to SMS 2.0: Novell NDS support is only available for Windows 95 and Windows 98 clients, not Windows NT 4.0 Workstation; Windows 3.1 and Windows for Workgroups 3.11 support is available for SMS 2.0, but may not be of the same quality as the support for other client operating systems; although Windows NT 2000 Systems have been tested as a both server and client platforms, they should not be assumed to work fully. Windows NT 4.0 Service Pack 4 is the recommended server environment under which other clients are assumed to work most reliably; software metering is not available for NetWare clients or 16-bit Windows clients; and SMS 2.0 does not support Windows Terminal Server clients or Windows CE clients at this time. Check Microsoft SMS Website WWW.MICROSOFT. COM for updated client information.

SMS TOOLS AND ADMINISTRATOR • SMS automatically installs the SMS Administrator and other SMS tools on the site server when you install a primary site. Other than a site server, you can, however, install the SMS Administrator and tools on other servers. You can do this to more evenly distribute SMS administrative tasks to other people in your organization or to reduce the load on the site server. The computer onto which you want to install the SMS Administrator and tools must meet the system requirements shown in the following sidebar, "Recommendations and System Requirements."

Study Break

Recommendations and System Requirements

SMS systems as in all backoffice products require powerful resources to help the administrator run a smooth operation, not only from a central location but from resources across the network. Additional systems such as Component servers must be running Windows NT Workstation 4.0 SP4 or Windows NT Server 4.0 SP4/2000. This includes all the following RAM requirements to run Windows NT Workstation 4.0 or higher or Windows NT Server 4.0 or higher (Windows 2000):

- 64 MB RAM

- 50–100 MB free disk space

If you want to install the SMS Administrator Console on a computer that is already part of the SMS system (such as a secondary site server, Component server, SMS logon server, or client), do not install the SMS Administrator in an existing directory used by SMS. The SMS directories and components can be maintained separately from the SMS Administrator by placing the SMS Administrator in its own directory. This means that you can upgrade or remove the tools or SMS Administrator independently. If the SMS Administrator is installed in the SMS root directory, you cannot remove it. Further, if SMS is removed from that computer, SMS Administrator will be removed.

RUNNING SMS IN A TEST ENVIRONMENT • Before fully deploying the product across your organization, Microsoft recommends that you set up an SMS test environment (Pilot Site). This test environment requires SMS on a primary site server running Windows NT Server 4.0 (SP4) and Microsoft SQL Server Version 6.5 SP4/7 (or one that has access to a remote installation of SQL Server) and a number of test clients.

The hardware size guidelines for installing, running, and evaluating SMS within a test environment are higher than those listed at the beginning of this part of the chapter. This is to accommodate for stress testing and to ensure that you do not encounter hardware limitations when evaluating SMS. For a small (up to 60 clients) to medium (60–3000 clients) test environment using Intel x86-based computers, you will need 16–32 MB of RAM for each of the following software products:

- SNA Server, if installed
- SQL Server
- SMS
- Windows NT Server 4.0

This calculates to minimum of 32 MB RAM for SMS and Windows NT Server 4.0; 48 MB of RAM for SMS, Windows NT Server 4.0, and SQL Server; and 64 MB of RAM for SMS, Windows NT 4.0 Server, SQL Server, and SNA Server. If you install several optional network services (such as additional network protocols or Windows NT Server 4.0 Gateway Services for Netware), an additional RAM is needed.

Alpha computers require more RAM than the Intel x86-based computers. For these computers, use minimum of 32 MB of RAM per each software product listed above.

A physical disk each for Windows NT Server 4.0, SMS, SQL Server, and SNA Server is recommended. A fast disk (RAID) array could be substituted for the multiple disks if it has more than 16 MB per second throughput for each physical disk it is replacing. While it may be nonessential to have four separate disks for a test environment of up to 60 clients, having them makes it easier to measure disk performance and to predict the effects of increasing or decreasing disk capacity or speed. Physical disks should be on a Peripheral Component Interconnect (PCI) SCSI® card, not an Industry Standard Architecture (ISA) SCSI card.

In addition, add another processor to improve processing throughput, especially if the computer performing SMS tasks will be under constant heavy load from such things as continually taking inventory, processing Queries, and running Software Metering.

Now, let's look at the SMS system requirements for client computers.

CLIENT SYSTEM REQUIREMENTS

SMS can manage computers running a mix of network and desktop operating systems. You must have a site server computer running Windows NT Server 4.0 at each site in your SMS system in order to provide this support. This Windows NT Server 4.0-based computer contains the SMS components and services needed to manage the site, its resources, database, and the computers (servers and clients) in the SMS site boundary.

By adding to the appropriate SMS Site server, additional site servers are incorporated into SMS systems (Components Servers, CAP Client Access Point Servers, Distribution Servers, or Logon Point Servers (PDC Domain Controllers). By default, SMS discovers and manages three types of resources: system resources (which include computers and other tangible devices on the network, such as routers, hubs, and SNMP devices), user group resources (Windows NT user groups, and user resources), and individual Windows NT user accounts. Of all the objects that Systems Management Server views as resources, only computers can become full Systems Management Server clients.

As systems are powered up and logged onto the network they can be discovered and included in the SMS system resource list. Once SMS has discovered a resource, it needs to install the client software to drive management operations. Once the agent is installed, there are many operations that it can perform. To enable the components of the agent requires configuring client agents as shown in Figure 3.1. Remember, not all clients must perform

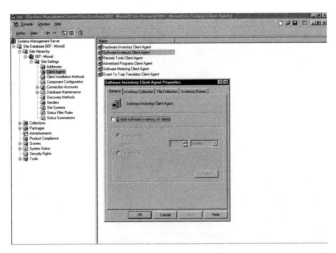

Figure 3.1 *32-bit Windows Client Software (Software Inventory)*

Figure 3.2   *32-bit Windows Client Software SMS Properties (in Remote Control)*

the same operation so an administrator can provide different setting using the SMS console, remote control can be enabled in the client properties as shown in Figure 3.2. SMS Client Components can also be checked in the clients control panel as shown on Figure 3.3; this is very helpful in diagnosing a problem of, for example, if software distribution was not running or remote control was not fully functional. These clients, once discovered and components installed, always run the client logon script at logon or they can manually run RUNSMS.BAT in the SMS local directory.

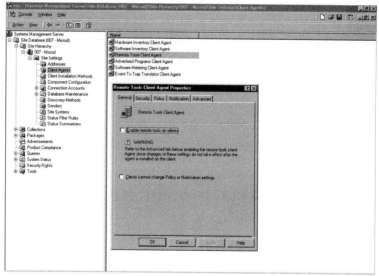

Figure 3.3   *32-bit Windows Client Software Remote Control (in Control Panel)*

Tables 3.3 and 3.4 list the supported desktop operating systems and required networking software for the following SMS logon servers:

- Windows NT Server 4.0/2000
- NetWare

 When clients are added to SMS, they typically have 1–3 MB of data copied to them. The exact amount of data copied depends on the client computer options (such as Advertised Programs Properties, SMS Client Properties, Remote Troubleshooting,) and the client operating system that you specify. SMS downloads all client software options by default. Using the Clients node, accessed through Site Properties, to control the options that are made available on a per-site basis.

Table 3.3 *Windows NT 4.0 Server System Requirements and Recommendations*

Desktop Operating System	Networking Software	Comments
Windows 3.1	Microsoft Network Client for MS-DOS 3.0, Using TCPIP	Microsoft Network Client for MS-DOS 3.0 is provided with Windows NT Server 4.0.
Windows for Workgroups 3.11 or higher	Microsoft Windows Network	
Windows 95 and 98	Client for Microsoft Networks	
Windows NT Server 4.0 SP4 / 2000		Windows NT Server 4.0 or higher is required for remote control. The SMS Service Account must have administrator privileges for remote control to work.
Windows NT Workstation 4.0 SP4 / 2000		Windows NT Workstation 4.0 or higher is required for remote control. The SMS Service Account must have administrator privileges for remote control to work.

 SMS supports only Program Manager 16-bit Clients or Explorer on 32-bit Clients. Other types of desktop shells are not supported. Microsoft recommends that you use the latest NetWare shell.

Table 3.4 shows the desktop operating system and networking software that must be present on the client for SMS to support clients logged on to a NetWare server 3.12 or 4.1 (NetWare 3.x Bindery Emulation Mode is required).

Table 3.4 *Novell NetWare System Requirements and Recommendations*

Desktop Operating System	Networking Software	Comments
MS-DOS 5.0 or higher	NETX	
	VLM	Bindery mode only
Windows 3.1	NETX	
	VLM	Bindery mode only
Windows for Workgroups 3.11 or higher	NETX	
	VLM	Bindery mode only
Windows 95 and 98	Either: MS Client for NetWare Networks	
	Or: NetWare Client 32 for Windows 95 and 98	Bindery mode only
	Or: MSNDS.95	Bindery mode only
	Or: NETX	32-bit client software recommended
	Or: VLM	Bindery mode only

For SMS to support clients logged on to a server running Microsoft NT, client must belong to a domain.

Table 3.6 shows the desktop operating system and networking software that must be present on the client for SMS to support clients logged on to a computer running Microsoft NT Server.

You must create a Windows NT Server user accounts for SMS services before you install SMS on the site server as shown in Figure 3.4. (Some of these are automatically created during SMS installation.) In order for users to have access to the database, create an SQL login ID for the SMS services. As an option, you can then create an additional SQL login ID that identifies you as a user on the SQL Server and gives you access to the database.

When you install and log on to SMS, you will need to enter the names and passwords of the user accounts and SQL login IDs as shown in Figure 3.5. (Some of these are automatically created during SMS installation.) Doc-

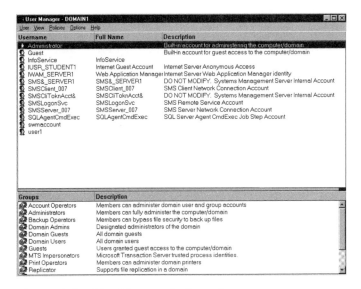

Figure 3.4   *User Manager for Domains*

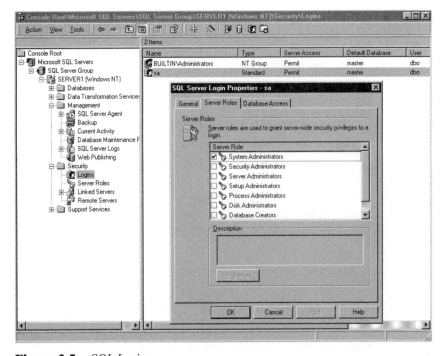

Figure 3.5   *SQL Logins*

ument these account names and passwords so that you have them on hand during the installation, log on processes, and for recovery purposes. In the procedures described in this chapter, you will create the information shown in Table 3.5.

 Each site must have an **SMS Service Account** that provides access to all of the servers and Windows NT client in SMS. This account operates with the same user name and password on all SMS servers within the site. Chapter 5, "SMS Security Strategy Design," describes how to create a Windows NT user account for SMS services.

Table 3.5 *Filling in the Account/Login ID Information*

Account/Login ID Needed	Location and Prompt for Input	Information to Input
Windows NT Server user account for SMS services	Primary Site Configuration Information dialog box when you install SMS	Example name: SMSUserServices
SQL login ID for use by SMS services to access the database	SQL Database Configuration dialog box when you install SMS or the SMS Administrator Login dialog box when you log on to SMS	Example name: SMSLoginServices
	Alternatively, the existing SQL Server systems administrator login ID	Type: sa
SQL login IDs for users of SMS Administrator	SMS Administrator Logon dialog box when you log on to SMS.	Example name: Administrator

Configuring SQL Server on a Remote Computer

SMS installation has been combined with Microsoft SQL Server installation to dramatically ease the setup and maintenance required for SMS. SQL is tightly integrated with SMS to ensure the most efficient data storage possible. If you want to use a Microsoft SQL Server that is installed on a computer other than the site server, you'll need to complete the following SQL Server configuration tasks:

1. Create a data device and a log device.
2. Synchronize the time on the SQL Server computer with the time on the site server.
3. Optimize SQL configuration settings.

Let's look at each of these tasks in more detail.

The SQL Server procedures described here are for Microsoft **SQL Server** 6.5 and 7.0. If you are using a different version of SQL Server, the procedures may vary. If you purchased SMS as part of Microsoft BackOffice, SQL Server cannot be installed on a remote computer and must be installed on the site server computer.

SMS DATA DEVICE CREATION

To create the data device to be used by SMS, perform the following steps:

1. Start the SQL Enterprise Manager.
2. From the Manage menu select Devices.
3. The Manage Database Devices window appears.
4. Choose New Devices.
5. Enter a name for the device; for example, `SMSXfile`.
6. Type "20 MB" as a minimum size for this device.

 Allocate 20–35K of the site's data device space for each computer in the database. The amount of space depends on a number of factors, including how much history is retained for each computer and how busy the site is based on the number of administrators accessing the database.

7. Accept the remaining default settings by choosing Create Now.
8. The `SMSXfile` device is created.

 If you use an existing data device, the SMS Setup program will delete all objects in this device. The SMS Setup program uses the entire database device for the site database.

SMS LOG DEVICE CREATION

To create the log device to be used by SMS, perform the following steps:

1. Start the SQL Enterprise Manager.
2. From the Manage menu, select Devices. The Manage Database Devices window will appear.
3. Choose New Devices.
4. Enter a name for the device; for example, `SMSCapLog`.
5. Type "10 MB" as a minimum size for this device.

The site database log device should be at least 10% of the size of the site data device.

6. Accept the remaining default settings by choosing Create Now.
7. The SMSCapLog device is created.

If you use an existing log device, the SMS Setup program will delete all objects in this device. The SMS Setup program uses the entire transaction log device for the transaction log.

TIME SYNCHRONIZATION

To synchronize the time on the SQL Server with the time on the site server, at the SQL Server computer system prompt, type the following where server name is the computer name of the SMS site server:

```
net time \\servername /set
```

To ensure efficient operation of SMS and SQL Server, the time on the site server should be synchronized with the time on the SQL Server computer each day. Windows NT Server 4.0 has a Command Scheduler (WINAT.EXE) and a Time Synchronizing Service (TIMESERV.EXE) that allow you to automate this procedure.

CONFIGURATION SETTINGS OPTIMIZATION

Optimum performance of SQL Server is dependent on a number of factors. The SQL Server settings shown in Table 3.6 apply to a remote installation of a SQL Server dedicated to SMS and where SMS is comprised of a single site with up to 3,000 clients.

If the resources shown in Table 3.6 are underallocated, error messages are displayed. You can trace SQL Server error messages by looking in the SQL Server error log MSSQL\LOG\ERRORLOG.

Table 3.6 *Minimum Settings for SQL Server with SMS*

Item	Requirements
Data device	20 MB minimum. Allocate 30–45K of a site's data device space for each computer. The amount of space depends on several factors, however, including how much history is retained for each computer in the database.
Log device	10 MB minimum
tempdb data device	At least thirty percent of the size of the site data device
tempdb log device	At least thirty percent of the size of the tempdb data device
SQL memory allocation	9 MB of RAM on startup
Open objects setting	600 (the SQL default)
Locks	6000 (the SQL default)
SQL connections	Thirty connections for each SMS site using SQL Server. If possible, try to allocate enough connections so that at least eleven are free at any given time.
Select Into/Bulk Copy	Enabled
Truncate Log on Checkpoint	Enabled for the tempdb database and the SMS database

Configuring Clients

The time on each client should match the time on the site server to ensure that all SMS processes are activated at the expected times. To synchronize the time on the client with the site server, type the following at the client system prompt, where "sitesservers" is the name of the site server:

```
net time \\sitesservers /set
```

The time on the client reflects the time where the user logs on to the NetWare server for NetWare clients. You should also ensure that the time on any NetWare logon server matches the time on the site server. Now, let's look at the additional computer support that is available to you.

Providing Additional Computer Support

If you want to include Macintosh clients, Microsoft LAN Manager servers, or IBM LAN Server computers in your SMS system, you'll need to set up SMS 1.2 server site to transfer information to primary SMS 2.0 site.

NOVELL NETWARE CLIENTS AND SERVERS SUPPORT

You must do the following for SMS to support Novell NetWare servers and the clients that log on to these servers:

- Install the Windows NT 4.0 Gateway Service for NetWare on the site server.
- Create an SMS Service Account on each NetWare server (with Supervisor rights).
- Group NetWare servers into SMS domains.
- Configure NetWare 4.x.
- Ensure the clients log on correctly.

GATEWAY SERVICE FOR NETWARE INSTALLATION • The Windows NT 4.0 Gateway Service for NetWare must be installed on the site server and on all other sites for which you want NetWare support. With installation of this component, SMS can connect to and manage the NetWare servers in a site.

SMS SERVICE ACCOUNT ON NETWARE SERVERS CREATION • Create an SMS Service Account on each NetWare server in each site. This is because the majority of NetWare servers do not share the same user account database allowing a single network logon. This account must have the same name and password as the SMS Service Account created before installation. The account requires SUPERVISOR privileges and must have all permissions for all volumes on each server.

GROUPING NETWARE SERVERS INTO SMS DOMAINS • Servers must be grouped into one or more SMS domain so that SMS can manage NetWare servers and the clients that log on at those servers. All servers in the SMS domains for a site must be on the same LAN.

CREATION OF SMS SITE TO INCLUDE NETWARE SERVERS • To create the SMS sites, SMS must be installed. From the SMS Administrator toolbar on the site server, perform the following steps:

1. Choose Open Window: Sites.
2. In the Sites widow, select the site in which you wish to create the domain.
3. Include the NetWare servers.
4. Choose Properties from the toolbar. The Site Properties dialog box appears as shown in Figure 3.6.
5. Choose Domains. The Domains dialog box appears
6. Select Proposed Properties, and then choose Add. The Domain Properties dialog box appears as shown in Figure 3.7.
7. In the Name box, type a name for the domain.
8. In the Type list, select Novell NetWare.
9. Under Logon Servers, select Use Specified Servers. This option allows you to specify the servers you want to include in the domain.

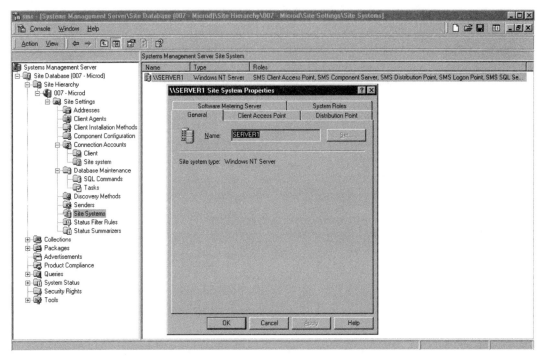

Figure 3.6 *The Site Properties Node.*

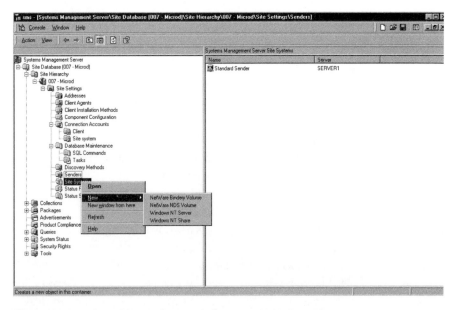

Figure 3.7 *The Additional Sites Node using SMS Console.*

Select Use All Detected Servers with caution. When enabled, SMS finds all NetWare servers within 18 router hops of the site server and adds them to the SMS domain you are creating.

SMS continues to monitor the network for any new servers and the Net-Ware servers are added to each SMS domain. This causes duplication of configuration and inventory information if you create NetWare SMS site at more than one site and the sites are within 18 router hops of each other. To avoid this, do not select Use All Detected Servers when creating SMS domains that group NetWare servers.

10. In the New Logon Server box, type the name of the server to be added to the SMS domain.

11. Optionally, in the Volume box you may type the NetWare volume where you want the SMS components (files and directories) to be installed. If you leave this field blank, SMS chooses the volume with the most free disk space.

12. Choose Add. The server and the volume (if specified) appears in the Use These Logon Servers box.

13. Choose OK to close the open dialog boxes.

14. Choose Yes when prompted for confirmation to update the site.

After the servers have reported their inventory and SMS has updated the database, the servers appear in their SMS domain in the Sites window.

NETWARE 4.X SERVERS CONFIGURATION • To run in Bindery Emulation Mode, ensure that NetWare version 4.x servers have been configured. For users to run the SMS client installation program from their logon script and monitor its progress, you must create a NetWare 3.x group called ALLINONE on each NetWare 4.x server and add all users to this group. You may use the NetWare 3.x bindery emulation capabilities of NetWare 4.x to create this group in 3.x format. SMS grants permissions to the SMS directories on NetWare logon servers by assigning trustee rights to the ALLINONE group.

ENSURING CLIENTS LOG ON CORRECTLY • To run SMS, users at NetWare clients must log on and connect to NetWare servers. NetWare supports two logon shells: NETX and VLM. For clients using the VLM shell, users must log on using the /b option. This tells NetWare that the client is using the bindery services, not the NetWare Directory Services. NETX users do not have to specify any special logon options.

A NetWare client cannot access SMS by logging on to a Windows NT Server 4.0 running the File and Print Services for NetWare (FPNW).

MICROSOFT LAN MANAGER SERVERS SUPPORT

For SMS to support computers running LAN Manager 2.2c or higher, first create an SMS Service Account in each domain that contains LAN Manager. The SMS Service Account must have the same password and user name as the site's SMS Service Account. Add the account to the ADMINS group.

Next, monitor the maximum password age setting so that it does not expire. Track the age of the password for the Maximum Password Age setting and the SMS Service Account. If the SMS Service Account's password expires, the SMS services will not be able to access the LAN Manager servers in the domain. If the SMS Service Account's password expires, you must reactivate the SMS Service Account in the LAN Manager domain.

IBM LAN SERVER COMPUTERS SUPPORT

For SMS to support IBM LAN Server computers, create an SMS Service Account in each domain that contains IBM LAN Server computers. The SMS Service Account must have the same user name and password as the site's Service Account. Add the account to the ADMINS group.

Study Break

SMS Upgrade Plan

If you are upgrading an existing version of SMS, you must consider the version of SQL Server that you are using for the SMS database. The different versions of SMS require the following versions of Microsoft SQL Server:

- SMS 1.0 supports SQL Server 4.21a only.
- SMS 1.1 supports SQL Server 4.21a and SQL Server 6.x.
- SMS 1.2 supports SQL Server 6.x. SQL Server 4.21a is supported, but only during the upgrade phase to version 6.x. SQL Server 4.21a is not supported for usage with SMS 1.2.
- SMS 2.0 supports SQL Server 6.x and higher. SQL Server 4.21a is supported, but only during the upgrade phase to version 6.x and higher. SQL Server 4.21a is not supported for usage with SMS 2.0.

For detailed information on upgrading, see the SMS Setup help file located in your `SMS\SMSSETUP\platform` directory (where platform is the processor type of the site server).

Designing an SMS Site

SMS 2.0 has a broader concept of managed devices than previous versions. It uses the idea of *resources*. In SMS 2.0, resources are the hardware, Windows NT 4.0 user groups, and Windows NT 4.0 user accounts that you can manage with SMS. Hardware resources include personal computers, servers, and network devices such as routers.

Location of Resources

The first elements that must be included to design an SMS site are the *locations of resources*. SMS must first know what resources there are and the properties of each resource for it to manage resources on your network. The process by which this information is gathered is called *resource discovery*.

SMS provides several methods to discover resources on the network, each of which detects as many details as possible about these resources. The information found by the various discovery methods is then correlated to produce a complete and accurate list of the resources on the network.

The process begins with the creation of a discovery data record (DDR) that provides a short list of known properties about each discovered resource. The specific properties vary according to the type of resource and the discovery method by which the resource was found. The discovery data manager (DDM) then reads the DDRs as they accumulate. They are compared to the records already entered in the discovery database. The information in the DDR is used either to create a new record in the discovery database or to update an existing record. After that, the DDR file is deleted. Finally, new or changed information in the discovery database is periodically replicated up through the SMS site hierarchy. This allows composite images to be built up of a resource even though the information is gathered through many different discovery processes.

The type of resource to be discovered and the specified configuration settings dictate the discovery methods. The various discovery methods available are accessed under the Site Settings for a particular site.

Types of Resources

The second elements that must be included to design an SMS site are the *types of resources*. SMS 2.0 discovers and manages three types of resources by default:

- *System* resources, such as Servers, Client computers, printers, and other tangible devices on the network, routers, switches, hubs, and SNMP devices.
- *User group* resources, included Windows NT 4.0 user groups.
- *User* resources, included individual Windows NT 4.0 user accounts.

Out of all the objects that SMS views as resources, only computers can become full SMS clients. Clients are the computers that match the criteria for inclusion in at least one site and have had the SMS client software installed. Other types of resources are discovered and added to the site database so that you can specify them when targeting software distribution and other management tasks. For example, you can advertise a program to install a purchasing software application to every member of the Purchasing user group. In this case, the application would be advertised to any client on which a member of Purchasing is connected.

SMS Features to Be Implemented

The third element that must be included to design an SMS site are the *features of SMS to be implemented*. SMS site designers may modify the features to focus less on design and more on the creation and testing of software and hardware components.

You should establish two SMS site design groups for the implementation of SMS features. Developers will probably modify each of the SMS features before implementation. The developers and testers must be different individuals; never mix these two roles.

Once you have established the SMS design groups, you should create a testing laboratory. The testing laboratory should consist of SMS infrastructure servers and SMS test clients. These test clients must be complete representations of the organization's client hardware and software.

You should also create specification documents for each SMS feature component to be implemented. These documents ensure that each component is installed in a compatible way and that they can be recreated.

Microsoft Visual SourceSafe™ version control system should be incorporated into the SMS laboratory environment. Visual SourceSafe will assist in the creation, control, modification, and tracking of SMS software distribution packages.

If the SMS feature to be implemented is to include upgrading operating systems, you should create specification documents for each of the proposed operating systems. These specification documents should address all aspects of the operating systems and should be used as a guide for the creation of unattended installation packages that SMS will deliver.

Once the new operating systems have been installed, you can use an unattended application installation package to layer desktop applications onto these operating systems. Perform careful testing after installing each application to ensure that no single application causes a problem on the desktop.

Once the developer and tester teams have created and tested a complete desktop configuration, the external testing teams can begin to test it. Typically, the types of external teams that will test the desktop configuration are:

- Deployment staff representatives
- Help desk staff representatives
- Production staff representatives
- User representatives

Each of these groups must test and approve the desktop configuration. If the external testers find any errors or if they recommend any modifications, the desktop configuration must be sent back to the developer and tester teams for adjustments. Once the developer and tester teams have made the corrections, the external testing team must once again test the desktop configuration. This process ensures the most stable, usable, and accurate desktop configuration and enables external teams to participate in technology transfer.

You should also use the SMS testing laboratory to test all SMS features relevant to the organization's implementation. This testing can be a vehicle for technology transfer to external teams (such as the operations team).

Once the desktop configuration is finalized and all testing is complete, training on the desktop can commence. This training ranges from user to support level.

The following describes some of the site system resource discovery methods. These fall into two categories: discovering site system resources and discovering user and user group resources.

Training cannot commence until the desktop configuration is finalized. Training is a very important aspect of SMS testing.

Site System Resources

The final elements that must be included to design an SMS site are *site system resources.* These resources are hardware resources, such as computers, routers, and other tangible devices on the network. Let's discuss some of the methods available for discovering system resources.

WINDOWS NETWORKING LOGON DISCOVERY, NETWARE BINDERY SERVER, AND NET-WARE NDS LOGONS (see Figure 3.8) • SMS collects information about each computer when it logs on to a Windows-based network, a NetWare bindery server, or the NetWare NDS context.

DISCOVERING NETWORKS • SMS collects information about 32-bit resources on the network from the Dynamic Host Configuration Protocol (DHCP)

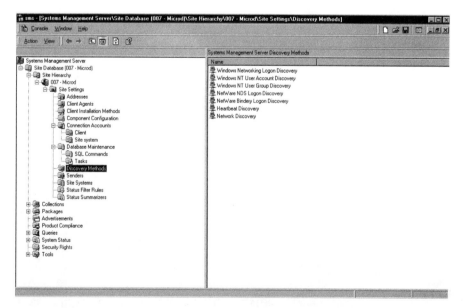

Figure 3.8 *Discovery Methods Node Using the SMS Administrator.*

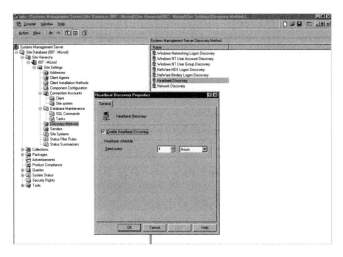

Figure 3.9 *Heartbeat Discovery Methods Node Using the SMS Administrator.*

server (a server that automatically administers client TCP/IP addresses and related settings for a network), from domain enumeration, and by similar means. This means you can discover computers that are not currently turned on. Network discovery also finds SNMP and IP devices on your network.

HEARTBEAT DISCOVERY • The heartbeat discovery method supplements the other methods; Windows networking logon discovery, in particular. Once a client has been discovered using a logon method, heartbeat discovery periodically checks and updates discovery data on this resource. This allows for a more up-to-date record of resource information on systems that are not regularly logged off and on as shown on Figure 3.9.

USER GROUP AND USER RESOURCES DISCOVERY

To discover user and user group resources, SMS searches the Windows NT 4.0 domains you specify as shown on Figure 3.10. All users and user groups in the specified boundaries are added to the discovered resources database. It uses the Windows networking user group discovery and Windows networking user account discovery methods to collect these data.

Discovery mechanisms are modular. New ones can be added as needed. For example, a new discovery mechanism may access information from the Windows NT 4.0 Active Directory when it is available.

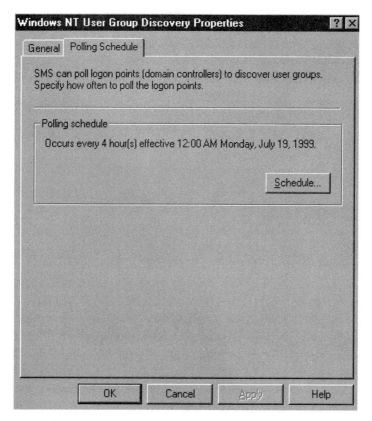

Figure 3.10   *User or Group Discovery Methods Node Using the SMS Administrator.*

SITE BOUNDARIES ASSIGNMENT

Resources can be discovered across your entire network, and all discovered resources are included in the resource discovery database. Before you can manage these resources, however, they must be assigned to SMS sites. If a discovered resource is found within the boundaries of a site, it is assigned to that site.

As part of the site configuration settings, the site boundaries are a set of IP and/or IPX networks that you specify. Each site is composed of one or more subnets. You have the option of setting overlapping site boundaries and resources can be included in more than one site.

Resource Management

Component Agents running on client systems are required to manage clients using SMS. Version 2.0 has the flexibility to specify which management facilities should run on each system. For example, you can do just software distribution without doing inventory or metering. To install the specific components requires:

- Finding the resources
- Installing the agent on the appropriate resources
- Enabling components of the agent

Configuring discovery methods are required to find the resources. To install the agent on the resource requires configuring *client installation methods*. To enable the components of the agent requires configuring *client agents*. These concepts are discussed next.

Installing the Client

Once discovered, a resource can have a client installed. An administrator, however, can decide not to install clients on every discovered resource. For example, employees' home computers may be discovered when they connect through RAS, but may not be considered appropriate machines to manage. The client installation methods allow an administrator to decide which resources are to be managed and how. The available client installation methods are accessed under the Site Settings for a particular site as shown on Figure 3.11.

The client installation process begins by examining the prospective client and then transferring SMS client files to the client. The client executive is started with the required parameters to complete the client installation once the files are transferred. The remainder of the installation takes place locally at the client and does not require network bandwidth.

 The client installation process also allows you to monitor the progress of client installation.

The methods available for client installation are analogous to the methods available for resource discovery. The client installation methods are shown in the following sidebar, "Client Installation Methods."

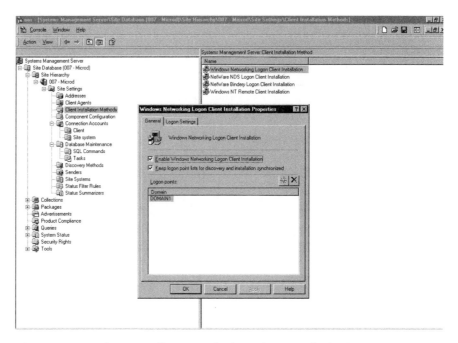

Figure 3.11   *Client Installation Methods Node Using the SMS Administrator.*

Client Installation Methods

- Windows networking logon client installation:
  When a computer within the site boundaries logs on to the Windows-based network, SMS installs the client software on that computer.

- Windows NT 4.0 remote client installation:
  SMS client software is automatically installed on Windows NT 4.0-based computers within the site boundaries. The Windows NT 4.0-based computers must be turned on and connected to the network. It is not necessary for anyone to be logged on to these computers.

- Manual Windows network connection client installation:
  The user must explicitly connect to a file on a Windows NT 4.0 logon point to install the SMS client software. This method provides for those cases where no logon script is used.

- NetWare Bindery server logon client installation:
  When a computer logs on to a NetWare bindery server, SMS installs the client software on that computer.

- NetWare NDS logon client installation:
  When a computer within the site boundaries logs on to the NetWare NDS context, SMS installs the client software on that computer.

- Manual NetWare NDS network connection client installation:
  The user must explicitly connect to a file on a NetWare NDS logon point to install SMS client software.

- Manual NetWare Bindery connection client installation:
  The user must explicitly connect to a file on a NetWare Bindery logon server to install SMS client software.

Configuring Client Agents

You need to decide how to configure the agent, once SMS has discovered the resources and installed agents as appropriate. These configuration options are accessed under the Site Settings node. For each SMS client component, you can choose one of these installation options:

- Install and automatically start the component on all computers. When you are ready to use the component, choose this option.
- Install the component but do not automatically start it. When you are not ready to use a component, but you know you will be using it in the near future, choose this option.
- Do not install the component. When you have no plans to use the component, choose this option.

Thus, the configuration options are different for each client component. For instance, administrators can separately configure software distribution options without changing inventory options. As different components are addressed, each case will be examined, such as remote diagnostics and software metering.

■ Summary

Before installing SMS 2.0, set up your environment to prepare for the installation of SMS. You will need to perform the following tasks:

- Check client and server system requirements.
- Create user accounts and login IDs.
- Configure SQL Server on a remote computer if it is not installed on the site server.

- Configure clients.
- Configure your environment to for additional computer support.

Thus, the reader should come away from this chapter with an in-depth knowledge of the preceding tasks and the following MCSE exam-specific main elements:

- Location of resources
- Types of resources
- SMS features to be implemented
- Site system resources

The first elements that must be included design an SMS site are the *location of resources*. For SMS to manage resources on your network, it must first know what resources there are and the properties of each resource for it. *Resource discovery* is the process by which this information is gathered.

The second elements that must be included to design an SMS site are the *types of resources*. SMS 2.0 discovers and manages three types of resources by default: system resources, user group resources, and user resources.

The third elements that must be included to design an SMS site are the *features of SMS to be implemented*. SMS site designers may modify the features to focus more on the creation and testing of software and hardware components and less on design.

The final elements that must be included to design an SMS site are *site system resources*. These resources are hardware resources, such as computers, printers, routers, and other tangible devices on the network.

SMS 2.0 has a broader concept of managed devices than previous versions. The notion of *resources* is also used by SMS 2.0. The resources in SMS 2.0 are the Windows NT 4.0 user accounts, hardware, and Windows NT 4.0 user groups that you can manage with SMS. Hardware resources include network devices such as routers, personal computers, and servers.

▲ CHAPTER REVIEW QUESTIONS

▲ True/False

1. *True or False? An NTFS volume is not required on client computers.*

2. *True or False? The contents of the distribution source directory should be exceeded by the free disk space.*

3. *True or False? If distributing packages with long file names on Windows NT Server or Windows NT 4.0 Workstation computers, an NTFS volume is not required.*

4. *True or False? To support Windows 3.11 clients, Windows NT 4.0 Server must be installed on the site server or on any Windows NT Server 4.0-based SMS logon servers and any distribution servers.*

5. *True or False? Use only SQL Server 6.5 and 7.0 on Windows NT Server 4.0, since SQL Server 6.0 is not supported on Windows NT Server 4.0.*

6. *True or False? Alpha computers require more RAM than the Intel x86-based computers.*

7. *True or False? With regard to installation and the configuration of logon points, the user must explicitly connect to a Windows NT 4.0 PDC Domain Controller to install the SMS client software. This method provides for those cases where a logon script is used.*

8. *True or False? A resource can have a client installed on it, once it is discovered. An administrator, however, can decide not to install clients on every discovered resource. For example, employees' home computers may be discovered when they connect through RAS, but may not be considered appropriate machines to manage. The client installation methods allow an administrator to monitor the progress of client installation and decide which resources are to be managed and how. The various client installation methods available are accessed under the Site Settings for a particular site.*

▲ Multiple Choice

1. *For each of the following software products, you will need 16 MB of RAM except:*

    A. SNA Server, if installed

    B. SQL Server

    C. SMS

    D. Windows NT Server 4.0

    E. Windows 95 Server

    F. SMS 1.3 supports SQL Server 4.21b only

2. *SMS 2.0 discovers and manages the following types of resources by default except:*

    A. System resources, which include computers and other tangible devices on the network, such as routers and SNMP devices.

    B. SMS Executive resources.

    C. User group resources, which include Windows NT 4.0 user groups.

    D. User resources, which include individual Windows NT 4.0 user accounts.

    E. None of the above.

3. *Agent components running on client systems are required to manage clients using SMS. Version 2.0 provides the flexibility to specify which management facilities should run on each system. For example, you can do just software distribution without doing inventory or metering. To get the specific components installed requires the following except:*

    A. Finding the resources

    B. Installing the agent on the appropriate resources

    C. Running applications from servers

    D. Enabling components of the agent

    E. None of the above

4. *You need to decide how to configure the agent, once SMS has discovered the resources and installed appropriate agents. These configuration options are accessed under the Site Settings node. For each SMS client component, you can choose one of these installation options except:*

    A. Install and automatically start the component on all computers. When you are ready to use the component, choose this option.

    B. Distribute and install software to the client.

    C. Install the component but do not automatically start it. When you are not ready to use a component, but you know you will be using it in the near future, choose this option.

    D. Do not install the component. When you have no plans to use the component, choose this option.

    E. None of the above.

5. *To design an SMS site, plan for the elements to be included except:*

    A. Location of resources

    B. Distribution of software to the client

    C. Types of resources, which consist of computers, printers, routers, users, and user groups

    D. Features of SMS to be implemented

    E. Site system resources

6. *Hardware requirements for site systems include the following except:*

    A. 64 MB of RAM minimum (128 MB recommended)

    B. 120 MHz Pentium processor

    C. 500 MB of free disk space on an NTFS partition and 100 MB on the system drive

    D. Access to any CD-ROM drive supported by Windows NT Server 4.0 or higher

7. *Software requirements for site systems include the following except:*

    A. Fresh install (recommended) of Windows NT 4.0, Service Pack 4

    B. Internet Explorer 3.0

    C. SMS 2.0 CD-ROM contains Microsoft Internet Explorer 4.01, Windows NT 4.0, Service Pack 3, and SQL Server 7.0

    D. SMS 2.0 CD-ROM contains SQL Server 7.0, Microsoft Management Console, and SMS 2.0

    E. Site system resources

SMS Site Hierarchy

Working in organizations from the smallest to the largest, the Systems Management Server (SMS) hierarchy model is scalable from the ground up. Every component is designed to be distributed, multithreaded, and modular. In documented tests, this allowed SMS 1.2 to scale beyond 100,000 clients. See http://www.microsoft.com/smsmgmt /showcase/sms_scale.asp for more information on this matter.

SMS 2.0 is designed to support even larger environments. To stop possible bottlenecks from occurring, a number of improvements have been made to the basic architecture. This allows SMS to work and grow in enterprises of any size by using the following key elements:

- Distributed components
- Industrial-strength database
- Integrated security model
- Integration with enterprise vendors and management standards
- Site communications

- Site hierarchy model
- Support for remote users and sites

MCSE 4.1 SMS Site Architectural Design

To ensure data integrity, SMS is built on top of SQL Server. To ensure the most efficient data storage possible, SMS natively uses the facilities of and is tightly integrated with SQL Server. The scalability of SQL Server can be exploited by SMS. To support data protection through clustering, it even works with SQL Server Enterprise Edition.

The administrator does not have to deal with the overhead of managing a database environment even though SMS uses SQL Server. So that you do not have to use SQL Server Enterprise Manager, SMS 2.0 has been designed to fully self-manage the database. This includes automatically creating the relevant database tables at installation and then sizing the tables as your system grows. Without having to stop the system and run separate administrative tools, it also contains a series of garbage collection facilities that ensure the data maintained by SMS is of a high quality.

The replacement of database polling with database triggers is a key new development in version 2.0. Previously, SMS components learned of database changes by regularly polling the database. In large systems, this could become a bottleneck. Now, any time there is a relevant database change, a process is specifically tasked with triggering all relevant SMS processes.

The Site Hierarchy Model

Your existing network can be organized into SMS sites through SMS itself. In large environments where different groups have different areas of responsibility, this network organization is key in helping you use the product. SMS is able to reflect your business structure.

Information gathered from computers is processed and stored on a site-by-site basis. It is also passed up through the site hierarchy. Management information and software distributions can be defined at one site in the hierarchy and passed down to child sites in a similar manner (see Figure 4.1).[1] It is more efficient for large networks or networks that include slow links to be organized into a hierarchy of SMS sites, because data passed between sites are often summarized or compressed.

---

1. Copyright © 1998 Microsoft and/or its suppliers, One Microsoft Way, Redmond, Washington 98052-6399 U.S.A. All rights reserved.

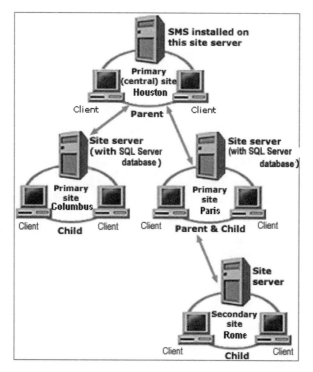

Figure 4.1 *Site Hierarchy Model.*

There are two main types of sites:

- A *primary site* stores system data for itself and its subsites in a SQL Server database.
- A *secondary site* has clients but no database. It passes its data to its parent primary site.

Sites can also be described by their relationship to other sites in the hierarchy. For instance, a *parent site* is a primary site that includes at least one other site beneath it in a SMS hierarchy. A primary site can have one or more child sites.

A *child site* on the other hand, is a site that reports to a site above it in the hierarchy. All information collected at a child site is copied to the parent site, which in turn reports all of the accumulated data to its parent site. While a secondary site cannot have a child site and must be a child site itself, a primary site can have one or more child sites.

The *central site* is the primary site at the top of the hierarchy. It is the one site in a hierarchy that is not a child to any other site. Therefore, the database at the central site acquires all the data of the entire hierarchy.

CENTRAL SITE

As just mentioned, the topmost site in the hierarchy is called the central site. The central site must be a primary site, which means that it must have its own SQL Server database. The central site database stores the inventory information for the central site and all its subsites. Inventory information is always reported from lower level sites up the hierarchy, all the way up to the central site. Thus, at the central site, you can view all sites and computers in the SMS system, and you can manage all sites in the hierarchy.

The central site is unique only in that it is the primary site at the top of site hierarchy. If you attach the current central site to a parent site, then the parent site becomes the new central site, assuming that it too does not have a parent site. If the parent site itself has a parent site, then the site at the top of the hierarchy becomes the new central site.

PRIMARY AND SECONDARY SITES

After you have installed a central site, you can add subsites beneath it. You can add both primary sites and secondary sites.

A primary site has its own SQL Server database to store site information for itself and its subsites. It also has administrative tools that enable you to directly manage the site and its subsites. You add a primary site to the site hierarchy by installing the primary site and then attaching the site to the central site or another primary site.

A secondary site is a site that neither has a database to store its site information nor has administrative tools for direct administration of the site. You add a secondary site directly from the primary site that will serve as its parent site. You cannot attach additional sites beneath secondary sites.

PARENT AND CHILD SITES

Sites are organized into a hierarchy by setting up parent-child relationships between the sites. By installing and attaching sites, you can create a hierarchy of sites that reflects your organization's structure. When you attach sites, you specify one site as the parent site and one site as the child site.

A parent site is a primary site that includes other sites beneath it in the site hierarchy. A parent site contains all pertinent information about its subsites and has the ability to control many operations of the child sites.

A child site is any site that reports to another SMS site in the hierarchy. A child site automatically reports its pertinent site information to its parent site.

A site may be both a parent (other sites report to it) and a child site (it reports to another site). A site can have many child sites, although it can have only one parent site.

A primary site can have one or more primary sites beneath it as well as one or more secondary sites beneath it. A secondary site cannot have any sites beneath it, meaning that it cannot be a parent site.

Figure 4.1 illustrates a site hierarchy with four sites. The Houston site, at the top of the hierarchy, is the central site. The Columbus and Paris sites are both primary sites, and both are child sites of the central site. The Rome site is a secondary site and is a child site of the Paris site.

UNDERSTANDING THE SMS SITE HIERARCHY MODEL

The site server and the SQL Server play a critical role in the site model. The site server runs the SMS services that manage the site and communicate with other sites. The database contains the computer inventory for the site and its subsites.

If the site server fails, SMS will not process inventory or jobs; it will not generate new events or alerts; and it will not send data to other sites in the system. If the SQL Server fails, you cannot run SMS Administrator, and you cannot add or delete data from the database. This means that you cannot create, modify, or even view SMS Advertisement, packages, queries, events, or inventory.

Even if the site server or SQL Server fails, however, most clients and servers will continue to run normally:

- New computers can still be configured to run Systems Management Server.
- Clients can continue to report inventory.
- Clients can continue to run commands from the Advertising Package Command Manager.
- Clients can continue to use network applications with Program Group Control.

In addition, once the failed site server or SQL Server is added back to the network, SMS will resume normal processing and all functionality will be restored to all computers and administrators.

Each site is comprised of one or more IP or IPX networks. In this way, they map to the Windows 2000 notion of sites.

There is no maximum limit to the number of sites you can have or to the number of child sites a parent site can maintain. With SMS 2.0, many companies have thousands of sites that report through a single hierarchy as shown in Figure 4.1.

SITE HIERARCHY MODEL BENEFITS

To fit your organizational and management requirements, you can organize your site structure. A hierarchy can be deep or nearly flat. You can include many or a few sites. The site hierarchy model provides many benefits.

First, it simplifies managing and viewing large numbers of computers. In the left window of the SMS Administrator, a hierarchical view of the site and all of its subsites can be seen.

Second, it scales to meet the needs of companies of all sizes. A single SMS site may be sufficient for some companies. For many organizations, however, the ability to divide the company into a number of related sites simplifies systems management, especially for those companies that are growing and experiencing rapid changes.

Third, the site hierarchy allows you to map SMS to your existing logical network. One or more IP and/or IPX subnets are contained in each site. You can set your site boundaries to avoid intrasite network traffic over slower WAN links and to permit distributed site management. For instance, if your network structure dictates that computers in Honolulu need to be managed independently of computers in Miami, you can create a site hierarchy to support this structure.

Fourth, while most actual management tasks are performed *within* a given site, management policies, software distribution packages, and inventory information are efficiently passed *between* sites. While maintaining centralized management over WAN links, this allows you to use a LAN for the tasks that require the greatest bandwidth. By using the SMS Courier Sender and removable media for intersite communications, even remote installations with no network connection to the rest of the organization can be administered as subsites.

Finally, it lets you phase the deployment of SMS. Before combining the sites into a hierarchy, you can install primary sites individually and verify that each site is working satisfactorily.

Distributed Components

Each component of SMS can be placed on a different physical computer. Individual threads within a site system can be placed on different computers in certain cases. If a management application is to work in a sizable environment, this distributed mechanism for processing management information is critical.

Each component—such as a server, share, or NetWare volume—that provides functionality to the SMS site is known as a *site system*. The site system's assigned roles determine the functionality contributed by a site system. The site server itself is a site system. By default, all SMS server components are installed on the site server.

You can expressly assign roles to other site systems. These include:

- Site server
- Software component server
- SQL Server
- Client access points
- Distribution points
- SMS Logon points
- Metering servers

SITE SERVER

The site server contains many of the threads associated with the processing of management tasks and is the key engine for SMS functions. As needed, it can be further subdivided and placed on to component servers.

COMPONENT SERVER

A component server is a server that runs some of the SMS threads in order to provide duplicate threads or to lessen the processing burden on the site server. This functionality is commonly used to offload sender capabilities. See the following sidebar, "Understanding Senders," for more information on Sender capabilities.

Study Break

Understanding Senders

Within a site, SMS requires that the network is fast and reliable. No special operations are implemented to communicate between servers within a site. When communicating between sites, however, the link between sites is presumed to be slow and potentially unreliable. Therefore, SMS sites use senders to communicate reliably with other sites shown in Figure 4.2.

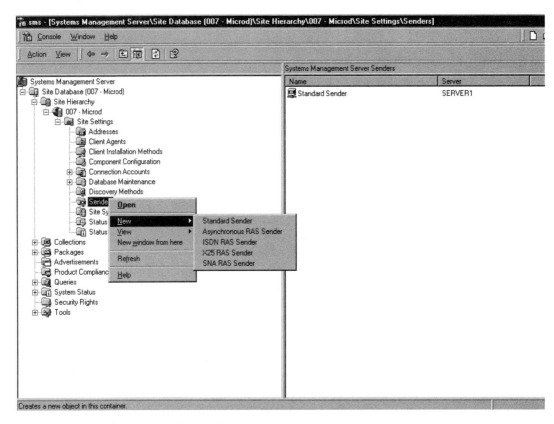

Figure 4.2 *Senders Options from Administrator Console.*

A *sender* is an SMS service that transmits instructions and data from one site to another. SMS always uses senders when transferring data between sites. When you set up a site, you must install the senders that the site uses to communicate with other sites. The sender uses the appropriate communications link to establish a connection to a target site and to transfer data to it. The sender manages the connection, ensures the integrity of transferred data, recovers from errors, and closes the connection when it is finished. You can install senders on the site server or on other Windows NT Servers. When you install senders to other servers, those servers are called *Component servers.*

SMS provides three basic types of senders: the LAN Sender, the RAS Sender, and the System Network Architecture (SNA) Sender. The senders do not provide connectivity to other sites. Instead, each type of sender uses a specific type of communications link to communicate with other sites. SMS supports three types of communications links: local area network, Remote Access Service (RAS), or SNA. If a sender requires another service to connect to other sites, that service must be installed on a computer at the site. For example, to use the SNA Sender, you must install it on a Windows NT 4.0 computer running Microsoft SNA Server.

By default, a LAN sender is created on all sites when they are created. You can install additional senders at a site. The senders you install depend on the other sites with which you need to communicate and the sender types used at those sites. You can install multiple senders of different types on a single computer. For instance, you can install a LAN and an SNA sender on the same computer. You can install more than one sender of the same type in a site, although you must install each sender on a different computer. If there is more than one sender available at a site, SMS selects the sender to use based on past throughput characteristics.

Different sender types use the network in different ways. For example, the SNA Sender can use batch or interactive mode. Using batch mode over an LU 6.2 session will not interfere with user's transactions from their terminals. However, using SNA INTER mode may impact users. This mode specifies that the SNA Sender may take as much bandwidth as it needs to complete sending the data as quickly as possible. Advertisements (Jobs) that use RAS will also monopolize the sending line (except for X.25 lines, which can send and receive at the same time). Even the LAN sender can consume all or most of the available bandwidth on a slow network.

All senders of a specific type manage a single outbox. Outboxes are directories where SMS services can place send request files. A send request file contains instructions that the sender uses to connect to a specified site and to transfer the specified data to the site. For example, all RAS Senders manage a single RAS Sender outbox.

Once you have installed a sender, you set up the sender addressing. An address contains specific information used to connect to the other site. A single site can have multiple addresses. For one site to be able to communicate with another site, the sending site must have at least one address defined for the receiving site. For example, if you want your current site to communicate with another site using RAS, you first must ensure that both sites have servers running the Windows NT 4.0 Remote Access Service. Then, you add a RAS Sender to your current site and create a RAS address for the other site. The RAS address specifies the phone number, RAS account, and RAS password used to dial in and connect to the RAS server at the other site.

If your company has a number of different physical locations connected by an SNA network, you might want to set up your site hierarchy so that each different physical location is a separate SMS site. Then you could use SNA Senders to communicate between your sites. SMS would send data between the sites over the SNA network, using the SNA Senders to ensure that the data were transferred correctly and efficiently. Installing an SNA Sender also installs the SNA Receiver, which is required at sites that receive data from the SNA Sender. Connecting SMS sites over an SNA network requires Microsoft SNA Server, an SNA Sender, and an SNA Receiver at each site.

SQL SERVER

The SQL Server database for a primary site can be installed on a computer. This is in addition to being installed on the site server. If you choose to install a dedicated version of SQL Server on the same site server for the SMS site database, network traffic can be reduced. This can also provide for easier backups and system maintenance. However, the computer used for the site server may not have the resources necessary to support both the site server and the SMS site database. If the site is very large, you may need use an instance of SQL Server on a different computer for your site database.

Installing SQL Server and the SMS site database on a computer other than your primary site server diverts some of the workload from your site server. If SMS was purchased as part of Microsoft BackOffice, you must install SQL Server on the computer used as the site server.

CLIENT ACCESS POINTS

A site system that provides a communication point between the site server and clients is known as a client access point (CAP). The client software contacts a CAP for management information from the SMS site, once it has been installed on a computer in a site. Status information, files, and inventory information collected at the clients are delivered to the CAPs. It is generally a good idea to assign this role to one or more computers other than the site server, since CAPs handle much of the communications between clients and the site server.

DISTRIBUTION POINTS

Site systems that receive package files from a site server are known as distribution points. After clients have received software distribution advertisements from the CAP, they contact distribution points to obtain programs and files. A distribution point can be a NetWare volume or a Windows NT 4.0 share. Like CAPs, distribution points handle much of the communication between clients and the site server. Other than the site server, it is generally a good idea to assign this role to one or more computers.

SMS LOGON POINTS

The initial point of contact between the client computer and the SMS environment is the logon point. The client runs the logon script, determines the sites to which it belongs, and finds a client access point. Microsoft Windows Networking clients run `smsls.bat` from the logon server. NetWare clients run `smsls.scr` from the system logon script. The client then determines the site or sites of which it is a member and looks for the possible client access points.

SOFTWARE METERING SERVERS

The SMS Software Metering feature enables you to monitor all applications running on the computers in your organization and to detect and monitor unregistered or unsupported software. You can also keep track of concurrent software usage to verify that you are within the license limits.

Site systems that maintain the software metering database and perform server-side software metering tasks are known as software metering servers. The software metering site database server must also be a server that has SQL Server installed. It can be installed on the same computer as a primary site, or to reduce the load, it can be installed on a computer other than the primary site server.

Site Communications

For the site hierarchy to function, the sites in the hierarchy must be able to communicate with each other. In particular, each site must be able to communicate with its parent site and its immediate child sites. There may be times when a site needs to communicate with other sites in the hierarchy as well. A site transfers data and instructions associated with a job directly to the target site. The job data and instructions are not forwarded through the hierarchy.

When you attach a primary site to a parent site, you need to define an address for the parent site so that inventory and status can be reported. You also need to define an address for the newly attached site at the parent site so that SMS network application information and inventory rules can be forwarded.

Security Model Integration

With many levels of configuration defining who can do what to whom, it is critical to make security as granular and flexible as possible. It is also important to make sure that any such model integrates with existing security.

In allowing you to grant permissions to Windows NT 4.0 users and user groups to perform specific SMS tasks, SMS 2.0 takes advantage of the Windows NT 4.0 security model. For instance, you can set SMS security so that members of the User Services user group can access only the Remote Tools features, but members of the System Administrators user group can also create packages for software distribution or alter the site hierarchy structure.

To open the administrator console, SMS 2.0 does not require a special login ID. Instead, the software permits or restricts access based on the Windows NT 4.0 account used to open the console. A user with limited permissions in the SMS site can open the console but can perform only the tasks for which that user account has permissions. Customized Administration consoles can also be created for allowing the user to view and use only specific SMS tasks.

SECURITY OBJECTS RIGHTS SPECIFICATION

You can set security levels by specifying the rights of Windows NT 4.0 users or user groups on various SMS security objects. SMS ships with the following default security objects:

- Advertisements
- Collections
- Packages
- Status objects

Remote Sites and Users Support

Large organizations work in distributed environments, often across WAN links. If you send sizable data across WAN links, you will find that these links are often slow, unreliable, or prohibitively expensive. SMS 2.0 is sensitive to the needs of remote sites and users, in businesses big and small.

REMOTE SITES

SMS is designed to work over WAN environments through the range of senders discussed previously. So that you can indicate the percentage of bandwidth used for a specific management task at a specific time, SMS offers bandwidth management capabilities. You could, for example, restrict bandwidth such that only 20% of it may be assigned to software distribution between the hours of 10:00 A.M. and 6:00 P.M., Monday through Saturday.

Furthermore, so that the full package does not need to be resent, SMS deals with network degradation by doing auto-restarts at the point of failure when there is a network break. Distribution packages are also compressed before being sent.

To make efficient use of bandwidth, SMS batches jobs into reasonably sized parcels. It carefully schedules packages to be distributed in a controlled manner to avoid bandwidth saturation. It does, however, offer a *send now* function in case a package needs to be at the top of the queue and be distributed in a hurry.

For software distribution that uses servers as routers of software, SMS 2.0 supports a fan-out mechanism. This means that a package going to multiple sites needs only to cross a slow link once before it is copied and routed to its various destinations.

SMS 2.0 also supports the new Courier Sender that allows software to be sent by *courier*. In other words, rather than across the wire, software is dispatched across land on CD-ROM. Courier Sender can be used in those situations where the package to be sent is too large or expensive to transmit or where the destination has no network connectivity. While the power of SMS is still available to the administrator, the software arrives by other means.

REMOTE USERS

SMS 2.0 has been developed with remote users in mind. The client agent has been modified to perform all processes locally rather than across the network. Only deltas of inventory—the difference between the current and the last measured state—are sent over the wire and are sent at a bandwidth-sensitive time.

When you log on to the network, SMS 2.0 avoids performing operations. It instead copies to the client only the information necessary to enable offline processing of information at less bandwidth-intensive and processor-intensive times.

Enterprise Vendors and Management Standards Integration

A key request of many enterprise environments is that SMS integrate with an existing heterogeneous management product, such as Computer Associates CA-Unicenter or IBM/Tivoli TME 10. By integrating with key industry standards such as the Common Information Model (CIM), SMS has been designed to share data with other management environments that support this model. It also allows access to existing data sources such as SNMP and DMI through CIM providers.

SMS is designed to act as a facilitator service to heterogeneous enterprise management products or to act as a stand-alone system. It can collect detailed objects from Windows-based environments and *provide* them to an enterprise management product; or it can be *driven* by an enterprise management product to perform specific operations from Windows-based environments.

MCSE 4.2 Adding Domains to a Site

When you add domains to an SMS site hierarchy model during the design phase, you select the type of domain being added and the method for specifying the logon servers to be included in the SMS domain. SMS differentiates between two types: Windows NT 4.0 and Novell NetWare environments. For each type, you can let SMS automatically detect the logon servers to be used or you can manually specify the logon servers.

SMS logon servers are configured automatically to run the discovery (Inventory) service when you add their domain to a site. This service configures SMS on each server and reports the server's inventory to the SMS system.

Automatically Detecting SMS Logon Servers

If you select Use All Detected Servers in a Windows NT 4.0, SMS automatically detects and includes all domain controllers. SMS attempts to use the NTFS drive with the most available space on each logon server. If an NTFS drive is not available on a particular logon server, SMS will use the largest non-NTFS drive.

For a Windows NT 4.0 domain, SMS lists only servers that are part of the domain: the computers running Windows NT Server 4.0 (primary domain controller, backup domain controllers, and member servers). As stated previously in Chapter 3, for a NetWare environment, SMS adds all NetWare servers within 18 router hops of the site server. On each server, SMS places files on the NetWare volume with the most free space.

When the Use All Detected Servers option is selected, SMS continues to monitor the SMS domain for any new servers. When it detects a new server, SMS configures it as an SMS logon server.

Automatic site configuration works best for small sites and for sites with simple Windows NT 4.0 domains. Automatically detecting all logon servers in a domain does not work as well for NetWare servers that do not support the concept of domains. Automatic site configuration does not work as well on complex Windows NT 4.0 domains, either—especially master user domain models, which call for domain controllers to be split across physical locations. In fact, automatically detecting the logon servers in a domain under these circumstances may cause serious problems, such as including some logon servers in more than one SMS site.

Manually Specifying SMS Logon Servers

If you manually specify the logon servers to use in an SMS domain, SMS includes only the servers you specify. When you specify the servers, you can also specify the drive on the server to use for SMS. If you choose this option, however, you must use the SMS Administrator to manually add new logon servers to the SMS domain as they are added to the network.

If you manually specify logon servers, you cannot specify that SMS automatically create the logon scripts. You can only automate the logon script creation when you the Use All Detected Servers option in the SMS domain.

If you manually specify logon servers, you can manually create the scripts, or you can have users manually run SMS Client Setup at their computers. In both cases, you must make sure that new computers and user logon scripts are added to the system.

Handling Windows NT 4.0 Domains that Span Sites

If you have implemented the master domain model for your organization, and you plan to have multiple sites, your master domain may need to span all your sites. This means that one or more servers from the master domain are in each site. You may decide to have a domain span multiple sites for many reasons, such as physical location or network topology.

When you add servers from the same domain to different sites, you must add the domain to each site using the Use Specified Servers option for Logon Servers in the Domain Properties dialog box. At each site, you add the specific logon servers that you want to include in the SMS domain in the Use These Logon Servers box in the Domain Properties dialog box.

For instance, assume that you have a Windows NT 4.0 domain named XFILECORP, with four network logon servers in it. You want the XFILE CORP domain to span the Arizona and Utah SMS sites, with the network logon servers FOX1 and FOX2 in the Arizona site and FOX3 and FOX4 in the Utah site. Add the XFILECORP domain to the Arizona site (it doesn't matter which site you do first), set Logon Servers to Use Specified Servers, and add FOX1 and FOX2 in the Use These Logon Servers box. Then add the XFILE CORP domain to the UTAH site, set Logon Servers to Use Specified Servers, and add FOX3 and FOX4 in the Use These Logon Servers box.

Do not use the Use All Detected Servers option for a domain that spans multiple sites. This will cause severe configuration problems, as the site that uses this option for the domain will conflict with the sites that explicitly contain the servers.

Adding Clients to a Site

Computers are added to the site hierarchy when a user at the computer connects to an SMS logon server and runs the RUNSMS batch file or when the user runs the SMSLS batch file through their logon script. Running either of these batch files also runs SMS Client Setup and the Inventory program. SMS Client Setup installs SMS at the client. The Inventory program scans the computer and reports its inventory to SMS. Remember if a computer's network connection is less than 40 Kbps, it is on a slow link and will not be discovered or installed during logon script processing. This entire process is known as the *registration process*. When a client is registered with SMS, its inventory records are added to a specific place in the site hierarchy. The place they are added depends on how the client is registered.

All clients run the RUNSMS or the SMSLS batch files to register with SMS. The RUNSMS program runs from the LOGON.SRV directory of a Systems Management Server logon server. The SMSLS program is run from a logon script. It runs from the NETLOGON share of a network logon server running Windows NT Server 4.0, and from the LOGON.SRV directory of NetWare logon servers.

There are five different ways for clients to register with SMS.

First, SMS can automatically configure logon scripts for your users. In this case, SMS automatically configures and replicates the SMSLS logon script. When you automatically configure logon scripts, you can choose whether or not to use SMSLS.INI for computer mapping. If you do not configure SMSLS.INI, computers are mapped to the network logon server domain.

Second, you can manually configure SMSLS-based logon scripts for your users. When you manually configure SMSLS-based logon scripts, you can also choose whether or not to use SMSLS.INI for computer mapping. If you do not configure SMSLS.INI, computers are mapped to the network logon server domain.

Third, you can configure the SMSLS.INI file to map computers in the site hierarchy. You can use SMSLS.INI whenever you use SMSLS-based

You must also set up a replication service for your Windows NT Servers. This service synchronizes a directory structure between machines in the domain, primarily the NETLOGON shares between the PDC and all BDCs. The NETLOGON share typically contains all the scripts associated with the logon process. Although this directory replication works well in a LAN environment, it can severely tax a dial-on-demand connection.

logon scripts. If you configure SMSLS.INI, computers are mapped to the SMS domain specified in the SMSLS.INI file. SMSLS.INI mapping is supported only in Windows NT 4.0 domains.

Fourth, you can manually configure RUNSMS-based logon scripts for your users. In this case, you configure each logon script to make an explicit connection to a specific SMS logon server. RUNSMS is run from the SMS_SHR share on the specified SMS logon server. The computer inventory is included in the site hierarchy in the same place as the SMS logon server inventory.

Finally, you can have users manually run the RUNSMS program from specific SMS logon servers. The users run the RUNSMS batch file directly from the SMS_SHR on the SMS logon server, or they can run the RUNSMS batch file through the AUTOEXEC.BAT file or the Start Up group within the Windows environment. In either case, the computer inventory is added to the SMS domain of the SMS logon server from which they ran the batch file.

Automatically Configuring Workstation Logon Scripts

You can use the Automatically Configure Workstation Logon Scripts option to include all clients in your SMS site. This option causes SMS to configure a logon script for each user that has an account in the domain, so that all users run the SMSLS file as they log on to the network. The SMSLS file runs the slow network detection program, SMS Client Setup (to install SMS components on the client), and the Discovery Inventory Agent (to collect inventory for a client from an SMS domain's logon server).

The option to Automatically Configure Workstation Logon Scripts is disabled by default when a site is installed. SMS does not create logon scripts unless you enable this option at your site. This option cannot be enabled unless you have also selected the option to automatically detect all logon servers in the domain.

If the Automatically Configure Workstation Logon Scripts option is enabled in a Windows NT 4.0, the SMSLS batch file (SMSLS.BAT) is added to the replication (REPL$) share. The SMSLS batch file is replicated to all network logon servers in the domain.

> SMS does not replicate the logon script itself. If you select the Automatically Configure Workstation Logon Scripts option, you must set up the Windows NT 4.0 Replicator service for each Windows NT 4.0 domain in the site.

SMS also adds the SMSLS batch file to all user profiles. If a user has an existing logon script, it modifies the existing script to call the SMSLS batch file. SMS adds the batch file to the logon script position specified by the Automatically Configure Workstation Logon Scripts setting. If a user has no logon script, it adds the SMSLS batch file to the user's profile.

SMS does not modify an existing logon script if the script file name does not have a file extension. For instance, if a user has a logon script specified as USER.BAT, SMS modifies the script to include the SMSLS batch file. If a user has a logon script named USER (instead of USER.BAT), SMS will not modify the script. If you want to set a user account so that the SMSLS batch file is not added to it, you can specify a logon script with no extension for that user.

In a NetWare environment, if the Automatically Configure Workstation Logon Scripts option is enabled, SMS modifies the system logon script on each NetWare logon server in the site. The SMSLS script file is called SMSLS.SCR on NetWare servers.

By default, when you use the Automatically Configure Workstation Logon Scripts option, client inventory is added to the site and domain of the SMS logon server from which the client runs the SMSLS script. You can control where the clients are included in the site hierarchy using the SMSLS.INI file. For more information, see "Mapping Computers to SMS Domains or Sites" below.

Manually Configuring Logon Scripts

If you do not want all clients in a particular domain to be included in the site, you can manually set up logon scripts for the clients you want to include. Before you configure the logon scripts for users in a Windows NT 4.0 you need to copy the SMS client files to the NET LOGON share of each SMS logon server in the domains where client users log on. You can then manually add the SMSLS batch file to logon scripts and assign a logon script to all users. If you manually configure logon scripts in a NetWare environment, you can manually add the SMS commands to the NetWare system script or to individual user logon scripts.

Mapping Computers to SMS Domains or Sites

When you run the SMSLS batch file as part of a logon script, the SMSLS file calls the SETLS program to make a connection to an SMS logon server. The SETLS program checks the SMSLS.INI file to see if it contains any entries about how to add computers to the hierarchy. These SMSLS.INI entries are called *mappings*, since they map computers to specific SMS domains or sites.

By default, SMSLS.INI does not contain any mappings, and SETLS runs SMS programs from the SMS logon server on which the SMSLS batch file was run. In this case, the computer inventory is reported to the SMS domain and site of the SMS logon server.

If an SMSLS.INI file is present and configured on an SMS logon server, then SETLS uses information in the SMSLS.INI file to choose an SMS logon server on which to run the SMS Client Setup and Inventory Agent programs. SETLS makes a universal naming convention (UNC) connection to the platform .BIN directory in the SMS_SHR share on the SMS logon server. The client is then added to the computer inventory of the SMS logon server's domain.

The SMSLS.INI file enables you to map existing configurations on a client to any domain and site that is part of a hierarchy. By using these mappings, a client appears in the specific site and domain that you want—regardless of which domain the client is actually logged on to. You can map computers to an SMS domain or to an SMS domain and site or to an SMS logon server. You can configure SMSLS.INI to map computers based on a number of different criteria:

- The client's specified workgroup
- The client's logon domain
- The client's machine name
- The SMS section in the client's WIN.INI file

Each type of mapping is a section in the SMSLS.INI file—for instance, [Machine]. Within each section, each entry maps the type of item in the section to an SMS domain or to a site domain combination. For instance, the following entry in SMSLS.INI would map the client FOXTO2 to the domain SKLYDOMAIN:

```
<PRE><FONT FACE="Courier" SIZE="2">[Machine]

FOXTO2= SKLYDOMAIN

</FONT></PRE>
```

In many cases, it may be enough to map a client to a specific domain. In other cases, you may want to map clients to a specific site and domain combination. For instance, if your organization uses a single master user domain that is split among multiple sites, specifying the SMS domain alone does not completely determine how computers are mapped into your site tree. A client could be mapped to a server in the correct domain but in the wrong site. To map a computer to a particular site and domain, you must specify a site in addition to an SMS domain on the right side of the entry in SMSLS.INI.

The domain name must be followed by a colon and the site code. For example, the following entry would map workstations that are part of the SKULLYGRP workgroup to an SMS logon server in the SKDOM domain that is in the site with the site code SK1:

```
<PRE><FONT FACE="Courier" SIZE="2">[WORKGROUP]

SKULLYGRP = SKDOM:SK1

</FONT></PRE>
```

You can also map a computer directly to an SMS logon server. In this case, the computer runs the SMS registration programs from the SMS_SHR on the specified server. The computer inventory is reported to the domain of the SMS logon server. The following entry would map computers that are part of the SKULLYGRP workgroup to an SMS logon server named DANAK1:

```
<PRE><FONT FACE="Courier" SIZE="2">[WORKGROUP]

SKULLYGRP = \\DANAK1

</FONT></PRE>
```

The SETLS program evaluates the SMSLS.INI file from top to bottom and uses the first successful match it finds. After it finds a match, it will attempt to find a server in the specified site and domain to use as the client's SMS logon server. If it finds a specified SMS logon server, SETLS connects to that server and runs SMS Client Setup and the Discovery (Inventory) Agent from that server. This adds the client to the mapped site and domain. If

SETLS does not find a matching SMS logon server, it proceeds to the next entry in the `SMSLS.INI` file. If it does not find any SMS logon servers that match the entries in `SMSLS.INI`, it adds the client to the SMS domain of the SMS logon server.

Because SMS evaluates the `SMSLS.INI` file from top to bottom, you can provide multiple paths for client mapping. The following example demonstrates how to set up an `SMSLS.INI` file with multiple mappings. The example maps clients in the workgroup MIS to an SMS logon server in the MISMAIN domain. If no SMS logon server is found in that domain, then it will map the clients to the SMS logon server named SMSBACKUP.

```
<PRE><FONT FACE="Courier" SIZE="2">[workgroup]

MIS=MISMAIN

MIS=\\SMSBACKUP

</FONT></PRE>
```

Once a computer has been mapped with `SMSLS.INI`, the mapping information is stored in the local `SMS.INI` file and is used for all SMS activities on the computer. The computer stays mapped according to the local information unless the `SMSLS.INI` file on its SMS logon server changes. In that case, the computer may be remapped the next time it runs the SMSLS batch file.

Configuring Logon Scripts to Use RUNSMS

You can use the RUNSMS program in logon scripts to map computers directly to specified SMS logon servers. You must modify the logon scripts for each user so that the script makes a connection to an SMS logon server and then runs RUNSMS from that server. You can connect with a drive letter or with a UNC path.

This option is useful if you want to map computers based on the users logging on to the network. For instance, if you have users in a Windows NT 4.0 domain that is split into two subnets, you can use this option to map users to an SMS logon server in their subnet. You create one logon script to map users in the first subnet to their SMS logon server and a second script to map users in the other subnet to the SMS logon server in their subnet. If the SMS logon server in one of the subnets is named SN1, the following command could be added to a Windows NT 4.0 logon script to map the users in the subnet to server SN1:

```
<PRE><FONT FACE="Courier" SIZE="2">\\SN1\SMS_SHR\RUNSMS

</FONT></PRE>
```

Manually Adding Computers to a Site

If you do not automate SMS client configuration, you must manually add each client to the SMS computer inventory. Clients are added when a user at the computer connects to an SMS logon server and runs the RUNSMS batch file. This file runs SMS Client Setup and the Inventory Agent. The computer inventory is added to the SMS domain and site of the SMS logon server.

You can manually add a client by running the RUNSMS batch file through the AUTOEXEC.BAT file or the Start Up group within the Windows environment. If you choose this method, modify the AUTOEXEC.BAT file or Start Up group at each client you want added to the site inventory.

How SMS Identifies Computers

Every computer in the hierarchy is assigned an SMS.INI file when it first registers with SMS. This file is hidden in the root of the primary partition on the computer. SMS uses this file to manage the computer and to uniquely identify the computer in the hierarchy.

One of the most important values in the file is the SMS ID. The SMS ID is assigned based on the site and the SMS logon server that initially configures the computer. SMS maintains a range of available IDs on every SMS logon server in every domain in the site. Each SMS logon server is assigned an ID range file consisting of the site code and five digits followed by the UID extension. The five digits can be any valid alphanumeric characters (0–9, A–Z). For example, the first SMS logon server added to the FOX site's inventory has a file called FOX00000.UID; the second SMS logon server has FOX01000.UID; the third SMS logon server has FOX02000.UID; the tenth server would have FOX09000.UID; the eleventh would have FOX0A000.UID; and so on.

When a client is logged on to SMS for the first time, SMS gives it an ID that matches the file (FOX00000, FOX00001, and so on) and then increments the last numerical digit in the file name. For example, if an SMS logon server has a file FOX00000.UID, the first client receives an ID of FOX00000. SMS renames the UID file to FOX00001.UID, which indicates the ID of the next client. SMS also writes the UID to each client's SMS.INI file.

If SMS detects that the client range is approaching its ID limit, it increments the range on the SMS logon server. In the previous example, if there were a total of three SMS logon servers available, FOX00000 would become FOX04000.UID.

The SMS ID is assigned to a computer in a way that guarantees it will be unique. The assignment is also permanent. Once assigned, the SMS ID is not reused. Since the SMS ID is contained in the SMS.INI file, you should not change this file in any way.

Study Break

Minimizing the Impact of SMS Deployment

The following are some specific actions you can take to minimize the impact of SMS deployment on your users:

- If you have not used logon scripts and you plan to introduce them to support SMS, enable a simple, friendly logon script well before you enable SMS in the logon script. This gives your users time to adjust to the logon scripts, and it gives you time to resolve any issues introduced by the logon scripts themselves.

- When you enable SMS in the logon scripts, customize the scripts so that your users know what is happening. For example, you might want to add a support contact name and phone number, an explanation and date for the last revision, a short description of the SMS features you are enabling, a reason for why you are enabling these features, and so on. You can even customize scripts to function differently for different users. You can use environment variables or file existence checks to trigger particular actions. For example, you can have a script run in a verbose mode for some users, while for other users it runs with almost no feedback.

- Give your users time to accept SMS. Do not immediately schedule major changes using SMS. Try not to schedule intrusive or time-consuming jobs unless you are sure that your users need the job functionality.

- Inform and educate your users about SMS before you deploy it on their computers. SMS includes an educational file that you can customize and distribute to your users. This file includes a complete description of what SMS is, why a company might want to use it, and how it affects clients. This file is called CLIENT.WRI. It is installed with the SMS help files.

In addition, control risk by putting the SMS site infrastructure in place before adding any clients to the sites. For instance, you could use the following model to build the site infrastructure:

1. Install SQL Servers for each site.

2. Install primary site servers.

3. Add secondary sites to primary sites.

4. Configure additional senders and addresses.

5. Add additional domains and logon servers to sites.

6. Verify the integrity of the site infrastructure.

7. Add clients.

This model allows you to implement and test the hierarchy before adding clients or moving on to more complicated uses of SMS. You can even disable client software when you add your clients. This causes SMS to set up the clients and run only hardware inventory. Enable the client software as you need it, phasing in new functionality and thereby reducing risk.

MCSE 4.3   Planning For Various Situations

When planning for various situations in the SMS site hierarchy design and defining site boundaries, the first thing to do is to construct a map or diagram showing all the locations where your company has an office facility. Then, identify the number and types of users at each location. In most cases, you can create an SMS site for each location. In some cases, you may want to split a single physical location into more than one SMS site—perhaps because of the number of users or because of different user needs. In other situations, different physical locations may be connected by a fast LAN, in which case you may want to create a single site for those locations. Although you cannot base your design decision entirely on location, it is an important factor to consider when planning your site boundaries.

Planning the Number of Resources

When planning the SMS site hierarchy design, account for the number of resources. This translates into much of the new software and hardware costs (not the cost of licensing). It includes the support costs accumulated as the software is deployed within an organization. This is especially true when upgrading to major new releases, such as Windows 98 or Windows 2000. By utilizing SMS Administrators, you can perform automatic, unattended upgrades of computers, overcoming many of the typical problems encountered when upgrading software. With SMS you can clearly target the computers that you wish to upgrade, specify any configuration options for the computer, indicate when the upgrade should happen, and verify whether or not the installation was successful. This reduces the costs and difficulties associated with upgrading software, and allows you to benefit immediately from the new technology.

Planning the Number of Layers

You must also plan for the number of layers needed for managing data, applications, and operating systems, as well as for performing other tasks such as scheduling system events, making sure there is enough capacity, and charging different departments for computer time. In the SMS environment, layering means that these tasks have been prioritized within the SMS architecture.

For instance, as businesses deploy more personal computers, systems management has lagged behind. While some basic issues have remained the same, managing distributed environments spread throughout many SMS primary and secondary site locations has created new problems. For example, an SMS site administrator might be concerned with user administration, automation of repetitive tasks for a large number of systems, and, of course, managing version control in many different systems and configuration files that may be different on every computer. Simply locating all the PCs within an organization is a common problem. Determining the hardware and software within each computer is even more difficult, since this should be done during nonworking hours so as not to affect the user. These procedures can take months to accomplish in a large distributed organization. In addition, installing and upgrading software on all the SMS sites has its own associated problems, such as making sure that the versions are correct and that the computers are capable of running the new software.

Even with the most comprehensive SMS design plan, things can go wrong. Therefore, you need tools to locate and diagnose problems so that a site is not left unavailable for any length of time. Equally important, you need to diagnose and resolve problems from a central site location, thereby reducing the cost of managing your systems. All these problems need to be addressed today for your existing SMS architectural environment and in the future as your business requirements change.

Planning Network Connectivity

The next factor to consider is network connectivity. Computers that are not connected together over a fast LAN (for instance, computers on different network segments) should be placed in different sites. If you have computers connected together across a fast LAN, you can place these computers in a single site or in different sites. Unless there are reasons for placing them in different sites, such as capacity or management issues, you should include all servers on the same LAN in the same site.

Planning for International Issues

Another factor to consider is *international issues*. Of course, the main international issue is language. The SMS server software is available in the following languages:

- English (U.S. and international)
- German
- French
- Japanese
- Korean
- Chinese

The SMS client software is available in these languages as well as in the following languages:

- Spanish
- Italian
- Swedish
- Dutch
- Norwegian
- Finnish
- Danish
- Brazilian

If you plan to use more than one language version of SMS within a site, you should consider the following:

- The U.S. English, French, German, and Korean versions of SMS do not support other languages within the site. In other words, you must use only French clients in a French site, German clients in a German site, and so on.
- If you want to run multiple client language types within an English site, the site server must be running the International English SMS server software.
- The Chinese version of SMS supports Chinese and English clients.
- The Japanese version of SMS supports English and Japanese clients within the site. The Japanese SMS CD-ROM contains Japanese and English language files.

Planning the Number of Sites

When you define your site boundaries, you also determine the overall number of sites in your system. In general, try to minimize the number of sites you create. Small companies (less than 60 computers) frequently find that a single site, single domain hierarchy works well for their environments. Large companies (more than 3000 computers) may well end up with many sites and multiple levels in the hierarchy.

Planning the Network Bandwidth Requirements

The final main factor to consider is planning the network bandwidth requirements. For example, planning for low bandwidth requirements reduces the bandwidth consumed by an application and its associated server. Low bandwidth is designed for the scenario where the client and server are separated by a low bandwidth link. The solution is to insert an intermediary (lbxproxy) between the client and server and place it on the client side of the low bandwidth link. This intermediary performs a number of actions that help reduce communication overhead. Its two main actions are to cache server information and to compress data between itself and the server. Caching server information reduces the number of interactions between the client and server while compressing the remaining data stream further reduces the communication overhead.

The decision to use reduction techniques is made at server connection time, meaning that the client chooses to use low bandwidth via the client's DISPLAY parameter. Once chosen, low bandwidth cannot be turned off; the bandwidth must be used for the duration of the connection. This can be somewhat limiting in a dynamic environment, like an SMS site in which varying network bandwidths dictate whether or not low bandwidth is used.

One solution to this problem is to add functionality to the low bandwidth intermediary to give it more dynamic behavior. A perfect place for this is in the compression control portion of the intermediary (lbxproxy). Compression control within lbxproxy is stateless, meaning that it can be turned on and off without informing the associated server. In this solution, the use of compression between the intermediary and the server would be dynamic, depending on the amount of bandwidth available. This can be achieved through the use of the Event Manager's (EM) Event Notification Interface in conjunction with lbxproxy. The intermediary is modified to listen for event notification messages regarding network bandwidth. Assuming that a mechanism exists that can measure network bandwidth and provide the Event Manager with this information, lbxproxy can be kept abreast of network resource changes through the use of the EM Notification Interface. The intermediary can use event notification messages to dynamically modify its use of compression between itself and the server.

This example demonstrates how the Event Manager's Event Notification Interface can be integrated easily into a preexisting application. In general, the infrastructure is usable with any application interested in mobile host state information, regardless of how the application intends to use this information.

Other Factors

There are many other factors to consider when planning for various situations in an SMS site hierarchy. Let's look at a few.

DOMAIN STRUCTURE

When you create your site boundaries, you specify which domains, logon servers, and computers are included in the site. Each site can contain one or more domains on the same LAN. Sites can also contain only some of the logon servers in a domain, so that the domain can, in effect, be split among different sites.

Domains are often a natural boundary for creating sites. You should not split a domain between sites unless it is required for some other reason. For example, if you have a single domain that spans one or more routers, you may want to install an SMS site on each subnet to ensure that your clients won't access distribution servers across the routers. This provides more efficient network performance within a site.

Also, if you use the Windows NT 4.0 master domain model, and you include domain controllers from the master domain at each physical location, you should consider creating an SMS site at each physical location. This gives you more flexibility when you want to map computers into specific SMS sites and domains.

NetWare servers do not support the domain concept. Before you can create sites with NetWare servers in them, you must group the NetWare servers into SMS domains. Group the NetWare servers into SMS domains and sites based on the guidelines in this chapter, such as physical location and network connectivity.

LOGICAL CONSIDERATIONS

Look for existing logical organizations in your current system. If you use management tools other than SMS, your use of these tools may suggest a particular grouping for SMS. For instance, if you already use a tool for network management, you probably have administrators in place to operate the tool. You may even have given the administrators responsibility for specific physical locations. If so, you can set up your SMS sites so that they match the existing management structure.

Consider both logical and physical elements when defining your site boundaries. For example, you may want to put all users in the Purchasing department into a single site. This is a logical preference that allows you to manage the Purchasing department as a single group. This only makes sense, however, if the physical environment allows for it. If the Purchasing department is actually located in several physical locations, connected over a slow network or not connected at all, physical constraints prevent this logical design choice.

SERVERS

When you are defining your site structure, consider the capacity and accessibility of your servers in the site. Each site needs the following types of servers:

- A site server (must be running Windows NT Server 4.0)
- Logon servers (network logon servers and SMS logon servers)
- Package servers (if you will be distributing software from or to computers in the site)
- A database server (primary sites only)
- One or more Windows NT 4.0-based computers to run the SMS administrative tools (primary sites only); by default, the administrative tools are installed on the site server
- Additional Site servers (optional)

These server roles can be met with a single server or with multiple servers. Define your site boundaries so that the servers in each site can adequately fulfill their roles. Ensure that all clients in a proposed site have access to the servers and services they need. In particular, all clients should have fast, direct access to an SMS logon server and to a distribution server.

CAPACITY GUIDELINES

As you do your site design, pay close attention to capacity issues for the computers and network at your sites. If you find that the capacity of a proposed site is inadequate, increase the hardware and network capacity of the site, or decrease the load on the site. Increase the capacity of a site by adding new servers or by upgrading the existing servers or network links. For instance, instead of making an existing server the SMS site server, add a new server to the site and make it the site server. Decrease the load at a site by dividing the proposed site into multiple sites. For instance, if you have many Windows NT 4.0 domains on a single LAN, create many sites (one per domain) instead of setting up a single site with numerous domains. Use the following capacity guidelines for configuring your SMS sites, domains, and servers.

First of all, the SMS site server is a Windows NT Server 4.0 domain controller that runs the SMS services. The site server usually experiences the heaviest load increase after SMS is installed. The load on the site server increases further with the size and activity of the site.

To get the best possible performance from your site server, install it in a private domain—a domain used exclusively for SMS. This approach has several benefits. It guarantees that the server will not be busy processing user logons, and it increases your flexibility to change the site structure. It also makes it easier to identify and fix system problems by isolating potential SMS problems from network logon problems.

If you install SMS on a server in an existing domain, pay attention to logon server load. SMS logon servers may replicate a large amount of data and are frequently polled for updates, availability, and inventory. If your logon servers are heavily stressed before implementing SMS, you may have to add more logon servers after you deploy SMS. This is not necessary in most cases.

If you install SMS into an existing domain and need to temporarily increase the performance of the site server, pause the NetLogon service on the site server. When paused, the NetLogon service is not the target for any pass-through authentication, allowing the computer to be available for other purposes. For example, you could pause the NetLogon service on the site server when a large package is being compressed. All logon servers in the domain must be running Windows NT Server 4.0 or higher to take advantage of this feature

The second capacity guideline allows you to consider whether you want to install SQL Server on the site server or on a different server. You can usually run both SQL Server and the SMS site server on the same high-end server with good results. However, if you have less-powerful servers or a large, busy site, you may want to run SQL Server and the SMS site server on separate servers.

There are advantages to both configurations. For example, running SQL Server on the site server makes it easier to install SMS. It reduces network traffic associated with the SMS services that access SQL Server, and it minimizes hardware requirements, since you need only one computer for both SQL Server and the site server. Running SQL Server on a server other than the site server is usually more flexible. It makes it easier to isolate SMS or SQL Server problems, and it may yield better performance, especially on low-end servers.

A third capacity guideline is to allocate separate physical drives for Windows NT Server 4.0, SQL Server, and SMS. Even if you install SMS and

If you are installing SMS and SQL Server from a single copy of the Microsoft BackOffice product, you must install both products on the same server.

SQL Server on the same computer, dedicating separate drives for each generally improves system performance.

The fourth capacity guideline is to allocate the best hardware to the site servers highest in the hierarchy. In the hierarchy, higher site servers generally have greater hardware needs. The fifth capacity guideline is to make sure that you maintain a fast network connection between the site server, the SQL Server, and any computers running the SMS Administrator. The sixth is that if you let SMS detect all servers in a domain, be sure that the servers (and the domain) are being detected only by one SMS site. If multiple SMS sites auto-detect the same servers, SMS will not work properly. The seventh guideline is that if you distribute packages to computers at the site, make sure that the distribution servers have enough capacity (especially disk space) to serve the clients in the site.

The eighth and final capacity guideline is that you can create an additional site server by moving the Scheduler, Despooler, Inventory Processor, Inventory Data Loader, and Sender components from the primary site server to another server. You should move the first four components to an additional site server only if you have determined that your site server is heavily loaded. Senders should be installed on servers configured to support the sender protocol.

If possible, you should use the Windows NT 4.0 Performance Monitor to determine which components are loading the site server, and then you should move those components to a helper server. If you cannot specifically determine which components are loading the site server, use the following guidelines to determine which components to move:

- First of all, if you are going to run multiple senders at a site, also install the senders on the additional site servers. Senders use a particular type of communications link, so the site server must be configured to support the sender. For example, a second site server for a RAS ASYNC sender would need to be configured with RAS and an async modem.
- Second, if the site server is consistently busy processing MIF files, move the Inventory Data Loader component to a component server.

- Finally, if the site server is busy accessing SQL Server, move the Inventory Data Loader and the Scheduler components to a second site server. If the site server is running SQL Server, you should also move the SQL Server to the same second site server.

PLATFORMS

You should evaluate the hardware and software platforms of the computers within your proposed site boundaries. Make sure that all computers meet the requirements for SMS (supported operating system, network operating system, hardware, and software).

Since each platform is managed in a different way—potentially by different administrators—each platform may require special access to certain types of servers and services. Be sure that your design can accommodate the different platform needs within each site. For example, if you include NetWare clients in a site, be sure that the clients have access to a NetWare logon server, a NetWare distribution server, and a computer running the Windows NT 4.0 Gateway Service for NetWare. You may also want to make sure that you have an administrator who is familiar with NetWare at the site or at the parent site.

SITE SIZE

The load on a site generally depends on the hardware in use at the site and on the number of users and computers included in the site and subsites. In general, the larger the site, the heavier the load on the site server and on other site components.

The site size is determined by the number of clients and resources.

If you create sites that are too large, you may find that SMS performs too slowly. If you create sites that are too small, you may find that you need to buy a lot of hardware (at least one site server per site), and that the hardware is generally not used to capacity.

Larger sites tend to put more of a burden on the administrator. Of course, the administrative burden depends on the number of jobs created, the amount of site maintenance required, and so on.

Microsoft generally considers that sites with less than 60 clients are small sites; sites with 60–3000 clients are medium sites; and sites with more than 3000 clients are large sites. Although you certainly can design sites with less than 60 users or with more than 3000 users, most sites fall into the medium range. If your design calls for less than 60 users in a site, you might want to see if you can combine them with other users at another location and create a larger site. If your design calls for more than 3000 users in a site, you might want to consider creating three or more sites.

 These limits should reflect computers reporting directly to the site. This does not include computers reporting to a subsite of the current site. For example, the database at a parent site with 3000 computers may have many more than 3000 computer records in the database, since the database contains records for all computers in the site and in all subsites.

USER NEEDS

You may find that user needs vary greatly, even within a single location. For example, a single location may include both advanced and novice computer users. The novice users may need frequent support. They may want you to install new software for them, to diagnose problems for them, and to otherwise manage their computers for them. You may want to install all SMS client software on the computers of these users, and you probably will want to frequently scan their computers for inventory.

The advanced users, however, may not want you to impact their computer use in any way. You may want to manage these users differently than you manage the novice users. In large part, the properties of a site determine how the site is managed. For example, the software to be installed on clients and the inventory scanning frequency are set in the SMS Administrator Site Properties dialog box. If you want to manage users in differing ways, put the users' computers into different sites and uniquely configure the site properties for each site.

■ Summary

You should come away from this chapter with an in-depth knowledge of the following MCSE exam-specific components needed to design the SMS site hierarchy model prior to installation for the enterprise.

First of all, SMS is built on top of SQL Server to ensure data integrity. Also, SMS natively uses the capabilities of SQL Server and is integrated with it to ensure the most efficient data storage possible.

Next, when you add domains to an SMS site hierarchy model, select the type of domain being added and the method for specifying the logon servers to be included in the SMS domain. SMS differentiates between two types of domains: Windows NT 4.0 and Novell NetWare environments. Thus, you can let SMS automatically detect the logon servers to be used, or you can manually specify the logon servers for each type of domain.

When planning for various situations in SMS site hierarchy design, you need to consider the following:

- Physical location
- Network connectivity
- Domain structure
- Logical considerations
- Servers
- Capacity guidelines
- Platforms
- Site size
- Number of sites
- User needs
- SMS network applications
- Multiple languages within a site

▲ CHAPTER REVIEW QUESTIONS

▲ True/False

1. *True or False? You should use the Use All Detected Servers option for a domain that spans multiple sites.*

2. *True or False? Site size limits should reflect computers reporting directly to the site. This does not include computers reporting to a subsite of the current site. For example, the database at a parent site with 3000 computers may have many more than 3000 computer records in the database, since the database contains records for all computers in the site and in all subsites.*

3. *True or False? Your existing network can be organized into SMS sites through the SQL Server.*

4. *True or False? Each component of SMS (known as a site system) can be placed on a different physical computer.*

5. *True or False? Computers that are not connected together over a fast LAN (for instance, computers on different network segments) should be placed in different sites. If you have computers that are connected together across a fast LAN, you can place these computers in a single site or in different sites. Unless there are other reasons for placing them in different sites (such as capacity or management issues), you should include all servers on the same LAN in the same site.*

6. *True or False? The initial point of contact between the client computer and the SMS environment is the configuration of the logon point. The client runs the logon script, determines which sites it is a member of, and finds a client access point. Microsoft Windows Networking clients run* `Smsls.doc` *from the logon server. NetWare clients run* `smsls.scr` *from the system logon script. The client then determines which site or sites it is a member of and looks for the possible client access points.*

7. *True or False? A site system that provides a communication point between the site server and clients is known as a client access point (CAP). The client software contacts a CAP for configuration management information from the SMS site once it has been installed on a computer in a site. Status information, files, and inventory information collected at the clients are delivered to the CAPs. It is generally a good idea to assign this role to one or more computers other than the site server, since CAPs handle much of the communications between clients and the site server.*

8. *True or False? When you attach a primary site to a parent site, define and configure an address to the parent site so that the inventory and status can be reported to the parent site. You also need to define and configure an address for the newly attached site at the parent site so that SMS network application information and inventory rules can be forwarded to the attached site.*

9. *True or False? Site systems that maintain the software metering database and perform server-side software metering tasks (like monitoring the progress of software metering) are known as software metering servers. Installing the software metering services on additional servers in an environment is recommended when there are a small number of clients being proactively checked for license compliance.*

▲ Multiple Choice

1. *If the SQL Server fails, you cannot run the SMS Administrator, and you cannot add or delete data from the database. This means that you cannot create, modify, or even view SMS advertisements, packages, queries, events, or resources (inventory). However, even if the site server or SQL Server fails, most clients and servers continue to run normally except:*

    A. New computers can still be configured to run Systems Management Server.
    B. Clients can continue to report inventory.
    C. Clients can continue to run commands from the Courier Sender.
    D. Clients can continue to use network applications with Program Group Control.

2. *SMS ships with the following default security objects, except:*

    A. Advertisements
    B. Collections
    C. Packages
    D. Inventory
    E. Status objects

3. *You can configure* SMSLS.INI *to map computers based on a number of different criteria except:*

    A. The client's specified workgroup
    B. The client's logon domain
    C. The client's machine name
    D. Windows NT Server

4. *You can map computers to an SMS site or to an SMS logon server. You can configure* SMSLS.INI *to map computers based on a number of different criteria except:*

    A. The SMS Server component settings
    B. A site server (must be running Windows NT Server 4.0)
    C. Logon servers (network logon servers and SMS logon servers)
    D. A database server (primary sites only)
    E. Additional Site servers (optional)

5. *There are several different ways for clients to register with SMS except:*

    A. You can configure SMS to automatically configure logon scripts for your users.

B. You can manually configure SMSLS-based logon scripts for your users.

C. You can ensure the clients log in correctly.

D. You can configure the SMSLS.INI file to map computers in the site hierarchy.

E. You can manually configure RUNSMS-based logon scripts for your users.

6. *Use the following capacity guidelines for configuring your SMS sites, domains, and servers except:*

A. To get the best possible performance from your site server, install it in a private domain—a domain used exclusively for SMS.

B. Consider whether you want to install SQL Server on the site server or on a different server.

C. Consider user group resources, which include Windows NT 4.0 user groups.

D. If you install SMS on a server in an existing domain, pay attention to logon server load.

E. If you install SMS into an existing domain and you need to temporarily increase the performance of the site server, you can pause the NetLogon service on the site server.

7. *There are advantages to the capacity guidelines in the previous question except:*

A. Running SQL Server on the site server makes it easier to install SMS.

B. Running SQL Server on a server other than the site server is usually more flexible.

C. Try to allocate separate physical drives for Windows NT Server 4.0, SQL Server, and SMS.

D. Allocate the best hardware to the site servers highest in the site hierarchy.

E. None of the above.

8. *If possible, you should use the Windows NT 4.0 Performance Monitor to determine which components are loading the site server, and then you should move those components to a helper server. If you cannot specifically determine which components are loading the site server, you can use the following guidelines to determine which components to move except:*

A. If you are going to run multiple senders at a site, install the senders on helper servers rather than on the site server.

    B. Distribute and install software to the client.

    C. If the site server is consistently busy processing MIF files, move the Inventory Data Loader component to a helper server.

    D. If the site server is busy accessing SQL Server, move the Inventory Data Loader and the Scheduler components to a helper server.

    E. If the site server is running SQL Server, you should also move the SQL Server to the same helper server.

9. *The SMS server software is available in the following languages except:*

    A. German

    B. French

    C. Japanese

    D. Korean

    E. Italian

▲ Open Ended

1. To stop possible bottlenecks from occurring, a number of improvements have been made to the basic architecture. This will allow SMS to work and grow in enterprises of any size by using which key components?

2. A server, share, or NetWare volume that provides functionality to the SMS site is known as a site system. The site system's assigned roles determines the functionality contributed by a site system. The site server itself is a site system. By default, all SMS server components are installed on the site server. You can expressly assign roles to other site systems. What are these roles?

SMS Security Strategy Plan

In the development of a Systems Management Server (SMS) security strategy plan for the support of large environments, it is critical to have the ability to make security as granular and as flexible as possible. This includes having many levels of configuration defining who can do what to whom. It is also important to make sure that any such security strategy model integrates with the security that is already pervasive in the environment.

SMS 2.0 takes advantage of the Windows NT 4.0 security model, allowing you to grant necessary permissions for specific SMS tasks to Windows NT 4.0 users and user groups. For instance, you can set SMS security so that members of the User Services user group can access only the Remote Tools features, but members of the System Administrators user group can also create packages for software distribution or alter the site hierarchy structure.

125

SMS 2.0 does not require a special login ID to open the administrator console. Instead, the software permits or restricts access based on the Windows NT 4.0 account used to open the console. A user with limited permissions in the SMS site can open the console but can perform only the tasks for which that user account has permissions.

Security levels are set by specifying the rights that a Windows NT 4.0 user or user group has on various SMS security objects. SMS has the following default security objects, which are discussed later in the chapter:

- Advertisements
- Collections
- Packages
- Status objects

Let's begin the first part of the chapter by taking a look at SMS accounts that are one of the elements of the security strategy plan. The discussion focuses on the creation of the user accounts for the SMS Server services. This was discussed in detail in Chapter 3, "SMS Site Design." It is included in this chapter not only because it is a big part of SMS security strategy plan, but also because readers may skip directly to this chapter to see how to set up such a plan.

MCSE 5.1   SMS Service Accounts

Each site must have an SMS Service Account that provides access to all the servers and Windows NT 4.0 clients in SMS. This account is the same (including user name and password) on all SMS servers within the site. The procedure for creating this account is explained in Chapter 3, "SMS Site Design."

To create a Windows NT 4.0 user account to be used by SMS services, you need to create this account at the site server. Make sure that you are logged in with an account that has administrator privileges. If you have trust relationships established between Windows NT 4.0 domains, the SMS Service Account needs to be added only to the master domain. If you do not have trust relationships in a multiple-domain environment, you must add a common SMS Service Account in each domain.

If using additional site servers the account name and password must be the same as those of the SMS Service Account on the central site server. For Novell NetWare, you must create an SMS Service Account with full permissions to all volumes on each NetWare server (equivalent to Supervisor). The account name and password must be the same as those of the SMS Service Account on the site server.

SQL Login IDs Creation

Create an SQL login ID for the SMS services to use to access the database. Instead of creating a new account, however, you can use the existing SQL Server system administrator (*sa*) account as the SQL login ID used by the SMS services.

You do not have to create accounts for users at the clients.

These SQL Server procedures are for Microsoft SQL Server 7.0 or higher. If you are using a different version of SQL Server, the procedures may vary.

CREATING AN SQL LOGIN ID FOR THE SMS SERVICES

The type of security you configure for SQL Server determines whether you need to create a new SQL login ID for SMS or if you can use the Windows NT 4.0 SMS Service Account. Your SQL Server will be configured to use standard, integrated, or mixed security. Standard security means that SQL Server manages its own logon validation process. Integrated security allows SQL Server to make use of Windows NT 4.0 security features and allows authorized users to bypass the SQL Server logon process. Mixed security allows logon requests to be validated using integrated or standard security.

SQL Server Integrated Security Use

With integrated security, SQL Server automatically uses the Windows NT 4.0 SMS Service Account as the SQL login ID for the SMS services. You do not need to create an additional account. This means that when you install SMS, leave the SQL Login and Password boxes blank in the SQL Database Setup dialog box as shown in Figure 5.1.

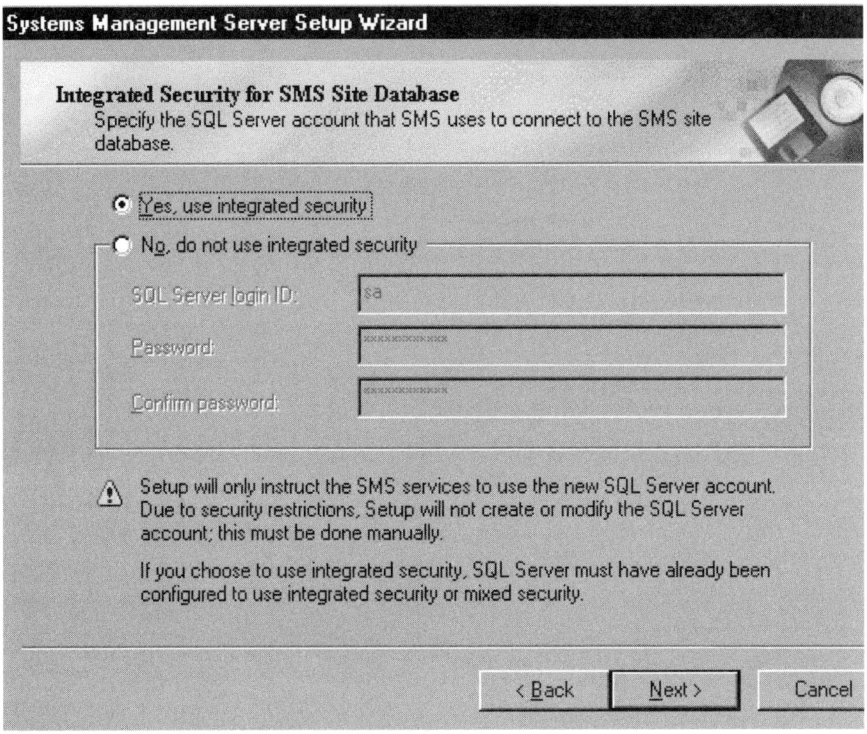

Figure 5.1   *SQL Database setup Dialog box.*

SQL Mixed Security Use

With mixed security you have two options: You can create an SQL login ID for the SMS services or you can use the Windows NT 4.0 SMS Service Account. To use the Windows NT 4.0 SMS Service Account, during SMS installation leave the Login ID and Password boxes blank in the SQL Database Configuration dialog box.

SQL Login IDs Creation for Additional Users

When you fully implement SMS across your organization, each administrator you allow to access the database must enter a login ID that identifies them as a user on the SQL Server and gives them access to the database. This login ID could be the SQL login ID you created for the SMS services. It is more likely that you will wish to create additional login IDs so that you can set access rights to specific SMS features for each user.

SMS administrative tools are installed on the site server of every primary site in an SMS system. They can also be installed on other computers running Windows NT Server 4.0 or higher, or Windows NT Workstation 4.0 or higher. This allows you to distribute administrative tasks throughout your SMS system. The procedures described in Chapter 3 show how to create additional login IDs for other users of SMS based on the three SQL Server security models.

Standard Security Use

To create an SQL login ID for an additional user, open the SQL Server Enterprise Manager and select the SQL Server computer as shown in Figure 5.2. You will have created an SMS SQL login ID that identifies the user on the SQL Server and gives the user access to the database. The new user could now log on to SMS, but would be unable to view the SMS system or use any of the SMS features. You must now assign access to SMS using the SMS Security Manager, a utility that is available once you install SMS. Access permissions for varying levels of SMS Administration are discussed in more detail later in the chapter.

Integrated Security Use

To create an SQL login ID for an additional user, open the SQL Server Enterprise Manager, select the SQL Server computer, and perform the appropriate procedure as shown in Figure 5.2. The existing Windows NT 4.0 user you selected has now been assigned an SMS SQL login ID that identifies them as a user on the SQL Server and gives them access to the database. The new user could now log on to SMS, but would be unable to view the SMS system or use any of the SMS features. You must now assign access to SMS using the SMS Security Manager, a utility available once you have installed SMS.

Mixed Security Use

To create an SQL login ID for an additional user, you can do either one of the following: Create an SQL login ID for an additional user using standard security (see "Standard Security Use") or create an SQL login ID for inte-

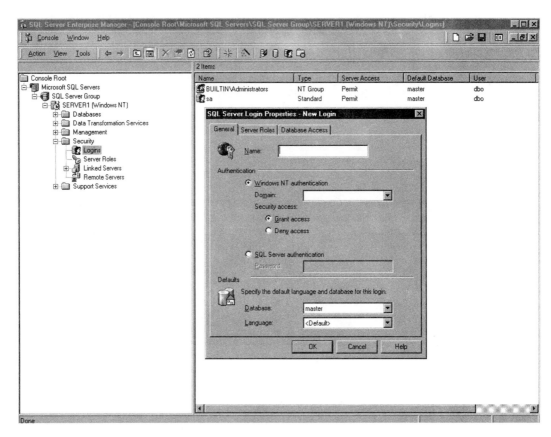

Figure 5.2 *SQL Enterprise Manager.*

grated security (see "Integrated Security Use"). Creating a SQL login ID is explained in the previous two sections.

Now, let's move on to the second SMS exam-specific element of the security strategy plan: the SMS Security Administrator.

MCSE 5.2 SMS Security Administrator

Security can be configured from the top-level Security Rights node. Permissions can be assigned to a particular instance and object type. Object types include collections, packages, advertisements, sites, and queries. Instances are examples of an object type, like the advertisement *"upgrade Purchasing machines to Windows 98."* Permissions can be assigned to any individual and include verbs such as read, modify, delete, distribute, and administer. A granular solution can be built through a sophisticated series of security rights in which the administrator can assign a particular person the rights to do only one type of operation to just one instance of one object type.

Collections

The collections node allows the creation and modification of collections. A collection is an arbitrary grouping of resources, such as machines and users, used to target software distribution and other tasks. The collections node can be used to drive operations on resources in that collection, such as generating inventory information on a resource or diagnosing resource problems.

Packages

The packages node allows the creation and modification of packages and programs that are subcomponents of packages. A package defines the software that is to be distributed to a particular collection, including the location of the source files and the servers that will be the intermediary distribution points. A package is made up of one or more programs that define the command line that the package uses to install the software on the target system.

Advertisements

The advertisements node is used to create or modify advertisements. Advertisements are the processes that tie collections, packages, and programs together and assign them to a particular schedule.

Status Objects

The status objects node provides detailed information on the status of SMS itself, including the status of system processes and software distribution advertisements. SMS 2.0 contains a sophisticated status engine that provides detailed information.

Security Rights

The security rights node allows the assignment of granular security rights. These can be specified on a per user, per target, and per operation basis. In addition, some tasks are launched directly from the Site Database node, rather than one of the top-level nodes. Particular tasks driven from this node

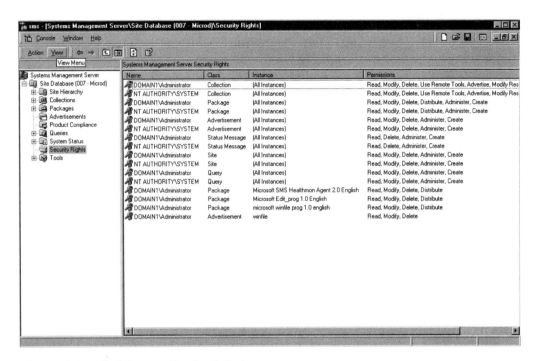

Figure 5.3   *Administrator Top-Level Options.*

are software metering and network monitoring. Figure 5.3 shows these top-level options in the administrator.[1]

SMS Administrator

The SMS Administrator is the primary tool used to manage the SMS system. The SMS Administrator provides access to the SQL Server database and lets you create, view, or modify any of the core SMS objects (such as packages, advertisements, and system status).

With the SMS Administrator, you can log on to the SMS system and administer the objects and properties for that site and its subsites. As discussed in earlier chapters, sites are collections of domains and computers that are managed together in SMS. An SMS system is composed of a central site and its subsites. The *central site* is a primary site that stores system-wide

1.   Copyright © 1998 Microsoft and/or its suppliers, One Microsoft Way, Redmond, Washington 98052-6399 U.S.A. All rights reserved.

information and manages all other sites. A *primary site* is a site that stores system data for itself and its subsites in a local SQL Server database. A *secondary site* is a site without a database. A *subsite* is a site that is beneath another site in the site hierarchy.

You can log in to the database for any site to which you have network access and permission. Once you have logged in, you can administer that site and all its subsites. If you log in to the database at the central site, you can administer the entire SMS system. By using the SMS Administrator, you can:

- Analyze network traffic.
- Create, modify, and delete SMS objects.
- Define resources to be collected.
- Manage computers using the Windows NT 4.0 Administrative Tools.
- Manage packages and advertisements.
- Receive SNMP traps.
- Set site and domain properties.
- View and provide remote support for all computers in the site and its subsites.

ANALYZING NETWORK TRAFFIC

You can use Network Monitor to capture network data from a computer in the inventory. Basically, what you're doing here is analyzing network traffic.

CREATING, MODIFYING, AND DELETING SMS OBJECTS

You can create SMS objects to be used at the primary site or its subsites. To modify and delete SMS objects, you must be logged in to the database of the site where the objects were created.

DEFINING RESOURCES TO BE COLLECTED

You can define how, when, and what resources (inventory) will be collected. SMS runs a discovery process depending on how the administrator has set up the discovery using different methods (Windows Networking Logon Discovery, Windows NT User Account, Windows NT User Group Discovery, Netware Bindery Logon Discovery, Netware NDS Logon Discovery, Heartbeat Discovery, and Network Discovery).

MANAGING COMPUTERS USING WINDOWS NT 4.0 ADMINISTRATIVE TOOLS

You can start Windows NT 4.0 Administrative Tools—Event Viewer, Server Manager, User Manager, and Performance Monitor—to manage Windows NT 4.0-based computers in the inventory.

MANAGING PACKAGES AND PROGRAM GROUPS

You can create, modify, and delete packages and program groups. Changes are made at a primary site and are applied to the site and its subsites.

RECEIVING SNMP TRAPS

You can configure the SMS Administrator to receive Simple Network Management Protocol (SNMP) traps and to store the traps in the database for later viewing. You can also configure the Event to Trap Translator to translate Windows NT 4.0 events into SNMP traps.

RAISING SNMP TRAPS IN ALERT RESPONSES • The extension agent, `SQLSNMP.DLL`, is a process that coordinates SQL Server 7.0 and Windows NT 4.0-based SNMP service. When the SNMP service is started, `SQLSNMP.DLL` is loaded and becomes accessible from management workstations via SNMP. The extension agent contains a trap mechanism that can be used to raise alerts from SQL Server. Traps are raised by defining alerts in SQL Enterprise Manager and by specifying that the alert raise an SNMP trap. To configure an alert to raise an SNMP trap, first go to the SQL Enterprise Manager, and choose Alerts from the Server menu. The Manage Alerts dialog box appears. Choose the New Alert icon or the Edit Alert icon. The New Alert or Edit Alert dialog box appears. Finally, configure the fields in the dialog box, and select the Raise an SNMP Trap When the Alert Occurs option.

Two extended stored procedures can also be used to raise SNMP traps: xp_snmp_getstate and xp_snmp_raisetrap.

SETTING SITE AND DOMAIN PROPERTIES

You can modify site properties for a site and all the sites below it in the site hierarchy. Site properties for a secondary site must be modified at a primary site above it in the site hierarchy.

VIEWING AND PROVIDING REMOTE SUPPORT

You can view the list of all computers in the site and its subsites. You can also view the inventory for each individual computer. If you need to remove a computer from the inventory, you can delete it. If you can directly connect to a computer in the inventory, you can provide direct support to the computer by using the remote troubleshooting utilities.

Installing the SMS Administrator

The SMS Administrator is installed on the site server in every primary site in the SMS system. You can also install and run the SMS Administrator on other computers running the Windows NT operating system (version 4.0 or higher). By default, you can run only one instance of the SMS Administrator. You can, however, configure a computer to run more than one instance of the SMS Administrator.

The SMS Administrator is composed of multiple windows that allow you to manage objects in the underlying database. The windows in the SMS Administrator are not refreshed automatically; they are updated only when you perform an action that retrieves data from the database. For example, the Sites window, which displays information about SMS sites, domains, and computers, is not updated when inventory is added to the database. You may need to refresh the display for the Sites window and the other windows in the SMS Administrator to see changes to the system.

When you open a window in the SMS Administrator (Figure 5.3), you see the top-level options under SMS. You can access any of the major windows in the SMS Administrator by picking any of the top-level options under SMS. You can also access these windows from the File Open menu item. The major windows in the SMS Administrator are described next.

SITES WINDOW

The Sites window shows a complete view of all domains and computers in the site hierarchy for the current site and any subsites. When you log in to a site's database, that site is the top site in the Sites window (appearing as a globe) even if there are parent sites above it.

You can navigate the Sites window to find any computer in the hierarchy. For each computer, SMS displays the name, the SMS Identifier (ID), the name of the last user to log on, the system type, and the system role (server or workstation). The computer icon also indicates the system role.

You can view the detailed hardware and software inventory properties of any computer in any site displayed in the Sites window. You also have access to utilities (such as remote troubleshooting, Network Monitor, and Windows NT 4.0 Administrative Tools) with which you can manage the computer.

Because the Sites window displays all of the computers, domains, and sites in the site hierarchy, it is often used in conjunction with other elements of the SMS Administrator. For example, if you want to run a query to find all Pentium servers in a specific site, configure a query to find all Pentium servers and then drag the query on to the specific site in the list. Dropping the query on the site will run the query, limiting it to the specified site. Similarly, to distribute a particular software package to a specific domain, you can drag the package onto that domain in the Sites window. This will create an advertisements to perform the software distribution.

MACHINE GROUPS AND SITE GROUPS WINDOWS

The Sites window groups computers by site and domain. Site groups and machine groups provide alternative ways of viewing and managing computers in SMS. You can create a machine group that serves as an alias for a set of computers. This can be used to specify the job targets and distribution servers for Run Command On Workstation and Share Package On Server advertisements. You can create machine groups by dragging computers from the Sites window or from a query results window to the Machine Groups window.

 A machine group is static; it contains only the computers that you add to it (unlike the Sites window, which contains all computers that belong in the site). For this reason, machine groups are often used in situations where you want to specify an exact number of computers, such as when distributing licensed software to clients.

You may also want to limit a job to a set of specific sites. SMS enables you to create *site groups* that serve as aliases for a set of sites. You can use a site group to limit an advertisement (job) to only the sites contained in the site group. For example, you may want to distribute software to servers at all your manufacturing sites. You can do this by creating a site group containing all the manufacturing sites and using this group to limit the job to servers at those sites. You can also use a site group to limit a query or an alert.

Site groups and machine groups can be nested, meaning that they can contain one or more groups. A site can be part of more than one site group and a computer can be part of multiple machine groups.

ADVERTISEMENTS WINDOW

Advertisements are used to define instructions for system actions. All Advertisements are stored in the database. You can create, modify, cancel, and delete Advertisements to manage the distribution, installation, and removal of software. Some Advertisements, called *system Advertisements*, are created automatically by SMS to manage and maintain the system. You cannot create or modify system Advertisements.

When you create an advertisements to distribute, install, or remove software, you must create a package before you create the advertisements. You may also need to create machine groups, site groups, or queries if you want to use these to limit the computers that receive the package. For instance, to create an advertisement to distribute Microsoft Office to all Pentium computers in your Research sites, you would first need to create a package for Microsoft Office, a query to find all Pentium computers, and a site group containing all Research sites. Then you could create the advertisement by dragging the Microsoft Office package to the Find All Pentium computers query, and selecting Research sites in the Limit to Sites field in the advertisements Details dialog box.

You can create three types of Advertisements to manage software: Run Command On Workstation Advertisements, Share Package On Server Advertisements, and Remove Package From Server Advertisements. All Advertisements are displayed in the Advertisements node in the administrators console as shown in Figure 5.3. The main window displays the primary properties associated with the advertisements, including the advertisements name, package, program, collection, available after, expires after, and advertisements id. Double-clicking a particular advertisements lets you view or modify its properties. There are three types of advertisements properties:

- *General:* Indicates the name of package, program to run, collection to use, and so on.
- *Schedule:* Indicates the advertisements start time, priority, and advertisements expiration date.
- *Security:* specifies security rights that users have on this advertisement (read, modify, delete, etc. . . .)

When you create an advertisements, SMS monitors the database and starts the advertisements after the Start time setting has expired. SMS determines the target sites (the sites where the target clients or target servers are located) and then sends the package and advertisements instructions to those sites. That is where the actions specified by the advertisements are carried out. As SMS carries out an advertisements, the advertisements's status is reported back to the site where the advertisements was created. Advertisements status can be viewed using the Status node in the administrator console. When you create a advertisements at one site and send it to another site, the data and instructions are sent directly to the target site. They are not routed through other intermediary sites. Thus, the site where the advertisements is created must have a direct address for the target site.

PACKAGES WINDOW

A *package* is an object that defines software distribution to the SMS system. SMS uses packages to store information about software so that the software can be identified, distributed, installed on clients, and shared from servers. When you create a package, you define the files that comprise the software, the package's configuration, and identification information. Packages are defined and maintained in the Packages window as shown in Figure 5.4.

Administrators can create distribution points for packages. Distribution points are the locations accessed by clients to obtain the files in the packages. The computer or share designated as a distribution point must have sufficient disk space for all the files that will be stored on it and must be assigned the role of distribution point. Systems Management Server client software can use any of the distribution points at a site that the client can access. You can configure rules for clients to use when connecting to site systems. After you create a package, SMS creates a PackageID.pkg file on the site server, in the Sms\Inboxes\Pkginfo.box directory. SMS then replicates the .pkg file to each of the CAPS. As you create programs for that package, SMS updates its .pkg file. You can use SMS to install the package on clients, share the package so that it is run from network servers, or maintain inventory on the package. You can create packages for commercial applications, applications you have developed, for batch or data files, and so on.

Package properties include the software name and version, the location of the package source directory, and group permissions for the distribution folder.

Packages are typically used to distribute software to Systems Management Server clients. A package defines the files and instructions for distribut-

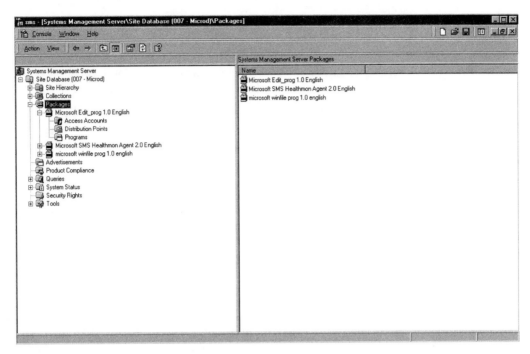

Figure 5.4   *Administrator Package Node.*

ing, installing, and running software. Once you create a package, you can create one or more programs for a package.

All packages are displayed in the Packages window. For each package, the window displays the package name, the package ID, the package setup status, and a comment. Double-clicking a particular package displays additional properties of the package. You can view or modify these additional package properties in the Package Properties dialog box.

The properties you define are determined by how the package will be used. A package can have one or more of the following properties:

- General information about the package, such as the name, version, and vendor of the software you plan to distribute
- If the package includes files, the package source directory that contains those files
- The distribution points for the package
- Whether a compressed copy of the files referred to in the package is created and stored on the site server at remote sites
- Whether the files in the package need to be periodically updated, and if so, when

All packages that you create are stored in the database at your site and at all subsites. All packages stored in the database are displayed in the Packages window.

When you create a package, you must define the package properties. For instance, when you install a package on clients, SMS uses the Workstations properties to determine which files comprise the package and the command used to install it.

After you create a package, you must create a advertisements to install the package on clients or share the package on servers. A advertisements defines the task you want to perform with a package. You do not need to create an explicit advertisements to perform software inventory. After you define Inventory properties for a package, the SMS system automatically creates a system advertisements to update the SMS inventory components so that they can maintain inventory on the package.

PROGRAMS WINDOW

Programs specify the command to be run at the client to perform the tasks that are described in a specific package (for example, install software, copy data files, or run a batch file). You can create several programs for one package (for example, one program can perform an express installation, while another executes a customized script you have created with Systems Management Server Installer).

The programs contained in a package are not run until you advertise those programs to a target collection.

For users with computers in Windows NT 4.0 domains, you assign program groups to global user groups.

QUERIES WINDOW

Queries are used to search for objects in the database. A *query* defines and stores the criteria used to identify the objects that you want to find. Queries are typically used to select target computers for a software distribution advertisements. They can also be used for other purposes, such as to select other types of objects, to create machine groups, or to trigger alerts. Queries are created and managed in the Queries window.

When you create a query, it is stored in the database. Queries are constructed by building a set of expressions combined by logical operators. The Query Expression Properties dialog box should be used for this purpose.

You can run a query without storing the query in the database. This type of query is known as an *ad hoc query* and is usually created for immediate use only. If you need to repeat the query, you should create and store a named query.

By running a query, you search the inventory for the objects that match the query's criteria. The results are displayed in a Query Results window.

The results displayed in the queries window are the actual objects that meet the query conditions. Deleting an object from the Query Results window also deletes the object from the database.

You can control how query results are displayed in the Query Results window by defining query result formats. Query result formats determine the attributes that are displayed for each object in the Query Results window.

Each query is specific to a predefined architecture. For example, you could create a query for the Personal Computer architecture to find computers that match a specified set of criteria, such as Processor Name is 486 and Operating System Name is Windows 98. You can also query system architectures, such as SMS Events and advertisements Details, or custom architectures that you have created. If you run a query for the Personal Computers architecture, you can save the results of the query to a machine group. For instance, this could be used later for advertisements targeting.

The query system in the SMS Administrator allows you to run *prompted* queries. These queries are constructed using a general expression, not a specific value. The SMS Administrator will prompt you for the actual value to be used when the query is run. SMS includes several default queries that take advantage of the new prompted query feature. For example, there is a query for Computers By Operating System. When you select and run this query, SMS will prompt you for the Operating System name to use in the query. You can select the name from a list that includes the names of all operating systems for all computers inventoried at that time.

EVENTS, ALERTS, AND SNMP TRAPS WINDOWS

The SMS Administrator contains separate windows for events, alerts, and SNMP traps. Each of these windows provides you with information and tools that you can use to better manage your network and your SMS system. Alerts are actions that are generated by SMS when certain conditions are detected. Events are logs generated by SMS that contain information, warnings, or error messages. SNMP traps are similar to SMS events, but SNMP traps are typically generated by other devices and systems on the network.

SMS SECURITY MANAGER

The SMS Security Manager is available in the SMS program group and from the SMS Administrator menu. Using the SMS Security Manager, you can view and set access rights to specific features in the SMS Administrator. Systems Management Server (SMS) grants access to its functionality based on security rights. Configuring SMS security means creating various security rights so that SMS administrators have access to certain functionality and data. For instance, a user may log in to SMS with full access to packages, queries, and Advertisements, but with view-only access to sites. This means that the user can view the Sites window and its contents (including viewing the site properties) but cannot create, modify, or delete any objects in the Sites window. The user can still view, create, modify, or delete any objects in the Packages, Queries, and Advertisements windows.

When you install a site, only the database owner account (DBOA) is granted all rights to the SMS Administrator. A new user is granted no access to any of the features in the SMS Administrator. You can use the SMS Security Manager to grant other database users rights to the SMS Administrator.

If you do not have full access to some objects, your view of those objects in the SMS Administrator will be altered. For example, if you have no access to the Packages window, you will not even see the Packages window in the SMS Administrator. If you have view access to objects in the advertisements window, you will be able to view the advertisements window but will not be able to modify advertisements in any way. Restrictions are enforced in the database as well as in the SMS Administrator.

Security settings are displayed on a per-user basis in the main window of the SMS Security Manager. For each object in the SMS Administrator, the SMS Security Manager displays the following information:

- User name: A Windows NT user name or user group to whom the security right applies.
- *Class Security*: An SMS security object class.
- *Instance Security*: An instance of an SMS security object. All instances appropriate to the current security object class are available in the list. This field is unavailable if you are viewing or modifying

an existing security right or if you are viewing or configuring a class security right

- *Permissions Field*: One or more SMS permissions for the security object. Only the permissions that apply to the current security object are displayed.

When you grant individual rights with the SMS Security Manager, you must be aware of dependencies between the security objects that restrict the sets of rights you can grant. For instance, to grant any rights to Alerts, a user must also have rights to Queries. To simplify the task of granting security rights to users, the SMS Security Manager includes templates you can use to grant a consistent set of rights to a user with a single action. The SMS Security Manager provides the following templates:

- Asset manager
- Advertisement manager
- Network monitor
- Software manager
- Tech support

SMS SERVICE MANAGER

The SMS Service Manager allows you to manage the SMS services and service components at a site. The SMS Service Manager is available in the SMS program group and from the SMS Administrator Tools menu. Using the SMS Service Manager, you can control and configure tracing on the SMS services and the components of the SMS Executive. SMS Service Manager can display the current run status and tracing status of the components. It can also start and stop the SMS services and components on the site server or on another server.

SMS SENDER MANAGER

The SMS Sender Manager allows you to control properties of the SMS senders. For example, you can control the sending bandwidth, the number of threads that each sender uses and how often the senders retry. The SMS Sender Manager is available in the SMS Administrator Senders Node menu as shown in Figure 5.5.

You can set the rate limits (maximum transfer rate per hour) to be used for each sender. For example, you can select a sender and set it to use no

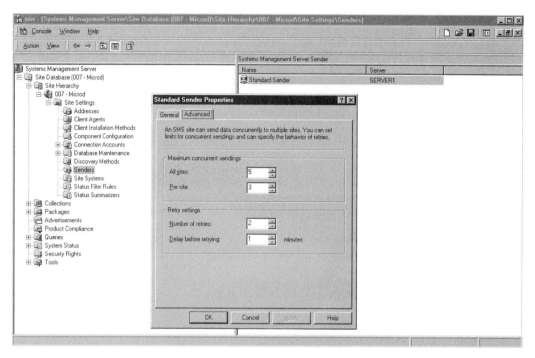

Figure 5.5   *Administrator Site Sender Node.*

more than 60% of the bandwidth during work hours and unlimited bandwidth after work hours. You can also set the number of concurrent sessions
for each sender, the maximum number of concurrent sessions to each destination site, and the retry settings for each sender.

You can also control properties of the sender addresses. For example,
you can limit the maximum transfer rate per hour on a per-address basis
instead of on a per-sender basis. You can further specify the maximum estimated bandwidth for the sender address. These options are useful when you
have more than one sender that can be used to communicate with a site, but
you want to limit the total amount of data sent to the site.

SMS DATABASE MANAGER

The SMS Database Manager allows you to delete most types of data from the
database. The SMS Database Manager is available in the SMS program group
and from the SMS Administrator menu.

The Collection views can also be set directly from within the SMS Administrator when you are viewing the Resource or Computer Properties.

MANAGEMENT INFORMATION FORMAT

To add or maintain items in a SMS database, the SMS system uses data in the Management Information Format (MIF). MIF files are ASCII text files that allow you to add objects with new architectures (such as printers or hardware routers) to the SMS database, add new objects with existing architectures (such as adding a new computer to the Personal Computer architecture), and add new groups and attributes to existing objects.

You can extend the SMS Administrator to display custom graphics for custom objects and groups in its Sites window and Properties window. If you want the new object to appear in the Sites window of the SMS Administrator, you must define at least seven specific attributes in the Identification group.

SMS SQL VIEW GENERATOR AND CRYSTAL REPORTS

The SMS SQL View Generator (`SMSVIEW.EXE`) is available in the SMS program group. This utility is used to set up views of the SMS database. These views can then be accessed by other database programs that use the Open Database Connectivity (ODBC) standard.

Crystal Reports is a tool for creating reports from databases. This tool can be installed from the SMS Setup program. Crystal Reports uses ODBC to extract data from the SMS database, and there are several ready-to-run reports included with Crystal Reports. To use Crystal Reports, you must first run the SMS SQL View Generator. For more information about using Crystal Reports, see Chapter 10, "Managing the SMS System Model."

Next, let's move on to the third SMS exam-specific element of the security strategy plan: Windows NT 4.0 Security Model.

MCSE 5.3   Windows NT 4.0 Security Model

SMS 2.0 takes advantage of the Windows NT 4.0 Security Model, allowing you to grant permissions to Windows NT 4.0 users and user groups who need to perform specific SMS tasks. With that in mind, this part of the chapter will focus on how to use the Windows NT 4.0 Security Model. The following sections also provide an overview of the security model and describe the components that make up the model. They also explain how Windows NT 4.0 tracks each user and each securable object. This overview helps you understand system messages and information found in the Event Viewer. This part of the chapter also provides examples of Windows NT 4.0 security, showing how Windows NT 4.0 validates access requests and how it audits activities performed on protected objects.

The Security Model

Security in Windows NT 4.0 was included as part of the initial design specifications for Windows NT 4.0 and is pervasive throughout the operating system. The security model includes components to control who accesses which objects (such as files and shared printers), which actions an individual can take on an object, and which events are audited. As shown in Figure 5.6, the Windows NT 4.0 security model includes the following components:

- Logon processes
- Local Security Authority
- Security Account Manager (SAM)
- Security Reference Monitor

Together these components are known as the security subsystem. This subsystem is known as an integral subsystem rather than an environmental subsystem because it affects the entire Windows NT 4.0 operating system.

The Windows NT 4.0 security model is designed for C2-level security as defined by the U.S. Department of Defense. The most important requirements of C2-level security are that the owner of a resource (such as a file) must be able to control access to the resource, and that the operating system must protect objects so they are not randomly reused by other processes. For instance, the system protects memory so that its contents cannot be read after it is freed by a process. In addition, when a file is deleted, users must not be able to access the file's data.

Another C2-level security requirement is that users must identify themselves by typing unique logon names and passwords before being allowed access to the system. The system must be able to use this unique identification to track the activities of users. Further, system administrators must be able to audit security-related events. Access to this audit data must be limited to authorized administrators. Finally, the system must protect

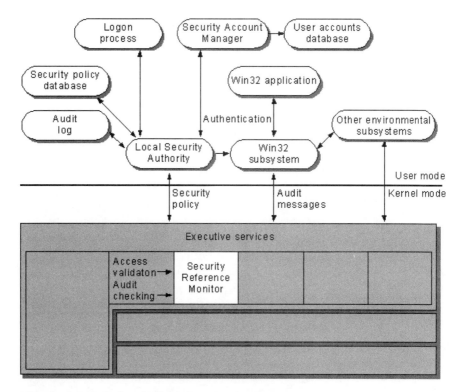

Figure 5.6 *Windows NT 4.0 Security Components.*

itself from external interference or tampering, such as modification of the running system or of system files stored on disk.

LOGON PROCESSES

Logon processes are those that accept a logon request from users. These include the initial interactive logon, which displays the initial logon dialog box to the user, and remote logon processes, which allow access by remote users to a Windows NT 4.0 server process.

LOCAL SECURITY AUTHORITY

The Local Security Authority ensures that the user has permission to access the system. This component is the center of the Windows NT 4.0 security subsystem. It generates access tokens (described later in this chapter), manages the local security policy, and provides interactive user authentication services. The Local Security Authority also controls audit policy and logs the audit messages generated by the Security Reference Monitor.

SECURITY ACCOUNT MANAGER

The Security Account Manager (SAM) maintains the user accounts database. This database contains information for all user and group accounts. SAM provides user validation services for the Local Security Authority.

SECURITY REFERENCE MONITOR

The Security Reference Monitor checks to see if the user has permission to access an object and perform an action. This component enforces the access validation and audit generation policy defined by the Local Security Authority. It provides services to both kernel and user mode to ensure the users and processes attempting access to an object have the necessary permissions. This component also generates audit messages when appropriate.

Permissions, Users, and Objects

The key objective of the Windows NT 4.0 security model is to monitor and control who accesses which objects. The security model keeps security information for each user, group, and object. It can identify access attempts that are made directly by a user, and it can identify access attempts that are made indirectly by a program or other process running on a user's behalf. Windows NT 4.0 also tracks and controls access to objects that users can see in the user interface (such as files and printers) and objects that users can't see (such as processes and named pipes).

As mentioned before, the security model controls not only which users can access which objects; it also controls how they may be accessed. An administrator can assign permissions to users and groups to grant or deny access to particular objects. For instance, these permissions may be assigned to a user for a particular file:

- Change permission
- Delete
- Execute
- No access
- Read
- Take ownership
- Write

The ability to assign permissions at the discretion of the owner (or other person authorized to change permissions) is called *discretionary access control*. Administrators can assign permissions to individual users or groups. For maintenance purposes, it's best to assign permissions to groups. For instance, an administrator can control access to the REPORTS directory by giving GROUP3 read permission and GROUP4 read, write, and execute permissions. To do this, choose Permissions from the Security menu in File Manager.

AUDITING SECURITY EVENTS IN THE SECURITY LOG

Windows NT 4.0 auditing features can record events to show which users access which objects, what type of access is being attempted, and whether or not the access attempt was successful. You can view audited security events through Event Viewer by selecting Security from the Log menu. You can see detailed information about a particular audited event in the security log by double-clicking on that event, as shown in Figure 5.7.

To set up auditing on your computer, use the Auditing and Security options in the User Manager, File Manager, Print Manager, and other tools. From these tools, you can specify the types of auditing events you want to include in the security log.

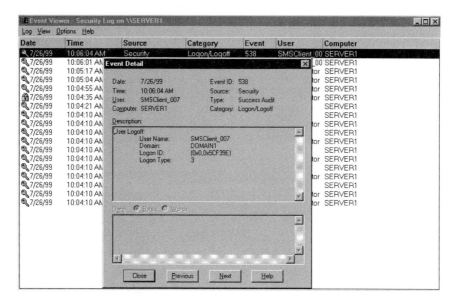

Figure 5.7 *Event Viewer and Event Detail Windows.*

While Event Viewer is adequate for most requirements, the security model is defined so that developers can write their own custom security event viewer/monitor.

Users Security Information

Users are identified to the system by a unique security ID (SID). SIDs are unique across time and space, meaning that there is no possibility of having two identical SIDs. For instance, suppose Dana, who has a Windows NT 4.0 account, leaves her job at a company but later returns to a different job at the same company. When Dana leaves, the administrator deletes her account, and Windows NT 4.0 no longer accepts her SID as valid. When Dana returns, the administrator creates a new account, and Windows NT 4.0 generates a new SID for that account. The new SID does not match the old one, so nothing from the old account is transferred to the new account.

When a user logs on, Windows NT 4.0 creates a security access token. This includes a SID for the user, other SIDs for the groups to which the user belongs, plus other information such as the user's name and the groups to which that user belongs. In addition, every process that runs on behalf of this user will have a copy of his or her access token. For instance, when Dana starts Notepad, the Notepad process receives a copy of Dana's access token as shown in Figure 5.8.

Windows NT 4.0 refers to the SIDs within a user's access token when he or she tries to access an object. The SIDs are compared with the list of access permissions for the object to ensure that the user has sufficient permission to access the object.

ACCESS TOKEN CREATION BY WINDOWS NT 4.0

Before a user can do anything on a Windows NT 4.0 system, he or she must log on to the system by supplying a username and password. Windows NT 4.0 uses the username for identification and the password for validation, as shown in Figure 5.9. The following procedure illustrates the interactive logon process for Windows NT 4.0.

The initial logon process for Windows NT 4.0 is interactive, meaning that the user must type information at the keyboard in response to a dialog

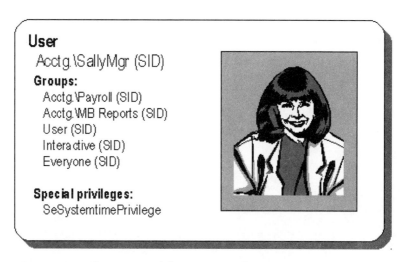

Figure 5.8 *Illustration of the Contents of an Access Token.*

box the operating system displays on the screen. Windows NT 4.0 grants or denies access based upon the information provided by the user.

The following list details the steps included in the interactive logon and validation process, as illustrated in Figure 5.9.

1. The user presses Ctrl+Alt+Del to gain the attention of Windows NT 4.0. This key combination before logon protects against Trojan Horse-type

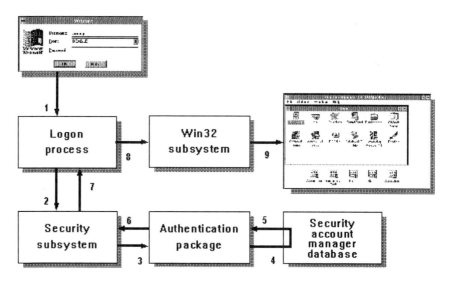

Figure 5.9 *Windows NT 4.0 Validation Process.*

programs that impersonate the operating system and trick users into disclosing their username and password.

2. When the user provides a username and a password, the logon process calls the Local Security Authority.

3. The Local Security Authority runs the appropriate authentication package.

4. The authentication package checks the user accounts database to see if the account is local. If it is, the username and password are verified against those held in the user accounts database. If not, the requested logon is forwarded to an alternate authentication package.

Windows NT 4.0 has the ability to support multiple authentication packages that are implemented as DLLs. This flexibility allows third-party software vendors the opportunity to integrate their own custom authentication packages with Windows NT 4.0. For instance, a network vendor might augment the standard Windows NT 4.0 authentication package by adding one that allows users to log on to Windows NT 4.0 and the vendor's network simultaneously.

5. When the account is validated, the SAM (which owns the user accounts database) returns the user's SID and the SIDs of any global groups to which the user belongs.

6. The authentication package creates a logon session and then passes the logon session and the SIDs associated with the user to the Local Security Authority.

7. If the logon is rejected, the logon session is deleted, and an error is returned to the logon process. Otherwise, an access token is created containing the user's SID and the SIDs of Everyone and other groups. It also contains user rights assigned to the collected SIDs. This access token is returned to the logon process with a Success status.

8. The logon session calls the Win32 subsystem to create a process and attach the access token to the process, thus creating a subject for the user account. Subjects are described later in this chapter in the section called "Impersonation and Subjects."

9. For an interactive Windows NT 4.0 session, the Win32 subsystem starts Program Manager for the user.

After the validation process, a user's shell process—that is, the process in which Program Manager is started for the user—is given an access token. The information in this access token is reflected by anything the user does or any process that runs on the user's behalf.

USER RIGHTS

Access to an object is typically determined by comparing the user and group memberships in the user's access token with permissions for the object. Some activities performed by users, however, are not associated with a particular object. For instance, you may want certain individuals to be able to create regular backups for the server. These people should be able to do their job without regard to permissions that have been set on those files. In cases like this, an administrator could assign specific user rights (sometimes called privileges) to give users or groups access to services that normal discretionary access control does not provide. Backing up files and directories, shutting down the computer, logging on interactively, and changing the system times are all examples of user rights defined by Windows NT 4.0.

You can use the dialog box from the User Manager tool to assign user rights (see Figure 5.10).

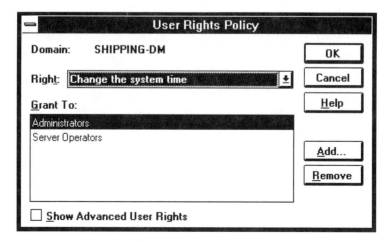

Figure 5.10 *User Rights Policy Dialog Box.*

In the current release of Windows NT 4.0, the set of user rights is defined by the system and cannot be changed. Future versions of Windows NT 4.0 may allow software developers to define new user rights appropriate to their application.

IMPERSONATION AND SUBJECTS

One objective of the Windows NT 4.0 security model is to ensure that the programs that a user runs have no more access to objects than the user does. That is, if users are granted only read access to a file, when they run a program, that program cannot write to the file. The program, like the user, is granted only read permission.

A subject is the combination of the user's access token plus the program acting on the user's behalf. Windows NT 4.0 uses subjects to track and manage permissions for the programs each user runs. When a program or process runs on the user's behalf, it is said to be running in the security context of that user. The security context controls what access the subject has to objects or system services.

To accommodate the client-server model of Windows NT 4.0, there are two classes of subjects within the Windows NT 4.0 security architecture. The first is a *simple subject*. This is a process that was assigned a security context when the corresponding user logged on. It is not acting in the capacity of a protected server, which may have other subjects as clients. The second is a *server subject*. This is a process implemented as a protected server (such as the Win32 subsystem), and it does have other subjects as clients. In this role, a server subject typically has the security context of those clients available for use when acting on their behalf.

In general, when a subject calls an object service through a protected subsystem, the subject's token is used within the service to determine who made the call. It is also used to decide whether the caller has sufficient access authority to perform the requested action.

Windows NT 4.0 allows one process to take on the security attributes of another through a technique called *impersonation*. For instance, a server process typically impersonates a client process to complete a task involving objects to which the server does not normally have access. In the scenario shown in Figure 5.11, a client is accessing an object on a Windows NT 4.0 server.

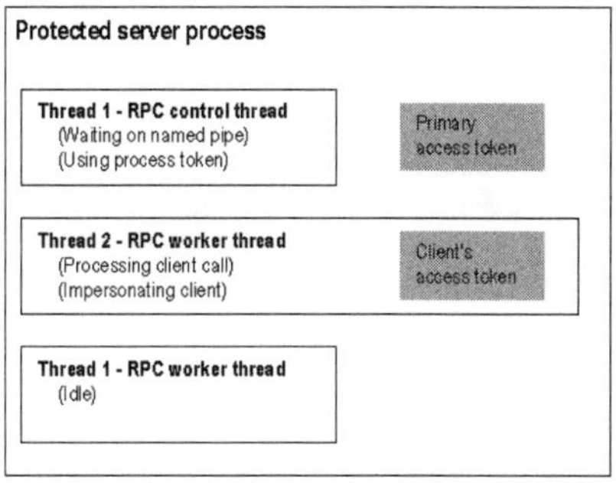

Figure 5.11 *Server Subject Security Context.*

The first thread in the process is a control thread. It is waiting to receive RPC calls via a named pipe. This thread is not impersonating another process, so any access validation to which Thread 1 is subjected will be carried out against the process's primary token.

The second thread in the process is currently handling a call from a client. This thread handles the client's call by temporarily using the client's access token to run with that client's access permissions (that is, the client's security context). While impersonating the client, any access validation to which Thread 2 is subjected is carried out in the client's security context.

The third thread in this scenario is an idle worker thread that is not impersonating any other process. You should use the Event Viewer to see this type of information for your system. Here, information for both the primary user and client user is recorded in the security log.

Objects Security Information

All named, and some unnamed, objects in Windows NT 4.0 can be secured. The security attributes for an object are described by a security descriptor. An object's security descriptor includes four parts as shown in Figure 5.13.

The first part is an owner SID (SallyMgr) that indicates the user or group who owns the object. The owner of an object can change the access permissions for the object. A group SID (not shown) is the second part. This part is used only by the POSIX subsystem and ignored by the rest of Windows NT 4.0. The third part is a discretionary access control list (ACL) that identifies which users and groups are granted or denied which access permissions. Discretionary ACLs are controlled by the owner of the object. These are described in the section called "Access Control Entries and Lists" beginning on page 157. Finally, there's a system ACL that controls which auditing

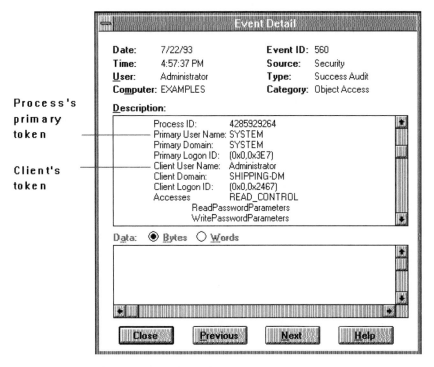

Process's
primary
token

Client's
token

Figure 5.12 *The Event Detail Window.*

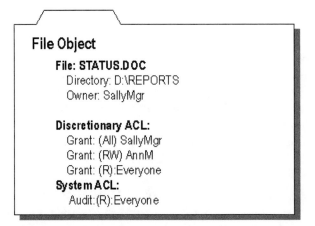

Figure 5.13 *Security Descriptor for a File Object.*

messages the system will generate. System ACLs are controlled by the security administrators. For more information about auditing objects, see "Security Events Auditing."

OBJECTS TYPES

The type of permissions that can be granted or denied for an object depend on the object's type. For instance, you can specify permissions like Manage Documents and Print for a printer queue, while for a directory you can specify Read, Write, Execute, and so on.

Another quality that affects the permissions of an object is whether that object is a container object or a noncontainer object. A container object is one that logically contains other objects. Noncontainer objects do not contain other objects. For instance, a directory is a container object that logically contains files and other directories. Files are noncontainer objects. This distinction between container and noncontainer objects is important since objects within a container object can inherit certain permissions from the parent container. For more information, go to the section called "Inheritance of Access Control."

NT File Systems (NTFS) support the inheritance of ACLs from directory objects to file objects that are created within the directory.

ACCESS CONTROL ENTRIES AND LISTS

Each ACL is made up of access control entries (ACEs) that specify access or auditing permissions to that object for one user or group. There are three ACE types—two for discretionary access control and one for system security. The discretionary ACEs are AccessAllowed and AccessDenied. Respectively, these explicitly grant and deny access to a user or group of users. Also, SystemAudit is a system security ACE used to keep a log of security events (such as who accesses which files) and to generate and log security audit messages.

ACCESS MASKS

Each ACE includes an access mask, which defines all possible actions for a particular object type as illustrated in Figure 5.14. Permissions are granted or denied based on this access mask. One way to think of an access mask is as a

There is an important distinction between a discretionary ACL that is empty (one that has no ACEs in it) and an object without any discretionary ACL. In the case of an empty discretionary ACL, no accesses are explicitly granted, so access is implicitly denied. For an object that has no ACL at all, there is no protection assigned to the object, so any access request is granted.

sort of menu from which granted and denied permissions are selected. Specific types include access options that apply specifically to this object type. Each object type can have up to 18 specific access types. Collectively, the access types for a particular object type are called the specific access mask. These are defined when the object type is defined. Windows NT 4.0 files have the following specific access types:

- AppendData
- Execute
- ReadAttributes
- ReadData
- ReadEA (Extended Attribute)
- WriteAttributes
- WriteData
- WriteEA (Extended Attribute)

Standard types apply to all objects and consist of the following access permissions:

- DELETE, used to grant or deny delete access
- READ_CONTROL, used to grant or deny read access to the security descriptor and owner

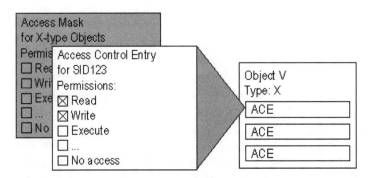

Figure 5.14 *Access Control Mask.*

Table 5.1 *Generic Types Mapped from Specific and Standard Types*

Generic Type...	...Mapped from These Specific and Standard Types
FILE_GENERIC_READ	STANDARD_RIGHTS_READ FILE_READ_DATA FILE_READ_ATTRIBUTES FILE_READ_EA SYNCHRONIZE
FILE_GENERIC_WRITE	STANDARD_RIGHTS_WRITE FILE_WRITE_DATA FILE_WRITE_ATTRIBUTES FILE_WRITE_EA FILE_APPEND_DATA SYNCHRONIZE
FILE_GENERIC_EXECUTE	STANDARD_RIGHTS_EXECUTE FILE_READ_ATTRIBUTES FILE_EXECUTE SYNCHRONIZE

- SYNCHRONIZE, used to synchronize access and to allow a process to wait for an object to enter the signaled state
- WRITE_DAC, used to grant or deny write access to the discretionary ACL
- WRITE_OWNER, used to assign write owner

Table 5.1 shows the generic types that are mapped from specific and standard types. Specific and standard types appear in the details of the security log.

Generic types do not appear in the security log. Instead, the corresponding specific and standard types are listed.

INHERITANCE OF ACCESS CONTROL

Objects can be classified as either container objects or noncontainer objects. Container objects (such as a directory) can logically contain other objects; noncontainer objects (such as a file) cannot.

By default, when you create new objects within a container object, the new objects inherit permissions from the parent object. For instance, in the

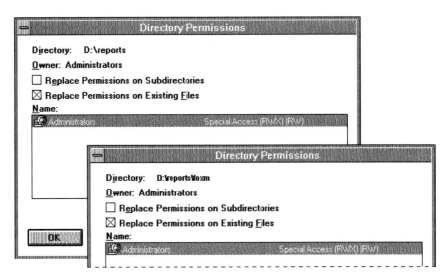

Figure 5.15 *Directory Permissions Dialog Box.*

dialog box shown in Figure 5.15, D:\REPORTS\FOXM inherited permissions from its parent directory, D:\REPORTS.

In the case of files and directories, when you change permissions on a directory, those changes affect that directory and its files but do not automatically apply to existing subdirectories and their contents. They do apply if you check the Replace Permissions On Existing Files check box, as shown in Figure 5.15.

You can apply the changed permissions to existing subdirectories and their files by selecting the Replace Permissions On Subdirectories check box. The dialog box shown in Figure 5.15 shows the file permissions that are inherited from the parent directory by a file within that directory.

Validation of Access

When a user tries to access an object, Windows NT 4.0 compares security information in the user's access token with the security information through access validation, as shown in Figure 5.16.

A desired access mask for the subject is created based on what type of access the user is attempting. This desired access mask, usually created by a program that the user is running, is compared with the object's ACL.

Each ACE in the ACL is evaluated first by comparing the set of security IDs in the user's access token to the SID in the ACE. If a match is not found,

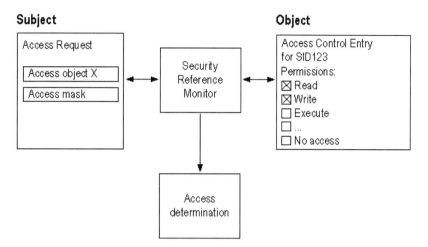

Figure 5.16 *Access Validation.*

All generic access types in the ACL are mapped to standard and specific access types.

the ACE is skipped. Further processing is based on the type of the ACE. AccessDenied ACEs are ordered and processed before AccessAllowed ACEs.

Next, if access is denied, the system checks to see if the original desired access mask contained only a ReadControl and/or WRITE_DAC.

If so, the system also checks to see if the requester is the owner of the object. In this case, access is granted.

Third, for an AccessDenied ACE, the accesses in the ACE access mask are compared with the desired access mask. If there are any accesses in both masks, further processing is unnecessary and access is denied. Otherwise, processing continues with the next requested ACE.

For an AccessAllowed ACE, the accesses in the ACE are next compared with those listed in the desired access mask. If all accesses in the desired access mask are matched by the ACE, no further processing is necessary, and access is granted. Otherwise, processing continues with the next ACE.

Finally, at the end of the ACL, if the contents of desired access mask are still not completely matched, access is implicitly denied. Examples of this access validation process are described next.

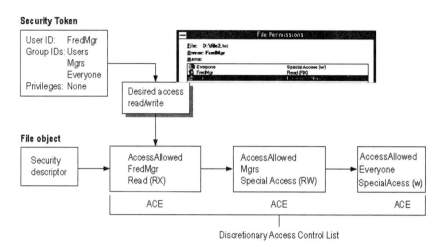

Figure 5.17 *Read and Write Access (Allowed).*

WRITE AND READ ACCESS REQUEST

A user with the user ID FredMgr tries to gain Read and Write access to
G:\FILE1.TXT which has the discretionary ACL shown in Figure 5.17. The
FredMgr access token indicates that he is a member of the groups Users,
Mgrs, and Everyone.

> The order in which permissions are listed by the File Permissions dialog
> box doesn't necessarily reflect the order in which ACEs are processed by
> Windows NT 4.0. It is important to note, however, that the Permissions
> Editor (controlled by means of this dialog box) orders all AccessDenied
> ACEs first so that they are the first to be processed within each ACL.

In this example, Windows NT 4.0 evaluates the ACL by comparing
the desired access mask with each ACE and processing the desired mask as
follows:

1. Windows NT 4.0 reads FredMgr's desired access mask to see that he is
   trying to gain Read and Write access.
2. Windows NT 4.0 reads the AccessAllowed ACE for FredMgr and finds a
   match to the Read permission requested in the desired access mask.
3. Windows NT 4.0 reads the AccessAllowed ACE for Mgrs and finds a
   match to the Write permission requested in desired access mask.

At this point, processing of the ACL stops even though there is another ACE in the ACL. Processing stops and access is granted because Windows NT 4.0 found matches for everything in the desired access mask.

DENIED ACCESS

In this example, FredMgr wants Read and Write access to the file whose discretionary ACL is shown in Figure 5.18. FredMgr is a member of the Users and Mgrs groups.

The File Manager Permissions Editor always orders AccessDenied ACEs first in the ACL.

In this example, the ACL is evaluated as follows:

1. Windows NT 4.0 reads FredMgr's desired access mask to see that he is trying to gain Read and Write access.
2. Windows NT 4.0 reads the AccessDenied ACE that denies all access (No Access) to Mgrs.

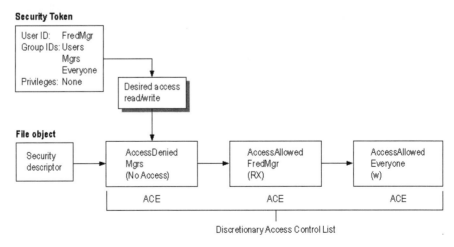

Figure 5.18 *Read and Write Access (Denied).*

At this point, processing of the ACL stops even though there are other ACEs in the ACL that grant permissions to FredMgr.

OBJECT OWNER WRITE AND READ ACCESS REQUEST

In the example shown in Figure 5.19, Windows NT 4.0 knows by reading FredMgr's access token that he is a member of the Mgrs group. Processing of the ACL will stop as soon as Windows NT 4.0 sees that NoAccess (None) is assigned to the Mgrs group, even though the other two ACEs allow Read, Write, and Execute access for FredMgr.

After failing to gain access via the discretionary ACL, Windows NT 4.0 notices that FredMgr is the owner of the object. Because of this, he is automatically granted ReadControl and WRITE_DAC. Since this is all the access he is asking for, his request is granted.

If FredMgr had asked for any other access in addition to ReadControl and WRITE_DAC, the request would be denied even though Fred is the object's owner. In this case, FredMgr receives the following message:

```
G:\FILE2.TXT

You do not have permission to open this file.

See the owner of the file or an administrator to obtain
permission.
```

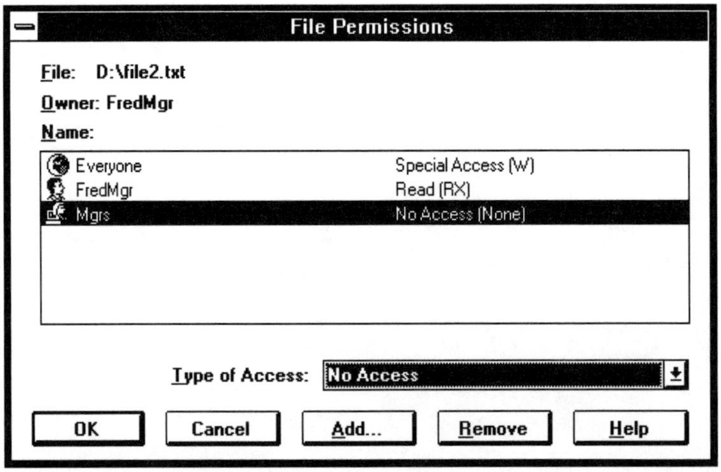

Figure 5.19 *Requesting Read and Write Access as Object Owner.*

In this case, because FredMgr is the owner, he can change his own permissions to grant himself appropriate access to the file.

PERMISSIONS ASSIGNED BY A CUSTOM APPLICATION

It's important to note that the three preceding examples demonstrate discretionary access control for file and directory permissions that are applied through the Windows NT 4.0 Permissions Editor either directly or by inheritance. If you use a custom application that sets and changes permissions on files and directories, the Windows NT 4.0 Permissions Editor may not be able to handle the ACL that the custom application creates or modifies.

Even though the logic just discussed still applies, there is no way of precisely determining the access to the object. The next example illustrates this point. The user BobMgr wants Read and Write access to the file object with the discretionary ACL shown in Figure 5.20. The access token for BobMgr indicates that she is a member of the groups Users, JnrMgrs, and Everyone.

In this example, a custom application has been used to update the ACL for a file, thus confusing the usual order in which the ACEs for this file are processed. Normally, all AccessDenied ACEs are processed first. Windows NT 4.0 evaluates this ACL as follows:

1. Windows NT 4.0 reads BobMgr's desired access mask to see that she is trying to gain Read and Write access.
2. Windows NT 4.0 reads the AccessAllowed ACE for BobMgr and finds a match to the Read permission requested in the desired access mask.

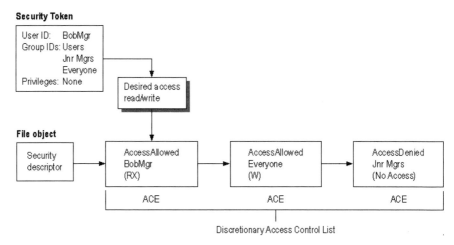

Figure 5.20 *Custom Application Assigns Permissions.*

3. Windows NT 4.0 reads the AccessAllowed ACE for Everyone and finds a match to the Write permission requested in the desired access mask.

BobMgr is granted Read and Write access to the file object, even though the third ACE explicitly denies JnrMgrs access to it. If the Windows NT 4.0 Permissions Editor had been used to apply the same permissions to the file object, the AccessDenied ACE for JnrMgrs would have been ordered first in the ACL, and BobMgr would have been denied access to the file.

Security Events Auditing

Windows NT 4.0 includes auditing features you can use to collect information about how your system is being used. These features also allow you to monitor events related to system security, to identify any security breaches, and to determine the extent and location of any damage. The level of audited events is adjustable to suit the needs of your organization. Some organizations need little auditing information, while others would be willing to trade some performance and disk space for the detailed information they can use to analyze their system.

Remember that when you enable auditing, there is some small performance overhead for each audit check the system performs.

Windows NT 4.0 can track events related to the operating system itself and to individual applications. Each application can define its own auditable events. Definitions of these events are added to the Registry when the application is installed on your Windows NT 4.0 computer.

Audit events are identified to the system by the event source module name that corresponds to a specific event type in the Registry and by an event ID. In addition to listing events by event ID, the security log in Event Viewer lists them by category. The categories of events shown in Table 5.2 are displayed in the Security Log. Those functions found in the Audit Policy dialog box of User Manager are shown in parenthesis in the "Category" column.

AUDIT EVENTS HANDLE AND PROCESS IDS

One of the most important aspects of security is determining who is actually behind operations of security interest, such as file writes or security policy

Table 5.2 *Categories of Events and Their Meaning*

Category	Meaning
Account Management (User and Group Management)	These events describe high-level changes to the user accounts database, such as User Created or Group Membership Change. Potentially, a more detailed object-level audit is also performed (see Object Access events).
Detailed Tracking (Process Tracking)	These events provide detailed subject-tracking information. This includes information such as program activation, handle duplication, and indirect object access.
Logon/Logoff (Logon and Logoff)	These events describe a single logon or logoff attempt, whether successful or unsuccessful. Included in each logon description is an indication of what type of logon was requested or performed (that is, interactive, network, or service).
Object Access (File and Object Access)	These events describe both successful and unsuccessful accesses to protected objects.
Policy Change (Security Policy Changes)	These events describe high-level changes to the security policy database, such as assignment of privileges or logon capabilities. Potentially, a more detailed object-level audit is also performed (see Object Access events).
Privilege Use (Use of User Rights)	These events describe both successful and unsuccessful attempts to use privileges. It also includes information about when some special privileges are assigned. These special privileges are audited only at assignment time, not at time of use.
System Event (System)	These events indicate something occurred that affects the security of the entire system or audit log.

change. With Windows' client/server model, user account identification can be rather tricky. Although a thread that requests access to a resource is identified by the user ID, the thread may be impersonating someone else. In this case, it would be misleading to log events by user ID and may not be useful in finding the perpetrator in the case of a security breach.

To prevent this problem, there are two levels of subject identification used in Windows NT 4.0 auditing and in the security log—the user ID (also called the primary ID) and the impersonation ID (also called the client ID), as applicable. These two IDs show security administrators who are performing auditable actions. In some cases, a security administrator wants to see what is happening with each process. To meet this need, auditing information also includes a subject's process ID where possible.

When process tracking is enabled (through the Audit Policy dialog box of User Manager), audit messages are generated each time a new process is created. This information can be correlated with specific audit messages to see not only which user account is performing auditable actions, but also which program was run.

Many audit events also include a handle ID, enabling the event to be associated with future events. For example, when a file is opened, the audit information indicates the handle ID assigned. When the handle is closed, another audit event with the same handle ID is generated. With this information, you can determine exactly how long the file remained open. This could be useful, for example, when you want to assess damage following a security breach.

This list shows some of the information that Windows NT 4.0 tracks within the access token of a process, which can also be used for auditing:

- Authentication ID, assigned when the user logs on
- The group security IDs and corresponding attributes of groups to which the user is assigned membership
- The names of the privileges assigned to and used by the user and their corresponding attributes
- The SID of the user account used to log on

EXAMPLES OF SECURITY EVENT

As described earlier, you can track several categories of security events. This part of the chapter provides examples for most of these categories. This set of examples does not constitute a strategy for using the auditing capabilities of Windows NT 4.0; they merely serve as an introduction to help you interpret these events when you enable auditing for your Windows NT 4.0 system.

OBJECT ACCESS AND TRACKING FILE • In this example, auditing is enabled as follows, assuming you are logged on as an administrator:

1. From Windows Explorer, select the .TXT file, and then choose Auditing from the Security menu. Assign Full Control permission to the user accessing the .TXT file and enable auditing for Success and Failure of Read and Write events.
2. From User Manager, choose Audit from the Policies menu. Next, enable auditing for Success and Failure of File and Object Access and Process Tracking.

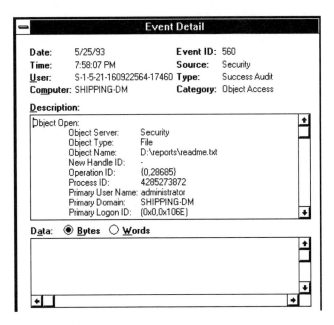

Figure 5.21 *Audit Events.*

This results in audit events shown in Figure 5.21.

From this view of the security log, you get a quick summary of security-related events that occurred. Double-click the first event to examine the details. Details of this first event are shown in the Event Detail box.

The data to be interpreted is listed in the Description list box. Table 5.3 summarizes the audited events for this example, in the order in which they occurred.

USER RIGHTS USE • User Manager is used to enable auditing for Success and Failure of Use of User Rights. When the user tries to change the system time, event is generated, as shown in Figure 5.22.

This event indicates that a privileged service was called and that a server component named Kernel has called an audit check on the primary username of the user. The audit type is a Success Audit, meaning that the user successfully exercised the right to use the SeSystemtimePrivilege (the right to change the system time).

GROUP MANAGEMENT AND USER • In this example, a new user account is added to the user accounts database. Auditing is enabled in User Manager by specifying both Success and Failure of User and Group Management. This generates new audit events, as shown in Figure 5.23 and Table 5.4.

Table 5.3 *Example of Security Events for File Access*

Event ID and Description	Analysis
Event 560: Object Open Event 561: Handle Allocated Event 562: Handle Closed	In this sequence of events, Windows NT 4.0 is doing some internal checks, such as seeing if the file exists and that there is no sharing violation.
Event 592: A New Process Has Been Created Event 560: Object Open Event 561: Handle Allocated Event 562: Handle Closed	In this series of events, a new process is created for NOTEPAD.EXE. This process opens the .TXT file for reading. Next, the process allocates and then closes a handle to the file. Note that from the security log it is clear that Notepad does not keep an open handle to the file; it simply keeps a copy of the file in memory.
Event 560: Object Open Event 561: Handle Allocated Event 562: Handle Closed	The process opens the file for reading and writing, and since the event is a successful audit, new data is written to the file. Next, the handle is allocated for the open file, and then closed.
Event 593: A Process Has Exited	This event indicates that the process, whose process ID relates to NOTEPAD.EXE, has ended.

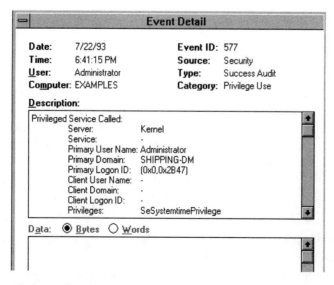

Figure 5.22 *Event Detail Window.*

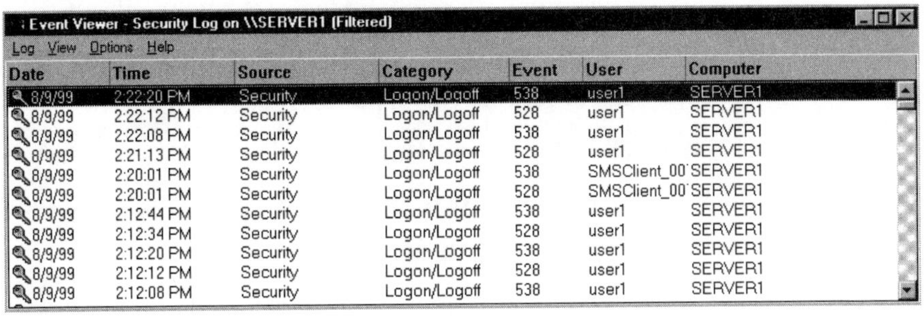

Figure 5.23 *Event Viewer Window.*

Table 5.4 *Security Events for Added User Account.*

Event ID and Description	Analysis
Event 632: Global Group Member Added Event 624: User Account Created	A new security ID (member) is created and added to the group represented by the target account ID. This is a default global group Domain Users. At this point, the security ID does not have a username allocated to it.
Event 642: User Account Changed	This event indicates that the account name of the security ID represented by the Target Account ID has been changed to the new user's.
Event 636: Local Group Member Added	This event indicates that the account represented by the new user's security ID is created. The new user is added to the local group represented by the security ID under Target Account ID (Users).

SYSTEM, RESTART, AND SHUTDOWN • The examples shown in Figure 5.23 have auditing enabled in User Manager for both Success and Failure of Restart, Shutdown, and System.

Audit Determination

Windows NT 4.0 has an audit determination process similar to its access determination process, described earlier in this chapter. Following access determination, Windows NT 4.0 evaluates the following information for possible auditing:

- The audit ACL associated with the target object.

- The desired accesses with all generic access types mapped to standard and specific access types.

- The final determination of whether access is granted or denied.

- The subject attempting the access (that is, the set of identifiers representing the subject).

Each ACE in the audit ACL is evaluated as follows:

1. Windows NT 4.0 checks to see if the type is SystemAudit. If not, the ACE is skipped.

2. Windows NT 4.0 compares the identifier in the ACE to the set of identifiers representing the subject. If no match is found, the ACE is skipped.

3. The desired accesses are compared to the access mask specified in the ACE. If none of the accesses specified in the ACE's mask were requested, the ACE is skipped.

4. The SUCCESSFUL_ACCESS_ACE_FLAG and FAILED_ACCESS_ACE_FLAG flags of the ACE are compared to the final determination of whether access was granted or denied. If access was granted but the SUCCESSFUL_ACCESS_ACE_FLAG flag is not set, or if access was denied but the FAILED_ACCESS_ACE_FLAG flag is not set, the ACE is skipped.

If Windows NT 4.0 performs all of these steps successfully, an audit message is generated. Figure 5.24 illustrates this process. In this scenario, a system access ACL is being evaluated. Here, Write access to the file object is granted, and the SUCCESSFUL_ACCESS_ACE_FLAG is set in each ACE.

In this example, Windows NT 4.0 evaluates the ACL by comparing the desired access mask with each ACE and then processes the desired mask through the following steps:

1. Windows NT 4.0 evaluates an ACE for SnrMgrs (of which FoxMgr is a member). However, when the desired access is compared to the access mask of the ACE, no match is found, and the ACE is skipped.

2. Windows NT 4.0 evaluates the ACE for FoxMgr and finds a match.

3. Windows NT 4.0 checks access flags and finds the SUCCESSFUL_ACCESS_ACE_FLAG is set. Processing stops, and an audit message is generated.

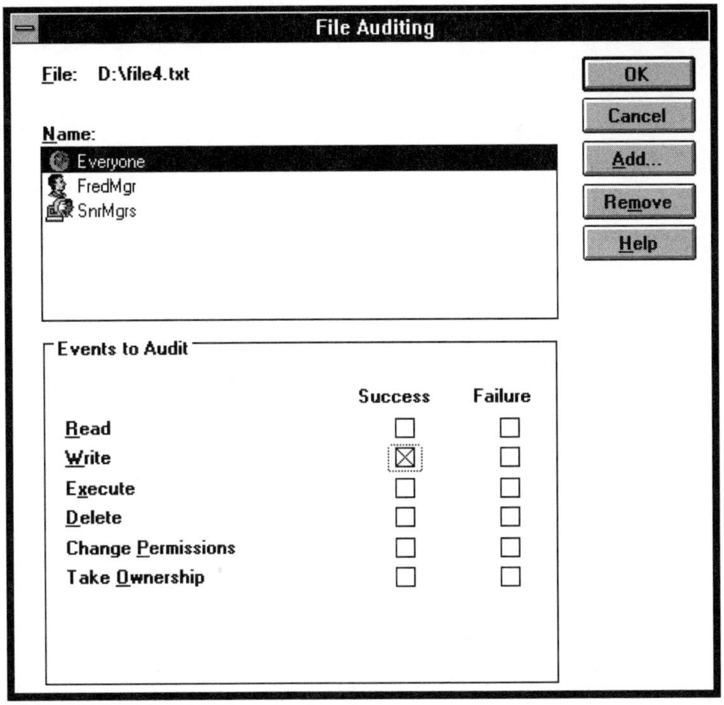

Figure 5.24   *File Auditing Window.*

■ Summary

The reader should come away from this chapter with an in-depth knowledge of the MCSE exam-specific components that are needed to design the SMS security strategy plan prior to installation for the organization. For instance, by specifying the rights that a Windows NT user or user group has on various SMS security objects, you set the security levels SMS has the following default security objects:

- Advertisements
- Collections
- Packages
- Status objects

Next, you can log in to the database on any site to which you have network access and permission. You can administer that site and all its subsites once you have logged in. You can administer the entire SMS system if you log in to the database at the central site. By using the SMS Administrator, you can do the following:

- Analyze network traffic
- Create, modify, and delete SMS objects
- Define resources to be collected
- Manage computers using the Windows NT 4.0 Administrative Tools
- Manage packages and program groups
- Receive SNMP traps
- Set site and domain properties
- View and provide remote support for all computers in the site and its subsites

Finally, as part of the initial design specifications for Windows NT 4.0, security in Windows NT 4.0 was included and is pervasive throughout the operating system. In the security model, components audit who accesses which events, who accesses which objects (such as files and shared printers), and which actions an individual can take on an object. The Windows NT 4.0 security model includes the following components.

- Local Security Authority
- Logon processes
- Security Account Manager (SAM)
- Security Reference Monitor

▲ CHAPTER REVIEW QUESTIONS

▲ True/False

1. *True or False? You do not have to create accounts for users at the clients.*

2. *True or False? A machine group is not static; it contains only the computers that you add to it (unlike the Sites window that contains all computers that belong in the site).*

3. *True or False? The Collection cannot be set directly from within the SMS Administrator.*

4. *True or False? While Event Viewer is not adequate for most requirements, the security model is defined so that developers can write their own custom security event viewer/monitor.*

5. *True or False? Windows NT 4.0 has the ability to support multiple authentication packages that are implemented as DLLs. This flexibility allows third-party software vendors the opportunity to integrate their own custom authentication packages with Windows NT 4.0. For instance, a network vendor might augment the standard Windows NT 4.0 authentication package by adding one that allows users to log on to Windows NT 4.0 and the vendor's network simultaneously.*

6. *True or False? In the current release of Windows NT 4.0, the set of user rights is defined by the system and can be changed. Future versions of Windows NT 4.0 may allow software developers to define new user rights appropriate to their application.*

7. *True or False? NT File Systems (NTFS) support the inheritance of ACLs from directory objects to file objects that are created within the directory.*

8. *True or False? When you come to fully implement SMS accounts across your organization, each administrator that you do not want to access the database must enter a login ID that identifies them as a user on the SQL Server and gives them access to the database.*

▲ Multiple Choice

1. *SMS has the following default security objects, except:*
   A. Advertisements
   B. Collections
   C. Packages
   D. Clients
   E. Status objects

2. *There are three types of Advertisements properties. Which of the following is not one of the three types?*
   A. Details
   B. Schedule
   C. Status
   D. Object type
   E. All of the above

3. *Which of the following properties is not defined for packages?*
   A. Workgroup
   B. Users

   C. Sharing

   D. Workstations

   E. All of the above

4. *The SMS Administrator contains separate windows for events, alerts, and SNMP traps. Each of these windows provides you with information and tools that you can use to better manage your network and your SMS system. Which one of the following statements does not belong here?*

   A. Alerts are actions that are generated by SMS when certain conditions are detected.

   B. A site server must be running the Windows NT Server 4.0.

   C. Events are logs generated by SMS that contain information, warnings, or error messages.

   D. SNMP traps are similar to SMS events, but SNMP traps are typically generated by other devices and systems on the network.

   E. All of the above.

5. *Security settings are displayed on a per user basis in the main window of the SMS Security Manager. Which of the following is not displayed by the SMS Security Manager?*

   A. Current rights

   B. Proposed rights

   C. Scales

   D. Security object

   E. All of the above

6. *Which of the following is not a part of the Windows NT 4.0 security model?*

   A. Local Security Authority

   B. Logon processes

   C. Security Account Manager (SAM)

   D. Change Permission

   E. Security Reference Monitor

7. *Specific types include access options that apply specifically to this object type. Each object type can have up to 18 specific access types. Collectively, the specific access types for a particular object type are called the specific access mask. These are defined when the object type is defined. Which of the following is not a Windows NT 4.0 file access type?*

   A. AppendData

   B. Execute

   C. Allocate separate physical drives

   D. ReadAttributes

   E. ReadData

▲ Open Ended

1. You can log in to the database for any site to which you have network access and permission. Once you have logged in, you can administer that site and all its subsites. If you log in to the database at the central site, you can administer the entire SMS system. By using the SMS Administrator, what are the steps you can perform?

Interoperability and Upgrade Plan

When planning an SMS site, you need an interoperability and upgrade strategy for various situations. Among those situations are the following:

- Planning the upgrade of an SMS 1.2 site to an SMS 2.0 site
- Planning the interoperability of a mixed SMS 1.2 and SMS 2.0 site

The situations identified in this chapter generally apply equally to primary and secondary mixed SMS 1.2 *and* SMS 2.0 sites and to the upgrade of an SMS 1.2 site to an SMS 2.0 site. In the former scenario, secondary sites do not generate any more network traffic than primary sites. In the latter scenario, when you upgrade a primary site, its secondary sites are also upgraded. This means that you have less control over upgrading secondary sites.

Remember, if you are upgrading an existing version of an SMS site, you must consider the version of SQL Server that you are using for the SMS database. This is discussed in detail in the Sidebar, "Microsoft SQL Server Upgrade for SMS Databases."

This chapter explains how to maintain your existing SMS 1.2 mixed in with SMS 2.0 sites. Since SMS will automatically upgrade existing sites there may be instances to block an automatic upgrade. Sometimes we need to allow for a manual upgrade in those situations where an automatic upgrade is not appropriate, such as when many secondary sites are reporting to a single primary site across a slow link.

Quick Refresher: An SMS secondary site is a limited SMS installation. Secondary sites provide SMS connectivity with minimal administrative requirements. There are many advantages, in terms of maintenance and bandwidth, to having a SMS secondary site. SMS sends packages to a secondary site in a compressed format, and Maintenance Manager does not poll secondary site servers during every cycle, which reduces network traffic. Therefore, an SMS secondary site can be created only from a primary site, and there can be no child sites under a secondary site. A secondary site does not have an SQL Server database, and it usually does not have a local administrator. Although you can install SMS Administrator Utilities on the secondary site server, you must remove them before you can upgrade the secondary site.

You will come away from this chapter with a clear understanding of two distinct MSCE design requirements: *interoperability of mixed sites* and *upgrading sites*. Let's take a look at how all of this works.

MCSE 6.1   Upgrading an SMS Site

When upgrading an existing version of an SMS site, you must consider the version of SQL Server you are using for the SMS database. Different versions of SMS require different versions of Microsoft SQL Server as follows:

- SMS 1.0 supports SQL Server 4.21a only.
- SMS 1.1 supports SQL Server 4.21a and SQL Server 6.x.
- SMS 1.2 supports SQL Server 6.x. SQL Server 4.21a is supported, but only during the upgrade phase to 6.x. SQL Server 4.21a is not supported for usage with SMS 1.2.
- SMS 2.0 supports SQL Server 6.x or higher.

Also consider that when a new version of SMS (like 2.0) is installed at the primary site, the secondary sites reporting to the primary site are typically updated automatically to this new version.

Primary and Secondary SMS Sites

For each site, decide if you want a local administrator at the site. If you want an administrator at the site, it should be a primary site. If you do not want an administrator at the site, it should be a secondary site. Let's quickly cover some other reasons for making a site primary or secondary.

POSITION IN THE HIERARCHY

Often, the site's position in the hierarchy will help you decide what type of site it should be. For instance, a site that has subsites must be a primary site. The central site must be a primary site as well. A site with no subsites can be a primary site or a secondary site. If a site currently does not have any subsites, but you may add subsites to it in the future, you should make the site a primary site. Remember that you cannot upgrade a secondary site to a primary site, and you cannot add subsites to a secondary site.

HARDWARE REQUIREMENTS

A primary site server generally has greater hardware requirements than a secondary site server. This is because primary sites store all site data in a SQL Server database. Managing the database creates overhead at the primary site and thus requires a more powerful site server. Each primary site will have its own SQL Server, although it is possible for multiple sites to store their databases on the same SQL Server.

Hardware requirements also tend to be greater at primary sites because they can have subsites. Subsites make the site larger and thus increase the load on the parent site server.

UPGRADING SYSTEMS MANAGEMENT SERVER

SMS 1.2 can be upgraded to SMS 2.0, or it can interoperate with SMS 2.0. There are good reasons both to upgrade and to interoperate. This chapter examines an SMS 1.2 to SMS 2.0 upgrade performed on a single, central site server.

There are several preinstallation requirements before an SMS 1.2 primary site server can be upgraded to an SMS 2.0 site server. The best strategy is to upgrade the operating system and database to the latest versions supported by SMS 1.2. Then consolidate all SMS 1.2 site server functions back to the SMS primary site server. For example, the SMS Executive threads running on SMS 1.2 helper servers should be returned to the site server. Upgrading the site server operating system and SMS database and consolidating SMS services will increase the likelihood of a successful upgrade to SMS 2.0. SMS 1.2 clients can be converted to SMS 2.0 client computers. Before conversion begins, you must be aware of which clients can be upgraded to SMS 2.0 client computers. You should consider the impact of future SMS upgrades on your site structure.

Only SMS 1.2 is designed for an upgrade to SMS 2.0. If you are running SMS 1.0 or 1.1, upgrade to SMS 1.2 before starting an upgrade to SMS 2.0. SMS 1.2 is designed to run on the x86, Alpha, or MIPS platform. Since SMS 2.0 does not include installation files for MIPS computers, an SMS 2.0 upgrade cannot be performed on this platform. Backup the SMS 1.2 registry keys and update the emergency repair disk (Rdisk) and the SMS directory structure. Ideally, run a full system backup and maintain this tape until a successful SMS 1.2 to SMS 2.0 upgrade has been completed.

An SMS 1.2 site server is designed for Windows NT Server 3.51 running SP3 (or later) domain controllers or Windows NT Server version 4.0 domain controllers. An SMS 2.0 site server can be installed on Windows NT Server version 4.0 running SP4 or Windows 2000 Server. The SMS 2.0 site server does not have to be a domain controller but it must be a member of a domain (member server). Remember, a Windows NT/2000 Server acting as a domain controller cannot be converted into a member server. Therefore, after the upgrade process, Windows NT/2000 Server will remain a domain controller.

Because of the overall difference between SMS 1.2 and SMS 2.0, some data in the SMS 1.2 site database cannot be converted to the SMS 2.0 site database. The following SMS 1.2 settings are lost in the upgrade: security settings configured through the SMS Security Manager; client disk inventory; named queries; and jobs, excluding system jobs. Since the SMS 1.2 directory structure is deleted, collected files, package definition files (PDF), custom management information format (MIF) files, and SMS logon scripts are deleted. It is therefore important to document all critical settings and make sure that you have performed a full system backup before performing an upgrade.

Modifications to the setup options cannot be made during the upgrade process. So installation modification must be performed after the upgrade is complete. The upgrade process should not be interrupted after a database conversion has begun. The upgrade routine will prompt you to start the database conversion. An upgrade can be cancelled before database conversion has begun.

To run the online help system and the Microsoft Management Console, you must install IE 4.01 on the computer that will be upgraded. IE 4.01 will not disrupt the normal function of an SMS 1.2 server.

Upgrading primary sites requires a local administrator to perform the upgrade at the site server. Secondary sites must be can be upgraded locally through the network or remotely using SMS CD-ROM setup program.

When you upgrade SMS to a new version, each secondary site is also upgraded from new code installed at the parent site. If you have many secondary sites reporting to a single primary site, this could put a heavy load on the primary site during the upgrade process.

Study Break

Microsoft SQL Server Upgrade for SMS Databases

While SMS 1.2 was designed for SQL Server version 6.x, it can run on SQL Server version 7.0. Therefore, you must upgrade SQL Server to either version 6.5 running SP4 or SQL Server version 7.0 before starting the SMS 2.0 upgrade process. Since SQL Server version 6.0 is not supported on Windows NT version 4.0, upgrade SQL Server to version 6.5 running SP4 before running a Windows NT Server version 4.0 upgrade. Ideally, upgrade to SQL Server version 7.0 and Windows NT Server version 4.0 running SP4 before performing any SMS 1.2 to SMS 2.0 upgrade. Once SMS 2.0 is installed on a computer running a local copy of SQL Server, that computer cannot service any SMS site servers running SMS 1.2.

The SQL Server version 6.5 tempdb (temporary database) must be expanded to support an upgrade from SMS 1.2 to SMS 2.0. You must first determine the size of the current SMS 1.2 site database. To do this, run the sp_spaceused stored procedure through SQL Server version 6.5's iSQL utility. When you have ascertained the value, increase the size of tempdb so that it is 20% larger than the site database. For example, if the SMS 1.2 site database is 200 MB, then tempdb should be at least 240 MB. This procedure is only necessary on SQL Server version 6.5, since SQL Server version 7.0 will dynamically grow the tempdb database as the upgrade installation requires it.

To protect your site database, run a database backup against the site database and the master database before starting a SQL Server upgrade. Run the SMS 1.2 DBCLEAN utility to delete obsolete or unused data from the database. Further, run database consistency checks in SQL Server Enterprise Manager and set the site database transaction log to "Truncate at checkpoint" before performing the SQL Server upgrade. This last option keeps the transaction log from growing out of control during the upgrade process.

Primary Site Upgrade

As previously stated, installing a service pack or a new version of SMS on a primary site automatically upgrades all secondary sites attached directly to it. This is the supported method of upgrading the sites, as it guarantees that all sites are running the same version of SMS.

The automatic upgrade process is usually quick and efficient. Sometimes, however, a primary site connected by a slow network link requires additional time to complete file transfers and to report. Concurrently upgrading multiple primary sites may adversely impact network bandwidth. SMS 2.0 includes enhancements to the upgrade process that allow a selective upgrade of individual primary sites.

Secondary Site Upgrade

While the standard upgrade process is designed to be quick and efficient, a secondary site at the end of a slow link can cause the automatic upgrade to take a long time. When multiple secondary sites (like primary sites) are being upgraded concurrently, network bandwidth can be impacted.

BLOCKING THE AUTOMATIC UPGRADE

When you upgrade an SMS primary site on a SMS 1.2 Server, the standard process invokes an automatic upgrade for all the secondary sites that report to the primary site. The process produces a number of jobs that download the new files required by the secondary site for its upgrade to take effect. The total size of the downloaded images is approximately 20 MB. This load is inappropriate in environments with slow links or with many secondary sites attached to a single primary across a slow link.

There is a way to stop this automatic process so that the secondary sites can be upgraded in a more controlled fashion. The process is very simple: It requires the use of a modified `setup.exe` with a command line switch to block the automatic secondary site upgrade. This `setup.exe` replaces the one found on the standard SMS CD in the SMSSETUP\X86 directory. This executable must be run from the command line and also must be passed additional parameters to tell it the location of the `SYSTEM.MAP` file. The command line is:

```
% setup /SYSMAP:system Map Path\SYSTEM.MAP /NOAUTOUPGRADE
```

This causes the primary site to upgrade normally, but blocks the request to upgrade the secondary sites that report to the primary.

CONTROLLING AN UPGRADE

Once the blocking operation is complete, there are two options for upgrading the secondary sites: upgrading across the network and upgrading from the CD.

CONTROLLING A NETWORK UPGRADE • To upgrade a selected secondary site from the primary site, use the `preinst.exe` utility found in the `$Systems Management Server/site.srv/x86.bin` directory of SMS. It takes a single parameter, which is the Secondary Site's site code:

```
% preinst /UPGRADE:SiteCode
```

This initiates a normal upgrade of the secondary site in which the 20 MB of upgrade files are downloaded to the site over the network.

For slow links, this upgrade will still take some time.

For sites with large numbers of secondary sites, it is advisable to start multiple upgrades that run overnight in order to reduce the time required to upgrade the entire hierarchy. It is worth experimenting on a test network to ascertain the number of secondary sites that can reasonably be upgraded at any one time in a particular environment.

CONTROLLING A CD UPGRADE • The alternative method of upgrading the secondary sites is to use a new utility called `upg2site.exe`, which is found in the same directory within the SMS CD. This allows the upgrade to be run from the SMS-CD. The CD can be either resident in or mounted on a secondary site server. This method is preferable for networks where the secondary sites are connected to their primary sites through slow WAN links. The utility takes a number of parameters as shown in Table 6.1:

```
UPG2SITE [/CD:path] [/SS:site-server] [/PDO] [/SDO] [/CEO]
```

Table 6.1 *CD Upgrade Parameters*

Parameters	Description
/CD:path	Specifies a path to the root of the SMS release CD-ROM; otherwise, the local machine's drives are searched.
/SS:site-server	Specifies the machine name of the site server; otherwise, the local machine is assumed to be the site server.
/PDO	Allows the purge directories override; otherwise, the default is to remove directories marked as purgeable in the system map file.
/SDO	Allows the shutdown site override; otherwise, the default is to require a successful site shutdown prior to starting the upgrade.
/CEO	Allows the critical error message box override; otherwise, the default is to let the operating system display a message box for all critical errors, such as the CD-ROM being removed from the drive.

For general use, the CD path is the only parameter that needs to be supplied.

MCSE 6.2   Planning the Interoperability of a Mixed Site

Planning the interoperability of a mixed SMS 1.2 and 2.0 site requires upgrades that are initiated automatically when you add a component or upgrade to the primary site above the secondary site using SMS Setup program. SMS 1.2 and 2.0 include enhancements to the upgrade process that permit greater control over primary and secondary site upgrades. This part of the chapter describes the normal automatic upgrade process with regard to mixed SMS 1.2 and 2.0 sites.

During a normal upgrade, once the primary site upgrade has been completed, the Setup program adds upgrade instructions to the database for all secondary sites directly beneath the primary site. The primary site's Hierarchy Manager polls the database periodically to detect these instructions. It then waits for all secondary sites to become Active, indicated by <status=1>.

Hierarchy Manager will not start the upgrade process if there are any secondary sites in the process of being created, in the process of being deleted, or otherwise involved in processes that cause them to be reported as inactive.

Next, a primary and secondary site upgrade goes through four phases:

- Phase 1: The primary site Bootstrap system job installs and starts the bootstrap service on the secondary site.
- Phase 2: The primary site Install system job sends upgrade component files to the secondary site.
- Phase 3: The primary site Control system job sends site configuration information to the secondary site.
- Phase 4: The secondary site Control system job reports site configuration and the primary site updates its database.

This part of the chapter describes each phase in detail.

Phase 1: Bootstrap Service Job

When all secondary sites are active, Hierarchy Manager creates a Bootstrap job for each secondary site. The SMS bootstrap service is sent to each secondary site, where it shuts down the site in preparation for the upgrade.

The SMS administrator cannot edit site properties for sites in the process of being upgraded.

At this point, you can select the secondary site in the SMS Administrator program Sites window and click Properties on the File menu to display the current status:

```
Phase 1: Site Upgrade Initiated
```

The primary site's Hierarchy Manager reports site control file processing in the `Hman.log` file. The site Preinstall system job installs the bootstrap service `SMS_UPGRADE_BOOTSTRAP_SERVICE` on the target secondary site server. The primary site's LanSender actually starts the upgrade bootstrap service.

Account problems may cause site upgrades to fail at this point, because installing the service involves accessing the registry of the target computer. Watch the Lansend.log file for any connection or access problems.

After installing the Upgrade bootstrap service on the secondary site server, the site Preinstall system job reports completion to the primary site. The primary site's Hierarchy Manager then changes the site status to *2 12* in the `Hman.log` file. You can select the secondary site in the SMS Administrator program Sites window and click Properties on the File menu to display the current status:

```
Phase 1: bootstrap service job completed
```

Corresponding entries are also made in the `Hman.log` file. You can verify that the bootstrap service has completed its tasks by connecting to the target server in Windows NT 4.0 Server Manager and verifying the following: `SMS_UPGRADE_BOOTSTRAP_SERVICE` has been installed and started and other SMS services have been stopped and removed.

You can also check the `Bootstrap.log` file for related entries. This log file is located on the root directory of the installation drive designated in the New Secondary Site dialog box. You can use any text editor to read this log, but you may find it more informative to use the SMSTrace utility. SMSTrace dynamically refreshes the display as processes append entries to the file, which allows you to view job progress.

A secondary site upgrade may fail because LanSender fails to install or start the bootstrap service.

Phase 2: Site Install Job

The site Install system job sends the SMS site package to the secondary site. This package contains all SMS site components. The primary site's Hierarchy Manager uses the `System.map` file on the primary site server to determine which files to include in the package.

Installing a service pack or a new version of SMS updates the System.map file.

At this point, you can select the secondary site in the SMS Administrator program Sites window and click Properties on the File menu to display the current status:

```
Job status is 2

Site <sitecode> new status is 2 12
```

The primary site's Hierarchy Manager begins copying files needed on a secondary site from the `$Sms\Site.srv` directory tree to the `$Sms\Prim site.srv\Rmotesrc.box` directory. Each file is logged in the `Hman.log` file as it is copied. When all files have been copied, they are compressed into a package that becomes the source for the site Install job that transfers the package to the secondary site.

$Sms refers to the SMS directory tree at the primary site.

When you create multiple secondary sites, this package is the source for all site Install jobs. The package is marked as read-only, and the Scheduler will not delete the package file until all secondary sites under construction have a status of Active.

The site properties for the secondary site reflect job progress. You can select the secondary site in the SMS Administrator program Sites window and click Properties on the File menu to display the current status:

```
Site install job started
```

The primary site's Hierarchy Manager monitors the status of this job just as it monitors the status of the Preinstall and Control jobs. As long as the Hman.log file reports a job status of 2, Hierarchy Manager considers the job to be still active.

When the compressed site source package arrives in the `$Sms\Site`
`.srv\Despoolr.box\receive` directory on the target secondary site
server, the bootstrap service moves it to the root of the SMS installation
directory and renames it `Bootstrp.pk1`. When the job reports that it is
complete, the primary site's Hierarchy Manager reports the updated status in
the `Hman.log` file as follows:

```
Job status is 4

Site <sitecode> new status is 2 22
```

At this point, you can select the secondary site in the SMS Administrator program Sites window, and click Properties on the File menu to display
the current status, as shown here:

```
Site install job completed
```

Phase 3: Site Control Job

The primary site's Hierarchy Manager now creates the final package for the
target secondary site containing the site control file for the secondary site as
defined by the existing secondary site properties in the primary site database.
The primary site's Hierarchy Manager reports site control file processing in
the `Hman.log` file.

At this point, you can select the secondary site in the SMS Administrator program Sites window and click Properties on the File menu to display
the current status, like so:

```
Phase 3: Site Configuration Job Started
```

When the target secondary site receives the site Control package, the
secondary site's bootstrap service takes over. It moves the package file to the
root of the SMS installation directory, renames it as `Bootstrp.pk2`, and
reports the site Control job as complete. The primary site now waits for the
secondary site to report configuration data and initiates no further activity at
the secondary site.

The bootstrap service decompresses the `Bootstrp.pk1` package file,
removes the existing SMS secondary site installation directory, and then fin-
ishes recreating the familiar SMS directory tree structure containing all the
updated files. It also decompresses the `Bootstrp.pk2` site control file and
moves it to the `$Secsite\Site.srv\Sitecfg.box` directory as a `.ct1`
file. Next, the bootstrap service starts the new secondary site's Site Configu-

ration Manager service, then stops and removes itself, and finally logs these actions, as shown in Listing 6.1.

Listing 6.1 *Deinstall Bootstrap Entries in the Bootstrap.log File*

```
Bootstrap v1.00.18 Log Mon May 10 15:42:59 1999
: Site Config Manager is running.
Bootstrap v1.00.18 Log Mon May 10 15:42:59 1999
: SMS Exec is running
Bootstrap v1.00.18 Log Mon May 10 15:43:30 1999
: Bootstrap has been executing for 63 minutes.
Bootstrap v1.00.18 Log Mon May 10 15:43:30 1999
: All operations completed. Terminating.
Bootstrap v1.00.18 Log Mon May 10 15:43:30 1999
: Deinstalling Service SMS_UPGRADE_BOOTSTRAP
```

Phase 4: Upgrade Completion

The secondary site's Site Configuration Manager reads the site control file, completes site and service installation (including the SMS Executive service), and then sends a status report to the parent primary site as a `.ct2` file. This action is the first secondary site job, indicated by `0000000.job` in the SMS Administrator program Jobs window for the secondary site. Site Configuration Manager reports a minijob creation in the `Scman.log` file:

```
created mini-job in <path to SCHEDULE.BOX> to send site
control file

<$SMS>\SMS_SHRD\SITE.SRV\SITECFG.BOX\00000001.ct2 to parent
site

DOM
```

The `.ct2` file is created in the `$Secsite\Sms\Site.srv\Schedule .box` directory. The secondary site's Scheduler, Despooler, and LanSender processes move the file to the parent primary site. The primary site's Hierarchy Manager and Site Configuration Manager process the file to mark the secondary site as active.

Until the secondary site's site control file is received and processed, you can select the secondary site in the SMS Administrator program Sites window and click Properties on the File menu to display the status. Hierarchy Manager reports the updated status in the `Hman.log` file:

```
Processing site <sitecode> <status = 2>
```

The secondary site creation may fail because the secondary site does not return the `.ct2` site control file to the primary site or the primary site fails to process it.

The <status=2> code is Hierarchy Manager's indication that the site is still *pending installation*. At this time, it is quite possible that the secondary site has completed its upgrade process and is operational but has not reported configuration data to the primary parent site. After the site control file from the secondary site is received and processed by the primary site, the Site Properties status changes to Active and the logs are updated to indicate that the site upgrade is complete.

MCSE 6.3 Upgrading Client Operating Systems Using SMS PDFs

SMS includes PDFs that specify setup programs, installation options, and execution command lines for certain applications and operating systems. When you import a PDF using the SMS Administrator, these options are displayed and can be modified. PDFs are available for all Microsoft operating systems supported on SMS clients. You can use PDFs to install operating system upgrades over your network with SMS. To use a PDF to upgrade client operating systems, you complete the following steps:

1. Create the package source directory on distribution servers.
2. Import the appropriate PDF for the operating system and select the sites that contain clients you want to upgrade.
3. Create a advertisement to distribute the upgrade package to clients.

Table 6.2 shows the operating systems you can upgrade with PDFs available from Microsoft. The table lists each operating system, the command you use to create the package source directory for the operating system, and the PDF file name for the operating system. The PDFs are available on the SMS 1.2 and 2.0 CD unless otherwise noted.

Table 6.2 *Supported Operating System Upgrades*

Operating System	Installation Command	PDF
MS-DOS 6.22 or higher	`xcopy#`	Dos622.pdf
Windows 3.1	`setup /a`	Win310.pdf
Windows 3.11 or higher	`setup /a`	Win311.pdf
Windows for Workgroups 3.11 or higher	`setup /a`	WfW311.pdf
Windows 95 or 98	`xcopy#`	Win95.pdf *or* Win98.pdf
Windows 95 or 98, Service Pack 1	`xcopy#`	Win95SP1.pdf *or* Win98SP1.pdf (available in the Admin\Tools\SMS directory on the Windows 95 or 98 Service Pack 1 CD)
Windows NT Server 3.5	`xcopy#`	WAS35_.pdf
Windows NT 4.0 Workstation	`xcopy#`	WNT35_.pdf
Windows NT Server 4.0	`xcopy#`	WAS351.pdf
Windows NT Workstation 4.0	`xcopy#`	WNT351.pdf
Windows NT 4.0, Service Pack 4	`xcopy#`	NT351SP4.pdf (available on the Microsoft BackOffice 2.0b CD)
Windows NT 4.0 or higher	`xcopy#`	NT40.pdf (available on the Windows NT 4.0 CD)

Note: Copy all files from all operating system disks to the package source directory. For example, if the operating system disks are placed in drive B and the package source directory is C:\MSDOS622, use the command xcopy /e b:\ c:\msdos622. Repeat this command for each operating system disk.

Package Source Directory Creation

In Table 6.2, you have a list of each command needed to create the package source directory for the operating system. The steps to create this package source directory are as follows:

1. On the server, create a package source directory for the operating system.
2. Share the directory using a share name that is identical to the directory name.

3. From a client or the server containing the package source directory, log on to the network and connect to the share you created.

4. Insert the disk of the operating system you are installing, and install the operating system files in the package source directory.

For Setup programs that request the location of the destination directory, specify the drive letter you assigned to the package source directory share. If the Setup program prompts for the location of shared files, choose Server.

Operating System Package Creation

To a create a package for the operating system, you must do the following:

1. In SMS Administrator, open the Packages window. From the File menu, choose New.

2. Click Import.

3. Select the PDF for the operating system and click OK. For information on which PDF corresponds to which operating system, see Table 6.2.

4. Choose Workstations.

5. In the Source directory box, type the location of the package source directory and click Close.

6. Click OK in all open dialog boxes.

After creating the package, select the sites that contain the clients you want to upgrade.

Package Distribution to Clients

If you're distributing the package to clients, first see Table 6.2 for information about which command line to choose. Next, install the operating system on one or more clients by distributing the package to the clients as follows:

1. In SMS Administrator, open the Packages window, and then open the Sites window.

2. In the Packages window, select the package you created for the operating system, and drag it onto a client or site in the Sites window.

3. In the Advertisment dialog box, choose the appropriate client command for the operating system of the clients on which the program will run.

4. Click OK in all open dialog boxes.

All Operating Systems Upgrading

Before upgrading an operating system, users should close all open applications and disconnect all shared resources on their computers. If an application has unsaved data or a shared connection is in use, the operating system Setup might not complete successfully.

RESTARTING THE COMPUTER AFTER UPGRADING

In an operating system setup program, the computer is restarted at the end of the upgrade process. The user must log back on to the network after the computer is restarted.

Clients running Windows 3.1 or Windows for Workgroups must exit Windows during the upgrade process. If the user is running an application with unsaved, altered data files open when the operating system upgrade job is run, user interaction is required to exit Windows. If a user is not present to provide this input, the job is delayed until the user is present.

Once a computer has been upgraded to a new operating system, the SMS software components residing on it locally must be upgraded. If the user has a logon script that runs the SMSLS.bat file, then the user's SMS client components will be upgraded the next time the user logs on to the new operating system. If the user does not have such a logon script, the user must connect to the SMS logon server and run the RunSMS.bat file manually.

Because operating system upgrade require the computer to be restarted when the upgrade is completed, any other mandatory SMS jobs scheduled on the client immediately after the operating system upgrade will not occur at the scheduled time. Therefore, be sure to leave adequate time between scheduling a mandatory operating system upgrade job and any other mandatory SMS jobs (such as application installations) on the same client.

UPGRADING CLIENTS WITH MORE THAN ONE OPERATING SYSTEM

Before upgrading an operating system for a client with more than one operating system, take the following steps:

1. The computer must be identified in the SMS inventory by the operating system that you want to upgrade and must be currently running that operating system.

2. The upgrade must be sent to that computer and specified as valid for the current operating system so that it shows up in Package Command Manager at the client.

3. The computer must be configured to restart to the current operating system so the upgrade script can be completed.

OPERATING SYSTEM UPGRADES STATUS

At some point during each operating system upgrade, control of the upgrade process is handed off from SMS to the Setup program of the operating system being upgraded. If the operating system Setup program fails after this point for any reason, the failure will not be reported back to SMS, and SMS will report the client status as completed.

When you create and send operating system upgrades, plan and test the process on a small sample of clients before attempting to distribute the job to a large number of clients. This gives you the opportunity to identify errors in the operating system-specific scripting components with minimal impact on the clients.

WINDOWS FOR WORKGROUPS

When you run an operating system upgrade on a client currently running Windows for Workgroups Clients, the client must have enough available disk space to accommodate the entire setup package in addition to what is actually needed for the new operating system components.

This upgrade can be an upgrade of MS-DOS running with Windows for Workgroups, or it can be an upgrade from Windows for Workgroups to another operating system, such as Windows NT 4.0 Workstation.

Extra disk space is required because SMS copies all the required operating system setup files before SMS exits Windows. These Setup programs run only in MS-DOS, and thus SMS must exit Windows before the operating system upgrade can begin. SMS assumes that the client will lose its network connection when Windows for Workgroups is exited.

Upgrading to MS-DOS 6.22 or Higher

SMS supports MS-DOS 6.22 Upgrade and MS-DOS 6.22 Step-Up or higher. MS-DOS 6.22 Upgrade can be used to upgrade from MS-DOS 5.0, while

You cannot use an automated Setup to upgrade a Novell NetWare client to Windows for Workgroups. These upgrades must be manual.

MS-DOS 6.22 Step-Up can be used to upgrade from MS-DOS 6.0. Therefore, the PDF for upgrading to MS-DOS 6.22 supports both of these products. However, when you create a package to install MS-DOS 6.22, be sure to choose the correct client command line or the upgrade may fail. If a package with a client command line for MS-DOS 6.22 Step-Up is distributed to a computer that currently has a version of MS-DOS earlier than 6.0, the upgrade will fail to complete.

Both MS-DOS 6.22 Upgrade and MS-DOS 6.22 Step-Up require some user interaction to complete the installation. Table 6.3 shows the installation methods to upgrade to MS-DOS 6.22 and specifies whether user interaction is required. Use this table to determine the method to use when distributing the upgrade package to clients.

Upgrading to Windows for Workgroups or Windows

The processes for upgrading to Windows 3.1, Windows 3.11, and Windows for Workgroups 3.11 or higher using PDFs are similar.

Table 6.3 *PDF for Upgrading to MS-DOS 6.22 or Higher*

Installation Method	Existing Operating System	User Interaction
Step-Up Windows and Windows for Workgroups Client	MS-DOS 6.0 and Windows or Windows for Workgroups	Upgrade unattended by user.
Batch Upgrade Windows and Windows for Workgroups Client	MS-DOS 5.0 and Windows or Windows for Workgroups	Upgrade unattended by user.
Batch Upgrade/Step-Up MS-DOS Client	MS-DOS 5.0 without Windows	Upgrade unattended by user.
Manual Step-Up Windows and Windows for Workgroups Client	MS-DOS 6.0 and Windows or Windows for Workgroups	User interacts with upgrade process.
Manual Upgrade Windows and Windows for Workgroups Client	MS-DOS 5.0 and Windows or Windows for Workgroups	User interacts with upgrade process.
Manual Upgrade/Step-Up Windows and Windows for Workgroups Client	MS-DOS 5.0 without Windows	User interacts with upgrade process.

Do not confuse this file with the Upgrade.bat file in the Logon.srv directory.

Table 6.4 shows the installation methods to upgrade to Windows 3.1 and Windows for Workgroups 3.11 or higher. It specifies whether or not user interaction is required. Use this table to determine the method to use when distributing the upgrade package to clients.

Table 6.4 *PDF for Upgrading to Windows 3.1 and Windows for Workgroups 3.11 or Higher*

Installation Method	Existing Operating System	User Interaction
Automated setup for MS-DOS client	MS-DOS without Windows	Installation unattended by user.
Automated setup for Windows and Windows for Workgroups client	MS-DOS and Windows	Upgrade unattended by user.
Manual setup for MS-DOS client	MS-DOS without Windows	User interacts with installation process.
Manual setup for Windows and Windows for Workgroups client	MS-DOS and Windows	User interacts with upgrade process.

MODIFYING SETUP.SHH FOR AUTOMATED SETUP

The product disks for Windows 3.1 and Windows for Workgroups 3.11 or higher include a `Setup.shh` file that can be used to run Setup in batch mode. This is an answer file that is used during the batch mode setup to define how the operating system is to be set up. The `Setup.shh` file does not provide for a fully automated setup. If you want to distribute jobs that are likely to proceed in a fully automated manner, you must make modifications to this file after creating the package source directory. You can use a standard text editor to modify the `Setup.shh` file in the package source directory. Review the entire `Setup.shh` file and make any changes necessary to match your configuration. For example, for Windows 3.1 or Windows for Workgroups 3.11 or higher, make the following changes to the `Setup.shh` file:

```
[ENDINSTALL]
ConfigFiles=MODIFY
EndOpt=REBOOT
[OPTIONS]
```

```
;SetupApps
;AutoSetupApps
;Tutorial
```

For Windows for Workgroups, you must also add the following to the `Setup.shh` file:

```
[SYSINFO]
ShowSysInfo=NO
```

The Windows for Workgroups upgrade also sets initial values for the user name, workgroup name, and computer name. If the upgrade of Windows for Workgroups will be attended by the user, the user can provide these names when prompted. If the upgrade will be unattended, these values can be provided in one of the following ways:

- Provide these values in the Username, Workgroup, and Computername lines of the `Setup.shh` file. If you do this, you will need to create a new package for each computer that will receive Windows for Workgroups so the Username and Computername values are unique.
- If the computer already has a version of Windows or Windows for Workgroups and the Username, Workgroup, and Computername lines are blank, the values are taken from the computer's `System.ini` file.
- Default values are used if the values are not provided using the previous methods described.

Automated setup of Windows for Workgroups 3.11 using the SETUP /H:*filename* command—where *filename* is the name of the `Setup.shh` file used in the automated setup—does not work correctly when you specify a network card with the setting netcardid=*number*. To work around this, complete the following steps:

1. Run the full setup on one computer. Make sure Windows for Workgroups is installed and working correctly with the network.
2. Copy the `Protocol.ini` file to the end of the `Setup.shh` file you are using for the automated setup. An example follows:

   ```
   copy setup.shh + c:\windows\protocol.ini new setup.shh
   file
   ```

3. Open the `Setup.shh` file and change makeprotocol=no to makeprotocol=yes. This tells the Setup program to create a

`Protocol.ini` file with the settings in the `Setup.shh` file and strip out the settings in the `protocol.ini` section.

 This Setup.shh modification works only if all clients have identical network cards and configurations. If they have different network cards, you must do this for each configuration.

PACKAGE SOURCE DIRECTORY CREATION

To automatically upgrade Windows 3.1 and Windows for Workgroups 3.1 clients or higher to Windows for Workgroups 3.11, you must make a number of changes if the package source consists of expanded files (e.g., `User.exe` instead of `User.ex_`). SMS includes a PDF (`WfW311.pdf`) to upgrade these clients to Windows for Workgroups 3.11 or higher. The default command line for the automated setup for Windows and Windows for Workgroups clients is as follows:

```
winstart setup /H:setup.shh
```

To upgrade clients with either Windows 3.1 and Windows for Workgroups 3.1, you must change the actual location of the Windows for Workgroups 3.11 files and the command line specified in the PDF.

The Windows for Workgroups 3.11 files must be moved to a directory just below the location specified in the Source Directory box of the Setup Package window. For example, if the source directory is C:\WfW311, you should move the files to C:\WfW311\Files. This hides the new Windows for Workgroups files from the version of Windows running on the client computer during the upgrade. Once you move the files, you must also modify the command line to include the relative path to the files as illustrated in the following example:

```
winstart files\setup /H:setup.shh
```

Upgrading to Windows 95 or 98

Table 6.5 shows the installation methods you can use to upgrade to Windows 95 and 98 and specifies whether user interaction is required. Use this table to determine the method to use when distributing the upgrade package to clients.

Table 6.5 *PDF for Upgrading Windows 95 or 98*

Installation Method	Existing Operating System	User Interaction
Automated Windows 95 or 98 upgrade	Windows 95 or 98	Upgrade unattended by user.
Automated setup for Windows and Windows for Workgroups client	Windows 3.1 and Windows for Workgroups and higher	Upgrade unattended by user.
Automated setup for MS-DOS client	MS-DOS without Windows	Upgrade unattended by user.
Manual Windows 95 or 98 upgrade	Windows 95 or 98	User interacts with upgrade process.
Manual setup for Windows and Windows for Workgroups client	Windows 3.1 and Windows for Workgroups or higher	User interacts with upgrade process.
Manual setup for MS-DOS client	MS-DOS without Windows	User interacts with upgrade process.

Table 6.6 shows the installation methods you can use to install Service Pack 1 for Windows 95 or 98 and specifies whether user interaction is required. Use this table to determine the method to use when distributing the upgrade package to clients.

Table 6.6 *PDF for Upgrading to Windows 95 or 98, Service Pack 1*

Installation Method	Existing Operating System	User Interaction
Automated Windows 95 or 98 upgrade	Windows 95 or 98	Upgrade unattended by user.
Manual Windows 95 or 98 upgrade	Windows 95 or 98	User interacts with upgrade process.

UPGRADE PREPARATION

Check the Windows 95 or 98 Release Notes for any new information about upgrading. You should also identify the target computers that will be upgraded to Windows 95 or 98. Your SQL database should contain the current inventory of computers administered by SMS. Query the database to determine the computers that are appropriate for this upgrade and check for the following:

- Available hard disk space
- CPU
- Installed RAM
- Operating system

Ensure that all applications have been closed before starting the automated Windows 95 or 98 upgrade. If an application is open, Setup will pause until the user closes the application. Finally, ensure that the target computers have enough hard disk space or the upgrade will not be able to complete successfully.

PACKAGE SOURCE DIRECTORY CREATION

When creating the Package Source Directory, you must copy all relevant files from the Windows 95 and 98 CDs to the new source directory. To do this, first use the NetSetup program to decompress and copy the necessary files to the source directory. This gives you maximum flexibility in customizing your installed components. Use the NetSetup program if you want to create a setup directory to install shared Windows 95 or 98 configurations (where clients run Windows 95 or 98 across the network).

You could also copy the compressed files directly from the Win95 or Win98 directory on the CD to the source directory. This saves disk space, but you lose flexibility in customizing the installation options.

Copy the `Msdos.inf` file to the package source directory and modify this file to tell the Windows 95 or 98 Setup program that the listed programs are *safe* to be running during Setup. In the KnownOkTasks section, list the following files.

- PCMWin16.exe
- SMSRun16.exe
- UserTSR.exe

If needed, also add the following:

- Fastboot.exe (from Microsoft Office)
- FindFast.exe (from Microsoft Office)
- MSOffice.exe (from Microsoft Office)
- Sage (from Microsoft Plus!)

Finally, from the site server, copy the following files from the `Logon.srv \MSTest` directory to the source directory:

- `Win95.inf` (for automated installations) or `Win98.inf`
- `Win95min.inf` (for manual installations) or `Win98min.inf`
- `Dos2W95.exe` (to set up MS-DOS clients) or `Dos2W98.exe`

MODIFYING THE WIN95.INF, WIN98.INF, WIN95MIN.INF, AND WIN98MIN.INF FILES • The `Win95.inf` or `Win98.inf` and `Win95min.inf` or `Win98min.inf` files are Windows 95 or 98 setup script files that follow the `MSBatch.inf` format. The `Win95min.inf` file is used in manual installations where the user provides or verifies installation choices. The `Win95.inf` file is used for automated Windows 95 installations where installation choices are determined by the file contents. This file defaults the network client installation to support both Microsoft networks and NetWare networks. It also sets clients to validate logons to Windows NT 4.0 domains.

The automated Windows 95 or 98 Setup process attempts to determine specific client information where possible, although you might need to modify the `Win95.inf` file for your network attributes or machine group configuration. You will probably need to modify the product ID and time zone. Review the default network client configuration and logon domain settings, and add information to the file to override default installation settings. For example, you can specify a network printer in the Printers section.

The Windows 95 or 98 installation process requires the UserName, Domain/Workgroup Name, and Computer Name for the targeted client. In the `Win95.inf` template, these values have been left blank. You can provide one or more of the values in the `Win95.inf`. If any of these values are blank in the `Win95.inf`, the installation program will attempt to fill them in using values in either the client's `SMS.ini` file or the `System.ini` file. The installation program searches for the User Name in the following order:

1. UserName in the input Windows 95 or 98 script file (i.e., `Win95.inf`).
2. UserName in the `SMS.ini` file on the client.
3. UserName in the `MSBatch.inf` file in the Windows directory (Windows 95 or 98 clients will have this file from the previous installation).
4. UserName in the `SerialNo.ini` file in the Windows directory (Windows for Workgroups clients have this from the previous installation).
5. If a user name cannot be located, the Computer Name specified in the `Win95.inf` file or the MachineName field in the `SMS.ini` file is used. If the client computer is running NetWare, the installation program uses the logon name of the current user.

If any of these values cannot be found, the user is prompted to enter them during the upgrade process. Be sure to add your Windows 95 or 98 product ID to the `Win95.inf` and `Win95min.inf` files.

When you upgrade a computer to MS-DOS 6.22 or higher, the MS-DOS setup program archives the previous MS-DOS directory as \OLD_DOSx (where x is a number). If the target computer has this directory, the Windows 95 or 98 installation program will pause and ask the user if this directory should be deleted. If you want to automatically install Windows 95 or 98, make sure the target computers do not have this directory. You can use SMS to query for computers with an old MS-DOS directory and delete these directories.

Windows NT 4.0 Upgrading

Windows NT 4.0 requires 120 MB or more disk space during installation. At least 6 MB of this space must be on drive C of the computer; the rest can be on any local hard drive. This extra disk space is used to store files during the upgrade.

When upgrading a computer running Windows NT 4.0, the computer must retain the same role. For example, if the computer uses Windows NT 4.0 Workstation, it cannot be upgraded to Windows NT 4.0 Server. You must do a clean installation to change the role of a computer.

Table 6.7 shows the installation methods to upgrade to Windows NT 4.0 and specifies whether user interaction is required. Use this table to determine the method to use when distributing the upgrade package to clients.

Table 6.7 *PDF for Upgrading to Windows NT Workstation 4.0 and Windows NT Server 4.0*

Installation Method	Existing Operating System	User Interaction
Automated setup of MS-DOS client	MS-DOS without Windows	Upgrade unattended by user.
Manual setup of MS-DOS client	MS-DOS without Windows	User interacts with upgrade process.
Automated setup of Windows client	MS-DOS and Windows, Windows for Workgroups, or Windows 95 or 98	Upgrade unattended by user.
Manual setup of Windows client	MS-DOS and Windows, Windows for Workgroups, or Windows 95 or 98	User interacts with upgrade process.
Automated upgrade of (x86) Windows NT 4.0 client	Windows NT 4.0	Upgrade unattended by user.
Manual upgrade of (x86) Windows NT 4.0 client	Windows NT 4.0	User interacts with upgrade process.
Automated upgrade of (Alpha) Windows NT 4.0 client	Windows NT 4.0	Upgrade unattended by user.
Manual upgrade of (Alpha) Windows NT 4.0 client	Windows NT 4.0	User interacts with upgrade process.
Automated upgrade of (MIPS) Windows NT 4.0 client	Windows NT 4.0	Upgrade unattended by user.
Manual upgrade of (MIPS) Windows NT 4.0 client	Windows NT 4.0	User interacts with upgrade process.

Table 6.8 shows the installation methods you can use to install Service Pack 4 for Windows NT 4.0 and specifies whether user interaction is required. Use this table to determine the method to use when distributing the upgrade package to clients.

Table 6.8 *PDF for Upgrading to Windows NT 4.0, Service Pack 4*

Installation Method	Existing Operating System	UserInteraction
Automated upgrade of (x86) Windows NT 4.0 Client	Windows NT 4.0	Upgrade unattended by user.
Automated upgrade of (Alpha) Windows NT 4.0 Client	Windows NT 4.0	Upgrade unattended by user.
Automated upgrade of (MIPS) Windows NT 4.0 Client	Windows NT 4.0	Upgrade unattended by user.

Table 6.9 shows the installation methods you can use to upgrade to Windows NT 4.0 or higher and Windows NT 4.0 Workstation, and specifies whether user interaction is required. Use this table to determine the method to use when distributing the upgrade package to clients.

Table 6.9 *PDF for Upgrading to Windows NT Workstation and Server 4.0 or Higher*

Installation Method	Existing Operating System	User Interaction
Automated upgrade of (x86) Windows NT 4.0 client	Windows NT 4.0	Upgrade unattended by user.
Manual upgrade of (x86) Windows NT 4.0 client	Windows NT 4.0	User interacts with upgrade process.
Automated upgrade of (Alpha) Windows NT 4.0 client	Windows NT 4.0	Upgrade unattended by user.
Manual upgrade of (Alpha) Windows NT 4.0 client	Windows NT 4.0	User interacts with upgrade process.
Automated setup of Windows client	MS-DOS and Windows, Windows for Workgroups, or Windows 95 or 98	Upgrade unattended by user.
Manual setup of Windows client	MS-DOS and Windows, Windows for Workgroups, or Windows 95 or 98	User interacts with upgrade process.
Automated setup of MS-DOS client	MS-DOS without Windows	Upgrade unattended by user.
Manual setup of MS-DOS client	MS-DOS without Windows	User interacts with upgrade process.

UPGRADING TO WINDOWS NT WORKSTATION 4.0 OR HIGHER

When preparing to upgrade, follow these steps:

1. Check the Windows NT 4.0 Release Notes for any new information about upgrading.
2. Identify the target computers. Query the database to determine the computers that are appropriate for this upgrade. This query should check for the following:

   a. Current operating system
   b. Processor type (Intel, Alpha)
   c. Available hard disk space
   d. Installed RAM

When creating the package source directories follow these steps:

1. Create a source directory for the Windows NT 4.0 operating system files. Within this source directory, create subdirectories for each processor type (I386, Alpha).
2. Share the directory using a share name that is identical to the directory name.
3. Copy all relevant files from the I386 and Alpha directories on the Windows NT 4.0 CD to their corresponding source directories. You can ignore directories for those processors you will not support.
4. Copy the Unattend.txt file from the Windows NT 4.0 CD to the source directory as follows:

   a. If you will be targeting Windows NT 4.0 systems for upgrade, copy Unattend.txt to NTUpgrd.400.
   b. If you will be targeting MS-DOS or Windows 3.1, Windows for Workgroups, or Windows 95 or 98 clients for upgrade, copy Unattend.txt to Unattend.400.

5. Modify the Unattend.400 and NTUpgrd.400 files for installation as required by your configuration.

In the Unattend.400 file, leave the ComputerName entry in the [UserData] section blank if you want SMS to fill in this value using the one specified in the SMS.ini file.

WINDOWS NT 3.1 TO 3.5 TO 3.51 OR 4.0 UPGRADES

On TCP/IP networks, when performing an automated upgrade of a Windows NT 3.1 client to version 3.5 to 3.51 or 4.0, you must specify an upgrade script. You do this by modifying the command line for the automated upgrade in WAS35_.pdf or WNT35_.pdf. In this command line, specify the upgrade script by adding a colon and the name of the script to the /U: option at the end of the command line. The following is an example of the command line after making these changes.

```
ntencap /NTW winnt32.exe /U:ntupgrad.scr
```

The upgrade script you specify must include the !UpgradeEnableDhcp setting, with either yes or no as the value. This setting indicates whether this client will have its TCP/IP address dynamically allocated by DHCP. The NTUpgrad.scr file in the Logon.srv\MSTest directory is a sample script file you can use to upgrade 3.1 to 3.51.

SMS 1.2 and 2.0 do not support clients running Windows NT 3.1.

WINDOWS NT 3.51 UPGRADES

When you are upgrading to Windows NT 4.0 on a computer that is currently running MS-DOS, Windows, or Windows for Workgroups, first copy the Unattend.scr file from the SMS\Logon.srv\MSTest directory to the package source directory. If the target computer runs only MS-DOS but not Windows or Windows for Workgroups, you must also copy DosNTUpg.exe from the SMS\Logon.srv\MSTest directory to the package source directory.

Next, modify the Unattend.scr file to make changes as needed for unattended installation of the operating system. You do not need to specify a value for the [UserData] !ComputerName key in the script. SMS will obtain the computer name from the SMS.ini file.

You can prepare a single package source directory to be used to upgrade clients running Windows NT 4.0, MS-DOS, and Windows. In this case, just be sure both the additional files DosNTUpg.exe and Unattend.scr are copied to the package source directory.

Use the Windows NT 4.0 Server Manager to add the computer name of the upgraded computer to the domain. You can upgrade a group of computers from MS-DOS, Windows, or Windows for Workgroups with a single job. When you do so, all computers being upgraded will use a single Unattend.scr file. Unattend.scr includes data about the operating system, network card type, and card parameters. If you want the setup to be automated, each job must target only computers with identical operating systems and identical network card setup information. You can query the SMS computer database to find computers with identical configurations. Computers targeted by a single upgrade job must also join the same domain or workgroup as specified in `Unattend.scr`.

The default `Unattend.scr` file documents the settings you need to make in this file. Examine it if you want more information. It is in the Logon.srv\MSTest directory. When you upgrade computers running Windows NT 4.0 using an upgrade script, you only need to specify keys that are new or that have new values. When you upgrade from one version of Windows NT 4.0 to another, and you do not specify an existing key in the upgrade script, the Setup program will preserve the existing system value for the key. So, if you do not want to explicitly change values for existing keys (such as network card settings, video mode settings, or server role), do not specify these values in the upgrade script.

WINDOWS NT 4.0 UPGRADES

When using SMS to install Windows NT 4.0 on a client previously running MS-DOS, Windows, Windows for Workgroups, or an earlier version of Windows NT, follow the instructions for 3.51 with a few exceptions. First, use the `Unattend.txt` file from the 4.0 CD (not the `Unattend.scr` file from the SMS CD). As with 3.51, you should edit the `Unattend.txt` file to make changes as needed for unattended installation.

Second, rename the `Unattend .txt` file to `Unattend.351` for MS-DOS or Windows upgrades. If the !ComputerName key in the [UserData] section of the upgrade script is left blank, the setup program will fill it in with the MachineName from the `SMS.ini` file. The `DosNTUpg.exe` file is still needed—copy it from the Logon.srv\MSTest directory to the package source directory.

Finally, for upgrades from previous versions of Windows NT, rename the `Unattend.txt` file to `NTUpgrd.351`. In the NTUpgrd.351 script, comment out the !ComputerName key. Do not leave this key blank as you did with the `Unattend.txt` script. SMS does not fill in the !ComputerName key when you do an upgrade from a previous version of Windows NT. Nevertheless, all unattended upgrades to 4.0 require an upgrade script.

■ Summary

You should come away from this chapter with an in-depth knowledge of the MCSE exam-specific design components needed to use upgrade an SMS site to a newer version, to plan the interoperability of a mixed SMS 1.2 and 2.0 site, and to upgrade client operating systems at an SMS site.

For instance, SMS environments must have both primary and secondary sites, as well as a version of SQL Server that's being used for the SMS database. Typically, the secondary sites reporting to the primary are automatically updated to a new version of SMS when it is installed at the primary site.

▲ Chapter Review Questions

▲ True/False

1. *True or False? Because operating system upgrade jobs require the computer to be restarted when the upgrade is completed, any other mandatory SMS jobs scheduled on the client immediately after the operating system upgrade will not occur at the scheduled time. Therefore, be sure to leave adequate time between scheduling a mandatory operating system upgrade job and any other mandatory SMS jobs (such as application installations) to the same client.*

2. *True or False? When you run an operating system upgrade on a client not currently running Windows for Workgroups Clients, the client must have enough available disk space to accommodate the entire setup package, in addition to what is actually needed for the new operating system components.*

3. *True or False? When you upgrade a computer to MS-DOS 6.22 or higher, the MS-DOS setup program archives the previous MS-DOS directory as \OLD_DOSx (where x is a number). If the target computer has this directory, the Windows 95 or 98 installation program will pause and ask the user if this directory should be deleted. If you want to automatically install Windows 95 or 98, you should make sure the target computers do not have this directory. You can use SMS to query for computers with an old MS-DOS directory and delete these directories.*

4. *True or False? SMS 1.2 and SMS 2.0 do not support clients running Windows NT 3.1.*

5. *True or False? During the process of site planning, you must choose an interoperability/upgrade plan for various situations.*

6. *True or False? The various situations identified for an interoperability plan generally do not apply equally well to primary and secondary mixed SMS 1.2 and 2.0 sites or to the upgrade of an SMS 1.2 site to a 2.0 site.*

7. *True or False? To automatically upgrade Windows 3.1 and Windows for Workgroups 3.1 clients or higher to Windows for Workgroups 3.11, you will need to identify and make a number of changes if the package source consists of expanded files (for example, User.exe instead of User.ex_). SMS includes a PDF (WfW311.pdf) to upgrade these clients to Windows for Workgroups 3.11 or higher.*

▲ Multiple Choice

1. *When you use a PDF to upgrade client operating systems, you will complete the following steps except:*
   A. Add the package source directory on distribution servers.
   B. Create the package source directory on distribution servers.
   C. Import the appropriate PDF for the operating system.
   D. Select the sites that contain clients you want to upgrade.
   E. Create a advertisement to distribute the upgrade package to clients.

2. *You can install the operating system on one or more clients by distributing the package to the clients as follows except:*
   A. In SMS Administrator, open the Packages window and then open the Sites window.
   B. In the site server, run the Windows NT Server 4.0 operating system.
   C. In the Packages window, select the package you created for the operating system, and drag it onto a client or site in the Sites window.
   D. Click OK in all open dialog boxes.

3. *Before upgrading an operating system for a client with more than one operating system, the following must be done except:*
   A. The computer must be identified in the SMS security object by the operating system that you want to upgrade, and it must currently be running that operating system.
   B. The computer must be identified in the SMS inventory by the operating system that you want to upgrade, and it must currently be running that operating system.
   C. The upgrade job must be sent to that computer and specified as valid for the current operating system so it shows up in Package Command Manager at the client.

    D.   The computer must be configured to restart to the current operating system so the upgrade script can be completed.

    E.   All of the above.

4. *You should check the Windows 95 or 98 Release Notes for any new information about upgrading. You should also identify the computers that will be upgraded to Windows 95 or 98. Your SQL database should contain the current inventory of computers administered by SMS. Query the database to determine the computers that are appropriate for this upgrade. This query should check for the following except:*

    A.   Local Security Authority

    B.   Available hard disk space

    C.   CPU

    D.   Installed RAM

    E.   Operating system

5. *You should copy the Msdos.inf file to the package source directory and modify this file to tell the Windows 95 or 98 Setup program that the listed programs are safe to be running during Setup. In the KnownOkTasks section, list the following files except:*

    A.   PCMWin16.exe

    B.   SMSRun16.exe

    C.   SMSDelete.exe

    D.   UserTSR.exe

    E.   All of the above

6. *CD upgrade parameters consist of the following except:*

    A.   /CD:path

    B.   /SS:site-server

    C.   /QEP

    D.   /SDO

    E.   /CEO

▲ Open Ended

1. You can use PDFs to install operating system upgrades over your network with SMS. SMS 1.2 and 2.0 support the upgrades of which operating systems over a network?

2. Name the steps to create a package for the operating system.

Installing and Configuring SMS Server

The goal of this part is to provide information on how to install SMS and include clients in your SMS system by adding them to the database. Using and managing SMS is covered in this part as well. This part also explores the administrator's and the client's abilities to configure, modify, and navigate the SMS site.

Establishing a Primary SMS Site

When you implement SMS across your entire organization, you will likely consider creating a hierarchy of sites through the establishment of a primary site. This chapter goes through a basic SMS installation, suitable for implementing SMS across a single site.

To ensure a successful installation of SMS, you must first complete the tasks described in the chapters contained in Part 2 of this book, "Site Planning." This chapter begins Part 3, "Installing and Configuring SMS Server," by providing information on how to install SMS and include clients in your SMS system by adding them to the database. Using and managing SMS is also covered in this chapter.

During the installation process you will create a single SMS domain and a central site. You will configure the Windows NT Server 4.0 computer that will be the site server. You will also configure the local SQL Server for use by SMS, and install all the SMS files and services.

215

MCSE 7.1   SMS Preinstallation Procedures

SMS is a flexible and extensible system that can be structured to meet your systems management requirements. However, as with any large-scale enterprise management system, a considerable planning effort should precede the actual installation process. This section provides background information dealing with preinstallation procedures.

So, before you actually install the necessary programs and components that are presented in Section 7.2, take a moment to read this first part of the chapter to familiarize yourself with the terminology, components, and the basic architecture of the product.

Components

SMS is comprised of several Windows NT 4.0 services as well as a few platform-specific applications. These components communicate with each other by writing information to the database or files, thus creating a batch-oriented management system. Each service or application polls the database or a directory for specific files and records its results in the database or files destined to be picked up by another service. The operation is much like that of an assembly line in an automobile factory; as the automobile moves through the line, each station specializes in completing a task. In the case of SMS, the finished product can be a client computer inventory or a successfully installed software package. The SMS component configurations and processes stored in the SQL Server database can be viewed and monitored using SMS Administrator, the Status Message Viewer, or through other SQL Server front-end tools, such as Microsoft Access.

Architecture

The SMS architecture has been discussed at length in the first six chapters. Nevertheless, it is covered here again briefly for those readers who have skipped directly to Part 3.

As you know by now, SMS is organized into a hierarchy of sites. At the top of the hierarchy is the central site, which must be a primary site. A primary site has a SQL Server database where hardware and software inventory information for the site and all subsites beneath it in the hierarchy is stored. A secondary site does not have a database and is administered from any site above it in the hierarchy (Using the Administrator Console). A parent site is any SMS site that has one or more subsites below it. A child site is any SMS site that has a parent site.

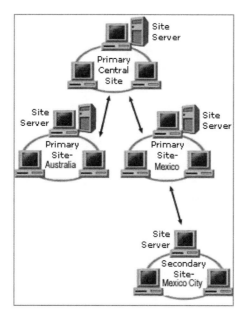

Figure 7.1 *SMS Architecture.*

Figure 7.1 illustrates a possible SMS hierarchy.[1] In this enterprise, the main Technology Information Systems department manages two other groups, one in Mexico and one in the Australia, each with its own ITS staff. By making these locations primary sites, the local staff can administer the network and allow SMS to report information to the central site. The group in Mexico City is a satellite office with no ITS staff and is implemented as a secondary site. All administration for Mexico City is done from either the main Mexico site or the central site office.

When you create a hierarchy by installing and attaching sites, you can build the ideal architecture to meet your management requirements. The example in Figure 7.1 illustrates a flexible solution in which the Mexico office can be detached easily from the central site. It would then become the central site for Mexico and manage Mexico City. Likewise, if an Acapulco office were opened, a SMS site could be installed and attached to the Mexico site or any other primary site. One of the great advantages of SMS is that this site structure is reflected in the Administrator User Interface. Using this tool, an administrator can easily select and view a computer based on location.

---

1. Copyright © 1998 Microsoft and/or its suppliers, One Microsoft Way, Redmond, Washington 98052-6399. All rights reserved.

Details of Installation

In using this book to explore SMS, you have the option of installing SMS on your network and inventorying your existing clients. In other words, you can set up one server and then add the preconfigured site data and inventory information. You'll need to install the following components first:

- Configuration of Windows NT Server 4.0 (SP4) and SQL Server
- Windows NT 4.0 Server installation
- Domain controller setup
- Service account creation
- SQL Server installation
- SMS installation on the primary site server

CONFIGURATION OF WINDOWS NT SERVER 4.0 AND SQL SERVER

Before installing SMS, SQL Server and Windows NT Server 4.0 (SP4) must be properly configured. If you have already installed Windows NT Server 4.0 (SP4) and SQL Server, read through this part of the chapter to verify that you have the correct configuration, making the appropriate changes where needed.

WINDOWS NT 4.0 SERVER INSTALLATION

If you have not yet installed Windows NT Server 4.0 (SP4) and SQL Server, do so at this time, making sure to configure the systems as described next. To prepare for the installation of SMS, you must be aware of these following Windows NT 4.0 options.

DOMAIN CONTROLLER SETUP

An SMS site server must be a computer running Windows NT Server 4.0 (SP4) that is configured as a primary domain controller (PDC), backup domain controller (BDC), or a member server (must be logged onto a domain controller). To set up a primary domain controller, follow these steps:

1. Start the Windows NT 4.0 Server Setup program, and choose the Express Setup option. SMS requires an NTFS partition. Windows NT 4.0 Setup gives you the opportunity to convert to NTFS. If you are familiar enough with Windows NT 4.0, you can convert to an NTFS partition at a later time, although it is easiest to convert during Setup.

2. When prompted to select the Windows NT 4.0 Server Security Role, choose the Domain Controller (Primary or Backup) option. For future reference, make a note of the Computer Name you choose to enter.
3. Enable Automatic DHCP Configuration (if appropriate).
4. In the Domain Settings dialog box, click Primary Domain Controller and type a Domain Name. For future reference, make a note of this name.
5. In the Administrator Account Setup dialog box, you will be prompted for a password for the Administrator user account. If you choose to enter a password, be sure to make a note of it. A password is not required.
6. Be sure to choose the correct Time Zone from the drop down list in the Date/Time dialog box. The default is Greenwich Mean Time.

SERVICE ACCOUNT CREATION

The SMS services run in the context of a Windows NT 4.0 user account. The account is typically called the SMSAdmin account and is created from the Windows NT 4.0 User Manager. After you have successfully installed Windows NT Server 4.0, choose New from the User menu and supply the appropriate information in the User Properties dialog box.

SQL SERVER INSTALLATION

If you have not already installed SQL Server, do so at this time. When installing SQL Server, there are a few things you must take into account for SMS, which are described next. When the SQL Server Setup for Windows NT 4.0 Installation Options dialog box appears as shown in Figure 7.2, select Auto

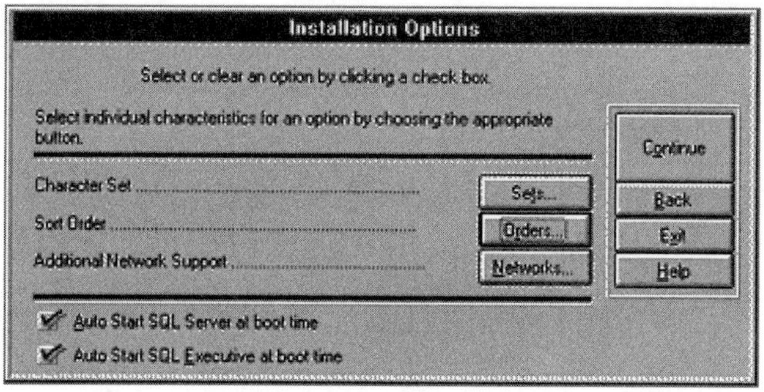

Figure 7.2 *Installations Options Dialog Box.*

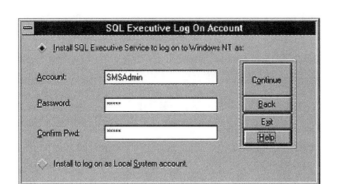

Figure 7.3   *SQL Executive Log On Account Dialog Box.*

Start SQL Server at boot time and Auto Start SQL Executive at boot time, which produces the dialog box in Figure 7.3.

If you are running SQL Server 4.21a or higher, you must upgrade to SQL Server 6.5, SQL Server 7.0, or higher. Also, if you run SQL Server and SMS on the same server, SMS gives you the opportunity to automatically create the SQL devices and databases during Setup.

Study Break

SMS Terminology

SMS has a unique set of terms to describe the roles played by computers in the system and how they are structured within the management architecture. The following are some basic terms that are important to understand.

Distribution Server

This server is used as a configured distribution point when sending packages for clients to install or run. For Run Command On Workstation packages, the package is stored on the distribution server and made available to target clients. The system administrator has to send only one copy of the software (package) to each group of computers connected to a distribution server, thus reducing network traffic. A distribution server can be a Windows NT Server 4.0, a NetWare NDS Server, or Netware Bindery Server.

Domain

An SMS site domain is a set of servers and client computers that have been grouped together. A domain is primarily used to organize servers and clients into manageable groups and provide logon validation, inventory collection, report generation, and package distribution. Within any one site there is always at least one domain. Each site, however, can have multiple domains to meet your management requirements. Valid domains are Windows NT 4.0, and NetWare.

Additional Site Server (Helper Server)

To help ease the load on the site server, you can move some of the SMS components from the site server to a logon server running Windows NT Server 4.0. When you move these components to a logon server, it becomes a site server and continues to function as a logon server.

Logon Server

A logon server supports configuration, inventory collection, package distribution for the client computers in its domain. Any supported network server can act as a logon server. For example, a Novell NetWare server can act as a logon server for its existing client computers. Within a small SMS site, the site server will likely also function as the logon server, the distribution server, and the SQL Server.

Primary Site

A site that has a Microsoft SQL Server database is called a primary site. Primary sites create and own the database for all the computers in that site and in any sites below it in the hierarchy. A primary site can be managed by a local administrator. The primary site located at the top of the hierarchy is called the central site. An unlimited number of subsites can exist below a primary site.

Secondary Site

A site without a SQL Server database is called a secondary site. Secondary sites report information to the primary site directly above it in the hierarchy. Secondary sites do not install the SMS Administrator utility. Instead, a secondary site must be created, configured, and administered through one of the primary sites above it in the hierarchy. A secondary site cannot have sites beneath it.

Site

A site is a group of computers on the network. It includes a site server and at least one domain. Sites provide structure in the inventory database by matching the organization or the physical locations of all the LANs to their own SMS site. SMS uses a three-character site code to identify each site in your SMS system.

Site Server

Each site has at least one site server. A site server is a computer running Windows NT Server 4.0 containing the SMS components needed to monitor and manage the site, its domains, and its computers. The site server also serves as a collection point for instructions and inventory information.

SQL Server

Each primary site must have a SQL Server for Windows NT 4.0 installed. SMS uses Microsoft SQL Server to store the site database. SQL Server can be installed on the site server or on a separate server. While each site must have its own database, different sites can share the same SQL Server. It is more efficient for SQL Server to be on the same LAN as the sites using its databases.

MCSE 7.2 Setting Up and Installing SMS

To install SMS on the site server, you must first log on to the computer running Windows NT Server 4.0 that you will use for the site server. The user account that you log on with must be a member of the Administrators group and the Domain Admins group.

Next, you need to insert the SMS 2.0 CD-ROM. The CD contains everything you need to install and run SMS. SMS 2.0 has version 7.0 of SQL Server on the CD-ROM and it can be installed automatically with SMS.

If you are using **SQL Server** on a remote computer, make sure that the user account you use to log on has access to the **SQL Server** and that the **SMS Service Account** you created has access to the **SQL Server**. If any of these conditions are not met, the **SMS** installation will be incomplete.

Before you start the install of SMS 2.0, you must prepare some important information. First, determine the *name and password for your SMS Service account*. SMS Setup can create this account and password for you during the setup process.

SMS uses SMSService as a default account name.

If you prefer, you can create a service account by going to Start: Programs: Administrative Tools: User Manager for Domains and then specifying that name during Setup. You can specify a local domain account by typing only the account name when prompted. You specify a trusted domain account by typing the domain and account name separated by a backslash. A trusted domain must be trusted by all domains within the site.

The second piece of information you need prior to installation is the *three-character Systems Management Server site code.* SMS uses a three-character site code to identify each site in your SMS system. Each site code needs to be unique. SMS does not prevent you from reusing a site code, but you cannot build a site hierarchy that includes two sites with identical codes.

The third piece of information to gather is the *SMS site name.* The site name is the friendly name used to label each site. You can use up to 50 characters, including spaces, except the following:

    { } < > " /

SMS Installation on the Primary Site Server

If you have not already installed SMS, do so at this time. SMS requires an NTFS partition and at least 200 MB of free disk space. If you did not choose to have Windows NT 4.0 Setup convert a partition to NTFS, convert it before beginning the SMS Setup program.

SMS Setup can be accomplished through one of two different setup scenarios: Express or Custom. The type of setup scenario your server will use is dependent on whether or not you have SQL Server 7.0 or higher installed on your computer before you begin SMS Setup. This part of the chapter takes you through the Express setup option.

Express Setup is a fast and easy way to install SMS for smaller sites (fewer than 500 clients in the hierarchy). Express Setup prompts you to install Microsoft SQL Server 6.5 or SQL Server 7.0 locally. The local installation prompts you to insert the SQL Server installation CD when it is needed. If you installed SQL Server 6.5, it installs Service Pack 5.

You can also access the SMSSETUP directory. Run SETUP.BAT. This batch file examines your system to determine which platform to install: X86 or Alpha.

Log on to the server with an account that has administrator privileges, which is an account that is a member of the Administrators group. This com-

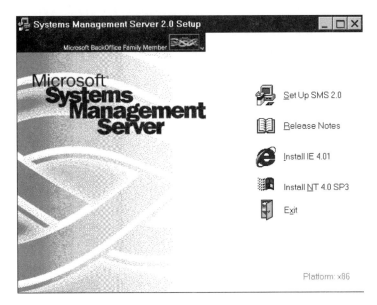

Figure 7.4 *SMS 2.0 Setup Window.*

puter can be set up as a Primary Domain Controller, a Backup Domain Controller, or a stand-alone server. If you are using a member server, make sure that you log on to the proper domain. Insert the SMS CD into the server's CD-ROM drive, and setup should start automatically. The screen in Figure 7.4 appears allowing you to set up Windows NT 4.0 Service Pack 3, or move on to SMS.

Study Break

Installing Microsoft Internet Explorer 4.01

Internet Explorer 4.01 with Service Pack 1 (SP1) is a customized version of IE 4.01 containing Snap-specific enhancements, such as bookmarks to Snap Online Channels. IE 4.01's support for key Internet standards, such as Dynamic HTML, Java, and the Channel Definition Format (CDF), means you can watch videos, listen to real-time broadcasts, and play games on the Internet through your browser. IE 4.01 works with your Windows 95 or 98 operating system to bring new functionality and Active Channels to your desktop. During Active Setup, you can choose which elements of the full install you want, including Active Desktop, Outlook Express, NetMeeting, FrontPage Express, and Microsoft Chat 2.0. SP1 adds year 2000 fixes, security and bug fixes previously released as patches and changes requested by specific corporations and Web sites for their intranet and Internet users.

You should note that IE 4.01 features Active Setup (a 433K file) that requires that you maintain your Internet connection after you double-click `ie4setup.exe`. Microsoft recommends that you uninstall any preview releases of this software before installing the latest version. Also note that the displayed version number remains as 4.0. To install Microsoft Internet Explorer 4.01, click on the *Install IE 4.01* icon as shown in Figure 7.4.

Install IE 4.01 Preview

In most cases, the Internet Explorer download page will recommend a specific browser for your computer. Simply click the Next button and run the program from its current location (Windows users) or download it to your hard drive (Macintosh and UNIX users). If you don't see a recommendation, follow the instructions below. During the setup, you can customize your installation to add components by choosing the Customize Your Installation option. Windows users can add components later by choosing Microsoft Internet Explorer from the Add/Remove Programs list in the Control Panel or by visiting the Windows Update site at http://windowsupdate.microsoft.com.

IE Install Instructions

1. On the Internet Explorer download page, click the offering you want to download.
2. When the list of platforms appears, click the one for your computer.
3. On the next pages, you see the name of the offering you want or a drop-down box.
4. If you see the name only, continue to step 4.
5. If you see a drop-down box, click the installation option you want, and then continue to step 4.
6. Click the button next to the language option you want.
7. If you choose English, click Next and continue to step 5.
8. If you choose Other, click Next. You will see a page with a list of languages. Click the language you want, and then click Next and continue to step 5.
9. On the page that appears, click the Download button next to one of the sites in the list.
10. When the dialog box appears, follow the directions below for your Windows, Macintosh, or UNIX computer.

Windows Users

For Windows users, Microsoft recommends you click *Run this program from its current location*. If you choose Save As, select the location on your hard drive where you want to save the Internet Explorer setup files. After the setup files have been saved, and while you're still connected to the Internet, run Setup by double-clicking the `ie4setup.exe` now located on your hard drive. In the first Setup dialog box, select which package of Internet Explorer Components to download.

Macintosh Users

For Macintosh users, perform the following tasks:

1. Click Download link to disk.

2. Click Desktop then click Save. After the download is complete, a .bin or .hqx file will appear on your desktop.

3. Use your decompression program to decompress and decode the file. If you have installed StuffIt Expander, you will need only to drag the file onto the Expander icon, and the file will unstuff to reveal an installer icon. If you are running Internet Explorer 4.0 or higher, the file will decompress automatically.

4. Double-click the Installer icon.

5. Read the End User License Agreement and click Accept.

6. Read the detailed instructions and click Next. If you are installing with the Active Setup Installer, choose whether to download only or to install completely, and then click Next. Choose one of the following installation options:

    • Choose a preconfigured installation option.
    • Choose Custom Install to change the configuration, and then click the boxes to the left of each component you want to install. To view a component's description, click the box containing an i to the right of the component.

7. In the Install Location area, go to the pop-up menu and choose the disk and folder where you want to install Internet Explorer. Now do one of the following:

    • If you are using the Active Setup Installer, click the Use Proxy checkbox if you use a proxy server to connect to the Internet; you must also enter the server name and port. Click Next. Select the download location closest to you and click Next to download your customized installer. Then click Next again to launch your customized installer. When the installation is complete, you are ready to run Internet Explorer.
    • If you have not using the Active Setup Installer, click Install. After installation is complete, click Restart. You are now ready to run Internet Explorer.

UNIX Users

Finally, for UNIX users, perform the following tasks:

1. In the File Download dialog box, you must choose the default Save this file to disk.

2. Use chmod +x ieXsetup (where X is the version number) to make the download executable.

3. Run the executable, as in ./ieXsetup.

4. When Setup prompts for an installation directory, either accept the default directory or type a new directory path and name. You should note that installing to the default directory /usr/local/microsoft may require that you be logged in as root.

5. After Internet Explorer is installed, you can start the browser by running installation directory/bin/iexplorer.

SETUP

To display the Setup window if you are running a previous version of Windows NT Server, change to your CD-ROM drive and double-click SETUP.EXE. You must also choose Set Up SMS 2.0. Again, the SMS Setup dialog box appears.

Choose Continue. Verification checks are performed, and the Registration dialog box appears. Type your name, your organization's name, and your product identification number. The product ID can be found on the registration card supplied with the product.

 After SMS has been installed, you can also find the product ID in the SMS Administrator Help menu by choosing About SMS Administrator.

Next, choose Set up SMS 2.0. When the Welcome SMS Setup Wizard screen appears, as shown in Figure 7.5, click Next. Setup then examines your computer to determine the current system configuration and informs you of any current SMS installations on the computer. When the System Configuration screen appears, click Next.

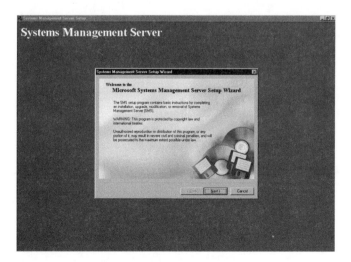

Figure 7.5 *Welcome SMS Setup Wizard Screen.*

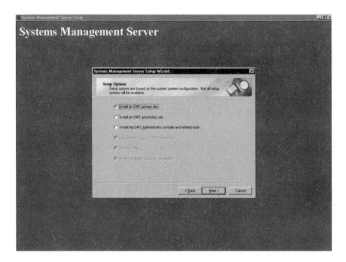

Figure 7.6 *Installation Options Dialog Box.*

INSTALLATION OPTIONS

The next step in the SMS 2.0 installation process is to choose Continue in the Registration dialog box, then choose Continue again to verify this information. The Installation Options dialog box appears as shown in Figure 7.6. Through the Installation Options dialog box, you create a primary site that will be the central site. This is the site where you will install the SMS administrative tools. When the Setup Options dialog box appears, choose Install a SMS Primary Site as shown in Figure 7.6, and then click Next.

SITE CODE

In the Site Code field in the Primary Site Configuration Information dialog box, enter a three-character code for the SMS system to identify the site. The site code for each site must be unique across your SMS system. This code is used as part of the addressing information in communication between sites. It is not case sensitive. The code cannot be changed once the site is created.

SITE NAME

Enter a name for the site in the Site Name field. This is used as the label for the site in the SMS Administrator.

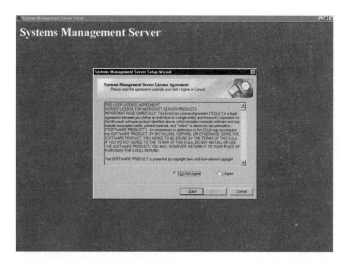

Figure 7.7 *Licensing Dialog Box.*

SITE SERVER AND SITE SERVER DOMAIN

The Site Server and Site Server Domain fields are already filled in. At this point, clear the Automatically detects all logon servers check box. Information on how to manually add computers is provided later in this chapter.

LICENSING

The Licensing window appears as shown in Figure 7.7. After reading the license and accepting its terms, select the *I agree that:* check box in the licensing dialog box, and then click OK.

An SMS Setup dialog box indicates that you should have completed some configuration tasks before installing SMS. If you have carried out the tasks described in Part 2 and you have all your site licenses in order, you should be sufficiently prepared to proceed with this installation. If you have not performed these tasks, SMS may not install correctly.

Assuming that you have performed the preceding tasks correctly, proceed with installation of by clicking OK in the Licensing window. The primary site installation will begin by the appearance of the Installation Options screen as shown in Figure 7.8.

Click Express Setup (this is not the default selection), and then click Next. Fill in the boxes in the Product Registration window, and then click Next. You must enter some alphanumeric text for the Product ID. For SMS

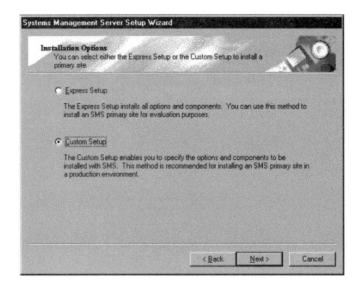

Figure 7.8 *Installation Options SMS Setup Wizard Screen.*

2.0, since there may not be a sticker with an associated CD-ROM key on the compact disk jewel case, just use any numbers.

When the SMS Site Information screen appears, enter the unique three-digit site code and the site name discussed earlier as shown in Figure 7.9. Enter correct information and Click Next. The SMS Service Account

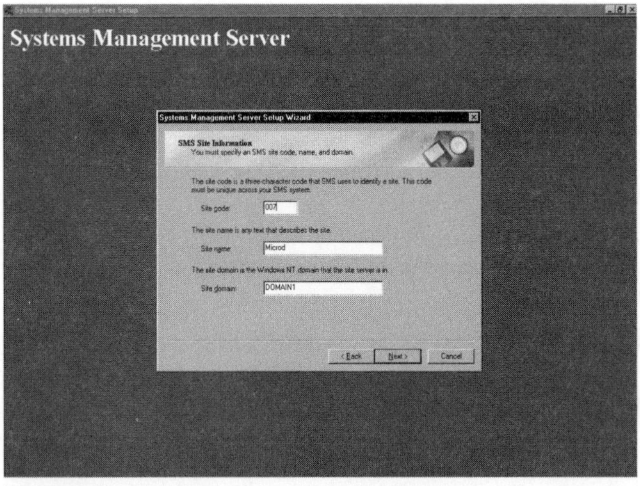

Figure 7.9 *SMS Service Site Information.*

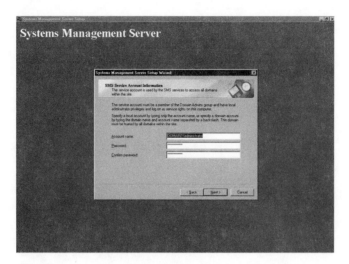

Figure 7.10   *SMS Service Account Information SMS
Setup Wizard Screen.*

Information screen appears as shown in Figure 7.10. Either keep the default
or enter your Service Account name in the first box of this screen. Press your
Tab key and enter your password. Press Tab again, reenter your password,
and then click Next.

INSTALLATION DIRECTORY

Now, let's proceed with the next part of the installation process by choosing
Next in the SMS Setup dialog box. The Installation Directory dialog box
appears.

The name of the default directory is SMS and is created at the root of
the NTFS partition with the most available space. You can specify another
directory by entering the drive letter and path of the desired location. You
must specify a path that uses the name format for its directories. This ensures
that the SMS root directory can be created properly on NetWare logon servers. SMS uses the name for the installation directory as the SMS root directory for all SMS logon servers in a site.

SETUP INSTALL OPTIONS

In the Installation Directory box, type a drive and directory, or accept the
default, and choose Continue. SMS Administrator Console Installation
Options dialog box appears as shown in Figure 7.11. This dialog box displays
a list of the default SMS components that can be installed. These compo-

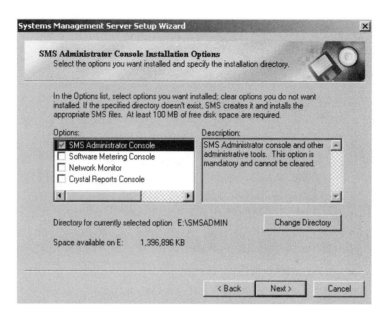

Figure 7.11 *Setup Installation Options Dialog Box.*

nents run on an x86 processor. If you install just the default components, SMS will be only able to support computers in your SMS system with x86 processors. You can also choose Continue to install the default SMS components. If you plan to use different components, select the Custom dialog box and choose the components that you plan to use.

At the SMS Primary Site Client Load screen, enter the number of client computers that will be managed from this SMS primary site, and then click Next. This information will be used to size the SQL Server database that is being created automatically.

The SQL Administrator Account screen appears. Enter a password for your SA account if you want to assign a password that is different from your SMS Service account, as shown in Figure 7.12. Click Next. The Concurrent SMS Administrator Consoles screen now appears. Enter the number of SMS Administrator consoles you expect to have at your site (usually one) and then click Next.

Finally, the Completing the SMS Setup Wizard screen appears, as shown in Figure 7.13. Review the choices you made throughout Setup. If you would like to make changes, click Back until you reach the screen that has the information you would like to change. Then, make the change and click Next until you come back to this screen.

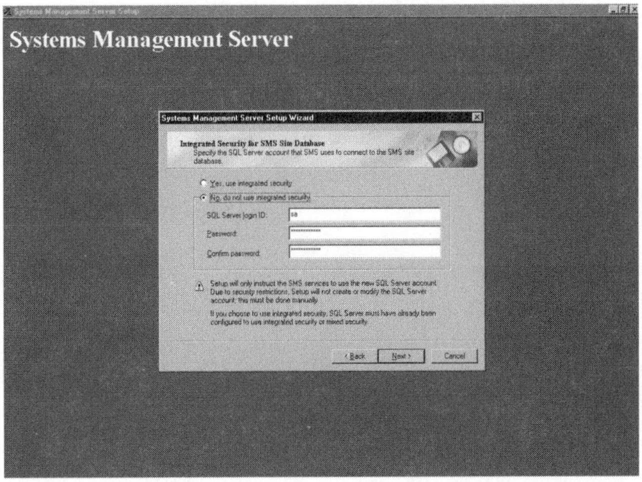

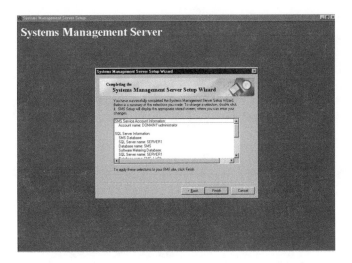

Figure 7.12 *Integrated Security for SMS Site Database Screen.*

When you are satisfied with your responses, click Finish. SMS will now be installed on your computer. Your next steps are to configure your site and your hierarchy. Before doing that, however, briefly familiarize yourself with the user interface.

Figure 7.13 *Completing the SMS Setup Wizard Screen.*

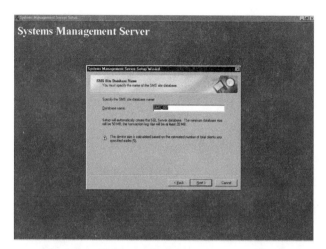

Figure 7.14 *SMS Site Database Name Dialog Box.*

SMS INSTALLATION ON THE SAME SERVER AS THE SQL SERVER

Now, if you are installing SMS on the same server as the SQL Server, the SQL Database Configuration dialog box (Figure 7.14) will display with the SQL Server configuration information. Accept the defaults.

The final SQL setting you may need to change is the number of connections. The SMS installation may prompt you to increase the number of SQL connections from the default. When you see the screen in Figure 7.15, make sure you will have enough administrative consoles and connections.

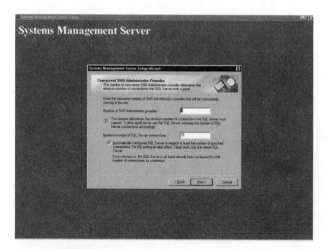

Figure 7.15 *SQL Connections Screen.*

Table 7.1 *Field Names Identification for the Primary Site Configuration Information Dialog Box*

Field Name	Description
Site Code	Any unique three character combination.
Site Name	A descriptive name.
Site Server	Leave as default.
Domain	Leave as default.
Automatically Detect All Logon Servers	Leave as default.
Username	The SMSAdmin account that you created.
Password	The SMSAdmin password that you specified when it was created.

If you choose software metering to be installed, an SQL metering database will be created automatically. Table 7.1 identifies the field names within the Primary Site Configuration Information dialog box.

The Setup program copies files, completes the database configuration, automatically installs the Network Monitor, and starts the SMS Services as shown in Figure 7.17.

Now, simply follow the directions and choose the Network Monitor agent from the Services tab as shown in Figure 7.18. Install as any other service on Windows NT and do not restart your system until Network Monitor

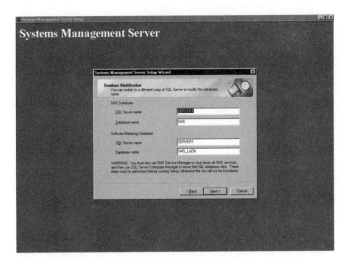

Figure 7.16 *SQL Software Metering database option.*

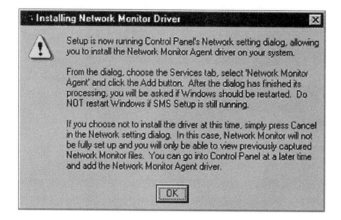

Figure 7.17 *Installing Network Monitor Driver Message Box.*

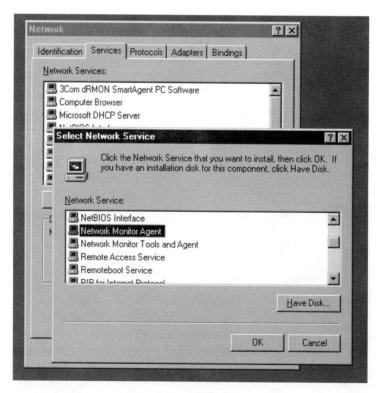

Figure 7.18 *Select Network Service Dialog Box.*

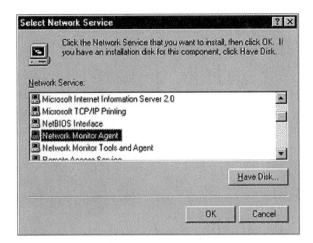

Figure 7.19 *Installing Network Monitor Drives message box.*

is completely installed as shown in Figure 7.19. Once SMS installation is completed successfully, then restart your computer.

SHUT DOWN, RESET, AND RESTART THE CURRENT PRIMARY SITE INSTALLATION

To shut down, reset, and restart the current primary site installation, a recovery plan using backup media should be considered. In many cases, SMS can be shut down, reset, and restarted to full functionality without resorting to backup tapes or the installation media. What might appear to be a catastrophic system failure may have been caused by incorrect settings in SQL Server or SMS Administrator during installation of the primary site or by problems elsewhere that caused SMS to fail.

The initial point of reference should be the Windows NT event logs and, if available, the SQL event window in SMS. The SMSTRACE utility, included on the SMS CD, will also prove useful here. These tools should provide an indication of the probable cause of the installation error of the primary site.

Access to the SMS database could be slow or denied for a number of reasons. Check the SQL event logs for warnings about the number of locks, open objects, full transaction logs, or physical memory allocation problems. You can correct the majority of these errors using SQL Enterprise Manager.

As an initial guideline, Microsoft Support recommends that the number of open objects should be set to 5000 (SQL 7.0 handles open objects allocation dynamically so there is no need to set parameters) and User

Connections to a minimum of 55 during the installation of the primary site. The amount of memory allocated to SQL Server will depend on the physical memory installed and whether or not the server is also running SMS. The administrator should certainly increase it from its default value of 8192 (2 KB) pages. If insufficient resources are allocated to SQL Server, the SMS Administrator program may fail. Typical symptoms include missing machine information or the user interface hanging during information retrieval. SQL Server 7.0 can be set to use memory dynamically, therefore it will check periodically to determine the amount of needed memory.

Occasionally you need to force a transaction to commit or abort to release a number of locks (minimum 1500 needed for normal operation) and make the SMS database resources available to other network users and applications. Furthermore, you need to put all SMS database transaction logs on a volume with some form of fault-tolerance to correct the majority of the errors previously mentioned. At this point, SMS is brought down and repaired; the SMS database is restored from a previous backup; and the SMS database is restored to the instant of failure by rolling forward committed transactions from the protected transaction logs.

If SMS cannot be recovered using something like a primary site reset, it may be necessary to restore some, if not all, of the server components from a backup. The amount of data that must be recovered depends on the type and nature of the error that occurred during current installation. There are two potential circumstances in which recovery may be required: the file system and registry keys have been corrupted, or the SMS database has failed. Database errors necessitate recovering the database device (DAT) files or the database and tables. System component failure requires the recovery of the Windows NT 4.0 registry, the file system, and the SMS database.

SMS DATABASE RECOVERY • Prior to recovering the database, it is necessary to shut down all SMS site services through the SMS Service Manager or by issuing a NET STOP command for each service in turn. You will therefore want the fastest way to restore the database, which is to recover the DAT files from the backup tape. To achieve this, stop the MSSQLServer service from the command line or by using the SQL Server Service Manager. Then recover the SMS database and log files from the backup device. The database device files are typically called `Smsdbdata.dat` and `Smsdbdata.log`. If the database spans more than one device file, restore these database device files at the same time.

After the file restore has been completed, restart SQL Server and check the SQL Server error log and Windows NT event logs to determine whether the database was successfully recovered. If there are no errors in the event

The database and transaction logs must be recreated and resized in the same manner as they were originally. This mechanism is best accomplished by using the *isql* scripts maintained during the lifetime of the SMS database. After the database structure has been recreated, restore the records using the information on the backup media.

log, check the database structure by issuing a DBCC CHECKDB statement to ensure the integrity of the data. If the database has been restored successfully, restart SMS and check the Windows NT 4.0 event logs once more.

This approach will be successful only if there have been no changes to the structure and size of the database since the backup was made. The master database records information about the database size, the extents, and the number and type of devices on which the SMS database is located. If the information in the master database does not match the physical structure of the SMS database, recovery will fail.

If the database will be recovered from backup storage rather than from the DAT file, remove the database and the device file using SQL Enterprise Manager. Then recreate the database, transaction logs, and device file on which they are stored through SQL Enterprise Manager or through the *isql* scripts maintained during the lifetime of the system.

After the database has been restored, check the SQL Server error log to verify that the database was successfully recovered. If there are no errors in the event log, check the database structure by issuing a DBCC CHECKDB statement to ensure data integrity.

The potential issue with the preceding approaches is that the master database may not accurately reflect the structure of the SMS database. This is likely if the database was recently resized and the backup does not reflect this change. In this case, both of the recovery methods will fail. It is then necessary to rebuild and recover the entire SQL Server, including the Master, MSDB, Model databases, and SMS database.

The mechanism for recovering an entire SQL Server is outside the scope of this book. Go to http://www.microsoft.com/SQL/Solpart.htm for more information.

FULL PRIMARY SITE RECOVERY • At this point, it is assumed that the site server itself has failed and there is no course of action other than to recover SMS from backup storage. Although it may be possible to recover just the system files and registry entries from the backup tape leaving the SMS database intact, this approach is not recommended.

To recover the server, build a base image of Windows NT Server 4.0 and install the backup software. Then perform a full system recovery, to include all system files, data files, and the databases necessary to bring SQL Server and the SMS database back on line. After the system has been recovered, check the event logs for error messages relating to SQL Server or SMS. Resolve these errors prior to putting the primary site server back into the production environment.

Software Installation Options

The Software Installation Options dialog box appears as shown in Figure 7.20. In the Available Software list, select the additional software components to be supported, and then choose Add. Next, click OK. The additional software components are added to the list of default components.

If you want to add components (configuring component servers) for additional processor types, such as Alpha, choose Custom from the Setup Install Options dialog box.

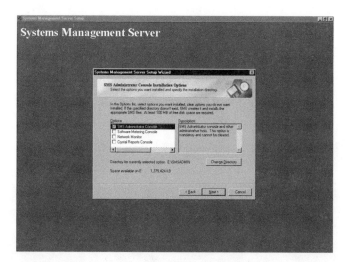

Figure 7.20 *Software Installation Options Dialog Box.*

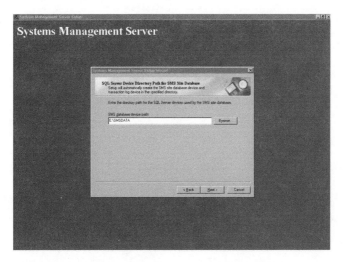

Figure 7.21 *SQL Databases Automatically Set up.*

SQL Database Configuration

SMS setup can automatically set up the SQL databases in specified directories as shown in Figure 7.21. If SQL Server is installed on a remote computer, you should have already created the databases.

Fields in the SQL Database Configuration dialog box are case sensitive.

SQL SERVER NAME

You also need to provide names for the SQL Server database and SQL Metering database if you choose to monitor licensing in SMS so that SMS can create them. If SQL Server is installed on a remote computer, you should have already created the databases.

SQL Database Configuration dialog box shown in Figure 7.22, You must fill in the correct settings. First, type in the name of the computer on which SQL Server is installed in the SQL Server Name field. If SQL Server is installed on the site server computer, this field is automatically filled in.

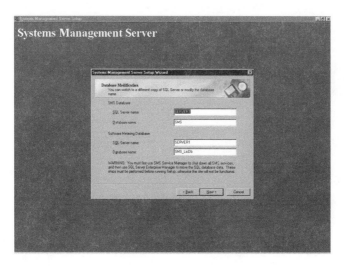

Figure 7.22   *SQL Database Configuration Dialog Box.*

SQL LOGIN

The next setting is the SQL Login. This is the SQL login ID you previously created for SMS services. In this dialog box, enter the information about the SQL Server you are using. You need to enter the SQL login ID and password you created earlier for the SMS services as shown in Figure 7.23.

PASSWORD

Type in the password. Again, this is the password you assigned to the SMS SQL login ID.

For the SQL Login and Password fields, you have the alternate option of using the SQL Server system administrator (sa) logon account and password.

CONFIRM PASSWORD

Now, confirm the Password. This is the same password you typed in the Password box.

DATABASE NAME

This field uses SMS as the default name for the database. Use this, or type another name. If you are using an existing database on a remote computer,

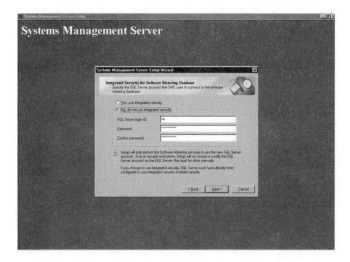

Figure 7.23   *SQL login ID and password.*

specify the name of that remote database. SMS will overwrite this database so make sure that it does not contain any data you want to keep.

DATABASE DEVICE

You also need to type in the database device. This the name (for instance, SMSData) for the SQL Server data device used to store SMS data. If you are using an SQL Server on a remote computer, type the name you have already assigned.

LOG DEVICE

This is the name (for example, SMSLog) for the SQL Server log device used for SMS transaction logs. If you are using an SQL Server on a remote computer, type the name you have already assigned. If the SQL Server is installed on the site server, you now need to create the data and log device.

SQL Device Creation

If SQL Server is installed on the site server, SMS can automatically create databases and its devices. The SQL Device Creation dialog box appears as shown in Figure 7.24. The names you just assigned to the database and log device are automatically created using information in Figure 7.22.

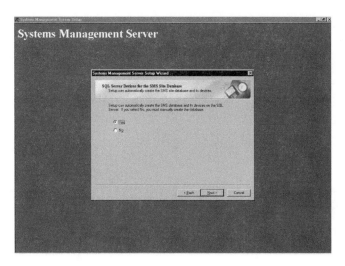

Figure 7.24 *SQL Device Creation Dialog Box.*

Primary Site Configuration Information

The Primary Site Configuration Information. You now need to enter identification information for the primary site (central site) you are creating.

USERNAME

Under Service Account as shown in Figure 7.25, type in the Username. This is the name of the Windows NT 4.0 account you created for SMS services (in this example, SMSService).

PASSWORD AND CONFIRM PASSWORD

In the Password field, type in the password for the SMS Service Account, and confirm it by retyping the same password in the Confirm Password field. Finally, click the Continue button.

SQL Connections

If SQL Server is installed on the site server, the SQL Connections dialog box appears. SMS needs a minimum of 55 connections for each site using SQL Server.

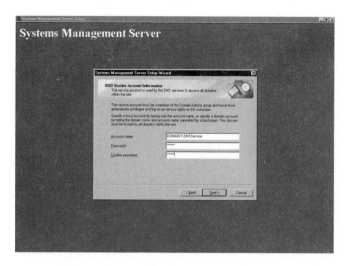

Figure 7.25 *SMS Service Account.*

If possible, allocate enough connections so that at least 20 are free at any given time.

For the purposes of this single site installation, type 55 in the Set Maximum User Connections To field, and choose Set. The SMS installation process installs the SMS files and sets up the database.

If you installed the SMS Network Monitor component, you are now prompted to install a device driver as shown in Figure 7.26. When you click OK in the Installing Network Monitor Driver window, the Windows NT 4.0 Server Network dialog box appears completed, as shown in Figure 7.27.

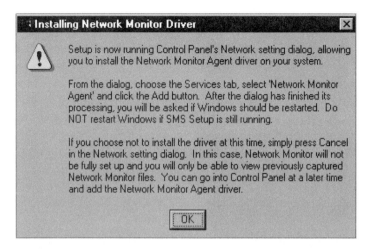

Figure 7.26 *Network Monitor Prompt.*

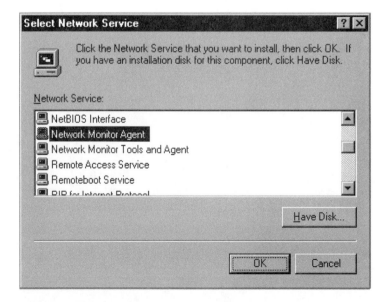

Figure 7.27 *Network Monitor Installation.*

Select Network Service

In the Network dialog box, choose the Services tab. Now choose Add. The Select Network Service dialog box appears as shown in Figure 7.27. In the Network Services list, select Network Monitor Agent, and choose OK. Choose OK to close the Network dialog box.

Now, wait for the driver processing to complete. A Windows NT Server 4.0 message is displayed asking you if you wish to restart Windows. *Do not restart Windows at this point.* If you do restart Windows, the SMS installation process will not complete. Choose No at this point.

When the Installing Network Monitor Driver message box shown in Figure 7.27 reappears, choose OK. A final completion message is displayed. You have now installed SMS.

SMS Services Verification

To verify that the SMS services are installed and running, click the Start menu, select Settings and then Control Panel. Now, double-click the Services icon. The Services dialog box is displayed. Ensure that the following list of services are shown and have been started:

- SMS_CLIENT SERVICE
- SMS_EXECUTIVE
- SMS_LICENSE_SERVER (SOFTWARE METERING)
- SMS_SQL_MONITOR
- SMS_SITE_BACKUP
- SMS_COMPONENT_MANAGER

If the installation does not complete successfully, or if any of the services did not start, use the Windows NT 4.0 Event Viewer to view SMS events in the application log. You can also use the SETUP.LOG file to trace the actions and errors logged by the SMS installation program.

Now, that you've installed SMS, let's take a detailed look at how to add clients to SMS.

Adding Clients

You now need to add clients to the database so that they can be managed. Clients can be added automatically and manually.

A convenient way to add clients to the database—especially in a large distributed environment—is to enable the Automatically network discovery of clients. When enabled, SMS detects a client as a user logs on, installs SMS software on the client, and automatically gathers an inventory of hardware and software information. Each time thereafter that a user at the client logs on, the Inventory Agent runs automatically via the logon script.

Manually adding clients to the database involves connecting the client to the SMS_SHR share of an SMS logon server and running RUNSMS.BAT. SMS downloads the appropriate client software to the client, inventories that client, and adds it to the SMS system.

Whether you add a client manually, or automatically via logon scripts, SMS downloads all the client software options by default, such as Remote Troubleshooting and SMS properties, in client's Control Panel.

The next section describes how to manually add clients to the database.

Manually Adding Clients

The SMS client software is installed into an MS\SMS directory. The way the user at the client accesses the SMS software depends on the desktop shell installed on the client. For example, for Windows 95 or 98 clients, the SMS software is accessed through the Start menu under Programs: SMS Client. The SMS client options allow the user to install software applications, run applications from a server, activate help desk options (such as remote control), and customize inventory information.

If you want to automate the above procedure for clients running MS-DOS or Windows 3.1 or higher, add the following lines to AUTOEXEC.BAT:

```
NET USE Z:\\servername\SMS_SHR

Z:

CALL RUNSMS

C:

NET USE Z: /DELETE
```

Here, z is the drive letter that you use to connect to the SMS logon server, and servername is the name of an SMS logon server in the SMS domain where you want to add the client.

ADDING NETWARE CLIENTS

To manually add NetWare clients to SMS, perform the following procedure:

1. Ensure that you have included the necessary support for NetWare.
2. At the client, map a drive to a NetWare server volume where SMS has installed the SMS logon server components (configured the component

server). The NetWare server must be an SMS logon server in an SMS NetWare domain.

3. Change to the `sms_dir\LOGON.SRV` directory, where `sms_dir` is the name of the SMS root directory.
4. Choose `RUNSMS.BAT`.
5. From the File menu, choose Run and then OK.

If you want to automate this procedure for clients running MS-DOS or Windows 3.1 or higher, add the following lines to AUTOEXEC.BAT:

```
MAP R: logonserver\volume

R:

CD \sms_dir\LOGON.SRV

RUNSMS.BAT
```

Here, `R` is the drive letter, `logonserver` is the server name of the SMS logon server, `volume` is the name of the volume where the SMS root directory is installed, and `sms_dir` is the SMS root directory.

Demo Database Installation

For a quick and easy way to see the full power of SMS, load the preconfigured data found on the CD-ROM that comes with this book. The demo database can be created using SQL Server 7.0 or higher, or SQL Server 6.5 running Service Pack 4 or higher. The demonstration data is stored in a separate SQL database so that it does not override any of your previous SMS operations. It also allows you to look at both preconfigured data and your real network by logging out and logging back into SMS with a different database name.

Here's how you can set it up: First, copy the files `SMSDMP.DAT` and `SMS.SQL` from the CD-ROM or from http://www.microsoft.com/SMS MGMT/demodata.htm to the directory C:\mssql\backup. If SQL is not installed on drive *C*, you need to change this accordingly and also alter the script as explained in the next section of this chapter, "Installation Modification." Now, you need to start SQL Enterprise Manager from the task list, and choose the SQL Query Tool from the Tools menu as shown in Figure 7.28.

Login to SQL using the *sa* account if you are prompted to do so, although this is usually unnecessary. With the Query window open, from the File menu choose Open as shown in Figure 7.29. Select the script file, `\mssql\backup\sms.sql`.

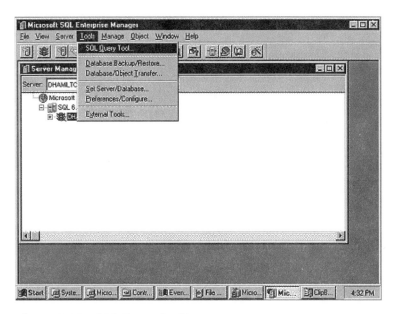

Figure 7.28 *SQL Enterprise Manager.*

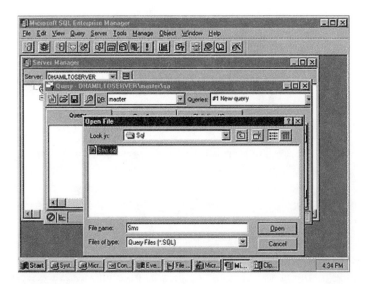

Figure 7.29 *Query Tool.*

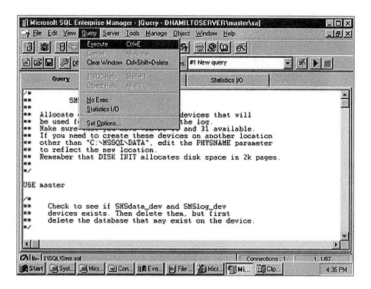

Figure 7.30 *Query Window.*

Now, from the Query menu, choose Execute to run the script as shown in Figure 7.30. It takes about five minutes to complete and updates its progress. When the script results state '100 percent loaded' in the query window, the process is complete (you may need to scroll down the window to see this message). Once it is complete, close the SQL Enterprise Manager.

INSTALLATION MODIFICATION

If you have installed SQL Server on a drive different than the C drive, or you are using SQL Server 6.5 Service Pack 4 or higher, you need to modify the SMS.SQL script file. Let's see how all of this is done.

EDITING THE SQL DRIVE LETTER • If you need to edit the script, use the SQL Query Tool to make your edits, as follows:

1. Open the `SMS.SQL` script file.
2. Find the DISK INIT statements. There are two of them.
3. Change the PHYSNAME to match your drive letter and SQL directory structure. Do not change the `.DAT` file name. For instance, change:

```
PHYSNAME =  'C:\MSSQL\DATA\SMSDATA.DAT',
```

   to

```
PHYSNAME =  '<your SQL location>\DATA\SMSDATA.DAT',
```

4. If necessary, find the last line in the script—the LOAD DATABASE statement—and change the path of the `SMSDMP.DAT` file.

SQL SERVER 6.5 HIGHER USE • If you are using SQL Server 6.5 higher, you can load the SMSDemo database, but you will need to make some changes to the `SMS.SQL` script and follow a different set of directions, as follows:

1. Copy the files SMSDMP.DAT and SMS.SQL from a CD-ROM or from http://www.microsoft.com/SMSMGMT/demodata.htm into the directory c:\sql65.
2. Start the SQL Query tool, ISQL/w.
3. Log in to SQL Server using the sa account if you are prompted to do so, although this is usually unnecessary.
4. Open the `c:\sql65\sms.sql` script file.
5. Find the DISK INIT statements. There are two of them.
6. Change the PHYSNAME path to match your SQL Server directory structure. By default it is "C:\SQL65\DATA\...".
7. Find the LOAD DATABASE statement. It is the last line in the script.
8. Change the path to match your directory structure. By default it should be C:\SQL65\SMSDMP.DAT.
9. From the Query menu, choose Execute to run the script.
10. It takes about six minutes to complete and updates you on progress as it goes. When the script results state '100 percent loaded' in the query results window, the process is complete. You may need to scroll down the window to see this message. Once it is complete, close ISQL/w.

MCSE 7.3   Using and Managing SMS

SMS installation has been combined with SQL Server installation to dramatically improve the setup required for SMS, making it the easiest to install enterprise-class solution. Without removing any of the flexibility of choosing where to install SQL Server, the setup options intelligently install and configure SQL Server in preparation for SMS. While SMS 2.0 specifically ships with an integrated SQL Server 7.0 setup, it also works with SQL Server 7.0 or higher. Furthermore, SMS can now be hosted on any Windows NT 4.0-based

Member Server, removing the previous Primary Domain Controller/Backup Domain Controller (PDC/BDC) requirement.

Microsoft Management Console Administrative User Interface

The administrator user interface has been redesigned to be task-oriented and intuitive. SMS now stores and presents information to indicate the progress of distributions, the number of managed clients, the success of installations, and other critical data used to manage itself. SMS 2.0 is integrated as a *snap-in* to the Microsoft Management Console (MMC). In fact, SMS is designed as a large series of integrated snap-ins which means that the administrator has the option of taking only part of the display offered by the console. For instance, a particular administrator may be responsible for software distribution. Rather than providing them with the whole console including remote control, only the snap-ins associated with software distribution are chosen. These snap-ins are then put into their own console window and sent to this administrator who has exactly the tool set needed to do the specific task at hand. Through this mechanism, different sets of administrators can be assigned different subsets of SMS easily and securely.

CONFIGURING THE SMS ADMINISTRATOR CONSOLE

The SMS Administrator console tree is an ordered hierarchical listing of related items and functionality. Each top-level node in the administrator display (directly beneath the Site Database node) represents a different SMS administrative function. Objects are grouped in a logical manner.

You begin to use the SMS Administrator by navigating and configuring the SMS Administrator console tree. You navigate by moving from item to item, expanding and collapsing branches as needed to expose the items whose functional scope meets your administrative objectives.

ADMINISTRATIVE TOP-LEVEL TASKS • The user interface is the administrator's primary tool for driving SMS operations. It is through this interface that software can be distributed, inventories collected, and problems diagnosed. The options in the following "Nodes" Sidebar are available from the top-level node in the administrator display.

Nodes

Systems Management Server

This is the root-level node in the Microsoft Management Console. From this point you can connect to a new database if you have more than one SMS database that is being managed. If you have HealthMon installed, it will also be at the root level.

Site Database (<name>)

This node is always directly below the SMS node. In a smaller system, there is only one site database node and management operations are accessed from below it. In larger networks, an administrator may have more than one site database to manage. At this level you perform database-wide operations, such as software metering, network monitoring, and service manager functions.

Site Hierarchy

This node allows the administrator to see and manage all the sites in SMS hierarchy. From here the administrator can perform such tasks as removing a site from the site hierarchy. This is a key area of functionality.

Collections

This node allows the creation and modification of collections. A collection is an arbitrary grouping of resources, such as machines, groups and users, used to target software distribution and other tasks. The collection node can also be used to drive operations on resources in that collection, such as generating inventory information on a resource or diagnosing resource problems.

Packages

This node allows the creation and modification of packages and also programs that are subcomponents of packages. A package defines the software to be distributed to a particular collection, including the location of the source files and the servers that will be the intermediary configured distribution points. A package is made up of one or more programs that define the command line that the package uses to install the software on the target system.

Advertisements

Use the advertisement node to create or modify advertisements, which are simply the processes that tie collections, packages, and programs together, assigning them to a particular schedule.

Y2K Products

This node contains a list of the software applications that are to be monitored for Year 2000 compliance and their compliance levels. This information can be updated or changed by loading a new Year 2000 or Euro-compliance database.

Queries

This node provides access to precanned queries as well as allowing the creation of new queries. A query is a question asked of the inventory and is often used to create a collection. A typical query would check to find which machines can be upgraded to a new version of an operating system based on an inventory of their memory and disk space.

System Status

This node provides detailed information on the status of SMS itself, including the status of system processes and software distribution advertisements. SMS 2.0 contains a sophisticated status engine to provide detailed information. This functionality is discussed in more detail later in this part of the chapter.

Reports

From this node in the interface, administrators can generate reports on any collected data.

Security Rights

As previously mentioned in Chapter 5, this node allows the assignment of granular security rights. These can be specified on a per user, per target, and per operation basis. They are discussed later in this part of the chapter.

When using the SMS Administrator, follow this general usage pattern:

1. Determine the task you wish to perform.
2. Find the console tree item that deals with the task. Use the online Help to assist you in identifying common SMS management tasks.
3. Expand the SMS Administrator console tree to expose additional items until you find the item you need to use.
4. Alter the item configuration by changing its properties.

Some management tasks with broad functional scope, such as site configuration, require viewing and configuring several different items in the SMS Administrator console tree. Also, some tasks are launched directly from the Site Database node, rather than one of the top-level nodes. Particular tasks driven from this node are software metering and network monitoring. Figure 7.31 shows these top-level options in the administrator. In addition to

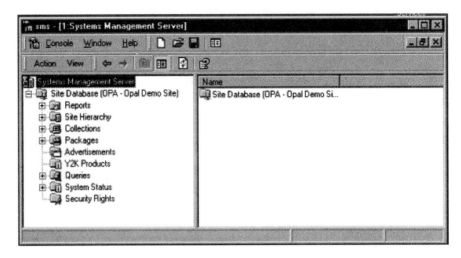

Figure 7.31 *SMS Administrator Console.*

driving operations from the top-level nodes in the user interface, SMS provides administrators with Wizards to execute common procedures.

WIZARDS FOR ADMINISTRATIVE USER INTERFACE

SMS 2.0 ships with a collection of 11 Wizards that are designed to walk administrators through the common tasks associated with managing a Windows environment. The available Wizards are:

- *Create a Direct Membership Rule Wizard*—Helps in the creation of collections

- *Create a Package from a Definition Wizard*—Allows the building of software packages to be distributed

- *Delete Package/Program/Collection Wizards*—Three distinct Wizards that not only delete critical software distribution processes but also explain the ramifications that deleting them will have on specific users before completing the operation

- *Manage or Configure a Distribution Points Wizard*—Allows for defining staging points for software distribution

- *Secondary Site Create/Upgrade/Delete Wizards*—Three distinct Wizards that allow the quick and easy building or modification of a SMS hierarchy

- *SMS Database Connection Wizard*—Allows a quick connection to a different SMS hierarchy in a large environment
- *Software Distribution Wizard*—Steps through all required functions to define a package, create a program, target a collection through an advertisement, and distribute software to users or machines

Client Nonintrusive Interface

The user experience is highly configurable in SMS 2.0. The administrator can choose exactly what the user sees, if anything. Typically the user might see:

- When advertised programs are made available
- When advertised programs are running or are counting down to run
- When a remote control operation is requested or is in progress

This experience has been integrated with other components of the operating system, such as Control Window and the status tray, so that working with SMS is effortless for the end user.

Systems Management Support

Key requirements from systems administrators are tools to develop exactly the systems management support they need. To address this issue, SMS 2.0 has added extensive configuration information. The default is always sensible, but for the more sophisticated administrator, the ability to fine-tune every component of the system is critical. This part of the chapter looks at the configurable nature of the system, concentrating on Site Settings, Security, Site Status, and Network Trace.

SITE SETTINGS

Site settings are the configurable settings that can be applied to a site in the SMS hierarchy. Each site can have different configuration settings. For example, remote sites may add and configure different senders, which consist of Standard, Courier, and RAS, or particular sites may have different functionality enabled for clients. Each site's configuration settings are accessed from the particular site node under the Site Hierarchy node in the administrator. These settings are designed to allow the administrator to create exactly the configuration required to meet the needs of their particular company's systems management environment. The settings described next can be configured at the site level.

ADDRESSES • Addresses can be configured through this node. They are used to enable sites to communicate via senders.

CLIENT AGENTS • Once the agent is installed, there are many operations that it can perform. Not all clients must perform the same operations—an administrator may want to provide software distribution but not remote diagnostics, for example. The configuration settings for these options are available under this node.

CLIENT INSTALLATION METHODS • Once SMS has discovered a resource, it needs to install the client to drive management operations. This node provides administrators with the ability to configure this to happen in one of many different ways.

COMPONENT SERVER CONFIGURATION • Some operations, such as metering and software distribution, have component-level server configuration settings in addition to client configurations. The component-level server configurations are set at this node.

CONNECTION ACCOUNTS • Server and client accounts used by SMS can be created and modified through this node.

DATABASE MAINTENANCE • SMS 2.0 greatly extends the database configuration available so that operations need not be performed directly on SQL Server Enterprise Manager. How this is executed is defined at this node.

DISCOVERY METHODS • This node allows the administrator to define how SMS discovers resources such as users and machines. For example, resources could be discovered by user logons or by listening for network activity.

ADD AND CONFIGURE SENDERS • This node provides access to sender creation and configuration changes, such as addition. Senders are mechanisms for communicating between sites. In a WAN environment RAS or Courier Senders may be needed in addition to the Standard LAN and WAN senders.

SITE SYSTEMS • This node allows the creation and configuration of site systems. A site system is a server, share, or NetWare volume that provides SMS functionality to the site. Under this node, administrators can indicate which functions are going to be performed by which site systems, therefore allowing the flexibly to distribute the management overhead through a computing environment. For example, one computer could handle the SQL Server processing, another drive the software metering facilities, and a third the sender functions. This node also allows analysis of an existing site system. For example, this could be running a network trace to understand how this system is related to another system in the site.

STATUS FILTER RULES • This node provides access to configuration information about the way status messages are filtered and forwarded to other sites in the hierarchy.

STATUS SUMMARIZER • This node provides access to configuration information about the way that status information is to be summarized and stored. Status is discussed in later in this chapter.

SECURITY

Security can be configured from the top-level Security Rights node. Permissions can be assigned to a particular instance and object type. Object types include collections, packages, advertisements, sites, and queries. Instances are examples of an object type, such as the advertisement "upgrade Purchasing machines to Windows 98." Permissions can be assigned to any individual and include verbs such as read, modify, delete, distribute, and administer. Through building a sophisticated series of security rights, an administrator can assign a particular person the rights to do only one type of operation to just one instance of one object type, which provides a very granular solution.

STATUS OF SITE

SMS 2.0 includes functionality to generate real-time status information and status reports on many aspects of the operation of the product. The SMS status system reports information about the health of the SMS system. As a component performs operations, it periodically generates messages about its performance. These messages are transmitted to the Status Manager, which decides where they should go based on a set of configurable rules. The messages can be written to the SMS database, they can be replicated to the parent site, or they can be written to the Windows NT 4.0 Event Log on the site server. The Status Manager includes two major components—status summarizers and status filters as discussed in the following sidebar, "Status Manager's Major Components."

Study Break

Status Manager's Major Components

Status Summarizers

Status summarizers are components responsible for collating certain groups of status messages into a meaningful summary. For example, statistics on the number of error and warning messages can be collated by the status summarizers to create a summary you can view through the Status item in the SMS Administrator console tree.

Status Filters

Status filters are used to route status messages through the status system based on filter rules. Each status summarizer registers a non-configurable status filter with the Status Manager. This filter limits the status messages the summarizer receives. Status Manager itself has a single configurable status filter. The filter determines which status messages are written to the SMS database, replicated to the parent site, or written to the Windows NT 4.0 Event Log on the site server.

Status information can be accessed from the System Status top-level node. Information generally is divided into site status, package status, and advertisement status. Site status provides real-time information on the actual SMS processes that are running in a particular site. It monitors the various threads that should be active and gives warning and critical error messages when unexpected events occur. This is an excellent source for troubleshooting information and for preemptive data used before embarking on major management task.

Package status provides details on the success or failure of software packages rolled out to resources. Advertisement status adds the program status information and scheduling details to the package status information.

NETWORK TRACE AND DISCOVERY

To aid in fully understanding the status of the SMS environment, new tools have been added that discover network information and display it to the administrator. This adds a network-aware component to typical tasks such as configuring software distribution points or managing SMS sites.

Network Discovery calculates Internet Protocol (IP) subnets between a SMS site server and a selected site system, allowing a view of the interconnectivity between SMS resources in a site. Network Trace can show all subnets, servers, routers, and other network devices along all the paths between the specified systems. It can also show the system roles of the servers and the status of the SMS components on the servers. Network Trace can be used to determine which servers are not reachable and to help diagnose server and network problems in the site.

Network Trace uses the server and network discovery information contained in the SMS Discovery Database to trace the SMS network, as shown in Figure 7.32. After server discovery is completed, Network Trace can map site systems within a site. After network discovery is completed, Network Trace

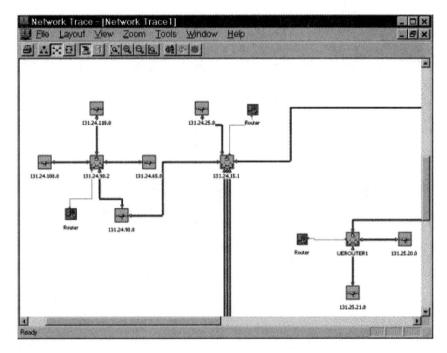

Figure 7.32   *Network Trace.*

can map routers and links between site systems. Network Trace can be accessed by selecting a site system under Site Settings or Site Status.

■ Summary

You should come away from this chapter with an in-depth knowledge of the MCSE exam-specific SMS installation and configuration components needed to establish the Primary SMS site. You can meet your systems management requirements by structuring SMS, although a considerable planning effort should precede the installation process, as with any large-scale enterprise management system. Thus, this chapter has gone into specific detail about the installation procedures.

The second part of the chapter discusses how to install SMS on the site server. Finally, the chapter discusses how SMS installation has been combined with SQL Server installation to dramatically ease the setup required for SMS. The setup options intelligently install and configure SQL Server in preparation for SMS without removing any of the flexibility of choosing where to install SQL Server. SMS 2.0 will also work with SQL Server 7.0 or higher. Furthermore, by removing the previous Primary Domain Controller/ Backup Domain Controller (PDC/BDC) requirement, SMS can now be hosted on any Windows NT 4.0-based Member Server.

▲ CHAPTER REVIEW QUESTIONS

▲ True/False

1. *True or False? If you have an existing SMS database in SQL Server 4.21a or higher they must be updated to SQL Server 6.5 before SMS 2.0 can be used.*

2. *True or False? If you run SQL Server and SMS on a different server, SMS gives you the opportunity to automatically create the SQL devices and databases during Setup.*

3. *True or False? If you are using SQL Server on a remote computer, make sure that the user account you use to log on with has access to the SQL Server and that the SMS Service Account you created has access to the SQL Server. If any of these conditions are not met, the SMS installation will still complete.*

4. *True or False? Once SMS has been installed, you cannot use the SMS Setup program to install additional SMS components.*

5. *True or False? If you plan to use different components, select the Custom Setup or Express Setup dialog boxes, then choose the components that you plan to use.*

6. *True or False? You should shut down, reset, and restart the current installation. After you have shut down and reset the current installation, during the wait for the driver processing to complete, a Windows NT 4.0 Server message is displayed asking you if you wish to restart Windows. Restart Windows at this point. If you do restart Windows, the SMS installation process will complete. Choose Yes at this point.*

7. *True or False? You should modify the SMS service account to a different user name or password. Under Service Account, you must type in the Username. This is the name of the Windows NT 4.0 account that you created for use by the SMS services.*

8. *True or False? When you type in the password for the SMS Service Account; you confirm it by typing in a different password than you typed in the Pass-*

word box. Next, choose Continue in the Primary Site Configuration Information dialog box.

9. *True or False? When you have completed the installation of SMS and are familiar with the functionality of the system, you will not be ready to install the demo data provided on the CD-ROM.*

10. *True or False? The inventory data and SMS component configurations stored in the SQL Server database can be viewed using SMS Administrator or through other SQL Server front-end tools, such as Microsoft Access.*

11. *True or False? The site systems node does not allow the creation and configuration of site systems. A site system is a server, share, or NetWare volume that provides SMS functionality to the site. Under this node, administrators can indicate which functions are going to be performed by which site systems, therefore allowing the flexibly to distribute the management overhead through a computing environment. For example, one computer could handle the SQL Server processing, another drive the software metering facilities, and a third the sender functions. This node also allows analysis of an existing site system. For example, this could be running a network trace to understand how this system is related to another system in the site.*

12. *True or False? Status summarizers (like the SMS Status Message Viewer) are components responsible for collating certain groups of status messages into a meaningful summary. For example, statistics on the number of error and warning messages generated can be collated by the status summarizers to create a summary you can view through the Status item in the SMS Administrator console tree.*

13. *True or False? The senders node does not provide access to sender creation and configuration. Senders are mechanisms for communicating between sites. In a WAN environment, RAS or Courier Senders may be needed in addition to the standard LAN and WAN senders.*

14. *True or False? A parent site is any SMS site that has one or more subsites below it. A child site is any SMS site that has a parent site.*

15. *True or False? A delete Wizard allows the quick and easy removal of a site from the SMS site hierarchy. SMS 2.0 ships with a collection of 15 Wizards that are designed to walk administrators through the common tasks associated with managing a Windows environment.*

16. *True or False? The SMS Log device is the name for the SQL Server log device that configures and uses SMS transaction logs to monitor SMS process activ-*

ity. If you are using an SQL Server on a remote computer, type the name you have already assigned. If the SQL Server is installed on the site server, you now need to create the data device and log device.

17. *True or False? If the installation does not complete successfully, or if any of the services did not start, use the Windows NT 4.0 Event Viewer to view SMS events logged to the application log and SMS error messages. You can also use the SETUP.LOG file to trace the actions and errors logged by the SMS installation program.*

18. *True or False? The inventory data SMS component configurations and processes stored in the SQL Server database can be viewed and monitored using SMS Administrator, the Status Message Viewer, or through other SQL Server front-end tools, such as Microsoft Excel.*

19. *True or False? Network Trace uses the server and network discovery information contained in the SMS Discovery Database to trace the SMS network. After server discovery is completed, Network Trace can map site systems within a site. After network discovery is completed, Network Trace can map routers and links between site systems. Network Trace can be accessed by selecting a site system under Site Settings or Site Status.*

20. *True or False? You can add components to your IE 4.01 installation during Setup by choosing the Customize Your Installation option. Windows users can also add components later by choosing Microsoft Internet Explorer 4.01 from the Add/Remove Programs list in the Control Panel or by visiting the Windows Update site at http://windowsupdate.microsoft.com.*

▲ Multiple Choice

1. *The user experience is highly configurable in SMS 2.0. The administrator can choose exactly what the user sees, if anything. Typically the user might see the following except:*

    A. When SMS 2.0 supports only SQL Server 6.0

    B. When advertised programs are made available

    C. When advertised programs are running or are counting down to run

    D. When a remote control operation is requested or its progress is being monitored

    E. All of the above

2. *A Wizard to help in the creation of collections is called a*
   A. Definition Wizard
   B. Manage Distribution Points Wizard
   C. SMS Database Connection Wizard
   D. Direct Membership Rule Wizard
   E. Software Distribution Wizard

3. *A process that allows the building of software packages to be distributed is called a*
   A. Manage Distribution Points Wizard
   B. SMS Database Connection Wizard
   C. Direct Membership Rule Wizard
   D. Definition Wizard
   E. Software Distribution Wizard

▲ Open Ended

1. In using this book to explore SMS, you have the option of installing SMS on your network and inventorying your existing clients, or you can set up one server and then add the preconfigured site data and inventory information. Whichever option you choose, name the components you'll need to install first.

Configuring, Modifying, and Navigating an SMS Site

This chapter explores the administrator's and the client's abilities to configure, modify, and navigate the SMS site. With that in mind, you can configure and modify your SMS site manually by connecting the client to an SMS logon server and running `RUNSMS.BAT`, or you can automate this procedure by configuring a user's logon script.

SMS automatically modifies the logon scripts for users in all Windows NT 4.0, LAN Manager, and Server domains in a site when you enable the Automatically Configure Workstation Logon Scripts option. The SMS Client Setup and Inventory Agent programs run when the user logs on to one of the site's SMS logon servers.

The system logon scripts for all the NetWare servers in the domain are automatically modified for SMS domains that contain NetWare servers. Each time thereafter that a user logs on, Client Setup and Inventory Agent automatically run via the logon script.

If you have NetWare 4.x or higher servers in your domain, you will need to edit the logon script once it is installed.

Inventory is scanned and reported according to the interval in the Inventory Frequency settings for each site, even though the Inventory Agent runs at each logon. The default setting is to scan and report inventory twice a week.

To automatically add clients to your SMS system, perform the following tasks to configure the appropriate logon scripts:

1. Configure the Windows NT 4.0 Directory Replicator service if your users are logging on to Windows NT 4.0 domains.
2. Configure Windows NT 4.0, LAN Manager, and Server domains to use the Use All Detected Servers option.
3. Enable Automatically Configure Workstation Logon.

 Log on scripts are not supported by Macintosh clients. You must manually add Macintosh clients to SMS 1.2 sites.

MCSE 8.1   Configuring and Modifying SMS

Configure the Windows NT 4.0 Directory Replicator service so the logon scripts can be replicated to the Windows NT Server 4.0 domain controllers, making them available at user logon. This is if you have users logging on to Windows NT 4.0-based computers. If you are in a NetWare environment, you do not need to configure the Windows NT 4.0 Directory Replicator service. Set up the LAN Manager Replicator service for LAN Manager domains.

Creating an Account

A Directory Replicator account must be created for each domain in a site. This is for use by the Directory Replicator service to access the logon servers in the domain. To create this account, log on with an account that has administrator privileges, and perform the following steps:

1. Open the Windows NT Server 4.0 User Manager for Domains.
2. From the User menu, select New User.
3. The New User dialog box appears. In the Username box, enter a name for the account, as in Replicate.
4. Enter a password, and confirm this password. You must provide a password for successful operation.
5. Select User Cannot Change Password and Password Never Expires.
6. Choose Groups.
7. Add the account to the Backup Operators, Replicator, and Domain Admins groups, and choose OK.
8. In the New User dialog box, choose Add.

Assigning Permissions

Now, let's look at how to assign Permissions to the Directory Replicator Account. You must perform the following steps:

1. Open the Windows NT 4.0 User Manager for Domains.
2. Select the Directory Replicator account you just created.
3. From the Policies menu, select User Rights. The User Rights Policy dialog box appears.
4. Select Show Advanced User Rights.
5. From the Rights list, select Log On As A Service.
6. Choose Add, and the Add Users and Groups dialog box appears.
7. In the Names box, select the Replicator group, and then choose Add.
8. Choose OK to close all open dialog boxes.

Create the Directory Replicator service for all SMS logon servers (except the primary domain controller) for each SMS domain in a site. This allows it to start automatically with the user account you've just created.

For each logon server running Windows NT 4.0, confirm that the NET LOGON share has at least Read permission assigned to the Domain Users group. If this is not the case, an error will occur when users log on to the domain, and users' computers will not be added to the computer inventory.

Setting up the Directory Replicator Service

To set up the Directory Replicator Service for each SMS logon server, perform the following steps:

1. Open the Windows NT 4.0 Server Manager.
2. Select the logon server and from the Computer menu select Properties.
3. Choose Replication.
4. Select Import Directories.
5. Confirm that the From List and To List boxes are empty. Remove items if they exist. The current domain is selected by default.
6. Choose OK to close all open dialog boxes.

Setting up the Replicator Service for the Primary Domain Controller

Now set up the Replicator Service for the Primary Domain Controller in each SMS domain in the site. To do this, perform the following steps:

1. Open the Windows NT 4.0 Server Manager.
2. Select the server and from the Computer menu select Properties.
3. Choose Replication.
4. Select Export Directories and Import Directories.
5. Confirm that the From List and To List boxes are empty. Remove items if they exist. The current domain is selected by default.
6. Choose OK to close all open dialog boxes.

This completes the process of setting up the Windows NT Server 4.0 Directory Replicator service for SMS. Let's test the correct operation of the Directory Replication Service by performing the following steps:

1. Place a small text file in the windows_dir\SYSTEM32\REPL\EXPORT \SCRIPTS directory on the primary domain controller.
2. Open the Windows NT 4.0 Server Manager and select the primary domain controller.
3. From the Computer menu, select Synchronize Entire Domain.
4. After some time has elapsed, change to the windows_dir\SYSTEM32\ REPL\IMPORT\SCRIPTS directory and see if the file exists on the primary domain controller and backup domain controllers in the domain.

Enabling the Use All Detected Servers Option

The Use All Detected Servers option must be enabled for the Automatically Configure Workstation Logon scripts to function on Windows NT 4.0 and LAN Manager domains. This section describes how to enable the Use All Detected Servers option so all logon servers detected on a domain are automatically added to SMS.

First, from the SMS Administrator, choose Sites. In the Sites window, select an appropriate site. Choose the Properties button from the node. The Site Properties window appears as shown in Figure 8.1.[1]

Using the collections node available server can be viewed Figure 8.2.

Choose Proposed Properties, and then choose the Properties button. The Server Properties dialog box appears as shown in Figure 8.3.

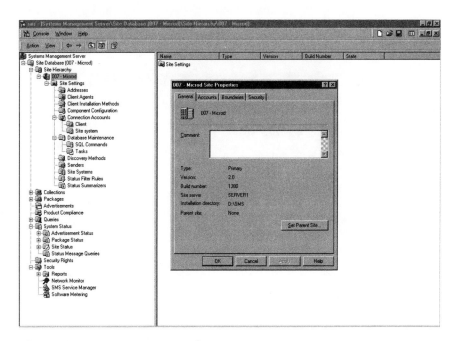

Figure 8.1 *Site Properties Window.*

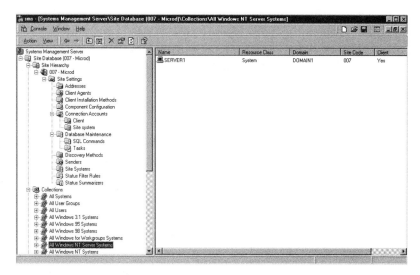

Figure 8.2 *Administrators Console and Collection of Servers Window.*

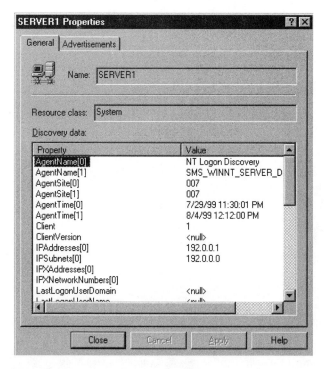

Figure 8.3 *Server Properties Dialog Box.*

For a given domain, you should have only one site detecting servers. If two sites detect the same server, and the server is added to each site, you will have severe site configuration problems at both sites.

If you select all servers including NetWare, SMS enumerates all NetWare servers on the network within 17 router hops. In addition, SMS will continue to monitor the network for any new servers within 17 router hops.

As each user logs on, the SMS client software is installed and the client's inventory information is taken. The inventory data is passed back to the SMS logon servers and to the database at the site server.

MCSE 8.2 Installing and Removing New SMS Components

There are occasions when a software application or a primary site server must be removed. This might be because it was configured incorrectly during the installation, or it should not have been installed on that client, or it does not accomplish the task it was supposed to perform.

With most commercial applications, a Setup program (like the SMS Setup under SMS Administrator) is used to both install and remove the application. The problem with most Setup programs is that they do not completely remove the application. Often they leave directories, as well as files, in the event that the application is installed again. The Registry is another area that is not restored completely during an application's removal. Registry entries that have been modified are not returned to preinstallation states, because the Setup program does not store which settings were changed during installation.

Removing SMS Components

The SMS Installer has a Rollback feature that can completely remove an application or an SMS component. If Rollback is configured for an installation file, then an `Install.log` file is generated during client and new SMS component installation. This log contains an entry for every file copied and every Registry entry that is created or modified. If a `.dll` file is replaced, the original file is archived to a known location as well. When the application is uninstalled, all copied files are removed, any `.dll` or other files that have been replaced by a newer version are returned to their original version, and all Registry modifications are reversed.

ENABLING ROLLBACK SUPPORT

Enabling rollback support is a simple process. Before compiling the installation script, select the Runtime Support attribute in the Installation Expert. Under Summary Information for Runtime Support, click Runtime Options, and then click Properties. In the dialog box that appears, verify that Uninstall Support is selected. The required file is included in the installation package and copied to the client desktop during the package execution.

USING THE ROLLBACK FUNCTION

Rolling back an SMS component installation is accomplished by using `Uninstal.exe`. `Uninstal.exe` is copied to the client computer during the application and new SMS component installation. To remove the application or SMS component, start `Uninstal.exe` from the application or SMS component's main directory. The Uninstall application or SMS component prompts for the name of the installation log file generated by the installation package if it is not in the application or SMS component directory. The default name is `Install.log`. It will then prompt for an Automated or Custom removal. If Automated is chosen, the application or SMS component is completely removed. If Custom is selected, prompts appear for those application and system files to remove, those directories to delete, and those SMS Registry values to remove.

As with the new SMS component installation, it is possible to configure the SMS Installer to create an SMS Status MIF file to indicate the status of the new SMS component. In this case, an uninstall MIF indicates that the application or SMS component has been removed. Configuration of the uninstall MIF file uses the Installation Expert's Installation Interface attribute in the same way as an install MIF file is configured.

Study Break

User Interface for SMS Administrator

The SMS Administrator utility is probably the most important and most often used tool. With this tool you can view the Site hierarchy; create packages, collections (jobs), queries, and alerts; and view the status of each ongoing process. You can also view and modify Machine, Site, Senders, Users, Groups, and view SMS Events.

From the SMS program group, start the SMS Administrator. You'll be prompted to provide information to enable SMS to access the SQL Server database. Choose the SMS Administrator icon from the SMS Program Group. The SMS Administrator Login screen appears. Default information is displayed by the Database and Login ID fields. Type in the password you created when you installed SQL Server. Change the Database field from SMS to SMSDemo, and choose OK if you want to use the new demo database you have created. If you have your own database, leave it as SMS.

When the Open SMS Window screen appears, use the arrow keys to scroll through the options in the Window Type and read its description. Each item listed represents a category in the SQL database. Take a few minutes to view these options and their respective screens. From any screen, you can press Cancel or Escape until you return to the Open SMS Window. Though you can use File: Open to access this screen, you'll notice that each item listed in the Window Type is also represented as a toolbar option. Point to any one icon in the toolbar and pause—the toolbar tip will display a short description of the icon.

Launching, Viewing, and Navigating SMS

You are given access to the SMS administrative tools after installing SMS. If you are running Windows NT Server 4.0 or higher, these tools can be accessed by clicking on the Start menu, selecting Programs, and then selecting SMS as shown in Figure 8.4.

These tools are installed on the site server in the primary (central) site by default. They can also be installed on other computers running Windows

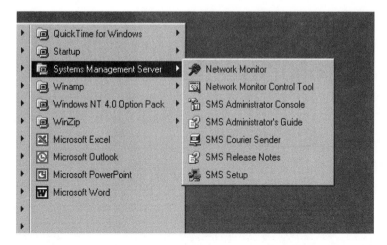

Figure 8.4 *Windows NT Server 4.0 Menu and SMS options.*

NT 4.0 located at other primary sites in your site hierarchy. This allows you to distribute SMS administrative tasks to other administrators at these locations. Table 8.1 describes the list of tools currently found under SMS Administrator in Figure 8.4.

Table 8.1 *SMS Administrator List of Tools and Their Description*

Tool Name	Description
SMS Network Monitor	Allows you to view statistics in real time about activity on your network, such as packets and bytes per second
SMS Network Monitor Control Tool	Allows you to identify network traffic patterns and network problems using real-time monitors
SMS Administrator Console	Allows you to log in to SMS and start the SMS Administrator. You use the SMS Administrator to perform the majority of SMS tasks.
SMS Administrator Guide	Allows you to access the SMS Administrators Guide Online that provide valuable information about SMS and how it works. The SMS Online help file is installed on all primary site servers and on each computer on which you install the SMS Administrator.
SMS Courier Sender	Allows you to control sender- and address-based bandwidth use. This feature allows a site to limit the link bandwidth consumed in sending SMS packages to another site.
SMS Release Notes	Allows you to access information about the current release of SMS
SMS Setup	Allows you to upgrade SMS, and install or remove SMS components. This includes adding support for additional processor types as they become available on your network, and installing SMS administrative tools on other computers.

SMS Login

You are actually logged onto the site's database automatically. This happens once you are authenticated using your domain server (based on your user or group permissions). Once inside the NT desktop you must first click the Start menu, select Programs: SMS, and then select SMS Administrator. As an administrator you can change site security as shown in Figure 8.5.

The password fields are case sensitive.

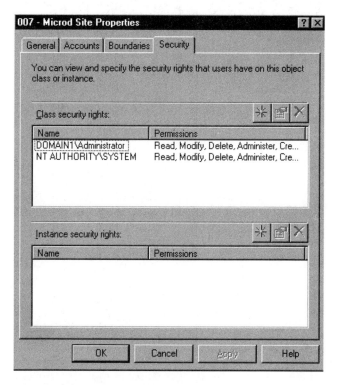

Figure 8.5 *SMS Security Dialog Box.*

SMS Navigation

The SMS Administrator is composed of multiple windows that allow you to manage information in the database. The Open SMS Window shown in Figure 8.6 displays a list of SMS Administrator windows.

You can view your SMS system by opening the Sites window after having logged on to SMS. Through this window, you can display the site and a hierarchical view of the SMS domains and computers beneath that site.

OPENING THE SITES WINDOW

To open the Sites window in the Open Systems Management Server Window dialog box shown in Figure 8.6, select Sites, and choose OK. The Sites window appears as shown in Figure 8.7.

When you log on to a site's database, that site appears at the top in the Sites window, even if there are parent sites above that site. Now, double-click the site at the top of the window. This is your central site, which is MICROD

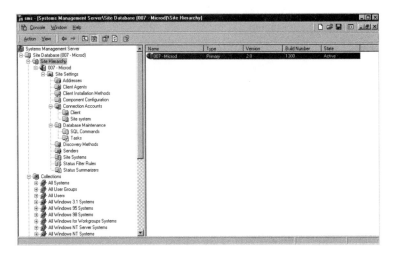

Figure 8.6   *Open SMS Window Dialog Box.*

in this example, This displays the site server SMS ID; 007 in this example, Next, double-click the site server SMS site beneath the site. In the right pane of the Sites window, you see the clients currently registered in the database for the selected site and SMS domain.

In the right pane, double-click the computer name, as shown in Figure 8.8, to display more detail for each client. The details for the computer are displayed.

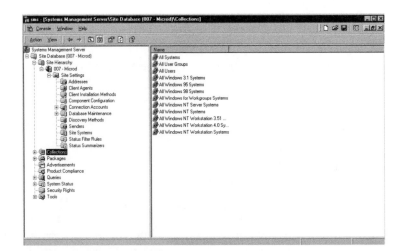

Figure 8.7   *The Sites Window.*

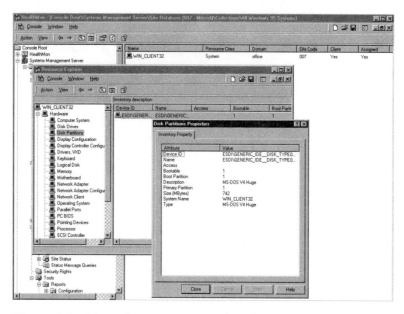

Figure 8.8   *SMS Administrator Console and Resource Explorer.*

To open additional windows, select Open from the File menu. The Open SMS Window screen is redisplayed. You can also use the buttons on the SMS Administrator to open windows and access SMS functions.

Updating the windows in the SMS Administrator requires retrieving data from the database. The SMS Administrator does not automatically refresh the windows when there are changes in the database. For instance, the Sites window is not updated when inventory is added to the database. You may need to refresh the display for the Sites window and the other windows in the SMS Administrator to see changes to your SMS system. To refresh a window, press F5: the **SMS Administrator Toolbar.**

Table 8.2 describes the SMS functions on the SMS Administrator Console toolbar. SMS Administrator Console displays available buttons depending on the currently active window. All operations that can be performed through the toolbar can also be performed from the menu bar.

Table 8.2 *SMS Functions and Description for Each of the Buttons on the SMS Administrator Toolbar*

Function Name	Description
Open Window: Sites	Opens a window that displays a hierarchical view of the site for the database and the SMS domains and computers beneath that site
Open Window: Collection (Jobs)	Opens a window through which you can create and monitor jobs throughout your SMS installation. A job contains instructions for SMS to perform. For example, a job can contain instructions to install a software application at a client.
Open Window: Packages	Opens a window through which you can create and manage SMS packages. A package contains diverse information about the software to identify and install the software.
Open Window: Queries	Opens a window through which you can manage stored queries. A query contains criteria used to locate information in the SMS database.
View All Details	Displays all available details in the current window
View Partial Details	Displays partial details for the current window
Sort	Sorts the current window by a selected field
Filter	Allows you to specify the items you see in the current window
Refresh	Updates the selected window with current information from the database. You can also use F5.
Cascade	Cascades all windows
Tile Vertically	Tiles all windows

Anyone who uses the SMS Administrator can make and save changes to the console settings. These settings are set on a per-session basis, not a per-user basis. To ensure that you can see all the tools in the toolbar, select Customize Toolbar from the Options menu, and then choose Reset to return the buttons to their original settings.

SMS: The Client's View

When a client is added to an SMS system, SMS client software is automatically installed on the client into a MS\SMS directory. The user experience is very configurable in SMS 2.0. The administrator can choose exactly what the user sees, if anything. Typically the user might see an advertised programs as they are made available. Also, when the advertised programs is running and is counting down to run. Administrator may request for a remote control operation and show it in progress. This experience has been integrated with other components of the operating system, such as Control Window and the status tray, so that working with SMS is effortless for the end user. The way the user at the client accesses this software depends on the desktop shell installed on the client. For example, Windows 95 and 98 clients access the SMS software is by clicking the Start menu, setting and selecting control panel were additional icon for sms have been placed. From the perspective of the user at the client, SMS provides the following benefits:

- Attended or unattended software installation
- Faster, automated software installation (no disks to shuffle)
- SMS shared applications, presented in the same way that locally installed software applications are presented
- Timed installations to fit around work schedules

The impact on the user is as follows:

- A slightly longer logon process
- Automatic periodic inventory of the client with no input required by the user
- When advertised programs are made available

ADVERTISE PROGRAMS MONITOR

When an advertised program is made available, a taskbar icon appears in the client's taskbar status tray. When remote control is requested, an icon appears on the desktop, or a dialog box appears requesting permission to begin a remote control session programs are made available.

A user at a client is required to perform SMS-related tasks when you:

- Advertise an SMS package containing software for installation that requires user input
- Need the user to provide specific inventory information
- Want to perform remote troubleshooting operations at the client and the client is configured so that the user needs to provide verification

When a new advertised program is made available at a client, the user can use the Advertised Programs Monitor to reschedule the program or to run it immediately as shown in Figure 8.9. If they choose to run it immediately, a wizard walks the user through the installation steps. This distribution methodology is closely aligned to the approach used with Windows 2000.

REMOTE CONTROL AND HELP DESK UTILITIES

Reducing total cost of ownership requires centralized problem diagnostics and resolution. SMS includes utilities that enable you to directly control and monitor remote clients running Windows 95, Windows 98, Windows NT

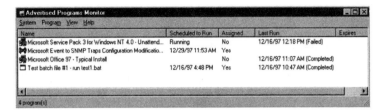

Figure 8.9 *Advertisement Client Monitor.*

 The more distribution servers you have in your SMS system, the longer clients take to initialize.

3.51 and 4.0, or Windows 3.x operating systems and utilities that allow you to diagnose network and server problems.

Help Desk SMS includes Remote Tools and Diagnostics utilities shown in Figure 8.10 that allow you to directly control and monitor remote clients using Windows 16-bit/32-bit and the Windows NT 4.0 operating system. The Help Desk utilities provide direct access to a client as shown in Figure 8.11. The Diagnostics utilities enable you to view a remote client's current configuration.

SMS provides a series of Help Desk utilities to enable administrators to troubleshoot user problems. These include the following utilities.

REMOTE CONTROL

Using the Remote Control utility, administrators can view the display of a remote SMS client and take control of its keyboard and mouse.

REMOTE REBOOT

When administrators are providing support for a remote client, they may need to restart the client to test a change to a start-up procedure, to load a new configuration, or to restart when a client has locked up due to a hard-

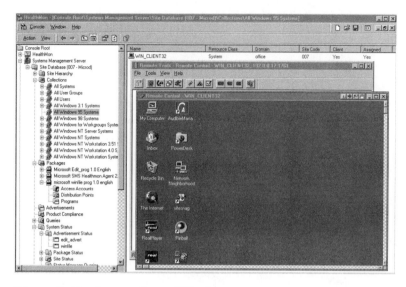

Figure 8.10 *Remote Control Window.*

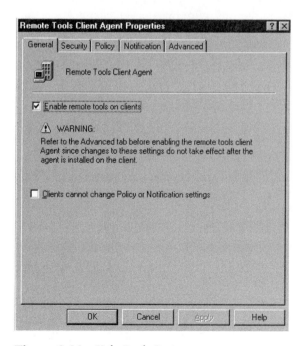

Figure 8.11 *Help Desk Options.*

ware or software malfunction. Using the Remote Reboot utility, administrators can restart the selected client.

REMOTE CHAT

Using the Remote Chat utility, administrators can communicate with a user at the selected client. When an administrator starts a chat session, the Remote Chat windows appear on both the SMS Administrator computer and the selected client. When either the administrator or the user at the client types text in the Remote Chat window, that text is displayed in the other computer's Remote Chat window.

FILE TRANSFER

Using the File Transfer utility, administrators can transfer files between the SMS-based console computer and the selected client.

REMOTE EXECUTE

The Remote Execute utility enables administrators to run an application or batch file on a remote Windows-based client. When administrators use Remote Execute instead of Remote Control, the user does not see the command being executed, and the command may complete more quickly.

Administrators can also perform Windows 95 and Windows 98 diagnostics via the Remote Tools utilities, and can run Windows NT administrative tools, such as User Manager, remotely.

Remote Control is a powerful tool, so security is critical. This feature of SMS is tightly integrated with operating system security, making it impossible for improper use of the tool. Different administrators can be assigned different levels of remote administration over different groups of users. Logs are kept as to what actions administrators performed while a remote control session was active. Configuration is extensive, allowing exactly the level of security that a corporation requires, from the end user having no knowledge a remote control session is happening to specific users never allowing remote control to take place, and everything in between.

For security purposes, the Help Desk utilities are disabled by default and can be enabled by administrator or a user at the remote client.

For more detailed information about the Help Desk and Diagnostics utilities, see Chapter 13, "Diagnosing and Resolving SMS Problems."

REMOTE CONTROL

Remote control must be enabled in the Help Desk Options dialog box at the client before you can remotely control the client. In addition, the Remote Control Agent program must be running at the client. To start the agent, the user double-clicks the Remote Control icon. The Remote Control Agent window in Figure 8.12 is minimized during the remote control session.

For clients running Windows NT 4.0, the Remote Control feature is automatically started.

A user can terminate a remote troubleshooting session by choosing Terminate Viewer. Again, for more detailed information about remote control, see Chapter 13.

SMS CLIENT HELP

The SMS Client Help icon allows a user to look up information about any of the SMS software that is installed on their computer. SMS Client Help is installed on all clients running SMS, and it describes all features of the software. Be sure that your users know about SMS Client Help.

Figure 8.12 *Remote Control Agent Window.*

■ Summary

You should come away from this chapter with an in-depth knowledge of the MCSE exam-specific SMS configuration and modification components that are needed to install and configure the SMS site. With that in mind, you need to configure the Windows NT 4.0 Directory Replicator service so that the logon scripts can be replicated to the Windows NT Server 4.0 domain controllers. This makes them available at user logon if you have users logging on to Windows NT 4.0-based computers. You do not need to configure the Windows NT 4.0 Directory Replicator service if you are in a NetWare environment. For LAN Manager domains, you must set up the LAN Manager Replicator service.

The second part of the chapter examines how you are given access to the SMS administrative tools after installing SMS. These tools can be accessed by clicking on the Start menu, selecting Programs, and then selecting SMS. The tools are located in Program Manager, in an SMS program group if you are running an earlier version of Windows NT 4.0.

▲ CHAPTER REVIEW QUESTIONS

▲ True/False

1. *True or False? For each logon server running Windows NT 4.0, confirm that the NETLOGON share has at least Read permission assigned to the Domain Users group. If this is not the case, an error will occur when users log on to the domain, and users' computers will not be added to the computer inventory.*

2. *True or False? For a given domain, you should have only one site detecting servers. If two sites detect the same server, and the server is added to each site, you will have severe site configuration problems at both sites.*

3. *True or False? Updating the windows in the SMS Administrator requires retrieving data from the database. The SMS Administrator does not automatically refresh the windows when there are changes in the database. For instance, the Sites window is not updated when inventory is added to the database. You may need to refresh the display for the Sites window and the other windows in the SMS Administrator to see changes to your SMS system. To refresh a window, press F5: the SMS Administrator Toolbar.*

4. *True or False? The Allow DOS Diagnostics and Allow Windows Diagnostics features are applicable to Windows NT 4.0. For current configuration information, client users should use the Windows NT 4.0 Diagnostics. The Allow Ping Test feature is not supported for Windows NT 4.0.*

5. *True or False? For clients running Windows NT 4.0, the Remote Control feature is automatically started.*

6. *True or False? SMS Setup allows you to upgrade SMS and install or remove SMS components. This includes adding support for additional processor types, as they become available on your network, and installing SMS administrative tools on other computers.*

▲ Multiple Choice

1. *When a client is added to an SMS system, SMS client software is automatically installed on the client into a MS\SMS directory. The way the user at the client accesses this software depends on the desktop shell installed on the client. For example, for Windows 95 and 98 clients, the SMS software is accessed by clicking the Start menu and selecting Programs: SMS Client. Therefore, from the perspective of the user at the client, SMS provides the following benefits except:*
   A.   A slightly longer logon process
   B.   Attended or unattended software installation
   C.   Faster, automated software installation with no disks to shuffle
   D.   Timed installations to fit around work schedules

2. *This tool allows you to log on to SMS and start the SMS Administrator:*
   A.   SMS Administrator
   B.   SMS Books Online
   C.   SMS Database Manager
   D.   Helper Server
   E.   SMS Frequently Asked Questions

3. *This tool runs the MIF Form Generator. It allows you to create forms and distribute them to clients. Users at clients can use the forms to enter customized information, which is then collected at inventory time.*
   A.   SMS Network Monitor
   B.   Manage Distribution Points wizard
   C.   SMS Release Notes

    D. SMS Security Manager

    E. SMS MIF Form Generator

4. *This tool allows you to view statistics in real time about activity on your network, such as packets and bytes per second:*

    A. SMS Release Notes

    B. SMS Security Manager

    C. SMS Sender Manager

    D. SMS Network Monitor

    E. SMS Service Manager

5. *This tool allows you to access information about the current release of SMS:*

    A. SMS Release Notes

    B. SMS Security Manager

    C. SMS Sender Manager

    D. SMS Service Manager

    E. SMS Setup

6. *This tool allows you to grant user rights to SMS Administrator functions:*

    A. SMS Sender Manager

    B. SMS Service Manager

    C. SMS Security Manager

    D. SMS Setup

    E. SMS SQL View Generator

▲ Open Ended

1. Describe the tasks to automatically configure logon scripts so that clients are automatically added to your SMS system.

2. To create the Directory Replicator account, you must be logged on with an account that has administrator privileges. Describe the other steps you must perform to complete the creation of the account.

Configuring and Managing Resources

Part 4 details how to automatically collect
information on personal computer
configurations, and how to test for Year 2000
compliance. It further explains the new SMS
feature that allows administrators to track and
control application use. It also outlines the
various facilities available to aid an administrator
in the use of SMS as a help desk tool.

The chapters in Part 4 also cover such topics as:

• SMS discovery and installation

• How to enable the agent and perform
management tasks through the distribution
and installation of software

• How to create database reports

• How to view the SMS database with utilities
other than the SMS Administrator Console

• How use Crystal Reports to view data and
create reports

Configuring, Auditing, and Controlling Network Clients with SMS

This chapter begins Part 4, "Configuring and Managing Resources," by taking you through a series of common user scenarios for configuring, auditing, and controlling network clients with SMS. For example, the first part of the chapters details how to automatically collect information on personal computer configurations and how to test for Year 2000 compliance.

The second part of the chapter explains the new SMS feature that allows administrators to track and control application use, such as Network Trace to trace the SMS network and SMS Trace to track and view application log files.

Finally, the third part of the chapter outlines the various ways an administrator can use SMS as a help desk tool.

MCSE 9.1 SMS Inventory

The SMS inventory process helps monitor an enterprise's PCs and their related hardware and software. In the process, this saves you a great deal of time and money. SMS automatically retrieves detailed information about both the hardware and software for every computer within your enterprise, and then stores all the information in a standard SQL Server database. You can select, sort, and view the data, or you can extract the data and create custom reports and graphs with popular desktop applications like Microsoft Access or Lotus 1-2-3. A few of the business benefits are maintenance, service tracking, and planning your upgrades.

You can alter this automatic inventory list of all computers in your business to suit your needs. For example, you can supplement this information by adding your company asset numbers, the cost of each computer, and any maintenance that has been performed. If you want to install a new adapter, you can tell the technician what the exact configuration of the computer is, thus ensuring that the device will work correctly and reducing any downtime of the computer.

Let's say, for example, that you decide you want to upgrade all computers in your organization to Windows 95 or 98. Some of your computers may need a hardware upgrade. You want to plan your budget for this now so you can order the hardware you need. With SMS, just define a standard computer configuration, and run a query on the database to find which computers meet your requirements and, more importantly, which computers need the upgrade.

Hardware and Software Inventory

By offering the administrator access to comprehensive computing information, hardware and software inventory capabilities have been substantially improved in SMS 2.0. In addition, a new Year 2000 (Y2K) compliance-checking tool has been included that evaluates the inventory data against a compliance database and generates reports and graphs on Y2K status.

HARDWARE INVENTORY

Hardware inventory is based on the Common Information Model (CIM) in SMS 2.0. Microsoft is supporting the CIM specification developed by the Desktop Management Task Force, as part of the Web-Based Enterprise Management (WBEM) initiative. This provides a common way of presenting management information from multiple sources, such as SNMP, DMI, and the Microsoft Win32 application programming interface. Microsoft is building CIM into the Windows NT 2000 and Windows 98 operating system environments, and thus it is helpful that SMS 2.0 has been designed to collect data in a CIM format. SMS also uses a CIM-based agent to get information out of all 32-bit Windows operating systems.

This means that SMS 2.0 has access to data from many sources, including Win32, SNMP, and DMI, and administrators have a much richer collection of inventory information available. Given the large number of inventory objects, filtering options have been added so that an administrator can choose which data is most important.

Client agents collect an inventory of the hardware on the client and store the results on the client. This information is passed through a Client Access Point to the site database. Over 200 properties are collected and reported with graphs and reports, including details such as:

- Amount of memory
- BIOS information
- Computer name and IP address
- Information about peripherals connected to the resource
- Monitor and display settings
- Network type
- Number of disk drives
- Operating system
- Type of processor

A Hardware Inventory Processor running on each primary site server enters the collected data into the SMS database. Once client inventory has been added to the SMS database, Resource Explorer or queries can be used to view inventory for any client.

SMS maintains an inventory history for each client computer. Inventory history can help you diagnose problems at clients by enabling you to view the configuration changes to individual computers. Changes to the hardware inventory are evaluated on clients, and only the delta between the current and last inventory files is written to a file and sent to the site server.

COLLECTING HARDWARE INVENTORY • The Inventory Agent detects all hardware that resides within each networked computer, running any supported operating system on any supported network environment. The hardware inventory includes the main components of the computer, such as the microprocessor, the various drives, the network adapter, the memory, and the IRQ table. SMS supports Management Information Format (MIF) files. Any device can appear within the properties of the computer where it resides, as long as the hardware vendor writes a MIF file for that device.

HOW THE INVENTORY IS PROCESSED • The inventory collection process begins when a client computer runs RUNSMS.BAT, or logs on to the network in the case of automatic inventory collection. SMS then installs an Inventory Agent program on the computer, and the Inventory Agent builds a binary inventory report and graph of the hardware and software configuration of the computer. From then on, at an interval set by the administrator, the Inventory Agent inspects the computer for inventory information.

The intervals for checking hardware and software can be set independently of one another. For example, you can check for hardware inventory once a day, and check for software inventory once a week.

In the second part of the inventory collection process, the Inventory Agent places the inventory report and graph on the logon server. During this process, the client computer uses its native network logon server. For instance, a NetWare client works directly with its existing NetWare server. It doesn't need to access a Windows NT 4.0, LAN, or other server.

Now, in the third part of the inventory collection process, the primary site server collects the inventory files from all its logon servers. The primary site server determines what hardware and software changes have taken place since the last inventory and updates the database with the new information. This changed information is passed up the hierarchy to the central site.

Large enterprise networks need to take advantage of SMS's ability to automatically detect computers on the network, inventory their software and hardware, and install the client components on each computer. For smaller networks, it is easy for a user at the client computer to manually add the computer to the inventory.

CLIENT COMPUTER MANUAL ADDITION • Now, let's look at how to manually add a client computer to the SMS inventory. In other words, here's how you manually install SMS client software on a computer running Windows, Windows NT 4.0, or Windows for Workgroups:

1. From the client, connect to the share \\server\SMS_SHR on your SMS primary site server.

2. From the share connection, run RUNSMS.BAT. This batch file installs the client components on the client and then inventories the computer's hardware and software.

The SMS Client program group is automatically created in the Program Manager on each client computer included in the inventory. These configuration changes appear after the client computer has been restarted.

If you are currently running the demonstration database, you must restart SMS for this change to show. The demonstration database (SMS-Demo), is designed to give you an example of SMS sites. When you restart SMS and choose the real database (SMS), this new client will be shown.

VIEWING THE CLIENT HARDWARE INVENTORY • Hardware inventory adds complete details of the hardware detected on each client in the site database. Hardware inventory is enabled by default.

For SMS 2.0, the interval between the installation of the hardware inventory agent and the inventory collection is sixteen minutes.

To view the client inventory using SMS Administrator, navigate to the hardware inventory information, and choose the following in numeric order as each option comes up:

1. SMS
2. Site Database (<name>)
3. Collections
4. All Systems

Now, perform the following steps:

1. The Results window displays all discovered systems. This should include both the site server and the Windows-based client computers. In the Results window, select the client computer, and then select Task from the Action menu. A new submenu appears.
2. Click Explore Resources. The Explorer window appears.
3. In the Scope window, expand Hardware. The inventoried hardware classes appear. Investigate these classes. Interesting ones include:

    a. Logical Disk
    b. Network Adapter Configuration
    c. Operating System
    d. Processor

  4. Close the Explorer window.

Notice the detailed information being returned from the Common Information Model.

SOFTWARE INVENTORY

To deliver better software inventory, SMS 2.0 searches for version resource information on every executable on the client machine, rather than checking against a predefined database. This provides a dynamic, efficient mechanism for getting detailed information on every application on every PC.

Administrators are returned a list of all software packages on a client machine, grouped under the company that manufactured them. This allows easy identification of the applications installed across the network, and provides a database against which administrators can easily check for specific applications, such as those that are not Y2K compliant.

As well as returning information on recognized applications, SMS returns a list of unknown applications. Specific custom applications may not have full header information, although they are still important to trace. With SMS, they can still be discovered.

The software inventory can also collect files. In this case, rather than returning a list of applications and the files that reference them, the actual files are collected and forwarded from the client back to the SMS database. This is an easy way to gather a set of configuration files from each system.

COLLECTING SOFTWARE INVENTORY • Two types of software inventory information are collected by SMS: detailed identification and comprehensive audit. These are explained in detail in Chapter 10 in the section called "Using Software Inventory in SMS 2.0," beginning on page 347. As with hardware inventory, both types of software information are processed by the Inventory Agent program and loaded into the database.

A great feature of SMS is that when it is doing software inventory, it can also collect software. For instance, it can collect copies of the computer's configuration files, such as `CONFIG.SYS`, `AUTOEXEC.BAT`, or `WIN.INI`, and can add them to an archive. If a problem occurs on a computer, a technician can review the archived files to see if a change in a configuration file might have caused the problem, and can replace corrupted files. This is the ideal way to manage a variety of configuration files. These processes require the creation of packages to collect the information and jobs to trigger the process. These processes, along with the concepts of distribution, are further explained in Chapter 10.

VIEWING THE CLIENT SOFTWARE INVENTORY • Software inventory is enabled by default. When you configure software inventory for a site, you can specify what file types to inventory and how often the inventory is to be performed.

 For SMS 2.0, the interval between the installation of the software inventory agent and the collection of inventory is thirty-one minutes.

To view the client inventory using SMS Administrator, navigate to the software inventory information, and choose the following in numeric order as each option comes up:

1. SMS
2. Site Database (<name>)
3. Collections
4. All Systems

Now, perform the following steps:

1. The Results window displays all discovered systems. This should include both the site server and the client computers. In the Results window, select the client computer, and then select Task from the Action menu. A new submenu appears.
2. Click Explore Resources. The Explorer window appears.
3. In the Scope window, expand Software. The Scope window displays software inventory elements, including Products, Unknown Files, and Collected Files.
4. In the Scope window, expand Products, and investigate each in turn.

Under Unknown Files, there is a list of products that do not define a header. You should still be able to retrieve basic information from them. Collected Files can be chosen just as easily to retrieve a similar listing.

INVENTORY DATABASE VIEWING

To explore the demo site and inventory data stored in your SMS database, follow these steps:

1. In the SMS Administrator, open the Sites window.
2. Double click on the Site to expand node.
3. Double click on Collection to expandNode.
4. Select one of the Collection Types in the left pane and Once the list appears on the right window pane choose system as shown in Table 9.1 and right click (Choose task). Run the Resource Explorer. This loads the computer inventory option to display hardware or software inventory as shown in Figure 9.1.[1]

Table 9.1 *SMS Administrator Personal Computer Properties Identification Details Screen*

Attribute	Value
Name	Computer name (Netbios name)
Resource Class	The class of the resource, such as System
Domain	The domain in which the resource exists
Site Code	The three-letter site code that "discovered" the resource
Client	Whether or not the resource has SMS client software installed
Assigned	Whether or not the resource has been assigned to the current site or a site below it in the hierarchy

Whether you choose hardware or software as you scroll down the list of Class (Name & Types) Properties you can see the wealth of information that is automatically detected. Take a few minutes to look at each property displayed for the computers in the database.

The inventory information uses a structure based on the MIF file that was created by the Desktop Management Task Force (DMTF).

---

1. Copyright © 1998 Microsoft and/or its suppliers, One Microsoft Way, Redmond, Washington 98052-6399. All rights reserved.

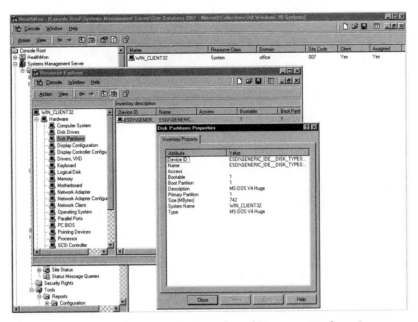

Figure 9.1 *SMS Administrator Console and Resource Explorer Screen.*

INVENTORY DATABASE QUERYING

You can use SMS query tools to search the database for a variety of criteria. You can identify an individual computer or a specific component or property of that computer, such as installed software or the network address of the network adapter. Most queries are run against the Personal Computer architecture, although other architectures can be searched for different criteria, such as the location of software packages or SNMP Traps. Combined queries can be created to see which computers meet a particular criteria. You can use combinations of AND, OR, and NOT operators to create a query.

QUERY CREATION • Using the following steps you can use predefined queries or create custom to show you almost anything based on the criteria set. The following steps show how to create a query to determine which clients have enough RAM (64 MB or more) and are using Windows NT 4.0 operating system.

1. Select site and expand node.
2. Select Queries node and expand node.
3. Click on predefined Query to edit or create a new one.
4. Using Query Builder tool set criteria for client (if needed).
5. Once completed, Save query and run to get results.

Figure 9.2 *Administrator Console and Query Node.*

The resulting query should look like the screen as shown in Figure 9.2.

If it does, choose OK. Using a similar procedure, you can create much more sophisticated queries.

QUERY EXECUTION • To execute the query you just created, choose query and right click to run Query from the File menu. The Query Results window displays the computers that meet the query search criteria, as shown in Figure 9.3.

You can edit or create a query anytime by using the Query Properties windows as shown in Figure 9.4.

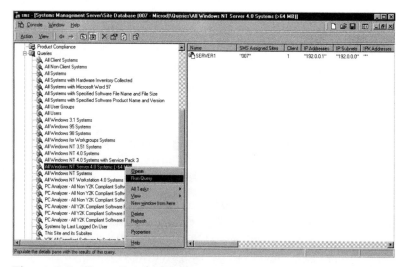

Figure 9.3 *Query Results Window.*

Figure 9.4 *Query Properties Window.*

PROMPTED QUERIES • SMS provides several default queries that take advantage of prompted queries. This is a query that prompts the administrator for a value when it is run. In the example shown in Figure 9.5, you can create this type of query by using a prompted criteria. When you select and run the predefined query, the administrator is prompted to specify an attribute. To edit this Query go to Properties tab as shown in the dialog box in Figure 9.6.

If a query contains more than one prompted expression, the expressions are resolved in sequence and the administrator can create specific attributes for each prompts as shown in Figure 9.7.

COMPLIANCE CHECKING FOR THE Y2K

Testing for Y2K software application compliance is a new feature added to SMS 2.0. SMS comes with a Microsoft database of applications and their Y2K compliance levels (compliant, noncompliant, compliant with issues), and allows administrators to input new databases from Microsoft or other vendors. This Y2K database is compared against the SMS software inventory generated by checking all machines on the network. A series of reports and graphs indicating Y2K compliance within a network is created.

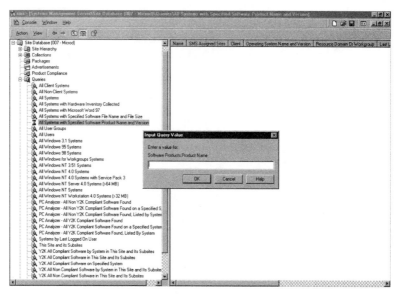

Figure 9.5 *Query Prompted Window.*

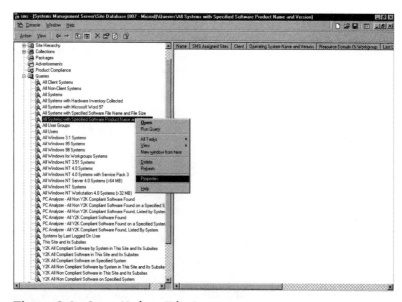

Figure 9.6 *Query Node to Edit Queries.*

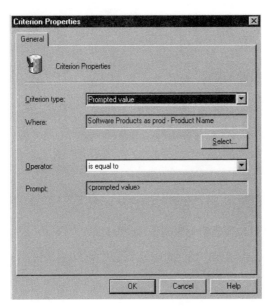

Figure 9.7 *Criterion Specific Attributes Dialog Box.*

The Y2K database can be found under the Y2K Products node. Replacement database can be imported. Y2K queries can be run from under the Queries node.

FUNCTIONALITY OF Y2K COMPLIANCE CHECKING • As previously stated, SMS 2.0 has added tools to check for Y2K compliance, based on the software inventory information. To investigate this functionality, navigate to the Y2K database, and choose the following in numeric order as each option comes up:

1. SMS
2. Site Database (<name>)
3. Y2K Database

Here you find a list of compliance levels for Microsoft products. This list is current as of SMS 2.0. To update this list, add compliance information from other vendors, or add checking for European compliance, first select the Y2K Database node, and then select Import from the Action. A dialog box appears in which you can specify a new tab-delimited database to load. The Microsoft Year 2000 site (http://www.microsoft.com/Year2000) provides the most up-to-date version of this file for Microsoft applications.

Once you have a database of compliance details (the database shipping with SMS 2.0 works fine for this operation), find out if you have Y2K compliance issues in your network. SMS does a comparison of this compliance data with information obtained from the software inventory scan. Navigate to the Queries node by choosing the following in numeric order as each option comes up:

1. SMS
2. Site Database (<name>)
3. Queries
4. Y2K Noncompliant Software on Systems by Version

Run the query by selecting Run Query from the Action menu. After the query runs, a list of applications with compliance problems appears in the Results window. This format will be modified by SMS specifically the value 2 maps to compliant with issues and the value 3 maps to noncompliant.

INVENTORY EXTENSION

Inventory is CIM-based and is designed to be easily extended by corporations or Integrated System Vendors. By collecting additional data on the client, new items can be collated and displayed on the administrator's console. Prompting the user for information or running additional discovery processes can collect additional data.

Study Break

Tales from the Y2K Crypt

No one knows for sure how much trouble there will be at the stroke of midnight, December 31, 1999, when computer clocks everywhere roll over to the Y2K. Even if planes don't fall from the sky and banks don't falter, experts say we will all experience inconveniences from what is becoming widely recognized as the *Y2K problem.* Some fear the worst.

As glitches go, the Y2K computer problem is simple enough. Fixing the Y2K problem is also simple...in concept: Someone must examine every line of code in every computer, locate the instructions regarding dates, and rewrite them to accept 2000 as a year designation. The problem is that despite the rising din of warnings, surveys indicate that too few managers in business and government recognize how little time is left to complete the task. Here's a look at five Y2K misconceptions that may promote this complacency and noncompliance.

Fable 1: There's plenty of time.

A world conference of Y2K problem managers in 1997 listed this as the foremost deadly fable they encounter. Sixteen months later, this is still being thrown about, especially in local government and health care. In the private sector, entire industries are bracing for the worst.

Fable 2: Someone will find a quick fix.

Despite obvious signs to the contrary, many managers are hoping for a miracle. Of course there are, and will be, some fixes for specific software. Still, there are tens of thousands of programs and applications out there. At least 700 different computer languages are in use throughout the world, containing several hundreds of billions of lines of code.

It gets worse: Many programs are written in *modular* style, meaning that one segment may be written in one language, like COBOL, while the next segment is written in another, like C++. A silver bullet for fixing COBOL would be very helpful in the COBOL segment but useless in the C++ segment. Having one uncorrected module is akin to a burned-out bulb in a string of cheap Christmas lights—the whole string goes down.

Fable 3: We are throwing enough money and people at the problem to fix it.

Even if enough money were allocated, there aren't enough debuggers and testing specialists who know ancient and varied programming languages to renovate the hundreds of billions of lines of code that need repair. Y2K boot camps are proliferating, where everyone from college kids to single moms gets crash courses in COBOL. Meanwhile, companies nationwide are raiding one another's staffs for programmers who command salaries of up to six figures.

Fable 4: With so many new computers out there, surely we can't be vulnerable to a problem created 26 years ago.

The notion that the Y2K problem applies only to old systems can give a false sense of security. Indeed, to many people, the Y2K problem sounds like a throwback to the era of punch cards and UNIVAC. Ironically, one reason the Y2K bug has survived is the concept of *backward compatibility* introduced in the 1960s to bring order to computer development. IBM and other computer companies, realizing they couldn't expect clients to buy new software every year, made sure that each new version was largely compatible with earlier programs. That, however, created an environment in which the old Y2K bugs have been able to worm their way—program by program—into the most modern equipment.

Fable 5: With luck, it won't affect me.

Not likely. Even if a system and its connected systems are Y2K compliant, they may still be brought to their knees by a noncompliant entity somewhere down the chain.

MCSE 9.2   ## Software Metering

Administrators require tools to track software usage by user, group, workstation, time, or license quota. SMS 2.0 provides new tools to analyze, monitor, and control the use of applications on servers and workstations. The administrator has many levels of control, ranging from simple alerts to actively preventing applications from running. This control can be exercised over specific applications with quota limits defined by the administrator, and can prevent the use of any application that is not specifically allowed by the administrator. Any application (.exe, .com, etc.) on any client or server can be monitored for compliance.

Software metering can help you find out how long applications are used to generate charge-back information. It can also be used to ensure that your company stays within the limits set by your license agreements for concurrent use of software packages. It does this by controlling the number of instances of each licensed software product that may be used at one time. Reporting tools help you identify your software needs so that you can more accurately estimate the number of concurrent licenses to buy.

Software metering *checks out* licenses for software to clients (including mobile clients using laptop computers) and notifies the client when the license is due to expire. If a program licensed to a client is not being used, the license can be reclaimed and made available to other clients. If a user is unable to use a program because all available licenses are checked out, the software metering server adds the user to a queue waiting for the program. When a license becomes available, the software metering server contacts the next user in the queue and offers them the use of the program. This is the software metering *callback* feature. You can assign a *callback priority* to each user that you specifically register in your system. Users with higher priority are offered an available software license before users with a lower priority. These priorities can age to let a lower priority user play through whenever higher-priority users are continually requesting a particular licensed program over time.

Since the software metering solution is unaffected by file renaming as it checks application resources, users cannot avoid monitoring. Further, the metering tools recognize different program versions and detect disabling of client agents, providing a comprehensive defense against tampering.

A report wizard, including graphs, is included to help you query the software metering database for information about the usage and attempted usage of each metered application. For example, you can view the number of licenses currently in use, the number of times licenses have been denied, and the number of callbacks currently waiting for licenses.

Software Metering Configuration

As previously mentioned, software metering is a new feature in SMS 2.0. It gives administrators the ability to monitor and prevent application use dependent on their criteria, and to track application use for charge-back purposes. To configure the software metering component for SMS 2.0, first define which of your servers is going to be the software metering server. Navigate to the site server, and choose the following in numeric order as each option comes up:

1. SMS
2. Site Database (<name>)
3. Site Hierarchy
4. Site Systems

Now, perform the following steps:

1. In the Results window, select your site server, and then select Properties from the Action menu.
2. Click the Software Metering tab.
3. Click Use Site System as a Software Metering Server.
4. In the Database Location box, type a path for the local software metering data cache (the default is fine), and then click OK.

You will need to wait for up to 31 minutes before this takes effect. While waiting you can modify the software metering configuration for the site. Navigate to the component configuration, and choose the following in numeric order as each option comes up:

1. SMS
2. Site Database (<name>)
3. Site Hierarchy
4. Component Configuration

Now, perform the following steps:

1. In the results window, click Software Metering.
2. On the Action menu, click Properties. The Software Metering Component Configuration Properties dialog box appears.
3. Under Program name policy, click Original Name, and then click the Local tab.
4. Set each of these schedules to 16 minutes, and then click OK.

Now you need to set the client agent configurations for this task. Navigate to the component configuration, and choose the following in numeric order as each option comes up:

1. SMS
2. Site Database (<name>)
3. Site Hierarchy
4. Client Agents

Now, perform the following steps:

1. In the Results window, click Software Metering, and then select Properties from the Action menu. The Software Metering Client Agent Properties dialog box displays General settings for the software metering client agent. Verify that Enable Software Metering on clients is selected.
2. Click the Timings tab. The Software Metering Client Agent Properties window displays Timing settings for the software metering client agent.
3. In the Configuration polling interval box, type 1.
4. In the Callback polling interval box at the bottom of screen, type 1, and then click OK.
5. Wait for shut down, and then restart the client computer. Log on as the domain user. The SMS client software executes, and the software metering client components are reconfigured to the new settings.

Software Usage Metering

Now let's indicate what you want to meter. Navigate to software metering, and choose the following in numeric order as each option comes up:

1. SMS
2. Site Database (<name>)

Next, perform the following steps:

1. On the Action menu, point to Task, and then click Software Metering. The Defining Metered Software dialog box appears.
2. Click the Add Product icon, and then click OK. The New Product dialog box appears. Complete the sections using the information in Table 9.2.
3. Click OK.
4. The Defining Metered Software window displays Notepad as a licensed program.
5. Under Licensed software, click Notepad, and then click Properties. The Properties dialog box displays Identification properties for Notepad.
6. Click the License Balancing tab. The Properties dialog box displays License Balancing properties for Notepad.
7. Click to cancel "Do not enforce the license limits for this product until a trend has been calculated," and then click OK. The Defining Licensed Software window displays Notepad as a licensed program.
8. On the Summary menu, click Software Metering Summary.
9. Click the Licensed tab. Notepad.exe appears with one available license at the site and none available at the software metering server. Leave this window open.

Table 9.2 *Defining Metered Software Dialog Box Information*

In This Box…	…Type or Select…
Product name	Notepad
Serial number	Blank
Purchase date	Default
Number of licenses	1
Enforce license limits for product [Program Name]	Click to select Notepad.exe (browse to get the app)

By default, licenses added at a site are not balanced to a server for seven days. This is to allow monitoring of applications for trend analysis. At the end of this trend analysis period, licenses are balanced to the software metering servers that need them. Trend analysis for Notepad was disabled by canceling "Do not enforce the license limits for this product until a trend has been calculated." With this canceled, the server does license balancing only after a request has been made for a license.

Thus, to force this balancing, you need to run Notepad on the client and receive a denial. At the client, start Notepad. A software metering message appears indicating no licenses are available. Click No Callback. Now that a denial has occurred, license balancing can take place. It is on a 16-minute schedule, so wait 16 minutes before continuing.

Now let's look at how metering controls application use on the client computer. Shut down, and then restart the *client computer* (unless it is unnecessary). Log on as the domain user, and start `Notepad.exe`. The Notepad window appears.

In the *administrator user interface* perform the following steps:

1. Click Refresh Now in the Licensed Software window. Notepad appears with one available license which is in use.

2. Start a second copy of Notepad. The license is refused and a callback is offered.

3. Try copying `notepad.exe` to another name and running it. The license is still refused, since it is checking the header information.

Software metering also has the ability to control software use based on time of day. For example, a corporation may want to disable game-playing during business hours, as shown in Figure 9.8. Experiment with this by double-clicking a licensed application (such as Notepad) under the Defining Metered Software window, and then selecting the Permissions tab. Also observe the other configuration options available under Permissions, Alerts and Rules.

Charge-back is another powerful feature of software metering. Not only is this tool able to monitor application use, it also monitors the length of time applications are used. This data is then available for an IS department

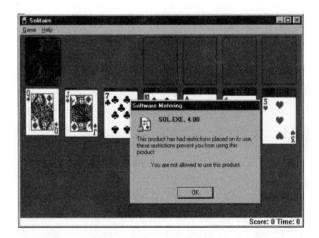

Figure 9.8   *Permissions for Software Use Are Set through Software Metering.*

to charge other departments for use of developed or deployed applications, or use of services such as the Internet. Experiment with this by examining the Duration column in the Software Metering Summary window.

Using SMS as a Help Desk Tool

SMS includes Help Desk and Diagnostics utilities that give you the ability to monitor and control certain remote clients. The Help Desk utilities provide direct access to a client and the Diagnostics utilities enable you to view a remote client's current configuration.

Remote Control Use

If you are viewing the computer properties of a Windows-based client and have already enabled the remote control features on the client, you can start working with the remote features of SMS. SMS provides a series of Help Desk utilities to enable administrators to troubleshoot user problems. As you explore the Collections node and view the list of available computers (clients) the Remote Tools option may be used for Help Desk and Diagnostics. Each feature detects whether or not the computer is running and then starts the Remote Tools.

The Help Desk option allows you to troubleshoot and support individual computers remotely. From a central location at the SMS administration console, you can take control of a remote Windows-based or Windows NT 4.0-based computer, or access the Windows NT 4.0 Workstation and Windows NT Server 4.0 management tools to perform management tasks. This can all be achieved across a LAN or WAN. You can:

- Check the memory map, the status of interrupts, and other operating system parameters
- Guide the user through a difficult task or perform the task directly, with or without the user being present
- Remotely execute commands
- Restart the computer
- Transfer files and install software

Client Computers Preparation for Remote Control

Client computers using Windows run a Terminate and Stay Resident (TSR) that is the remote control agent. The user at the client can set options for what kind of remote control is allowed. On Windows NT 4.0-based computers, the remote control agent is a service installed by SMS when the client is

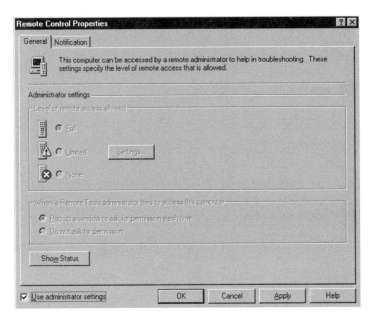

Figure 9.9   *Help Desk Options Dialog Box.*

first set up. Since it is still new to SMS 2.0, this part of the chapter demonstrates Windows NT 4.0 remote control.

Windows NT 4.0 Remote Control Configuration at the Client

For security reasons, the user may want to disable remote control before the administrator can take control of the computer. The process of disabling the security features is as follows:

1. At the client machine, log on to the network.
2. In the SMS Client control panel, start Remote Tools icon as shown in Figure 9.9.
3. Select all available check boxes.
4. Select Save As Default and Save As Current, and then choose Exit.

Accessing the Client Remotely

If you are currently running the demonstration database, restart SMS to remotely access a client. The demonstration database (SMSDemo) is designed to give you an example of SMS sites, and these are simulations of real computers. When you restart SMS, and choose the real database (SMS)

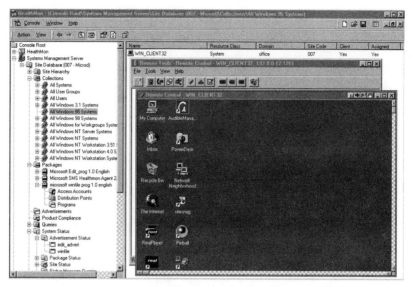

Figure 9.10 *Remote Windows Viewer.*

you can perform these operations or real, previously-inventoried computers. To remotely access the client from the SMS administrator, follow these steps:

1. Select site and expand node.
2. Select Collections node and expand node (Choose Collection type).
3. Select the client on right pane.
4. Right click on selected client and run Remote Tools.

The Remote Windows Viewer appears with several options, displaying the desktop of the remote client, as shown in Figure 9.10.

The site server has shared control with the client during the remote control session. If you move the mouse at the site server, the mouse pointer moves on the remote client. Likewise, either you or the user at the client computer can enter text with the keyboard. You also can use the remote control features to run an application on the client computer from the SMS console.

By remotely accessing the client, it is possible to take full control and work on the client computer just as if you were there. The cost savings are obvious. These features can work across X.25, ISDN, or standard asynchronous phone lines, as well as any normal routed network.

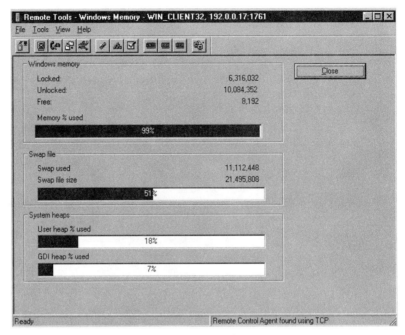

Figure 9.11 *Client Computers Properties.*

Once you have worked with the remote control feature, try some of the other features of the Help Desk option, such as File Transfer or Remote Execute. In addition to Help Desk, there are a number of tools available using the Diagnostics option. Figure 9.11 shows the amount of Windows Memory available on a Windows-based computer. These tools provide the ideal solution for help desk operators by enabling them to resolve problems from one central location, thus minimizing the need to physically visit the computers.

Remote Chat Utility

The Remote Chat utility enables you to communicate with a user at a client computer. When the chat session is started, a Remote Chat window appears on the SMS Administrator computer and on the selected client. Whatever is typed in the Local User box of either computer displays in the other computer's Remote User box. If you have inventoried client computers on your existing network, initiate a Remote Chat session from the site server by following these steps:

1. Open the Sites window.
2. Select the client.

3. From the File menu, choose Properties.
4. In the Groups (left) pane, choose the Help Desk icon.
5. In the right pane, choose Remote Chat.

When the Remote Chat session is successfully established, the Remote Chat window displays on each computer.

Network Monitor

The SMS Network Monitor allows you to analyze network traffic and pinpoint problems or potential bottlenecks. With Network Monitor you can:

- Capture frames (also called *packets)* directly from the network
- Capture frames on a remote computer and display the capture statistics on the local computer at intervals that you specify
- Display and filter captured frames
- Edit and transmit captured frames onto the network to test network resources or reproduce network problems

Network Monitor is entirely software-based. The only special hardware you need is a network card that supports *promiscuous* mode with a supporting Network Device/Driver Interface Specification (NDIS) driver.

Promiscuous mode enables the network adaptor card to be directed by a device to pass all frames going over the network to the operating system.

When you want to analyze traffic on a network segment, a *capture agent* puts its network card into promiscuous mode. A capture agent is a program running on a computer attached to the appropriate network segment. The agent makes a duplicate of frames that pass through that computer, stores the frames in a buffer, and sends the session summary statistics to the Network Monitor console (either local or remote) as shown in Figure 9.12. The summary statistics include: graphs of total network utilization and statistics of frames; bytes, broadcasts, and multicasts per second; and statistics for individual computers.

Network Monitor automatically builds an address database of friendly names to help you identify individual stations. You can filter captures based on computer address or address pairs, protocols, or data patterns within the frame. From the Network Monitor console, you can display each of the individual frames captured, including details of the protocols used to send it, and

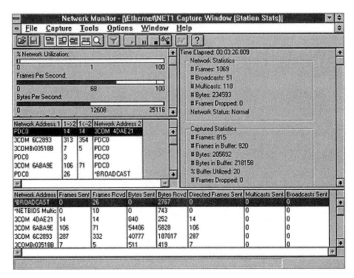

Figure 9.12 *SMS Site Database Tools Network Monitor Window.*

hexadecimal and ASCII representations of the captured data. The frames can also be filtered for display based on address, protocol, or contents.

Network Monitor capture triggers allow you to execute specific programs, or batch files, when the capture agent receives a frame containing a pattern you specify. You can also edit and retransmit frames you have already captured to reproduce network problems or to generate network activity to simulate specific test conditions. SMS includes Network Monitor console and agents for Windows NT 4.0 Workstation, Windows NT Server 4.0, and Windows for Workgroups.

NETWORK MONITOR USE

The following steps demonstrate how to capture and save network frames using Network Monitor:

1. In the SMS Administrator tool, open the Sites window.
2. Expand the tools node window for your site server.
3. Select Network Monitor, as shown in Figure 9.12.
4. Choose Start Network Monitor, as shown in Figure 9.12.

You can capture data from a remote computer by running the Network Monitor Remote Agent.

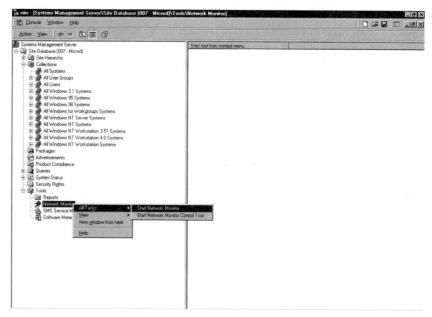

Figure 9.13 *Network Monitor Capture Window.*

TRIGGER SETTING • To set a trigger to stop capture when the buffer is full, select Trigger from the Capture menu in Figure 9.13, and then choose the options shown in Table 9.3.

Table 9.3 *Network Monitor Capture Window Options*

In This Box...	...Select This...
Trigger On	Buffer Space
Buffer Space	100%
Trigger Action</TD> Stop Capture	

Now, choose OK to return to the Network Monitor Capture Window shown in Figure 9.13.

NETWORK BROADCAST FRAMES CAPTURE • Now let's look at how to capture network broadcast frames. From the Capture menu in Figure 9.13, select Start. Network Monitor allocates buffer space for network data and begins capturing frames.

Next, place the cursor anywhere in the 1-->2 column, and click the right mouse button. Select Sort Column. Network Monitor sorts the contents of the Session Statistics window pane by the frames sent.

When the Trigger dialog box appears, stating the specified amount of buffer that has been filled, choose OK. Finally, place the cursor anywhere in the 1<--2 column, click the right mouse button, and select Sort Column. Network Monitor again sorts the frames that were sent. The first address in this list shows the source of the most frames.

CAPTURED DATA DISPLAY • To display the captured data, select Display Captured Data from the Capture menu in Figure 9.13. The Network Monitor Capture Summary window appears, displaying a summary record of all frames captured.

CAPTURED DATA HIGHLIGHTING • With the following steps, you can change the color of all NetBIOS protocol frames. This is useful in selecting frames of a particular protocol for viewing.

1. From the Display menu, select Colors.
2. Under Name, select NetBIOS.
3. Under Colors, set Foreground to Green.
4. Choose OK.

CAPTURED DATA FILTERING • To create a display filter to view only the frames that represent the conversation between your two servers, perform the following steps:

1. From the Display menu, select Filter.
2. Select the ANY<-->ANY line.
3. Under Edit, select the Expression button.
4. Under *ANY <--> *ANY, select the Address tab.
5. Under Station 1, select the primary site server name.
6. Under Station 2, select the secondary site server name.
7. Choose the OK button to return to the Display Filter dialog box.
8. Choose the OK button. The Network Monitor Capture Summary window appears, displaying all frames in the conversation between your primary and secondary site servers.

REMOTE WINDOWS NT 4.0-BASED COMPUTER CAPTURED DATA • Finally, to capture data from a remote Windows NT 4.0-based computer, first be sure the Network Monitor Agent is installed and started on the remote Windows NT 4.0-based computer.

On the site server, switch to the Network Monitor application. From the Capture menu, select Networks. Then select the line containing the node name REMOTE, and choose OK.

The Connect to Network Monitoring Agent dialog box appears. In the Agent Name box, type the name of the remote computer on which you

You can start the Network Monitor Agent by choosing the Services option in the Control Panel on the local server, selecting the Network Monitor Agent, and choosing Start.

started the Remote Agent service, and choose Connect. Network Monitor attempts to connect to the remote computer. A Select Agent Network Card might appear if the remote computer contains multiple network cards. If this happens, select any of the cards and choose OK.

Network Monitor allocates buffer space, and the Capture window appears. From the Capture menu, choose Display Captured Data. Capture a number of frames and choose Stop. Now, from the Capture menu, choose Display Captured Data, and then choose Networks. Finally, select the line containing the name of the remote computer, and choose Disconnect.

For more information on SMS's Help Desk and Diagnostics utilities, see Chapter 13.

■ Summary

You should come away from this chapter with an in-depth knowledge of the MCSE exam-specific SMS configuration, audit and control network client components needed to install, configure, and manage SMS resources. With that in mind, the first part of the chapter discussed the problems associated with simply determining the number of personal computers that exist in a large distributed enterprise, and then detecting all of the hardware and software in each computer. For every computer within your enterprise, SMS automatically retrieves detailed information about both the hardware and software. It also stores the information in a standard SQL Server database. With popular desktop applications, such as Microsoft Access or Lotus 1-2-3, you can select, sort, and view the data, or you can extract the data and create custom reports and graphs. Maintenance, service tracking, and planning your upgrades are a few of the business benefits.

The second part of the chapter examines tools to track software usage by user, group, workstation, time, or license quota. SMS 2.0 provides new tools to analyze, monitor, and control the use of applications on servers and workstations. Ranging from simple alerts to actively preventing applications from running, the administrator has many levels of control. Control can be exercised over applications with quota limits and over applications specifically disallowed by the administrator. Any application (.exe, .com, etc.) on any client or server can be monitored for compliance.

The third part of the chapter explores SMS's inclusion of Help Desk and Diagnostics utilities. These utilities monitor and control certain remote clients. The Diagnostics utilities allow you to view a remote client's current configuration, while the Help Desk utilities provide direct access to a client.

▲ CHAPTER REVIEW QUESTIONS

▲ True/False

1. *True or False? The intervals for checking hardware and software can be set independently of one another, which means that you can check for hardware inventory once a day and check for software inventory once a week.*

2. *True or False? For SMS 2.0 there is a 16-minute delay after the installation of the hardware inventory agent before inventory is collected.*

3. *True or False? For SMS 2.0 there is a 31–minute delay after the installation of the software inventory agent before inventory is collected.*

4. *True or False? Hardware inventory is not based on the Common Information Model in SMS 2.0.*

5. *True or False? To deliver better software inventory, SMS 2.0 searches for version resource information on every executable on the client machine, rather than checking against a predefined database.*

6. *True or False? The inventory information uses a software inventory on the MIF file that was created by the Desktop Management Task Force (DMTF).*

7. *True or False? A Hardware Inventory Processor runs on each primary site server, and enters the collected data into the SMS database. Once client inventory has been deleted from the SMS database, Resource Explorer or queries can be used to view inventory for any client. SMS maintains an inventory history for each client computer. Inventory history can help you diagnose problems at clients by enabling you to view the inventory data and the configuration changes to individual computers.*

8. *True or False? By default, licenses added to a site are not balanced to a server for 14 days to allow monitoring of applications to do trend analysis. At the*

end of this trend analysis period, licenses are balanced to the software metering servers that need them. You can disable the trend analysis by canceling 'Do not enforce the license limits for this product until a trend has been calculated.' With this canceled, the server does license balancing only after a request has been made for a license. To force this balancing, you need to run the application on the client and receive a denial.

9. *True or False? Software metering can also control software use based on time of day. For example, a corporation may want to disable game-playing during business hours.*

10. *True or False? A report wizard is not included to help you query the software metering database for information about the usage and attempted usage of each metered application.*

11. *True or False? When you want to analyze traffic on a network segment, a capture agent puts its network card into promiscuous mode. The agent makes a duplicate of frames that pass through that computer, stores the frames in a buffer, and sends the session summary statistics to the Network Monitor console. The summary statistics include: generated graphs of the total network utilization and statistics of frames; bytes, broadcasts, and multicasts per second; and statistics for individual computers.*

12. *True or False? You should diagnose and resolve installation problems involving the secondary site server.*

13. *True or False? In the inventory collection process, the first time a client computer runs RUNSMS.BAT, or logs on to the network in the case of automatic inventory collection, SMS deinstalls an Inventory Agent program on the computer. The Inventory Agent builds a binary inventory report and graphs of the hardware and software configuration of the computer. From then on, at an interval set by the administrator, the Inventory Agent inspects the computer for inventory information.*

14. *True or False? You can use SMS query tools to search the database for a variety of criteria. You can identify an individual computer or a specific component or property of that computer, such as installed software or the network address of the network adapter. Most queries are run against the Personal Computer architecture, although other architectures are searched for items such as the location of software packages, or SNMP integration Traps.*

▲ Multiple Choice

1. *To view the client hardware inventory using SMS Administrator, navigate to the hardware inventory information, and choose the following in numeric order as each option comes up except:*
   A. SMS Network Monitor
   B. SMS
   C. Site Database (<name>)
   D. Collections
   E. All Systems

2. *To view the client software inventory using SMS Administrator, navigate to the software inventory information and choose the following in numeric order as each option comes up except:*
   A. SMS
   B. Site Database (<name>)
   C. Collections
   D. SMS Network Monitor
   E. All Systems

3. *Once you have a database that contains compliance details, find out if you have Y2K compliance issues in your network. SMS does a comparison of this compliance data with information obtained from the software inventory scan. Navigate to the Queries node by choosing the following in numeric order as each option comes up except:*
   A. SMS
   B. Site Database (<name>)
   C. SMS Sender Manager
   D. Queries
   E. Y2K Noncompliant Software on Systems by Version

4. *To configure the software metering component for SMS 2.0, first define which of your servers is to be the software metering server. Navigate to the site server, and choose the following in numeric order as each option comes up except:*
   A. SMS
   B. Site Database (<name>)
   C. SMS Security Manager
   D. Site Hierarchy
   E. Site Systems

▲ Open Ended

1. Client agents collect an inventory of the hardware on the client and store the results on the client. This information is passed through a Client Access Point to the site database. Over 200 properties are collected and reported using reports and graphs, including details such as...

2. Create a query to determine which clients have enough RAM to be upgraded to Windows NT 4.0 stating that the operating system is Windows for Workgroups or MS-DOS and the total physical memory is equal to or greater than 27175.

Managing the SMS System Model

Managing clients using SMS requires agent components running on client systems. SMS version 2.0 has been designed to provide the flexibility to specifically decide which management tools should run on each system—you can just do software distribution without doing inventory or metering, for example.

To install the specific components installed requires finding the systems, installing the agent on the system, and enabling components of the agent. The first section of this chapter discusses discovery and installation. The second section of the chapter explains how to enable the agent and perform management tasks through the distribution and installation of software.

SMS 2.0 is not limited to discovering only personal computers. Many new discovery mechanisms are available to allow you to discover a wide range of different types of resources.

Finally, the last section of the chapter shows how to go about creating database reports and

325

explains how view the SMS database by using utilities like Crystal Reports rather than the SMS Administrator Console.

MCSE 10.1 SMS Network Architecture

In SMS 2.0, you can manage resources that include the hardware, Windows NT 4.0 user groups, and Windows NT 4.0 user accounts. Hardware resources include personal computers, servers, and network devices such as routers. Resources are discovered on your network according to their types. Different discovery methods are provided for the different resource types.

SMS discovers all resources throughout your network; it is not restricted to the site boundaries you define. The location of each resource is compared to the site boundaries you have set and the resource is assigned to the appropriate site or sites. Discovery mechanisms for SMS 2.0 include:

- Heartbeat Discovery
- Netware Bindery Server Logon Discovery
- Netware NDS Logon Discovery
- Network Discovery
- Windows Networking Logon Discovery
- Windows Networking User Account Discovery
- Windows Networking User Group Discovery

Other discovery mechanisms, such as using Active Directory, will be added in the future. For now, resource discovery methods are enabled, disabled, and configured under Discovery Methods in the SMS console tree. To navigate to this node, click on the following options in sequence:

1. SMS
2. Site Database (<name>)
3. Site Hierarchy
4. Discovery Methods

Use the Windows Networking Logon Discovery mechanism in this exercise. Before configuring it on the administrator console, ensure that there is a client machine to be discovered, and that the client machine you want to manage for the rest of these exercises is configured to allow discovery.

Create a user account for the client machine, or verify that there is a user account for this domain already available. This must be completed so that the administrator console changes we make are applied to all accounts.

In these exercises, assume that the client is a Windows NT 4.0 Workstation, but it could also be running Windows 95, Windows 98, or Windows for Workstations.

User Account Creation

You need to start User Manager for Domains and create a user account with the parameters shown in Table 10.1.

Table 10.1 *User Account Parameters*

For This Configuration Parameter...	...Use This...
Username	<choose a name>
Password	<choose a password>
User Must Change Password at Next Logon	Click to clear this check box
Domain membership	Domain Users

Once this user is in place, return to the administrator console and perform the following steps:

1. Expand the site node, click Discovery Methods.
2. In the Results window, click Windows Networking Logon Discovery, and then click Properties on the Action menu. The dialog box displays General settings for Windows Networking Logon Discovery.
3. Verify that Enable Windows Networking Logon Discovery is selected. Notice your local domain is configured automatically to use the Windows networking logon discovery method.
4. Click the Logon Settings tab.
5. Click to select Modify user logon scripts.
6. Click OK.

Agent on the Client Installation

Navigate to the area where you can install the Agent on the Client by clicking on the following options in sequence:

1. SMS
2. Site Database (<name>)
3. Site Hierarchy
4. Client Installation Methods

Now, SMS client software can be installed by any of these methods:

- Windows networking logon client installation
- Windows NT 4.0 remote client installation
- Manual NT client installation
- NetWare Bindery server logon client installation
- NetWare NDS logon client installation
- Manual NetWare NDS network connection client installation
- Manual NetWare Bindery connection client installation

INSTALLING THE WINDOWS NETWORKING LOGON CLIENT

When a computer within the site boundaries logs on to the Windows-based network, SMS installs the client software on that computer.

INSTALLING THE WINDOWS NT 4.0 REMOTE CLIENT

SMS client software is installed automatically on Windows NT 4.0 computers within the site boundaries. The Windows NT 4.0 computers need to be turned on and connected to the network. It is not necessary for anyone to be logged on to these computers.

INSTALLING THE MANUAL WINDOWS NETWORKING NETWORK CONNECTION CLIENT

The user must explicitly connect to a file on a Windows NT 4.0 logon point to install the SMS client software. This method provides for those cases where no logon script is used.

INSTALLING THE NETWARE BINDERY SERVER LOGON CLIENT

When a computer logs on to a NetWare bindery server, SMS installs the client software on that computer.

INSTALLING THE NETWARE NDS LOGON CLIENT

When a computer within the site boundaries logs on to the NetWare NDS context, SMS installs the client software on that computer.

INSTALLING THE MANUAL NETWARE NDS NETWORK CONNECTION CLIENT

The user must explicitly connect to a file on a NetWare NDS logon point to install SMS client software.

INSTALLING THE MANUAL NETWARE BINDERY CONNECTION CLIENT

The user must explicitly connect to a file on a NetWare Bindery logon server to install SMS client software. You can use more than one installation method. For example, let's use the Windows networking logon client installation mechanism in this exercise. Because the logon script has already been defined in the discovery process, there is nothing further to do. Other client setup methods require further configuration at this level. In the next procedure, verify that the account created earlier is ready to be used:

1. Start User Manager for Domains, and click the account you created.
2. On the User menu, click Properties.
3. The User Properties dialog box appears. Click Profile. The User Environment Profile dialog box appears. Notice that smsls has been added as the Logon Script Name.
4. Exit User Manager for Domains.

Client Computer Addition to the Site

In this exercise, add your client computer to your SMS site. Next, restart your client computer. Log onto your computer as the new account you created. A command prompt appears briefly as the SMS client software discovery and installation begins. This process is completed in stages, and even though the window is removed, the discovery and installation processes still execute for a few moments. In the next procedure, view the properties of the newly added SMS client.

Viewing the Properties of the Client

To navigate to where you can view the properties of the client, click on the following options in sequence:

1. SMS
2. Site Database (<name>)
3. Collections
4. All Systems

Now, you can view the properties of the client by performing these steps:

1. On the Action menu, click all Tasks. A new menu appears.
2. Click update Collection.
3. The All Systems collection is refreshed, and the client computer appears as a member along with the site server.
4. In the Results window, click the client, and then click Properties on the Action menu. The Properties dialog box displays the general settings for the client computer. Notice under Discovery data, all the discovered properties of the client are displayed.
5. Click Close.

While examining collections, it is worth looking at the results of other discovery processes. For example, investigate the resource information available under the following collections: All Users and All User Groups.

MCSE 10.2 Software Distribution Management

One of the most common management tasks that needs to be automated is the installation and upgrading of software. Distribution of the software can be based on any inventory information that SMS gathers. This means that you can clearly identify computers that need to have new software installed.

Software distribution involves creating a package. In a package you define the files that comprise the software application to be distributed and define package configuration and identification information. For your convenience, SMS provides package definition files (PDFs) for a number of popular Microsoft applications and operating systems. Each PDF has its package configuration and identification information already defined. You simply import the file to your new package. Once the package has been created, you generate an advertisement (job) to distribute and install the package on clients.

When a user at a client logs on to the network, the Advertisement Manager (installed when the client was added to the database) checks to see if there are any software installation advertisements (jobs) intended for that computer. If there are, Advertisement Manager follows the installation instructions specified in the job.

By using Advertisement Manager, the user at the client can select and schedule any optional packages to be installed. Advertisement Manager automatically installs mandatory packages for which the install time has been reached. Alternatively, if the advertisement (job) was configured for unattended, mandatory installation, the software can be installed when the computer is unattended—overnight, for instance.

Installation Capabilities and Software Distribution Use

The software distribution and installation features of SMS allow you to distribute and install software on clients, copy files to them, or enable them to run commands or programs as shown in Table 10.2.

Table 10.2 *SMS Software Distribution and Installation Features*

	Task	Feature
Distributing and Installing Software	Use SMS to identify the computers to which you wish to distribute the software, and then install the software.	Queries, Package, Run Command On Advertisement (job)
Viewing the Status of a Software Distribution/Installation Job	Identify, for example, whether the Advertisement (job) is pending, active, complete, or has failed.	Advertisement (job) Status, Advertisement (job) Details

SOFTWARE DISTRIBUTION AND INSTALLATION

The following procedure describes how to distribute and install Microsoft Office 97 on Windows 95 clients, and it involves theses steps:

- Creating a source directory to store the application.
- Running a query to identify clients that have the correct criteria.
- Creating a package (using a supplied PDF) to distribute the software.
- Creating an advertisement (job) to install on the Windows clients.

CREATING A SOURCE DIRECTORY • The source directory is not the location from which the client will install the software, the client will use distribution point servers. Therefore, to create a source directory to store Office 97, you must perform the following tasks:

1. On a site server, create a source directory for the application, and share the directory with the same name, such as \\servername\OFFICE97. The server on which you create the source directory does not have to be running SMS as long as the SMS Service Account has access to that server. Each application to distribute must have its own directory.
2. On the same server, create the directory for the embedded applications and share the directory with the same name, such as \\servername\MSAPPS32.
3. Connect to these shares. For instance, type net use \\servername\OFFICE97 and net use \\servername\MSAPPS32.
4. Insert disk 1 or the CD for Microsoft Office 97.

5. Click Start and select Run. The Run dialog box appears.
6. In the Open box, type x:\setup /a where x is the drive containing the Office 97 disk.
7. When prompted, enter the location of the two directories you created.
8. Complete the Setup program.

> The source directory is used by SMS to distribute the SMS package to distribution servers.

CREATING A QUERY • For the purposes of this procedure, the next section describes how to use a query that identifies all computers currently running Windows 95 that have at least 16 MB of RAM. From the SMS Administrator toolbar shown in Figure 10.1, follow these steps:

1. Expand Sites Node.
2. Choose Query Node and expand.

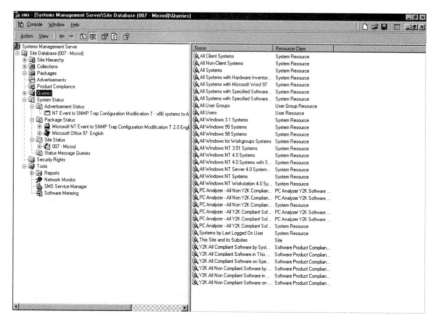

Figure 10.1 *SMS Administrator Screen.*

3. Look for a predefined query with (all Windows 95) right click to run query or click properties to edit.

4. Select Query and right click on properties to edit (we need to add an additional criteria (> 16 MB RAM).

The Query Properties dialog box appears as shown in Figure 10.2. There are many predefined queries to choose as shown in list on Figure 10.1 Since we need to edit this query for additional requirements, using the properties dialog will help us make all necessary changes. The Query Expression

Once inside the properties dialog box (General tab) we can change the name or add additional comments to help us identify this query for later use. Click on the Edit Query Statement button to modify results and expressions to be viewed on our SMS window pane. The Query Properties dialog box appears with the expression displayed as shown in Figure 10.3. Choose the asterisk to add an additional expression (equal to or greater than 16000 KB). The Query Criterion Expression Properties dialog box appears as shown in Figure 10.4. Select the values shown in Table 10.3.

Once the above expression is complete click OK and the Query Properties dialog box reappears with both expressions displayed as shown in Figure 10.3.

Next, choose OK. The query is displayed in the Queries window. You now need to create a package that defines the software to be distributed, and

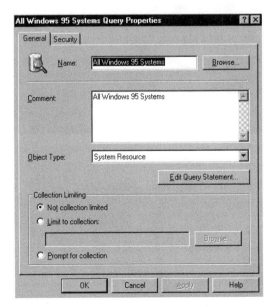

Figure 10.2 *Query Properties Dialog Box.*

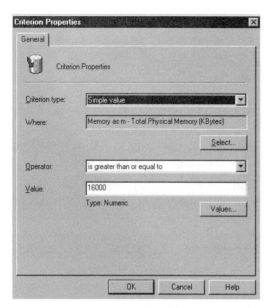

Figure 10.3 *General Tab of the Query Properties Dialog Box.*

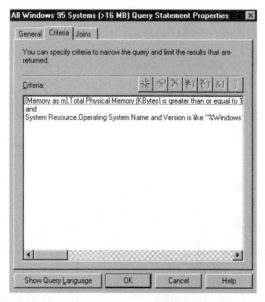

Figure 10.4 *Query Criterion Expression Properties Dialog Box.*

Table 10.3 *Adding Query Expression Properties*

Type	Where	Operator	Value
Simple Value	Memory as m-Total Physical Memory (KB)	is greater than or equal to	16000 **Type:** Numeric

then create the advertisement (job) that will include the query to install the software.

CREATING A PACKAGE • SMS 2.0 packages specify information about the software, the location of source files, the distribution points that will be used to distribute the software, and similar information.

Administrators can create distribution points (additional servers) for packages. Distribution points are the locations accessed by clients to obtain the files in the packages. The server or share designated as a distribution point must have sufficient disk space for all the files that will be stored on it and must be assigned the role of distribution point. SMS client software can use any of the distribution points at a site that the client can access. You can configure rules (criteria) for clients to use when connecting to site systems. For example, you can provide a specific list of distribution points to contact or allow random selection from available distribution points. If the client is already connected to a distribution point when it is ready to run an advertised program, it will use that distribution point.

Package properties include the software name and version, the location of the package source directory, and group permissions for the distribution folder. Packages are typically used to distribute software to SMS clients. A package defines the files and instructions for distributing, installing, and running software. Once you create a package, you can create one or more programs for the package.

To create a package from the SMS Administrator toolbar, perform the following steps highlighted in Figure 10.5:

1. First make sure to run a collection and see if client is available (Collection node).
2. Open Packages node .
3. Right click to choose new package or package from definition. If you Click on Package from definition (as shown on Figure 10.6), a wizard should start.

   If you choose New then the Package Properties dialog box appears as shown in Figure 10.7, and has the fields and buttons shown in Table 10.4.
4. You can also choose to Package from definition as shown in Figure 10.6. followed by a wizard as shown on Figure 10.7.

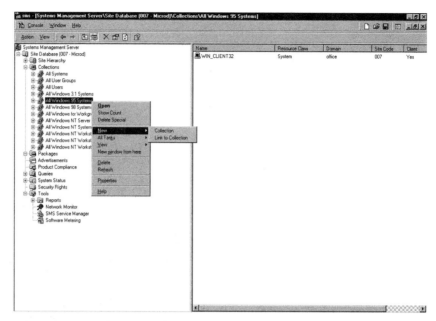

Figure 10.5 *Administrator Console and Collection Node.*

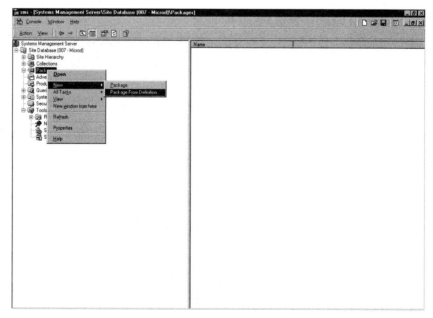

Figure 10.6 *Choosing a New Package or Package from Definition.*

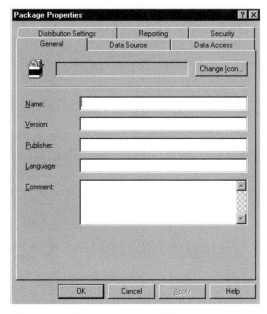

Figure 10.7   *New Package Wizard.*

 Before you create a package, check that the site servers at the sending and receiving sites have enough space to store package source files as well as to compress and decompress them.

Table 10.4 *Package Properties Dialog Box Elements and Description*

Element	Description
Name	The name of the package, up to 50 characters. This field is required.
Version	The version number of the software package, up to 32 characters.
Publisher	The name of the software publisher, up to 32 characters.
Language	The language version of the software, up to 32 characters.
Comment	Optional text about the package, such as a description. You can use up to 127 characters.

Follow the wizard and choose the predefined package definition for Office 97 then click next to specify that the package always contains files from a source location. Next you need to specify the source directory for Office 97. Choose Workstations. The Setup Package for Workstations dialog box appears. In the Source Directory box, type the location of the software, such as \\servername\OFFICE97.

If the directory is on the site server, you can type a local path. If the directory is on another server, type the Universal Naming Convention (UNC) path, such as \\servername\sharename. If the source directory is in a NetWare volume, type the server name, volume, and directory.

In the Command Lines box, select Typical as the type of installation to view the Typical command, and then choose Close when you're finished viewing the command.

The Command Lines box specifies the instructions for running of the package. A command line can be used to install a package by running a script or starting an application's Setup program. In this example, it runs the Office 97 Setup program for a typical installation. For the purposes of this example, the fields are completed using information from the supplied PDF. If you were creating this package from scratch, you would need to create one or more command lines.

Next, choose OK to close all open dialog boxes. Then, choose OK when prompted for confirmation to update sites. The new package is available now for distribution.

CREATING AN ADVERTISEMENT (JOB) • Advertisements are very important new feature of SMS 2.0. Programs that are available for distribution are advertised to clients. Advertisements make a program available to a collection and, optionally, its collections. Advertisements specify which collection will receive each program and the date and time when the software will be available to run on clients. You can assign an advertisement (make it mandatory) from the moment it is advertised or set it to be assigned after a specified date or time. You can also set an expiration date after which the advertisement will no longer be available. This section explains how to create an advertisement (job) and distribute a package to the appropriate clients. To create an advertisement (job) from the SMS Administrator console perform the following steps (see Figure 10.8):

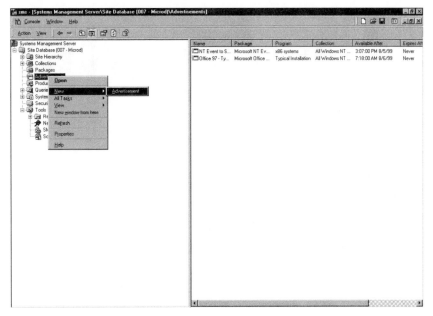

Figure 10.8 *Advertisements in the Administrators Console.*

1. Expand Queries Node.
2. In the Queries window, make sure that the clients based on your criteria are visible.
3. Click on advertisements node, then right-click and choose new advertisement.

The advertisement properties window will appear as in Figure 10.9 in an advertisement you specify:

- The package and program to run on the client
- The target collection
- The schedule of when the program is available to clients
- When or whet her the program is assigned (mandatory)

Each client that meets the criteria for the collection you specify will receive the advertisement. Because collection memberships are evaluated dynamically, new computers and new users automatically receive advertisements for programs if they meet the criteria for a collection to which the software has been advertised. Also, users that no longer meet the criteria may have programs removed from their system.

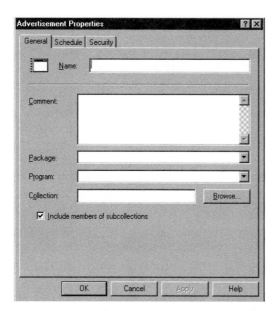

Figure 10.9 *Advertisements Properties Dialog Box.*

SMS ensures that everything required to respond to an advertisement is available on the distribution points. If the package referred to by an advertisement is not already on a distribution point at a child site, SMS sends a compressed package to that distribution point.

When you are ready to make a program in a package available to clients, you advertise the program to a target collection. SMS uses collections to determine which clients receive an advertisement for a program.

The advertisement (job) will be carried out at the times you specify. Package installation instructions for each client are placed at a collection point, and the package source directory is placed on servers and made available to the clients.

INSTALLING THE PACKAGE • If the software application package was configured for unattended installation, the installation does not require any user input. For some packages, the user at the client needs to run the package once it has arrived and Setup completes the installation with no input required from the user.

If you chose the Custom command when you created the job, the user is prompted for setup information. This is accomplished through the Package Command Manager under SMS Client.

To install the package on the client, perform the following steps:

1. At the client, click Start, select Settings, Control Panel: Advertisements Monitor.
2. Select the package and Execute. The application will start to install (for example Office 97 upgrade).

On completion, test the installation at the client by running the application.

CHECKING THE ADVERTISEMENTS (JOB) STATUS • To check the status of an advertisements (job) from the SMS Administrator, perform the following steps (Figure 10.10):

1. Choose system status node.
2. Expand node and choose advertisements.

The Advertisements (job) window appears as shown in Figure 10.11. It might take a few minutes for SMS to update the job status. You can choose Refresh the Jobs Status window at any time.

When the Advertisements (job) status appears, the advertisement can be checked for all types of messages. Now, let's examine the use of software distribution, installation and inventory in closer detail.

Using Software Distribution in SMS 2.0

As mentioned earlier in the chapter, for software distribution first create a package that contains the original copy of the software being distributed, plus instructions for installing the software on remote computers. Second, create a job telling the system where to send the package and when to send it. SMS can distribute packages to each site over any LAN or WAN protocol supported by Windows NT Server 4.0 (such as TCP/IP or IPX), over an SNA backbone, or over standard serial lines (including ISDN or X.25).

Third, the package is compressed before being sent to the target site, thus reducing the amount of traffic on the network as the package is passed through the hierarchy. SMS 2.0 also manages error detection and correction over the WAN. If the distribution requires more time than is available on the link you have specified between sites, SMS distributes segments of the package sequentially when the WAN is available.

Finally, when the target site server receives the package, it places it on one or more distribution servers, and places the installation instructions for the target computers on the appropriate logon servers. These instructions are then picked up by the client computers at logon time or at a given interval if the user has already logged on.

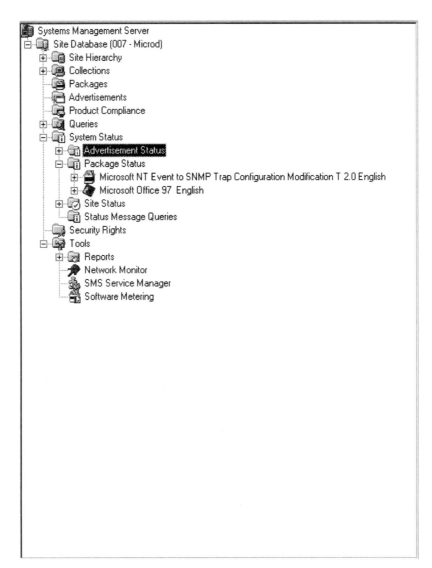

Figure 10.10 *Administrator Console and System Status Node.*

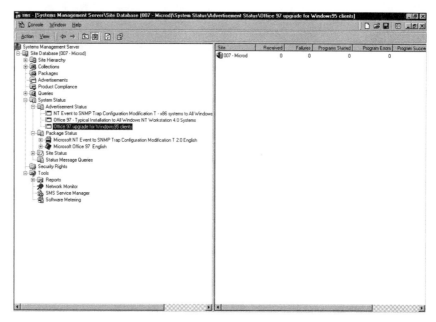

Figure 10.11   *Advertisement Status Window.*

These distribution tasks are common for all types of packages. It is in the second stage, the installation phase, that the system starts to differentiate the different types of packages, based on the properties defined by the administrator: Workstation, Sharing, or Inventory. Let's take a quick look at packages and jobs.

Packages

The object that defines the software to SMS 2.0 is a package. Remember, SMS uses packages to store information about software so that the software can be identified, installed on clients, shared from servers, or inventoried. When you create a package, you define the files that comprise the software, as well as the package's configuration and identification information. After you create a package, use SMS to install the package on clients, share the package so that it can be run from network servers, or maintain inventory on the package. You can create packages for commercial applications, applications you have developed, and data files. All the information about the software makes up the package properties. The properties you define are determined by how the package will be used.

A PDF is a text file that contains predefined Workstation, Sharing, and Inventory property settings for a package. When you create a new package, you can use the Import command from the Package Properties dialog box and use a PDF to define the properties for that package. SMS includes PDFs for some of the more popular applications, such as Microsoft Excel and Word. Other software developers are also creating PDFs.

ADVERTISEMENTS (JOBS)

Advertisements make a program available to a collection and, optionally, its collections. Advertisements specify which collection will receive each program and the date and time when the software will be available to run on clients. You can assign an advertisement (make it mandatory) from the moment it is advertised or set it to be assigned after a specified date or time. You can also set an expiration date after which the advertisement will no longer be available.

CREATING PACKAGES AND ADVERTISEMENTS (JOBS)

This part of the chapter demonstrates additional information on how to create the package and advertisements (job) pairs for distributing software. If you are currently running the demonstration database, restart SMS 2.0 to create real packages to distribute. The demonstration database (SMSDemo) is designed to give you an example of SMS sites. When you restart SMS 2.0, and choose the real database (SMS), you will be able to perform these operations.

CREATING A PACKAGE • The following shows you how to install Microsoft Word 97. The same process can be used for any application simply by substituting a different PDF file. So, to create a package to be installed on a workstation, perform the following steps:

1. Open the Packages Window in the SMS Administrator.
2. From the File menu, select New.
3. Choose Import to import a PDF file used to define the package.
4. Select the ENU directory then select WWD60C.PDF, and choose OK.
5. Choose Workstations.
6. In the Source Directory box, enter the location where the word installation files are stored—\\server\MSWORD, in our example. Close the dialog box.
7. Choose Inventory. You will notice that the PDF file has already defined rules to detect if the package has already been created on the computer.

8. Select OK to create the package.

9. A message box appears indicating that SMS will update this package at all sites. Click OK.

CREATING THE ADVERTISEMENT • Now, let's look at how to create the advertisement job to distribute the package to workstations. The steps for distributing the package to any number of workstations are listed as follows:

1. On the SMS Administrator, expand the advertisement node.

2. Right-click and choose new advertisement as shown in Figure 10.12.

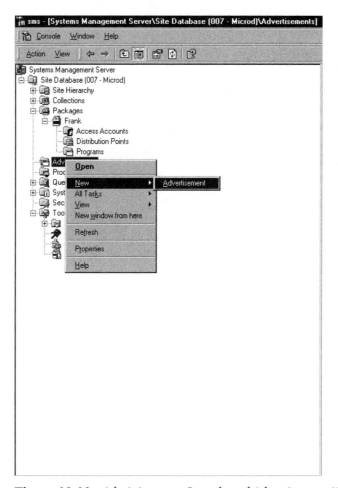

Figure 10.12 *Administrators Console and Advertisement Node.*

3. The Advertisement properties dialog appears as shown back in Figure 10.9.
4. Once completed choose OK to create the advertisement (job) and has the fields and buttons shown in Table 10.5.

Table 10.5 *Advertisement Properties Dialog Box Elements and Description*

Element	Description
Name	The name of the advertisement, up to 50 characters. This field is required.
Comment	Optional text about the advertisement, such as a description. You can use up to 127 characters.
Package	The package that contains the program that will be advertised to clients. This field is required.
Program	The program (within the specified package) to advertise to clients. This field is required.
Collection	The existing collection that will receive the advertisement. This field is required. *Note*: SMS will not advertise a program to 16-bit clients based on user groups or user accounts, but this is supported for 32-bit clients.

The Advertisement (job) is processed as soon as the Scheduler service checks on pending Advertisement (job). It is also possible to check the status of the job and where it is in its distribution cycle at all times. Once the Sending Status is Complete, the client can begin to install the software.

Using Software Installation in SMS 2.0

When a new advertised program is made available at a client, the user can use the Advertised Programs Monitor to reschedule the program or to run it immediately. If they choose to run it immediately, a wizard walks the user through the installation steps.

To run the advertised program the user at the client can do one of the following:

- Double-click the New Advertised Programs Available icon.
- Right-click the icon and choose the Run Advertised Program Wizard from the popup menu.
- Access the Advertised Programs icon from the Control Panel.

In addition, the user at the client can use the Advertised Programs Monitor (available in the same locations) to perform the following tasks:

- Monitor program run status
- Change configuration options for advertised programs
- View advertised program properties

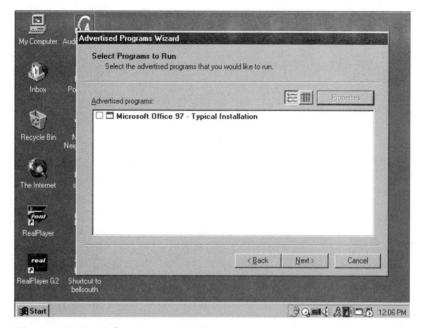

Figure 10.13 *Advertisement on clients computer.*

The process of installing the application is easy. If the administrator has configured the package for unattended installation, the installation will not require any user input. If installation requires client attention then a windows will appear at the target computer, the user can begin the installation by selecting the advertisement and following the wizard as shown in Figure 10.13. Next, the user selects the package and chooses Execute. If the package is mandatory, they just wait for the automatic start time.

For example a Word 97 Setup window can appear and execute automatically. Word for Windows will be installed on the drive with the most free space. When it is complete, the Word for Windows program group appears. To test the installation, start Word.

Using Software Inventory in SMS 2.0

As previously mentioned, SMS 2.0 can also collect software inventory. Two types of software inventory information are collected by SMS: detailed identification and comprehensive audit. As with hardware inventory, both types of software information are processed by the Inventory Agent program and loaded into the database.

While doing software inventory, SMS can also collect files. For instance, it can collect copies of the computer's configuration files—such as `config.sys`, `autoexec.bat`, or `win.ini`—and add them to an archive. If a problem later occurs on a computer, a technician can review the files in the archive to see if a change in a configuration file might have caused the problem and can replace corrupted files.

DETAILED ID

Detailed identification inventory looks for a particular set of files. For instance, if an accounting system requires a particular set of `.EXE` and `.DLL` files, detailed identification inventory can verify that all the required files are present and are valid versions. If you want to upgrade to the new version of an application, this type of inventory can tell you how many copies to buy and where to distribute them.

To gather this information, configure the Software Client Inventory Agent under the Client Agent settings that identifies the files you need to find. You can easily browse for and retrieve specific information to identify a file, such as the size, date, checksum, and other attributes. This information is then saved in the database.

Using this information, the Inventory Agent inspects a computer's hard disk(s) for any files that match the parameters that you have specified. The Inventory Agent then records all matches, and includes this information in the inventory for each computer that had a match.

COMPREHENSIVE AUDIT

A comprehensive audit is used to find out what applications are installed on networked computers. In this type of inventory, SMS 2.0 checks the files on the computer's disk against a list of applications that can be predefined in the Software Client Inventory Agent properties dialog. These Auditing tools and related files are installed, during SMS Setup, as part of the `SCRIPTS` component.

SMS 2.0 Software Distribution Problems

Software distribution and installation is a critical feature of SMS 2.0 and a key reason for choosing it. SMS 2.0 has become even more sophisticated at offering the administrator flexibility to install any application in any setting. SMS 2.0 addresses the following five administrative problems:

- Flexible targeting of software
- Rules-based distribution and deletion
- Scheduling distribution
- User context and elevated privilege
- WAN-aware software distribution

FLEXIBILITY SOFTWARE TARGETING

SMS 2.0 provides rich options for targeting software distribution. In addition to targeting machines (as in version 1.2), SMS 2.0 can now distribute to any combination of the following:

- Machines
- TCP/IP network segments
- User groups
- Users

This allows applications to be sent in a more directed manner. For instance, a particular Windows NT 4.0 user group could be sent a software patch that was only relevant to them, or all machines in a network segment could be sent a printer driver pertaining to the printer in that segment.

RULES-BASED DELETION AND DISTRIBUTION (DYNAMIC)

If a new user joins a user group, software now is automatically sent to them according to the group's policy. This is possible because, in addition to distributing to a wider range of targets, these targets are now assessed dynamically. Rather than the distribution target list being created at the central server, the rule-set itself is distributed to all sites and a small rule definition file is transmitted with every package. Each site is now aware of the rules, and as a new object joins the site it is evaluated against the rules.

In addition to distributing software when someone joins a group, it can be removed when they leave that group. The administrator can choose for a finance software application to only be installed while someone is a member of the finance group, for example. When they change groups, the dynamic assessment indicates that they should not have this software, and SMS starts the deinstall process on the client system.

DISTRIBUTION SCHEDULING

SMS 2.0 provides key tools to allow administrators to schedule distributions outside working hours. For example, a specific time of day can be indicated, or the installation can be set to happen when the user is not actually logged on. It is also possible to schedule distribution based on network bandwidth, therefore ensuring package delivery does not affect other network tasks.

ELEVATED PRIVILEGES AND USER CONTEXT

Some applications need to be installed in a user context in order to set up the appropriate icons; others need administrator rights to access system configurations. Often a user without local administrative privilege needs to install software that requires higher privileges. SMS 2.0 can deal with these situations as it is intelligent enough to be able to check to see if a currently logged-on user has the appropriate privileges, and, if not, to use its own domain administrator privileges on that machine to install the software.

This is a key capability of the system that has been further expanded in version 2.0. Previously, applications were installed by the user or by a service account with administrator privileges. Now, if SMS finds that a user without appropriate security rights is logged on, the program still is installed, and, importantly, the user context is still maintained. You can install software on Windows-based clients using accounts that have lower privileges than the SMS service account.

SOFTWARE DISTRIBUTION WAN-AWARE

SMS contains many capabilities geared toward supporting software distribution in a WAN environment, such as senders, bandwidth profiling, retries, compression, and batching. In addition, new capabilities have been added with version 2.0.

The new Courier Sender allows software to be sent by CD-ROM or other media rather than across the network. This is useful in those situations where the network bandwidth is too slow or too expensive to use for the delivery of a package. Courier Sender acts the same as a WAN Sender with the administrator indicating what type of media the software is placed on. Once the media manually arrives at the target destination the local administrator simply puts the CD-ROM in the drive and the process is completed automatically.

SMS 2.0 supports a fan-out mechanism for software distribution that makes use of servers as routers of software. This means that a package going to multiple sites needs to cross a slow-link only once before it is copied and routed to its various destinations.

COLLECTIONS

One of the features of SMS 2.0 is the concept of *collections*. In previous versions of SMS, sites were the main management construct used to address both logical and physical needs. In this version of SMS, sites are intended to more closely reflect the physical layout of your organization. SMS collections provide a way to reflect the logical aspects of your organization. Collections are arbitrary groupings of machines, users, user groups, and network information. These groupings are used to target software distribution.

You define and populate collections by setting *membership rules* for each collection. Membership rules are the criteria by which SMS evaluates whether a resource is a member of a particular collection. A membership rule can be a query, or it can explicitly specify a resource.

Once you set the membership rules for a collection, you can use it as a target for software distribution and other management tasks. A resource can belong to as many collections as you deem appropriate. You can define the rules for collections at any time. You do not need to wait until resources are discovered to create collections.

Collections are dynamic. Resources are periodically evaluated against the membership rules. As computers are discovered, they are included in any collection whose rules they satisfy. When hardware and software configurations on individual computers change, those computers are removed from or added to collections as appropriate. That means that your software distributions go to all the computers that meet your collection criteria—*even those computers that were added to the network after you created the collection.*

In a similar manner, a computer may no longer meets the criteria for a collection, perhaps because it is moved to a different group or no longer has the minimum free disk space specified in the collection criteria. Thus, it will no longer receive software targeted to that collection. In fact, if software has been installed to a particular collection and a resource leaves that collection (for example, the user moves from Finance to Marketing), the software can be deinstalled automatically from that system based on the fact that collection criteria is no longer met.

Collections can contain other collections called *subcollections* as well as resources. Collections are propagated automatically to child sites (either primary or secondary sites).

SMS enables you to distribute software to any collections you specify across one or more sites in your SMS site hierarchy. You can distribute a single command to be run on computers, a complete software application to be installed on individual computers, or a shortcut to a software package that is installed on and run from a network share.

SOFTWARE DISTRIBUTION STEPS

To perform software distribution using SMS 2.0, you need to create:

- Scripted install procedures
- Packages
- Programs
- Advertisements

SMS comes with a software distribution wizard to walk you through this process.

SCRIPTED INSTALLATION PROCEDURE • To install software without input from the user, you need to use a scripted installation procedure, like SMS Installer to produce installation scripts. Many commercial software packages, including operating systems such as Windows NT 4.0 Workstation, Windows 95, and Windows 98 support scripted installation. If you want to distribute a software application that does not support scripted installation, use the SMS 2.0 Installer to create your own installation script.

SMS PACKAGES • SMS 2.0 packages specify information about the software, the location of source files, the distribution points used to distribute the software, and similar information. Administrators can create *distribution points* for packages. Distribution points are the locations accessed by clients to obtain the files in the packages. The computer or share designated as a distribution point must have sufficient disk space for all the files that will be stored on it and must be assigned the role of distribution point. SMS client software can use any of the distribution points at a site that the client can access. You can configure rules for clients to use when connecting to site systems. For instance, you can provide a specific list of distribution points to contact or allow random selection from available distribution points. If the client is already connected to a distribution point when it is ready to run an advertised program, it will use that distribution point.

Package properties include the software name and version, the location of the package source directory, and group permissions for the distribution folder. Packages are typically used to distribute software to SMS clients. A package defines the files and instructions for distributing, installing, and running software. Once you create a package, you can create one or more *programs* for the package.

You can create packages for commercial software, in-house software, and data files. In each package, you define:

- General information about the package, such as the name, version, and vendor of the software you plan to distribute
- If the package includes files, the package source directory that contains those files
- The distribution points for the package
- Whether a compressed copy of the files referred to in the package is created and stored on the site server at remote sites
- Whether the files in the package need to be periodically updated and if so, how often

PROGRAMS • *Programs* specify the command to be run at the client to perform the tasks described in a specific package; for instance install software, copy data files, or run a batch file. You can create several programs for one package; for instance, one program can perform an express installation, while another executes a customized script you have created with SMS 2.0 Installer. The programs contained in a package are not run until you *advertise* those programs to a target collection.

ADVERTISEMENTS • Advertisements make a program available to a collection and, optionally, its collections. Advertisements specify which collection receives each program and the date and time when the software will be available to run on clients. You can *assign* an advertisement from the moment it is advertised or set it to be assigned after a specified date or time. You can also set an expiration date after which the advertisement will no longer be available. In an advertisement you specify:

- The package and program to run on the client
- The target collection
- The schedule of when the program is available to clients
- When or whether the program is *assigned*

Each client that meets the criteria for the collection you specify receives the advertisement. Because collection memberships are evaluated dynamically, new computers and new users automatically receive advertisements for programs if they meet the criteria for a collection to which the software has been advertised. Also, users that no longer meet the criteria may have programs removed from their system.

SMS 2.0 ensures that everything required to respond to an advertisement is available on the distribution points. If the package referred to by an advertisement is not already on a distribution point at a child site, SMS sends a compressed package to that distribution point.

When you are ready to make a program in a package available to clients, you advertise the program to a target collection. SMS uses collections to determine which clients receive an advertisement for a program.

SOFTWARE DISTRIBUTION WIZARD • SMS 2.0 provides a wizard to step you through the process of creating packages, programs, and advertisements and assigning them to collections. The wizard can be accessed from the site database level or on a per collection basis.

THE CLIENT VIEW

Typically, users at a SMS client are not aware that their computer is part of a SMS system. SMS 2.0 has been designed to be as unobtrusive to a user at a client machine as possible. Depending on how you configure each client, the user at the client may be made aware of none, one, or all of the following:

- When advertised programs are made available
- When advertised programs are running or are counting down to run
- When a remote control operation is requested, or in progress

When an advertised program is made available, a taskbar icon appears in the client's taskbar status tray. When remote control is requested, an icon appears on the desktop, or a dialog box appears requesting permission to begin a remote control session. A user at a client is required to perform SMS-related tasks when you:

- Advertise a SMS package containing software for installation that requires user input
- Need the user to provide specific inventory information
- Want to perform remote troubleshooting operations at the client and the client is configured so that the user needs to provide verification

AVAILABILITY OF ADVERTISED PROGRAMS • An advertised programs icon with the label *New Advertised Program* appears in a user's system tray if a program is available as shown in Figure 10.14. When a new advertised program is made available at a client, the user can use the Advertised Programs Monitor to reschedule the program or to run it immediately. If they choose to run it immediately, a wizard walks the user through the installation steps. This dis-

Figure 10.14 *New Advertised Program Icon in System Tray.*

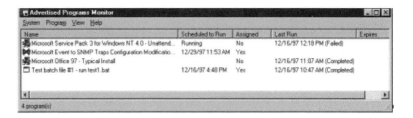

Figure 10.15   *Advertised Programs Monitor.*

tribution methodology is closely aligned to the approach used with Windows 2000. To run the advertised program the user at the client can do one of the following:

- Double-click the New Advertised Programs Available icon.
- Right-click the icon and choose the Run Advertised Program Wizard from the pop-up menu.
- Select Start: Settings: Control Window: Advertised Programs.

In addition, the user at the client can use the Advertised Programs Monitor in the same location to perform the tasks as shown in Figure 10.15:

1. Monitor program run status.
2. Change configuration options for advertised programs.
3. View advertised program properties.

The Advertised program Monitor displays a list of all scheduled programs and all programs that have already run at the client. The run status of each program appears in the *Scheduled to Run* and *Last Run* columns.

WINDOWS 2000 AND SMS DISTRIBUTION

SMS 2.0 has been aligned with many of the techniques and terminology that are used in the IntelliMirror technology that will be made available in Windows 2000. It has been designed to complement the facilities that are being released by building advanced software distribution facilities on top of the standard *just in time* facilities in the operating system.

SMS 2.0 is designed to provide a *push* mechanism that scales to meet the needs of any size organization by dealing with WAN and administrative issues that are not addressed by IntelliMirror. The combination of IntelliMirror providing on-demand installation of program components and SMS providing controlled administrator-based push meets the needs of any environment. In addition, SMS 2.0 is the ideal tool for rolling out a Windows

2000 environment, and for managing a heterogeneous mix of Windows 2000 and other operating systems.

Advanced SMS 2.0 Software Distribution and Installation Procedures Exercises

As previously stated, one of the key abilities of SMS 2.0 is to distribute and install software. SMS has the flexibility to distribute a software package to a collection that can contain machines, users, and user groups. A collection can contain a subset of one of these resources based on inventory information collected; for example, all machines that have more that 16 MB of RAM. There are a number of components to distributing software:

- Creating a collection (with or without a query)
- Configuring software distribution
- Advertising a program
- Creating a package
- Creating a program
- Creating an advertisement
- Installing the software on the client machine

SMS comes with a software distribution wizard that steps you through these operations. In the following exercise, a procedure is examined for rolling out Service Pack 4 of Windows NT 4.0 to a Windows NT 4.0 Workstation that is running Windows NT 4.0 and is in a local subnet.

Therefore, the ideal client to have is a Windows NT 4.0 Workstation. If you have a Windows 95-based client, you may be able to make substitutions as you move through the exercise.

COLLECTION CREATION VIA QUERY

Create a collection to be used as the target to advertise a software program. This collection will be dynamically created as a result of a query that checks to see which machines are currently running Windows NT 4.0 and are in the local subnetwork. Now, navigate to the Queries node, and click on the following functions in sequential order:

1. SMS
2. Site Database (<name>)
3. Query

Next, perform the following steps:

1. On the Action menu, point to New, and then click Query.
2. In the Query Properties dialog box, enter the name Local Windows NT 4.0 Clients and the comment, "All Windows NT Workstation 4.0 clients on the local subnet."
3. Click Edit Query Statement, and the Local Windows NT 4.0 Clients Query Statement Properties dialog box appears. Notice that under Results, all attributes of the System Resource class are displayed.
4. Under Results, click System Resource, and then click Delete.
5. The Local Windows NT 4.0 Clients Query Statement Properties dialog box appears. Notice no properties are displayed. Click New.
6. The Result Properties dialog box appears to select attributes to be displayed when the query runs.
7. Click Select, and the Select Attribute dialog box appears. In the Attribute Class box, click System. In the Attribute box, click Name.
8. Click OK, and the Result Properties dialog box appears. Notice the attribute System—Name is listed. Click OK.
9. The Local Windows NT 4.0 Clients Query Statement Properties dialog box appears. Notice the System class attribute of Name is to be displayed. Add the attributes to the list shown in Table 10.6.

Table 10.6 *Attribute Classes and Attributes for the Local Windows NT 4.0 Clients Query Statement Properties Dialog Box*

Attribute Class	Attribute
System resource	IPSubnets
Operating system	Name

In the following procedure, you will create the criteria to be used to determine all Windows NT Workstation 4.0 computers on the local subnet:

1. Click the Criteria tab. The Local Windows NT 4.0 Clients Query Statement Properties dialog box appears displaying the criteria used to determine which resources to display when the query runs. By default, there is no criteria, which means all resources will be displayed.
2. Click New. The Criterion Properties dialog box appears to assign the criteria used to determine which resources are to be displayed when the query runs.
3. Click Select. The Select Attribute dialog box appears. In the Attribute Class box, click System Resource. In the Attribute box, click IPSubnets, and then click OK. The Criterion Properties dialog box appears.

4. Notice the first part of the criteria is filled in as System Resource—IPSubnets is equal to. In the Value box, type your subnet, and then click OK.

5. The Local Windows NT 4.0 Clients Query Statement Properties dialog box appears and displays the criteria used to determine which resources to display when the query runs. Notice the statement added. Click New.

6. The Criterion Properties dialog box appears to assign the criteria used to determine which resources are to be displayed when the query runs. Click Select. The Select Attribute dialog box appears.

7. In the Attribute Class box, click System Resource. In the Attribute box, click OperatingSystemNameandVersion, and then click OK. The Criterion Properties dialog box appears.

8. Notice the first part of the criteria is filled in as "System Resource—OperatingSystemNameandVersion is equal to listed." In the Value box, type Microsoft Windows NT Workstation 4.0, and then click OK.

9. The Local Windows NT 4.0 Clients Query Statement Properties dialog box appears displaying the criteria used to determine which resources to display when the query runs. Notice the statement added to the criteria, with an *and* to join the two expressions. Click OK, and OK again when the Query Properties dialog box appears. The Local Windows NT 4.0 Clients query appears in the list of queries.

Test the query to verify it works successfully before creating the collection. In the console tree, click Local Windows NT 4.0 Clients, and then on the Action menu, click Run Query. The Windows NT Workstation 4.0 computers that are on the local subnet appear in the Details window. Verify this includes only the Windows NT 4.0 clients. You will need to scroll the Details window to view the computer names.

Next, create the collection and assign the Local Windows NT 4.0 Clients query as the membership rule for the collection. Navigate to the Collections node, by clicking on the following functions in sequential order:

1. SMS
2. Site Database (<name>)
3. Collections

Next, perform the following steps:

1. On the Action menu, click New, and then click Collection. The Collection Properties dialog box displays General settings for the collection.
2. In the Name box, type Local Windows NT 4.0 Clients.

3. In the Comment box, type "All Windows NT 4.0 clients on the local subnet," and then click the Membership Rules tab. Select the Query Rule icon (this is the second icon).

4. In the Query Rule Properties dialog box, select the Browse button and choose the Local Windows NT 4.0 Clients query. Then click OK.

5. Finally, click OK on the Collection Properties dialog box. When this is complete, select the new Local Windows NT 4.0 Clients collection in the left window, and from the Action menu choose the Update Collection option.

6. The collection members appear in the Results window. This should include the client computer you are going to upgrade. If it does not appear, you may have to select Refresh from the Action menu.

SOFTWARE DISTRIBUTION AGENT CONFIGURATION

Now configure the software distribution agent. You do not have to do this, but it makes the user experience more pleasant. Navigate to the Client Agents node and click on the following functions in sequential order:

1. SMS
2. Site Database (<name>)
3. Site Hierarchy
4. Site Settings
5. Client Agents

Next, perform the following steps:

1. In the Results window, click Advertised Programs Client Agent, and then on the Action menu, click Properties. The Advertised Programs Client Agent Properties dialog box displays General settings for the advertised programs client agent.

2. Verify Enable software distribution to clients is selected. In the Check for new programs every box, type 6.

3. Click the Notification tab.

4. Under "When new advertised programs are available," select "Display a visual indicator." This will inform the client when a program is available.

5. Under "When a scheduled program is about to run," verify Provide a countdown is selected, and the Minute Countdown box is set to 6.

6. Click to select Show status icon on taskbar, and then click OK.

SOFTWARE DISTRIBUTION WIZARD

In next exercise, let's create a package and program to be advertised to all computers that are part of the collection. Then let's assign distribution points for the package, and create the advertisement for the package. This will be accomplished using the Distribute Software Wizard. Navigate to the Software Distribution Wizard and click on the following functions in sequential order:

1. SMS
2. Site Database (<name>)
3. Collections
4. Local Windows NT 4.0 Clients

Before starting, make sure that the service pack you are about to install is available to be bundled in a package. To do this, create a directory on the hard drive and copy the directory Nt4sp4 from the SMS 2.0 CD-ROM. Also copy the three files off your hard drive from the \sms\scripts\enu\nt4\i386 directory to this same new directory. This new directory should now have _osw32rc.dll, ntencap.exe, w95ntupg, and Nt4sp4 at the top level. Share out this directory for a later exercise. Now, perform the following steps:

1. In the console tree, click the Local Windows NT 4.0 Clients collection, and then on the Action menu, point to Task. A new menu appears.
2. Click Distribute Software Wizard. The Distribute Software Wizard dialog box appears. Click Next.
3. The Distribute Software Wizard Package dialog box appears providing options for package distribution. Verify Create a new package from a definition is selected, and then click Next.
4. The Package Definition dialog box appears allowing you to select the package definition file to use. In the Publisher box, verify that Microsoft is displayed. Under Package definition, click Service Pack 4 for Windows NT 4.0, and then click Next.
5. The Source Files dialog box appears prompting for source file handling instructions. Click Always obtain files from a source directory, and then click Next.
6. The Source Directory dialog box appears allowing the designation of the source file directory. Click Browse. The Browse for Folder dialog box appears. Point the browser to Nt4sp4 in the newly created directory.

7. Click OK, and a message box appears indicating the path may not be accessible to other computers. Since you have the source files on your site server computer, this is fine. Click OK, and then click Next.

8. The Distribution Points dialog box appears allowing the designation of distribution points to store the package files. Under Distribution points, click to select the site server, and then click Next. If you have a detailed hierarchy, this is where you would specify a group of servers to act as distribution points.

9. The Advertise a Program dialog box appears allowing the configuration of advertisements. Click "Yes. Advertise a program," and then under Programs, click Unattended update for x86.

10. Click Next. The Current Advertisements dialog box appears. Click Create a new advertisement, and then click Next.

11. The Advertisement Target dialog box appears prompting for the collection to advertise the program. Click Browse.

12. The Browse Collection dialog box appears displaying all collections. Click Local Windows NT 4.0 Clients, and then click OK. The Advertisement Target dialog box displays the selected collection. Click Next.

13. The Advertisement Name dialog box appears prompting for a name and comment for the advertisement. In the Name box, type Windows NT 4.0 SP 4 Update, and then click Next.

14. The Advertise to Subcollections dialog box appears prompting for advertising to subcollections. Select 'Advertise the program only to members of the specified collection,' and then click Next.

15. The Advertisement Schedule dialog box appears prompting for a start and expiration time for the advertisement. In the Advertise the program after box, set the appropriate date and time. Verify that "No. This advertisement never expires" is selected, and then click Next.

16. The Assign Program dialog box appears prompting for program assignments. Click "No. Do not assign the program," and then click Next.

17. The Completing the Distribute Software Wizard dialog box appears, prompting you to complete the wizard. Click Finish.

Before moving to the client machine, verify that the advertised program is available by viewing the advertisement status in the SMS Administrator console. This is possible due to the new status engine that SMS 2.0 provides. Navigate to the Advertisement Status, and click on the following functions in sequential order:

1. SMS
2. Site Database (<name>)

3. System Status
4. Advertisement Status

Next perform the following steps:

1. The available advertisements appear in the console tree. Under Advertisement Status, click Windows NT 4.0 SP4 Update. The advertisement status summary appears in the Details window.
2. In the Details window, click the local site code, and then on the Action menu, point to Show Messages. A new submenu appears. Click All.
3. The SMS Status Message Viewer for local site code window appears displaying all messages for the selected advertisement at the local site. Expand the Description column to view more details on the description.

CLIENT MACHINE SOFTWARE INSTALLATION

Now let's install the software distribution components on the client computer. One of the key features that SMS 2.0 offers is the ability to work in elevated privilege. A user without administrative privileges on their workstation would not be able to install Service Pack 4, but that should not stop a successful deployment from happening. So first, try and run the program directly as a user, and then distribute it to the user through SMS. The first will fail; the second will succeed.

DIRECT PROGRAM RUN • On the server, first share out the Windows NT 4.0 Service Pack 4 from the CD-ROM so that the client can access this share. Next, log on to the Windows NT 4.0 Workstation as the user you created earlier. Then, connect to the server's NT4SP4 share. Run update.exe /u, which is exactly the command that SMS 2.0 runs. A Service Pack setup error occurs indicating you don't have permissions to update the system. Finally, disconnect from the NT4SP4 share. Thus, you cannot run it directly. When SMS encounters this problem, however, it automatically switches over to running at an elevated privilege level.

SMS PROGRAM RUN • From Control Window, start Advertised Programs. As illustrated earlier in the chapter, you can also click the Advertised Programs icon with the label New Advertised Program, which appears in the status tray (Figure 5.14).

The Advertised Programs Wizard window appears. Click Next. The Advertised Programs Wizard Select Programs to Run window appears. Under Advertised Programs, click Microsoft Service Pack 4 for Windows NT 4.0—Unattended update for x86, and then click Properties. The Microsoft

Service Pack 4 for Windows NT 4.0—Unattended update for x86 Properties dialog box appears showing properties for the selected advertised program.

Note the amount of time estimated to run this program and the required disk space.

Now, click Close, and then click Next. The Advertised Programs Wizard Run Programs Now or Later window appears prompting to run the program now, or to schedule it for a later time.

Click Run the selected program now, and then click Next. The Completing the Advertised Programs Wizard window appears, prompting you to complete the wizard. Next, click Finish. Service Pack 4 is installed using the same user account that could not manually run the program earlier.

No user input is required.

At the end of the upgrade, the computer automatically reboots. Now verify the system has been upgraded to Service Pack 4.

Study Break

Epilogue

Once a computer has been included in the inventory database, several operations can be carried out for that computer. One of the most common tasks administrators wish to automate is the software installation process. Software distribution can be based on any inventory information that SMS 2.0 gathers, allowing the administrator to clearly define the target workstations and servers that need to have a software upgrade or new installation. The tasks that can be successfully completed with SMS are many. Here are a few examples.

First of all, some salespeople are slow about downloading the new price list file every week. On a recurring basis, SMS can automatically copy this file to the computers you specify.

Second, the accounting department wants to switch to new travel expense software throughout the company next weekend. SMS allows you to target an installation for every computer at the same time, even when employees are not at their desks.

Third, you have decided that you want the appropriate computers to be running Windows 98. SMS identifies which computers need the upgrade and automatically installs the software, with minimal impact on the user.

Finally, you need to run a virus scan program or back up users' hard disks on a regular basis. SMS can do this for you too.

MCSE 10.3 Creating Database Reports

SMS 2.0 includes a single user, runtime version of Crystal Info Reports an application that allows you to create reports from information stored in an SMS database. SMS provides comprehensive report design, scheduling, and viewing capabilities to help you manage and present data. You can use reports to analyze and distribute inventory and SMS status data throughout your organization.

SMS includes several predesigned reports that you can run. Report topics include hardware and software inventory, network configuration, software distribution, the SMS status system, and product compliance. You can use these reports as they are, modify them, or create new reports by using Crystal Info Report Designer, a tool provided with SMS. You can use this tool to create many different types of reports, including cross-tab, sub, conditional, and form reports.

Reports must be scheduled to run. You can schedule reports to run immediately or at any time you choose. If a report successfully runs, the information obtained appears in the details pane of the SMS Administrator console.

Reports must be set to query your SMS site database. When you use the predesigned reports or you create a new report, the database location is automatically set to your SMS site database. However, if you import a report from another SMS site or another source, you must use the Set Location tool provided with SMS to reset the database location to your SMS site database. Using the Set Location tool also resets the default user rights.

To create a new report template file, you should have an understanding of the underlying WBEM data classes that SMS uses to obtain information. When accessing the SMS site database with Crystal Info, the "tables" of data you can base a report on are WBEM data objects called resource classes.

These are the same resource classes used by the SMS query builder. In the SMS Administrator console, navigate to any report object under Reports. Right-click the report object, point to Task, and then click Design New Report. The Info Report Designer splash screen opens. Click New Report. The Report Gallery dialog box opens.

Select the Standard report type. The Create Report expert will help you create this report. For more information about creating other types of reports, click Help from the Report Gallery.

The Create Report expert opens displaying the dialog box. The expert will guide you through the process of providing data for each tab in sequence. During this process, you will specify report properties such as the report data source, fields, and appearance.

Crystal Reports is a product of Crystal Computer Services, Inc. Microsoft does not provide support services for Crystal Reports.

Info Crystal Reports

You can create many different types of reports, including cross-tab, sub, conditional, and form reports. Using the integrated graphing capabilities of Crystal Info Report Designer, you can insert graphs that illustrate key SMS data. To make your reports more informative, you can choose from among 80 customizable styles, and display detail, group, or formula data as required.

If Crystal Info reports was not installed in the original setup then insert the SMS 2.0 CD-ROM in the CD-ROM drive on your Windows NT 4.0 computer. The SMS Setup window appears as shown in Figure 10.16. Therefore, to display the Setup window if you are running a previous version of Windows NT Server, go to your CD-ROM drive, and double-click SETUP.EXE.

Next, choose Set Up Crystal Info Reports from the SMS Setup window. The Installation Options dialog box appears as shown in Figure 10.17. Use the default directory or enter a new path and directory.

Now, choose Continue from the Installation Options dialog box until installation complete.

Configuring and Installing ODBC

Crystal Info for SMS can access a wide variety of data sources, but to report on SMS-specific data, you must use the ODBC-WBEM data source. If ODBC

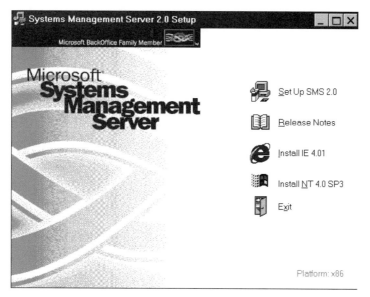

Figure 10.16 *SMS Setup Window.*

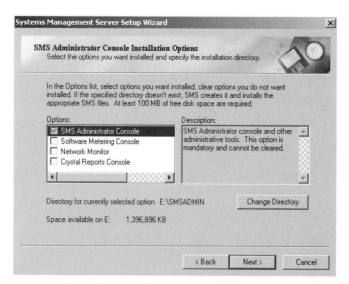

Figure 10.17 *SMS Installation Options Window.*

is not configured you now must install and configure ODBC using the control panel and select ODBC icon, which enables Crystal Info Reports to work with the database.

Select SQL Server as the driver and choose OK. The Data Source dialog box appears. In this dialog box you specify the data you want to access and the information needed to get to the data. You need to specify that the source is SQL Server, and the server on which it resides. Choose Add. Then, select SQL Server as the source, and choose OK. The ODBC dialog box appears as shown in Figure 10.18. In the Data Source Name field, type the name of the database data log where the information is currently stored. SMS 2.0 gives this log a default name of SMSData.

In the Description field, type a description of the data in the data source. If SQL Server is on the site server, from the Server list select (local). If SQL Server is on a remote computer, from the Server list, type the name of the computer, and enter the network address of the computer.

Choose Options. Further fields are displayed in the ODBC SQL Server Setup dialog box. In the Database Name field, type the name of the database you are using. The default name for the SMS database is SMS. Now choose OK, and the Data Sources dialog box is redisplayed.

Next, choose Close. In the confirmation message box, choose OK. You have now installed and configured ODBC to work with the SMS database.

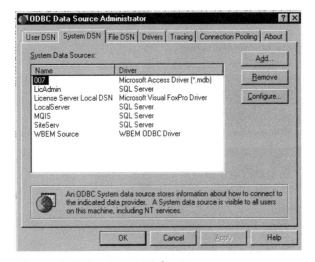

Figure 10.18   *ODBC Dialog Box.*

Running Crystal Info Reports

To run Crystal Reports, Start the SMS Administrator and expand the Tools node. Under Tools node, click on Reports as shown in Figure 10.19. Existing default Reports can be viewed directly from administrator's console or they can be modified using info designer as shown in Figure 10.20.

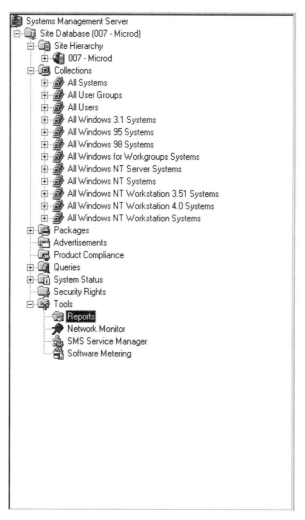

Figure 10.19 *SMS Administrator and Tools Node.*

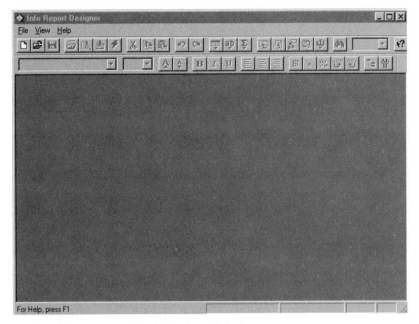

Figure 10.20 *Crystal Info Designer Window.*

Saving the Report

Crystal Info Reports enables you to save the data in a number of formats. To save the report in HTML format, perform the following steps:

1. From menu, select Print, and then select Export. The Export dialog box is displayed.
2. From the Format list, select an HTML entry (e.g., HTML for Internet Explorer 2.0).
3. Choose OK.
4. Type a name and location for the HTML file and choose OK.

The file is saved and you may distribute the file to the appropriate Web servers and view it using a Web browser.

■ Summary

You should come away from this chapter with an in-depth knowledge of the MCSE exam-specific components or functions of SMS architecture: managing inventory; software distribution and management; and creating database reports needed to install and configure and manage SMS resources. With that in mind, the first part of the chapter discussed how SMS discovers all the resources throughout your network, and how it is not restricted to the site boundaries that you define. The location of each resource is then compared to the site boundaries you have set. The resource is assigned to the appropriate site or sites. Discovery mechanisms for SMS 2.0 include:

- Heartbeat Discovery
- Netware Bindery Server Logon Discovery
- Netware NDS Logon Discovery
- Network Discovery
- Windows Networking Logon Discovery
- Windows Networking User Account Discovery
- Windows Networking User Group Discovery

The second part of the chapter examines how software distribution and installation provides an insight into the sophisticated tools that are available to allow an administrator to install any software on any desktop. It also differentiates the distribution mechanism used by SMS 2.0 to be offered in the operating system with Windows 2000.

The final part of the chapter examines SMS 2.0's inclusion of a single user, runtime version of Crystal Info Reports an application that allows you to create reports from information stored in an SMS database. The following procedures describe how to:

- Create a view on the SMS database that Crystal Info Reports can use to read the data.
- If not previously done, Install and configure Microsoft's Open Database Connectivity (ODBC) tool so Crystal Reports can access the data in the database.
- Create an SMS report using a supplied templates that can be published as a Web page.

▲ CHAPTER REVIEW QUESTIONS

▲ True/False

1. *True or False? To install Windows networking logon client, when a computer within the site boundaries logs on to the Windows-based network, SMS deinstalls the client software on that computer.*

2. *True or False? SMS client software is automatically installed on Windows NT 4.0 computers within the site boundaries. The Windows NT 4.0 computers need to be turned on and connected to the network. It is necessary to be logged on to these computers.*

3. *True or False? The user must explicitly connect to a file on a Windows NT 4.0 logon point to install the SMS client software. This method provides for those cases where no logon script is used.*

4. *True or False? To install the Netware Bindery server logon client, when a computer logs on to a NetWare bindery server, SMS installs the client software on that computer.*

5. *True or False? The following steps describe how to create a query that will locate all target computers currently running Windows 98 that have at least 50 MB of free disk space. From the SMS Administrator expand Queries and then right click and choose New. The Query Properties dialog box appears.*

6. *True or False? Once you set the membership rules for a collection, use it as a target for software distribution and other management tasks—like creating a collection of target computers. A resource can belong to as many collections as you deem appropriate. You can define the rules for collections at any time, and you must wait until resources are discovered to create collections.*

7. *True or False? You can create packages to distribute commercial software, in-house software, and data files.*

8. *True or False? When monitoring the software distribution process, use the SMS Status Message Viewer for local site code window. However, it doesn't display all messages for the selected advertisement at the local site.*

9. *True or False? SMS 2.0 ensures that everything required to respond to an advertisement (like removing advertised software) is available on the distribution points. If the package referred to by an advertisement is not already on a distribution point at a child site, SMS sends a compressed package to that distribution point.*

10. *True or False? To install software without input from the user, you need to use a scripted installation procedure (like SMS Installer to produce installation scripts). Many commercial software packages, including operating systems such as Windows NT 4.0 Workstation, Windows 95, and Windows 98 support scripted installation. If you want to distribute a software application that does support scripted installation, use the SMS 2.0 Installer to create your own installation script.*

▲ Multiple Choice

1. *Advertisements make a program available to a collection and, optionally, its collections. Advertisements specify which collection receive each program and the date and time when the software will be available to run on clients. You can assign an advertisement (make it mandatory) from the moment it is advertised or set it to be assigned after a specified date or time. You can also set an expiration date after which the advertisement will no longer be available. In an advertisement you specify except:*

   A.   The package and program to run on the client

   B.   SMS

   C.   The target collection

   D.   The schedule of when the program is available to clients

   E.   When or whether the program is *assigned* (mandatory)

2. *SMS 2.0 includes a single user, runtime version of Crystal Info Reports, an application that allows you to create reports from information stored in an SMS database. The following are procedures you can perform except:*

   A.   Create a view on the SMS database that Crystal Reports can use to read the data

   B.   Install Collections

   C.   Install and configure Microsoft's Open Database Connectivity (ODBC) tool so Crystal Reports can access the data in the database

   D.   Create an SMS report using a supplied template that can be published as a Web page

3. *One of the features of SMS 2.0 is to distribute and install software. SMS has the flexibility to distribute a software package to a collection that can contain machines, users, and user groups. A collection can contain a subset of one of these resources based on inventory information collected (for example, all machines that have more that 16 MB of RAM). There are a number of components to distributing software except:*

   A.   Creating a collection (with or without a query)

   B.   Configuring software distribution

   C.   Advertising a program

   D.   Creating queries

   E.   Creating a package

4. *To create a package and program to be advertised to all computers that are part of the collection, assign distribution points for the package, and create the*

advertisement for the package. This will be accomplished using the Distribute Software wizard. Navigate to the Software Distribution wizard and click on the following functions in sequential order except:

A. SMS

B. SMS Security Manager

C. Site Database (<name>)

D. Collections

E. Local Windows NT 4.0 Clients

▲ Open Ended

1. SMS discovers all resources throughout your network. It is not restricted to the site boundaries that you define. The location of each resource is then compared to the site boundaries you have set and the resource is assigned to the appropriate site or sites. What are the discovery mechanisms for SMS 2.0?

2. SMS client software can be installed by which installation methods?

Interoperability of an SMS Network

The chapters in this part cover areas, including the client experience during remote control; how to configure remote control agent at the site server; and the use of diagnostic utilities for clients. This part also explains how to configure remote control and start a remote control session.

Next, the part shows you how to install and configure Windows NT 4.0 Event to SNMP Trap Translator.

The part also shows you how to go about installing the HealthMon server monitoring tools as well as focusing on other remote management tools.

SMS Network Installation and Configuration

This chapter takes you through a series of common user scenarios for configuring and installing remote utilities with SMS. The chapter begins by discussing the client experience during remote control, which includes how to configure remote control agent at the site server, and how to use diagnostic utilities for clients. More importantly, it includes how to configure protocols on clients. The following section explains how to configure remote control and start a remote control session. This covers how to configure remote control settings at the client, and how to use remote tools.

The third part of the chapter shows you how to install and configure Windows NT 4.0 Event to SNMP Trap translator. This includes any Windows NT 4.0 Event, such as low disk space. It can now be forwarded as an SNMP trap translator to an SNMP management console, such as HP Openview, IBM Netview AIX, or Digital POLYCENTER Manager on Netview.

The chapter then covers how to go about installing the HealthMon server monitoring tools. This includes how to install and configure Health Monitor to monitor Windows NT Server 4.0 computers.

Finally, the chapter focuses on other remote management tools, such as remote reboot, remote chat, and remote launching of administrative tools.

MCSE 11.1 Installing and Configuring an SMS Client Computer

SMS 2.0 includes Remote Tools, which provides diagnostics and Help Desk utilities that allow you to directly monitor and control your inventoried computers as shown in Figure 11.1. When the client computer initializes Remote Control Agent, the user can be completely unaware or depending on setting, ask permission to allow remote control of their desktop.

Figure 11.1 *Remote Tools Window.*

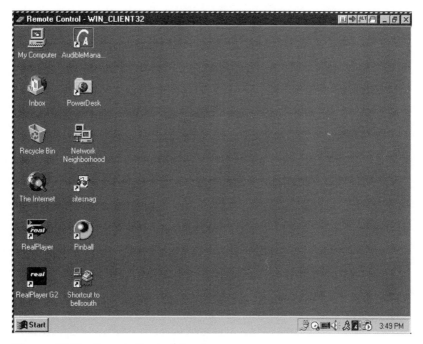

Figure 11.2   *Remote Control Session.*

The clients window shown in Figure 11.2 appears on the administrator desktop.[1] If you notice on the clients taskbar is a small SMS icon indicating active remote session. When Remote Control session ends the window task bar returns to normal. Double-clicking taskbar icon during active session displays the Remote Control Status dialog box shown in Figure 11.3.

Figure 11.3   *Remote Control Agent Dialog Box.*

Figure 11.4 *Clients desktop, use taskbar icon to close active session.*

Users may want to cancel session at anytime using the taskbar icon as shown in Figure 11.4. This will Close Session immediately. Pressing Unload Agent prevents any Remote Control operation until the agent is reloaded. Administrators always have the option of reconfiguring remote tools to connect without permission of client user.

While working with SMS 2.0 on a color monitor, the window title bar is gray, and the user is alerted to an active Remote Control session when the title bar turns red.

Configuring Protocols on Clients

In practice, two categories of problems present themselves: difficulties in configuring protocols on clients and difficulties with configuring and starting the remote control session itself (as discussed in the second section of the chapter). Therefore, before you start, first ensure that you have basic network connectivity between the SMS Administrator computer and the client computer you are trying to remotely control using the *protocol* you have configured for remote control. If you cannot establish a network connection between the machines, you cannot perform remote control.

Second, install the latest service pack (SP) for the version of SMS you are using. Next, make sure you have selected the proper options in the Help Desk Options section in the SMS client group on the client, and that the remote agent is loaded (minimized on the screen). These are not configured by default.

LOCATING THE CLIENT

To successfully locate a client computer, three conditions must be met:

- The computer must be inventoried correctly.
- The computer's remote agent must be *listening* for this session.
- The intervening network must establish and maintain the session.

INVENTORY PROBLEMS RELATED TO REMOTE CONTROL • Remote Control is initiated by double-clicking the Help Desk icon in the properties of an inventoried computer. The SMS Administrator program uses `Sightnt.dll` to attempt to initiate a session with the remote agent of the client by querying for the computer name (client name or IPX address) and the address type (NetBIOS name or IPX address) recorded in the inventory in the SQL database. The inventory information regarding the computer's network information and SMSID must correctly match an SMS client computer whose remote agent is currently *listening* on the network.

> If the computer is not listed in the inventory collection, it will not be located and, therefore, cannot be remotely controlled.

Common inventory problems include:

- The client has not been inventoried at all.
- The client is a duplicate with an invalid SMSID.
- The client shares an SMSID with another client.
- The client is running Windows for Workgroups 3.11 and has been inventoried with a computer name in lowercase letters.
- The client's network address has been incorrectly inventoried.

If the client has not been inventoried, it may be that the client computer does not have SMS Client files on it, and thus its name does not appear in the inventory. The client computer could also have the SMS Client files on it, and still not appear in the inventory. To troubleshoot these symptoms, you would install the SMS Client files on a computer without them by invoking `Smsls.bat` or `Runsms.bat`. If the client has the SMS Client files on it but does not appear in inventory, deinstall and reinstall the client.

Now, if the client selected is a duplicate with an old, invalid SMSID, the same computer name appears next to different SMSIDs in the Sites window, and the error message UNABLE TO LOCATE CLIENTNAME appears after Trying Additional Protocols. To troubleshoot these symptoms, you would first select the most recent occurrence of the computer name, and see if SMS can locate it. If SMS cannot locate it, you have additional problems, but should still remove your duplicate inventory. If the problem persists, check to see why the `Sms.ini` file is being deleted, or why it is being locked during the verification process.

Some MSTest scripts invoke Invdos.exe after installing a program to check to see if the program installed correctly. This can cause a new SMSID to be assigned, since the Sms.ini file is locked. Because SMS cannot read it, SMS thinks the Sms.ini file is not present, and the client will be reinstalled with a new SMSID.

If the client shares an SMSID with another client, the Help Desk and other icons may be missing in the affected client computer's properties. First check that the network is functioning correctly and that other clients on the same subnet can be remotely controlled. If that is not the problem, check to see if the clients have been cloned and have been preloaded with the SMS client files. All these clones will have the same assigned SMSID. Delete the Sms.ini file from all clones, and then check to see if the .uid files on two logon servers overlap, or if there are multiple .uid files on a logon server.

If you have Windows for Workgroups 3.11 clients inventoried with a computer name in lowercase letters, this is often the result of manually configuring the System.ini file on the client. The error message UNABLE TO LOCATE CLIENTNAME appears after Trying Additional Protocols.

Finally, if the client's network address has been incorrectly inventoried, the TCP/IP or IPX address of the client will be wrong or missing in the Network section of the Computer Properties. Also, the error message UNABLE TO LOCATE CLIENTNAME appears after Trying Additional Protocols.

The Trying Additional Protocols error message can indicate many types of problems and is not relevant only to what is covered here.

If no address appears, check to see if the computer has a dial-up adapter and if the dial-up adapter is first in the bindings for the protocol in question. If the dial-up adapter is first, SMS returns the address of the dial-up adapter, which should be 0.0.0.0. For Windows NT 4.0 clients, open Control Panel Network, and click Bindings to move the binding for the network adapter to the first position. If the wrong IP address appears, check for reasons the IP address might have changed, such as a DHCP problem. Re-inventory the client to get current address information.

CLIENT REMOTE AGENT CONFIGURATION PROBLEMS • Improper or unsupported client configurations are perhaps the most frequent cause of the

Unable to locate message. The server side (Sightnt.dll on the SMS site server) calls the client side (the Wuser.exe program). If anything interferes with Wuser.exe's properly loading, such as a third-party TSR or forgetting to load the remote agent, the client will not be listening for Sightnt.dll's call. If anything on the client, such as a third-party protocol stack, accepts Sightnt.dll's call before Wuser.exe hears it, the client will not be able to respond.

Neither Usertsr.exe or Useripx.exe is used with SMS 2.0 clients running Windows.

Common client configuration issues include:

- Other TSRs conflicting with Wuser.exe's supporting TSRs, Usertsr.exe or Useripx.exe
- Failing to configure remote viewer options or load the remote agent/service
- Hardware problems

If other TSRs are conflicting with wuser.exe's supporting TSRs, usertsr.exe or useripx.exe, the Help Desk Options and Remote Agent icons may be missing from the SMS program group on the client. The client may experience a GP fault during remote control. To troubleshoot this, remove all TSRs—such as virus scanners, virtual memory managers, and so forth—from the Autoexec.bat file and the load line of the Win.ini file, and reinstall the SMS Client software. If the client can now be remotely controlled successfully, add back in each TSR one at a time until the conflict reoccurs. Query the Knowledge Base on remote control, SMS, and the name of the TSR in question for any possible workarounds.

If a virus scanner is in conflict, consider using a daily SMS advertisement (job) to scan for viruses.

Also, USERTSR or USERIPX does not load in memory with SMS 2.0. In addition, the Remote Control service does not load on Windows NT 4.0 clients. To troubleshoot this, first check to see whether the Remote Troubleshooting check box is selected in the Clients section of the site's Current Properties dialog box. Second, check to see whether the Allow Remote Control option is selected in the Help Desk Options in the SMS Client program group on the client computer. This can be verified remotely by looking in the client's Sms.ini file for the entry Allow Remote Takeover=yes. Finally, check to see whether the Remote Agent is loaded on the client computer. The Remote Agent icon will be minimized. You can verify that the remote agent is loaded by typing mem /c at the command prompt and looking for USERTSR (NetBEUI, NWLINK, or IP) or USERIPX (NetWare's IPX clients).

This does not apply to SMS 2.0, in that these TSRs are no longer necessary for Windows-based clients.

With SMS 2.0, you have the added functionality of remote control as a service for Windows NT 4.0. Usually the only additional problem that surfaces is that the SMS service account, under whose context the remote control service installs, does not have administrator rights, nor does it have log on as a service right for the workstation. If this is the case, the SMS client files will install, but neither the inventory agent service nor the remote control service will start. (To see if the Remote Control service has started, see Control Panel Services, or type net start at the command prompt of the Windows NT 4.0-based client.) This lack of rights shows up in the Clicfg.log file on the SMS site server. Make sure the domain administrators are part of the local administrators group on the client, and that the SMS service account is a member of the domain admins group. Verify that it has log on as a service right.

Sometimes a bad network adapter or other hardware problem can cause remote control to fail. If everything else checks out, try swapping out the network adapter, or try an identical hardware configuration with a fresh installation of the network operating system. If you can isolate the problem to a particular piece of hardware, try querying the Knowledge Base on remote control, SMS, and the name of the offending hardware.

NETWORK PROBLEMS • SMS allows remote control over a variety of networking configurations using Microsoft's NetBIOS-capable protocols (NetBEUI, TCPIP-32, and NWLINK) and sockets with NetWare's IPX protocols (NETX and VLM). SMS 2.0 supports remote control using IP sockets for all the members of the Windows operating system family.

With SMS 2.0, in the Client section of the Site Properties dialog box, there is an Options section with three choices: NetBIOS, (IP) sockets, or IPX. These options are not just for Windows NT 4.0; they are relevant for the entire Windows operating system family. Selecting one of these options causes the corresponding entry to be written to all the Sms.ini files on your site: NetBIOS, IP (for sockets), or IPX. Also, if you select IP sockets, and the remote protocol specified in the Sms.ini file is not present on the client, SMS tries to bind to the next available protocol on the client. This means it finds NetWare's IPX and binds to it automatically.

For the remote session to be established, the network functions must be working properly. This could include such things as protocol initialization, name resolution, packet sequencing, session establishment, messaging, routing, and bandwidth availability.

Common network-related problems include:

- Unsupported or corrupted network client
- Protocol conflicts or binding order problems
- Configuration of the wrong LANA number
- NetBIOS name resolution problems
- Insufficient routing configurations

If the network client is unsupported or corrupted, the error message UNABLE TO LOCATE CLIENTNAME appears after Trying Additional Protocols. The error message UNABLE TO INITIALIZE may also appear on the client when the computer is restarted. To troubleshoot this, check your network client against the list of supported clients in SMS. Second, you may have to upgrade to a supported client. This includes upgrading to the latest Windows for Workgroups redirector and the MSTCPIP-32 stack (both found on your Windows NT Server 4.0 CD). Third, remove all third-party network client software or protocol stacks, and then add them back in one at a time until the offending stack is identified. If it is necessary to run the third-party stack, try a different load order, or try using a different protocol for remote control (for example, sockets with SMS 2.0). Occasionally, a network client can become corrupted. This can be especially true of specially configured *images* or *clones* that are stored on the network for administrative installations. Try a fresh installation from the manufacturer's original source media.

If you have protocol configuration or binding problems, the error message UNABLE TO LOCATE CLIENTNAME appears after Trying Additional Protocols. In addition, the error message Unable to initialize IP, IPX, or NetBIOS may appear during the boot process on the client. The error message "NetBIOS is not loaded on this workstation" may also appear during the boot process on the client. You should be aware that the error Unable to initialize on client boot can occur if unsupported protocol stacks are present. Troubleshoot this by completely removing them from the client; don't just remark them in the `Autoexec.bat` file. You can verify the protocol in use by selecting the remote agent icon while it is minimized and by checking the Default Protocol in the [Sight] section of the `Sms.ini` file.

If you receive the error "NetBIOS is not loaded," verify that the SMS client has been installed properly. In particular, check to see which operating system SMS detects the client is running. Check this by looking at the OS entry in the [SMS] section of the `Sms.ini` file, where 1=MS-DOS, 2=16-bit Windows, 3=OS/2, 4=Windows NT 4.0, 5=Windows 95, 6=Windows 98, and so on. If the operating system on the client is Windows, but SMS has an OS entry indicating it is an MS-DOS client, your Windows directory may be too far down in the path in your `Autoexec.bat` file. Move it to the beginning of the path, and reinstall the SMS client.

If Windows for Workgroups is configured to use both the NetWare Shell and the NWLINK protocol, NWLINK grabs the IPX packets, but does not pass them on to `Wuser.exe`. The solution is to remove NWLINK from the client. If a Windows 95 client receives the error message "IPX is not loaded for this workstation. Would you like to load the drivers for Win95?," use cliopts /set useripx /w to configure USERIPX according to the Remote Troubleshooting Utilities section of the `Readme.wri` file on the SMS CD. For Windows clients, be sure to remove any unsupported protocol stacks completely; don't just remark them.

Remote Control is not supported on any third-party TCP/IP stack. Always update clients running Windows for Workgroups to the latest redirector and MSTCPIP-32, found on the Windows NT Server 4.0 CD. Also, typing nbtstat -n is a quick way to verify that the TCP/IP stack is properly bound and the remote agent is running. If everything is working properly, nbtstat -n should return a <43> extension next to the computer name. If the <43> service does not show up, and no TSRs are conflicting, check for a dial-up adapter configured for TCP/IP, and remove the binding for TCP/IP to the adapter.

If the wrong LAN Adapter (LANA) number is configured, NetBIOS becomes an interface between an application and a protocol. It consists of a set of function calls. NetBIOS network applications, like remote control, set up logical network sessions between two computers by riding on top of a transport protocol that supports NetBIOS, such as NetBEUI, TCP/IP, and NWLink. Each NetBIOS-capable protocol binding can support one NetBIOS session at a time. If five pairs of NetBIOS network applications were communicating at a time, each would establish its own logical network session. Each computer running the network applications would need five distinct bindings of any protocols that support NetBIOS.

For a network application to know on which logical network session to send and receive its function calls, each is assigned a LANA number. The two network applications sharing a NetBIOS logical network session must be configured to send and receive on the same LANA number. If they are not configured to the same LANA number, you will receive the Trying Additional Protocols message. Each binding is then tried in turn, and when the proper binding is tried, the client will be located.

Although the client will probably be located, you want to avoid the Trying Additional Protocols message and the ensuing delay. Setting LANA numbers speeds up the location process. To do this, set the LANA number for both the client and the server using NetBIOS over TCP/IP. First, double-click the server's NetBIOS interface in Control Panel Network, and set Nbt to an available number—LANA 0, in our example. Second, for Windows for Workgroups clients, check the NBT section in System.ini and make sure LANABASE=0. Third, for Windows 95 or 98 clients, set TCP/IP as the default protocol. Fourth, for MS-DOS 3.0 clients, check the network.setup section in Protocol.ini.

If you're having NetBIOS name resolution problems, remote control works locally, but not across a router. Also, remote control may work only for those computers that share a primary WINS server with the Admin tools computer. In this scenario, you can also ping the IP address, but not the NetBIOS name. A captured Network Monitor trace would show that the CLIENTNAME C name query is failing. To troubleshoot this, first look at the Name Resolution and Routers. Verify that UDP Port 137 and UDP Port 139 are enabled by trying a *net use* from the server to the client or other clients on the same segment. Next, verify that UDP Port 138 is enabled by trying a *net send* from the server to the client or other clients on the same segment. For NWLINK networks, verify that the router is configured to pass type 20 packets for NWLINK NetBIOS support.

Second, you must look at the Name Resolution and WINS. From the server type nbtstat -a CLIENTNAME, and look for the CLIENTNAME <43> entry, which is the WINS registration of the Remote Control agent's extension. Next, if no <43> service registration shows up from the server, type nbtstat -n on the client itself and check for the <43> service. If the <43> service is present on the client, but cannot be seen from the server when you type nbtstat -a CLIENTNAME, look for problems with WINS or confirm that UDP Port 137, UDP Port 138, and UDP Port 139 are not disabled on your routers. Check all relevant WINS databases for the <43> service by CLIENTNAME. If the <43> service is not present on the client, there is a configuration problem on the client. Check for a modem on the client, and, if present, disable the NBT binding on the modem. Also, try reinstalling TCP/IP. For Windows for Workgroups clients, use the updated redirector and the MS32TCPIP-B stack. Check also for third-party TSRs and protocol stacks. Remove them, and try again. If the SMS Admin Tools computer and the client computer have different primary WINS servers, make sure WINS replication is not the cause of the problem. Check for the CLIENTNAME <43> entry in *both* WINS databases. Also verify that the LMHOSTS file is configured properly.

Only the server's LMHOSTS file needs to be configured with the remote extensions.

Also check the following:

- Verify that the IP address is correct.
- Verify that the computer name is spelled correctly and that the C entry is in the 16th place.
- Verify that there are not multiple entries for CLIENTNAME C.
- If there is another copy of the LMHOSTS file on a working server, rename the local copy and copy the file to the nonworking server. Type nbstat -R to reload the cache.
- Try creating a new LMHOSTS file, and then type nbtstat -R to reload the cache.
- Make sure there is a blank carriage return at the bottom of the LMHOSTS file.

Finally, for all networking configurations, routers must be functioning properly and adequately to support remote control. If your routers are dropping packets or corrupting the data portion of the packets, you may see symptoms like dropped sessions or GP faults on the clients during a remote control session. Furthermore, because remote control occurs in real-time, numerous hops can seriously impede its ability to function.

For remote control to function properly, certain ports must be enabled on the routers. Before further explanation, some misconceptions must be addressed. Enabling a port on a router is not necessarily the same thing as bridging a protocol. For example, for NetBIOS over TCP/IP name resolution to work, routers must have UDP Port 137 enabled. Thus any packet *specifically* sent to this port is forwarded. A sniff reveals that only name queries, such as requests for name resolution to WINS servers, are sent to this port. Thus, NetBEUI is not being bridged, as some users may think.

For NetBIOS over TCP/IP, UDP Ports 137, 138, and 139 must be enabled. Port 137 is for name resolution; Port 138 is for messaging (as in sending the screen image); and Port 139 is for sessions. For NetBIOS over NWLINK, Type 20 packets must be forwarded. Type 20 packets provide Net-BIOS support, and forwarding these *can* cause more traffic than desired. For TCP/IP sockets and IPX, no special configuration is required.

Clients can be located on the local segment, but not across the router. Therefore, you must verify UDP Port 137 and 139 are enabled by trying a net use from the server to the client or to other clients on the remote segment with only the TCP/IP bindings to the network card enabled. You must also verify UDP Port 138 is enabled by trying a net send from the server to the client or other clients on the same segment. Make sure Winpopup is enabled on the client, and only TCP/IP bindings are enabled. Check the number of hops on a TCP/IP network by using the TRACERT command. Also, verify that Type 20 packets are being forwarded by trying a net use to a computer across the router with only the NWLINK protocol bindings enabled.

MCSE 11.2 Installing and Configuring Remote Utilities in Clients

To configure the remote control component for SMS 2.0, navigate to the remote control client agent, and click on the following functions in order:

1. SMS
2. Site Database (<name>)
3. Site Hierarchy
4. Client Agents

Now, perform the following steps:

1. In the Results window, click Remote Tools Client Agent. Click Properties on the Action menu, and the Remote Tools Client Agent Properties dialog box displays General settings for the remote control client agent.
2. Verify Enable remote tools on clients is selected, and then click the Security tab. The dialog box displays Security settings for the remote control client agent. Notice that the Administrators group is permitted to remotely control Windows NT 4.0-based client computers.
3. Click the Policy tab. The dialog box displays Policy settings for the remote control client agent. In the Level of remote control allowed box,

click Full remote control allowed. Verify Display a message to ask for permission is selected.

4. Click the Advanced tab. The dialog box displays Advanced settings for the remote control client agent.

5. Click to select Install accelerated screen transfer, and then click OK.

On the client computer perform the following steps:

1. Shut down, and then restart the client computer. Log on as the domain user. The SMS client software executes, and the remote control client components are updated.

2. The Remote Control Agent appears inside the clients Control Panel.

Starting a Remote Control Session

In this part of the chapter, let's take over the screen and keyboard on the client machine. Navigate to the client machine and click on the following functions in order:

1. SMS
2. Site Database (<name>)
3. Collections
4. All Systems

Next, perform the following steps:

1. Select the All Systems Collection. In the Results window, select your client computer, and then point to Task on the Action menu. A new submenu appears.

2. Click start Remote Tools. The Remote Tools window appears as the remote control connection is being established with the client computer.

3. Click the Remote Control icon—this is the top left-hand icon. On the client machine, a Remote Control message box appears indicating permission is being requested.

4. Click Yes. You now have screen and keyboard control over the client machine.

 The remote control settings are configured in such a way that the user cannot change them, but can be set to ask the client for permission before a remote control session is started.

The remote diagnostics tools in SMS 2.0 are faster and more robust that in previous versions. Their configuration is also more granular, especially from a security context.

MCSE 11.3 Installing and Configuring Windows NT Event

SMS 2.0 extends its integration into the enterprise management environment by providing SNMP event forwarding and receiving. This means you can install and configure Windows NT 4.0 Event to SNMP Trap translator. Any Windows NT 4.0 Event, such as low disk space, can now be forwarded as an SNMP trap translator to an SNMP management console, such as HP Openview, IBM Netview AIX, or Digital POLYCENTER Manager on Netview. This alerts you to any predefined critical event. SMS can also receive SNMP traps from managed devices and other management consoles.

Cross-Platform Integration and Interoperability Management

System administrators are increasingly faced with the necessity of providing interoperability between systems supporting different network protocols. With Windows NT 4.0 Event, system integrators receive support for protocols such as TCP/IP, NetBEUI, IPX/SPX, NetWare Core Protocol, systems network architecture, LAN Manager, X Window System, and NFS.

SNMP TRAP TRANSLATOR-BASED SMS

To integrate Windows with SMS systems SNMP Trap translator service can be installed and configured within Windows NT 4.0 Event, Windows 95, and Windows 98. Network administrators of UNIX systems can thus use SNMP Trap translator management software, such as HP OpenView, to manage Windows systems.

The SNMP Trap translator service installed and configured within Windows NT 4.0 Event provides support for the Internet Management Information Base-II (MIB-II) and LanMan MIB II. Future support is planned for the Ethernet MIB, X.25 MIB, and Host MIB. HP OpenView and IBM NetView are examples of SNMP Trap translator-based management software available on Windows. Using such products, system administrators on Windows NT Server 4.0 can manage SMS clients.

SYSTEMS AND NETWORK MANAGEMENT

Across the board, support for the SNMP Trap translator in Windows NT 4.0 Event has reached critical mass, with HP OpenView, Ca UniCenter TNG, and IBM Tivoli available on Windows NT 4.0. In addition, Windows NT Server 4.0 and Windows NT 4.0 Workstation both include complete support for SNMP Trap translator Management Information Base (MIB) files, allowing them to be managed through these consoles.

For administrators trained in the management of UNIX systems, Windows NT 4.0 can now offer the same management paradigm by means of tools from MKS and Softway Systems. Both vendors offer UNIX-style commands, utilities, and shell environments that make a Windows NT 4.0-based system look, act, and feel like a UNIX-based system. Administrators uncomfortable without such tools as awk, grep, and ps can now be productive immediately when managing a Windows NT 4.0-based system. Windows 2000 will offer a full range of built-in command-line and scriptable management capabilities providing true lights out management of a Windows NT 4.0-based system.

Management and User Interface APIs

Routing and Remote Access Service (RRAS) provides for ease of administration with both an intuitive graphical user interface and a command-line user interface. A full set of APIs make RRAS management extensible, which is a great example of the potential for third-party development.

The built-in management features and APIs make it easy to deploy RRAS in existing or new network environments. Since RRAS supports SNMP Trap translator MIB II, it can be managed from an SNMP management console. RRAS running on a Windows NT 4.0 Event Server platform can appear, act, and be managed like many other routers in an organization. This allows RRAS to interoperate with existing networking systems. SNMP Trap translator standards allow devices from different companies to be administered from a central point, such as from an HP OpenView console.

Plugging into HP OpenView, NMS, and SMS via SNMP Trap Translator Agent

Windows 95 and 98 plugs cleanly into HP OpenView, Novell Network Management System (NMS), and SMS through the use of its SNMP Trap translator agent. Built-in support allows for easy management of workstations under these network management platforms.

SNMP Trap translator support in Windows 95 and 98 includes an SNMP Trap translator agent, an extensible MIB handler interface, and MIB I and MIB II support. Support of SNMP Trap translator makes it easy to add workstations into a formally managed network without having to struggle with special software on each workstation. In addition, the extensible MIB handler interface allows hardware or software vendors to instrument their components so they can be remotely managed via the SNMP management console. The Windows 95 and 98 SNMP Trap translator support works over TCP/IP and IPX transports.

MCSE 11.4   Installing and Configuring Health Monitor

SMS 2.0 includes a new server health monitoring feature called HealthMon. HealthMon is at preview quality in SMS 2.0 and should not be used in production environments. The following exercises examine HealthMon and remote control.

HealthMon

HealthMon is an example of the power of the WBEM infrastructure underlying SMS 2.0. It uses information populated through the performance monitor provider for CIM. It is at preview quality only for SMS 2.0. To investigate the potential of this tool, let's complete the following exercises:

- Installing the HealthMon Console
- Installing the HealthMon Agent
- Installing the HealthMon Snap-in
- Managing a server with HealthMon

We will also cover the monitoring of BackOffice services, which is not supported in SMS 2.0.

HEALTHMON CONSOLE INSTALLATION

Perform the following tasks:

1. Run `\Healthmon\I386\Healthmon.exe` off the SMS 2.0 CD-ROM. The Welcome window appears.
2. Click Next. The Select Destination Directory window appears.

3. Click Next to accept the default directory. The HealthMon console is installed, and then the Installation Completed window appears.
4. Click Finish.

HEALTHMON AGENT INSTALLATION

Next, install the Health Monitor agent software. You could do this on a remote Windows NT Server 4.0 (preferred) or on the same server on which SMS is installed. To do this, perform the following tasks:

1. Run `\Healthmon\ I386\Agent.exe` off the SMS 2.0 CD-ROM. The Welcome window appears.
2. Click Next. The Select Destination Directory window appears.
3. Click Next to accept the default directory. The HealthMon console is installed, and then the Installation Completed window appears.
4. Click Finish. Processing may take a few seconds to complete.

HEALTHMON SNAP-IN INSTALLATION

Next add HealthMon to the MMC by following these steps:

1. Close down SMS 2.0, and start up the Microsoft Management Console from the Run menu by typing mmc.
2. In the Microsoft Management Console, select the Console menu item, and then Add/Remove Snap-in. The Add/Remove Snap-in dialog box appears.
3. Click Add, and the Add Standalone Snap-in dialog box appears.
4. Select the HealthMon Snap-in option, click Add, and then click Close.
5. When the HealthMon Tool has been added to the display, select OK.

You may also want to add SMS to this display by choosing it as a snap-in and following the steps in the wizard. The display should now change to show both SMS and HealthMon immediately below the Console Root as shown in Figure 11.5.

HEALTHMON SERVER MANAGEMENT

Next, let's set up HealthMon, so it can be used to monitor the Server. Perform the following tasks:

1. In the HealthMon console tree, expand Managed Systems, and then click All Systems. Notice that there are no results displayed in the Details

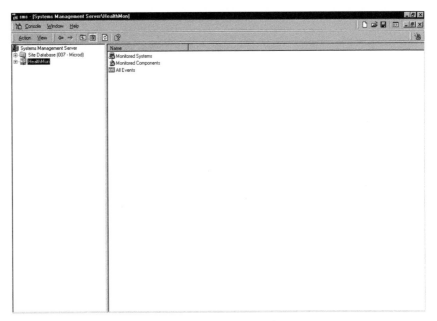

Figure 11.5 *Administrator Console and HealthMon Snap-in.*

window. This is because each managed system must be added to the console that is monitoring it.

2. In the console tree, click Managed Systems, and then point to New on the Action menu. A new menu appears.

3. Click Machine. The Configure Managed Systems dialog box appears.

4. In the Enter the name of the machine to manage box, type your server name, and then click Add. The Configure Managed Systems dialog box displays all managed systems, which now include the site server computer.

5. Click OK.

Navigate to the managed server, and click on these functions in order:

1. HealthMon Tool
2. Managed Systems
3. <server name>
4. All Objects

When you click on All Objects, the list of monitored objects is displayed in the Details window as shown in Figure 11.6.

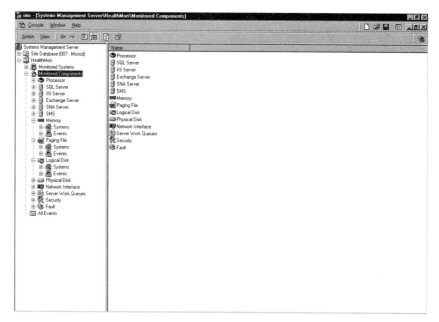

Figure 11.6 *Administrator Console and HealthMon.*

If you are working with SMS 2.0 on a color monitor, all enabled objects have green icons while the disabled objects (BackOffice services) have gray icons.

MONITORING OF BACKOFFICE SERVICES

Monitoring of BackOffice services is not supported in SMS 2.0. Therefore, you must perform the following tasks:

1. In the console tree, click the server name, and then point to Task on the Action menu. A new menu appears.
2. Click Edit Machine Profile. The Configure Managed Objects dialog box appears.
3. Under List of Managed Objects, click Processor, and then click Edit. The Configure Managed Object Policy dialog box appears displaying the implemented thresholds that determine whether the object is in a normal, warning, or critical state.

4. Under Managed Object Properties, click Processor: percent total system time. The dialog box displays all implemented thresholds that determine whether the Processor: percent total system time is in a normal, warning, or critical state.

5. Under Critical, set the Threshold to 30.

6. Under Warning, set the Threshold to 20.

7. In the Duration boxes, set both Critical and Warning to 20, and then click OK. The Configure Managed Objects dialog box appears.

8. Click OK, and under the server name, click All Objects. The list of monitored objects is displayed in the Details window. Notice Processor may not be at 100% normal. If Processor is still at 100% normal, generate CPU activity by switching between or starting additional applications.

9. Select the Object Events node and observe critical and warning events being generated in response to processor activity.

Distributing the agent was not performed here with HealthMon. It is better to simply install it manually. In an enterprise environment, a user would use SMS to distribute this agent. To enable this process, there is a package available for HealthMon that can be distributed through the software distribution wizard. Feel free to investigate this functionality.

Additional Remote Management Tools

There are other remote management tools available in SMS 2.0, including remote reboot, remote chat, and remote launching of administrative tools. Experiment with these from within the Remote Tools window.

The network-monitoring tool is particularly interesting for the way in which it has changed since SMS 1.2. This tool has added a series of monitors and experts that can evaluate the captured information and therefore lessen the work an administrator needs to do to research a problem. Monitors available include the Rogue DHCP Address Monitor and the IP Range Monitor which can help you find problem systems before they cause outages. To navigate to Network Monitor, click on the following functions in order:

1. SMS

2. Site Database (<name>)

3. Tools Node, and then click Network Monitor as shown in Figure 11.7.

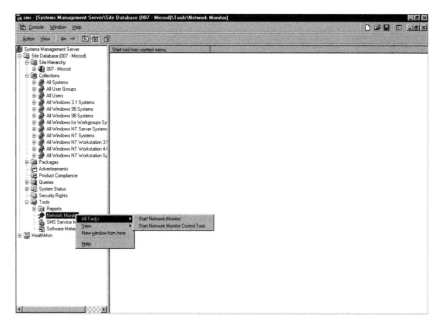

Figure 11.7   *Administrator Console and Network Monitor.*

■ Summary

You should come away from this chapter with an in-depth knowledge of the MCSE exam-specific components or functions of SMS network interoperability and integration needed to install and configure an SMS client computer; install and configure remote utilities in clients; and install and configure Health Monitor. With that in mind, the first part of the chapter discusses how SMS 2.0 provides diagnostics and Help Desk utilities that allow you to directly monitor and control your inventoried computers. It also discusses how to configure protocols on clients, configure a remote control agent at the site server, and use diagnostic utilities for clients.

The second part of the chapter examines how to configure the remote control component for SMS 2.0. It also examines how to configure remote control settings at the client and how to use remote tools.

The third part of the chapter shows you how to install and configure Windows NT 4.0 Event to SNMP Trap translator. Any Windows NT 4.0

Event, such as low disk space, can now be forwarded as an SNMP trap translator to an SNMP management console, such as HP Openview, IBM Netview AIX, or Digital POLYCENTER Manager on Netview.

The fourth part of the chapter examines the new SMS 2.0 server health monitoring feature called HealthMon. It examines how to install and configure Health Monitor to monitor Windows NT Server 4.0 computers.

▲ CHAPTER REVIEW QUESTIONS

▲ True/False

1. *True or False? The remote control settings at the client are configured in such a way that the user could change them and is asked for permission before a remote control session started.*

2. *True or False? The remote diagnostics tools in SMS 2.0 are slower and more robust than in previous versions.*

3. *True or False? The remote diagnostics tools' configurations are less granular, especially from a security context.*

4. *True or False? SMS 2.0 provides diagnostics and Help Desk utilities that allow you to directly configure, monitor, and control your inventoried computers or site servers. Therefore, when the site server is running Remote Control Agent, nothing appears on the users desktop or taskbar.*

5. *True or False? You can install and configure the Health Monitor agent software to monitor Windows NT Server 4.0 computers. You could do this on a remote Windows NT Server 4.0 (preferred) or on the same server on which SMS is installed.*

6. *True or False? One action that is not performed with HealthMon is distributing the agent. It is better to install it manually. In an enterprise environment, a user would use SMS to distribute this agent. To enable this process, there is a package available for HealthMon that can be distributed through the software distribution wizard.*

7. *True or False? You must make sure you have basic network connectivity between the SMS Administrator computer and the client computer you are trying to remotely control using the protocol you have configured for remote control. If you cannot establish a network connection among the machines, you will not be able to perform remote control.*

8. *True or False? SMS 2.0 extends its integration into the enterprise management environment by providing SNMP event forwarding and receiving. In other words, you can install and configure Windows NT 4.0 Event to SNMP Trap translator. Any Windows NT 4.0 Event, such as low disk space, can now be forwarded as an SNMP trap translator to an SNMP management console, such as HP Openview, IBM Netview AIX, or Digital POLYCENTER Manager on Netview. This alerts the administrator of any predefined critical event. SMS can also receive SNMP traps from managed devices and other management consoles.*

▲ Multiple Choice

1. *To configure the remote control component for SMS 2.0, navigate to the remote control client agent and click the following functions in order except:*

    A. SMS

    B. Site Database (<name>)

    C. Check the memory map, the status of interrupts, and other operating system parameters

    D. Site Hierarchy

    E. Client Agents

2. *To take over the screen and keyboard on the client machine, navigate to the client machine, and click on the following functions in order except:*

    A. SMS

    B. Log on to the network at the client machine

    C. Site Database (<name>)

    D. Collections

    E. All Systems

3. *There following are other remote management tools available in SMS 2.0 except:*

    A. SMS

    B. Remote reboot

    C. Remote chat

    D. Remote launching of administrative tools

    E. None of the above

4. *Experiment with the remote management tools mentioned in above from within the following window:*
   A. Capture frames window
   B. Creating source directory window
   C. Creating a query window
   D. Creating a workstation package window
   E. Remote Tools window

▲ Open Ended

1. HealthMon is intended to be an example of the power of the WBEM infrastructure underlying SMS 2.0. It uses information populated by the performance monitor provider for CIM. Explain some features of HealthMon for an administrator to improve server performance.

Monitoring and Optimization

This section examines the most essential part of administering a distributed network—the ability to analyze and maintain the integrity of the network itself. It explains how SMS tracks its own operation and generates events when something significant occurs within the system. This part discusses how to identify changes to a site server after SMS installation. Furthermore, it shows how to monitor and configure SMS status messages, and how to monitor or track the progress of SMS functions. Finally, this part shows how to configure the SMS database maintenance tasks.

Monitoring SMS

This chapter opens up Part 6, "Monitoring and Optimization," by taking you through a series of common user scenarios surrounding changes to a site server after installation, such as:

- Identifying types of site servers

- Identifying areas for change

- Monitoring Systems Management Server (SMS) 2.0 status reporting

- Monitoring the progress of SMS functions

- Using SMS utilities to monitor SMS functions

- Monitoring the SMS database

This chapter examines your ability to analyze and maintain the integrity of the network itself. The Network Monitor tool allows you to identify network traffic patterns, test your network, and quickly pinpoint network trouble spots.

405

The chapter then explains how SMS tracks its own operation and generates events when something significant occurs within the system. Events are logged both to the database and to the Windows NT 4.0 event log of the computer where the SMS component generating the event is installed. If the SMS component is not on the site server, the component also logs an event to the Windows NT 4.0 event log on the site server. Thus, SMS events logged to the Windows NT 4.0 event log are not forwarded to other sites.

You will also learn how to identify changes to a site server after SMS installation. This includes different types of site servers, such as domain controllers, nondomain controllers, and secondary site servers.

Further on in the chapter, there is a discussion about how to monitor and configure SMS status messages. This includes configuration and monitoring of SMS job status messages, SMS site installation status messages, and unwanted status messages.

The fifth part of the chapter shows how to monitor or track the progress of SMS functions. It provides you with information on how to monitor the progress of client installation, software distribution, inventory collection, and remote control.

Finally, this chapter shows how to configure the SMS database maintenance tasks. The more often you configure these tasks, the less time it will take to perform them.

MCSE 12.1 Maintaining and Analyzing SMS Network Data

Network Monitor monitors the network's data stream, which includes all the information transferred over a network at any given time. Prior to transmission, this information is divided by the networking software into smaller segments called frames or packets. These frames can be copied to a capture buffer as they are sent across the network. The captured frames are then displayed dynamically through the Network Monitor window.

Typically, you do not need to examine all captured frames. When you need to record just a segment of network data, you can design a capture filter to do this. Like inventory queries, you can single out only the network traffic in which you are interested. For instance, you might use a capture filter to capture only the frames sent between two specific computers.

Network Monitor included in SMS also allows you to capture information remotely by using the Network Monitor Agent. Network Monitor Agent gathers statistics from a remote computer and sends them to your local computer, where they are displayed in a local Network Monitor window. Network Monitor allows you to troubleshoot LANs or WANs running RAS.

If you want a capture to respond to events on your network as soon as they are detected, you can design a capture trigger. A capture trigger performs a specified action (such as starting an executable file) when Network Monitor detects a particular set of conditions on the network. You can also edit and retransmit frames you have already captured to generate network activity and to simulate specific test conditions.

Network Monitor Requirements

Before you can begin monitoring, the Network Monitor component must be installed. If you elected not to install this component when you installed SMS 2.0, do so now using the SMS Setup program. Choose Start Network Monitor, and the Network Monitor Capture window appears as shown in Figure 12.1. The Capture window displays the Pane and Description information shown in Table 12.1.

From the Capture menu, select Start. Network Monitor allocates memory (buffer space) for network data and begins capturing frames. To stop capturing data, select Stop or Pause from the Capture menu. Through the

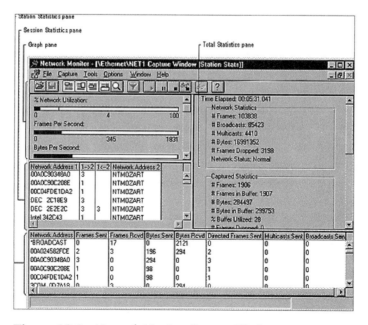

Figure 12.1 *Network Monitor Capture Window.*

Table 12.1 *Network Monitor Capture Window Pane and Description Information*

Pane	Description
Graph	A graphical representation of the activity currently taking place on the network
Session statistics	Statistics about individual sessions currently taking place on the network
Station statistics	Statistics about the sessions participated in by the computer running Network Monitor
Total statistics	Summary statistics about the network activity detected since the capture process began

Trigger option in the Capture menu, you can also set options that will automatically stop the capture process. For instance, you can set options that stop the capture process when the buffer becomes 60% full.

To view more detail on the captured data, select Display Captured Data from the Capture menu. The Network Monitor Frame Viewer window appears as shown in Figure 12.2. The Frame Viewer window displays the Pane and Description information listed in Table 12.2.

To focus on a particular pane in the Frame Viewer window, select the pane, and from the Window menu, choose Zoom. This causes the selected pane to fill the window. To restore the pane to its normal size, choose Zoom from the Window menu.

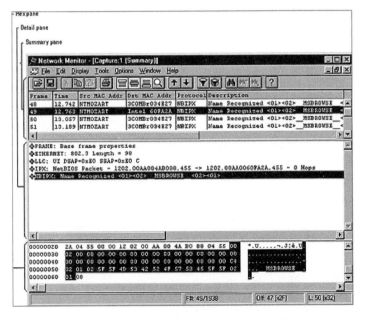

Figure 12.2 *Network Monitor Frame Viewer Window.*

Table 12.2 *Network Monitor Frame Viewer Window Pane and Description Information*

Pane	Description
Summary	General information about captured frames in the order in which they were captured
Detail	The frame's contents, including the protocols that were used to send it
Hex	A hexadecimal and ASCII representation of the captured data

You must also have a network adapter card that supports *promiscuous* mode. Promiscuous mode is a state in which the network adapter card can be directed by a device driver to pass on to the operating system all the frames that pass over the network. To determine this, see the documentation that accompanies the card. If you are using Network Monitor on a remote computer, this computer needs a network adapter card that supports promiscuous mode; the local computer does not.

There must be support for the network protocol in use. For a list of network protocols supported by Network Monitor, see the `PARSER.INI` file in the SMS\NETMON\platform directory where platform is the processor type.

Network Monitor Capabilities

This section provides an overview of the capabilities of Network Monitor. It also provides instructions on how to perform a number of common management tasks.

NETWORK DATA CAPTURE

This following section explains how to capture and save network frames. To capture network data, perform the following steps from the SMS Administrator Console as shown in Figure 12.3:[1]

1. Open Sites Node and Expand Site Node.

2. Expand Tools Node.

3. Click on Network Monitor and right-click and Start Network Monitor.

The Windows Program Menu also contains Network Monitor as shown in Figure 12.4.

---

1. Copyright © 1998 Microsoft and/or its suppliers, One Microsoft Way, Redmond, Washington 98052-6399. All rights reserved.

Figure 12.3 *SMS Administrator Console Toolbar.*

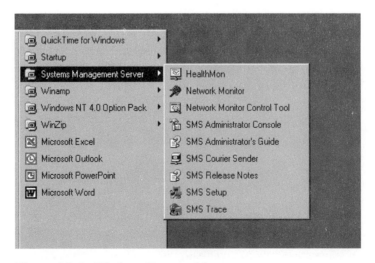

Figure 12.4 *Windows Program Menu.*

DATA CAPTURE ACROSS MORE THAN ONE NETWORK

Network Monitor captures only the traffic that passes through the NIC of the computer it is running on. This means that you can capture only the traffic of the local network segment. You can gather statistics about network traffic on other subnets by running Network Monitor Agent 2.0 on a computer in the other subnet and then connecting to that computer remotely. When a full installation of Network Monitor connects to a computer running the Network Monitor Agent, the Agent is used to capture network data. The Network Monitor Agent gives no visual indication that it is being used. The remote computer actually performs all capture operations, transfers statistics to you, and saves capture files to your local storage device.

To monitor remote networks or nonlocal subnets with Network Monitor, Network Monitor Agent 2.0 must be installed on the remote computer. Starting the agent on a remote computer enables you to use the computer's NIC as though the card were installed locally. When you use Network Monitor on a local computer, data capture, filters, and triggers function on the remote system just as they would locally. If you stop a remote capture and display the data, the capture data are displayed as if the capture were local. You can save the capture file to any location.

The Remote Agent simply creates a capture file, which you can view on your local computer.

The Network Monitor Agent is installed through the Network option in Control Panel. Choosing the Services tab, choose Add, and then select the Network Monitor Agent.

To capture data across more than one network from the SMS Administrator toolbar (Figure 12.5), follow these steps:

1. Connect to the remote computer that is running (Agent) or that the Network Monitor Agent driver must be installed on.

2. Start Network Monitor on the local computer.

3. On the Capture menu, click Networks. In the Networks window, expand the Remote item.

4. Double-click for remote NPPs.

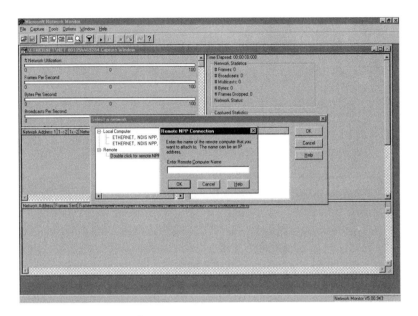

Figure 12.5   *Network Monitor.*

5. In the Remote NPP Connection window, type the remote computer name or IP address and then click OK.

6. To begin capturing data, on the Capture menu, click Start. The capture window title bar displays the NIC and machine name of the remote computer where you are capturing data.

Once you have captured a number of frames, stop capture and view Summary window. Remember to disconnect from the remote client, this will lower bandwidth on the network.

IDENTIFYING THE SOURCE OF THE HIGHEST NUMBER OF BROADCAST FRAMES • To identify the source of the highest number of broadcast frames, follow these steps from Network Monitor (Figure 12.6):

1. Choose Start Network monitor.

2. Network Monitor Capture window appears and start capture.

You can set a trigger that stops the Network Monitor when the buffer starts to fill up. Network Monitor begins capturing frames from the network. To stop capturing data, from the Capture menu, select Stop or Pause. The Capture window appears.

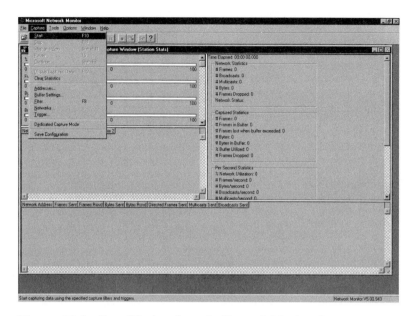

Figure 12.6 *Start Window from the Network Monitor Screen.*

In the Station Statistics pane (the lowest pane), scroll to the Broadcasts Sent column header. Double-click the Broadcasts Sent column. The row containing the highest number of broadcasts sent becomes the top row. The network address in this row represents the highest broadcaster on the network.

FRAME CAPTURING FROM SPECIFIC COMPUTERS

To use capturing effectively, you will often need to capture only those frames that originate with, or are destined to, specific computers. To do this, you must know the addresses of the computers on your network. You can use Network Monitor to associate a computer's hexadecimal address with its computer name. Once you create these associations, you can save them to an address database.

BUILDING AN ADDRESS DATABASE OF COMPUTERS ON YOUR NETWORK • To build an address database of computers on your network, follow these steps from the SMS Administrator toolbar (Figure 12.7):

1. Choose Start Network Monitor.
2. Network Monitor Capture window appears and start capture.

From the Tools menu, choose Resolve Addresses From Name. The Find Network Addresses From Name dialog box appears, as shown in Figure 12.8.

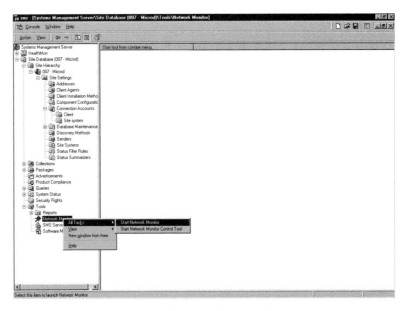

Figure 12.7 *SMS Site Database Tools Network Monitor Screen.*

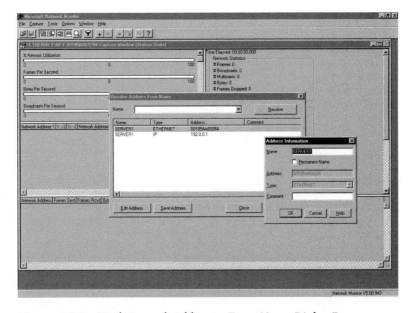

Figure 12.8 *Find Network Addresses From Name Dialog Box.*

In the Name box, type the name of the computer. You can also type an address in the Name box to resolve the computer name associated with that address.

Now, choose resolve. Network Monitor browses your network for the specified computer name or address. The address, name, and any aliases associated with the name are retrieved for the specified computer name or address. The Find Network Addresses From Name dialog box displays the retrieved items. To get the addresses for the computer on which you are currently running Network Monitor, choose Local Machine Information.

Next, choose Keep Names. The computer's name and address are added to the address database. Finally, choose close.

COMPUTER CAPTURE FILTER CREATION • A capture filter functions like a database query to single out specific types of network information. To monitor a subset of computers, use the address database created in the preceding procedure and add the target addresses to the capture filter. From the SMS Administrator Console (Figure 12.9), follow these steps:

1. From Administrators Console choose Expand Site Node.
2. From the Tools Node expand and Start Network Monitor.
3. From the capture menu, choose filter or click (F8).

The Capture Filter dialog box appears as shown in Figure 12.10.

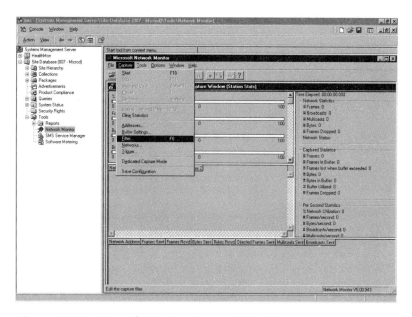

Figure 12.9 *Network Monitor Capture Filter Screen.*

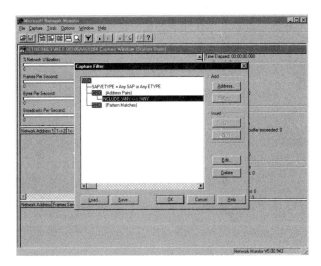

Figure 12.10 *Capture Filter Dialog Box.*

The Capture Filter dialog box displays filter expressions (the filter's logic). The Capture Filter dialog box has the fields and buttons shown in Table 12.3.

Next, double-click the ANY<-> ANY line. The Address Expression dialog box appears, as shown in Figure 12.11. The Address Expression dialog box has the fields and buttons shown in Table 12.4.

Table 12.3 *Capture Filter Dialog Box Fields and Buttons*

Element	Description
SAP/ETYPE	Specifies the protocols to capture
(Address Pairs)	Specifies the computer addresses on which you want to capture data
(Pattern Matches)	Specifies the data patterns to capture
Address	Displays the Address Expression dialog box to specify the address pairs between which you want to capture data
Pattern	Displays the Pattern Match dialog box to specify that you want to capture only those frames containing a specific pattern of ASCII or hexadecimal data
OR	Adds an OR operator to the filter; only applies to pattern matches
NOT	Adds a NOT operator to the filter; only applies to pattern matches
Line	Modifies or deletes the currently selected line
Load	Replaces the current capture filter with a capture filter that has been saved to a file
Save	Saves the current capture filter to a file

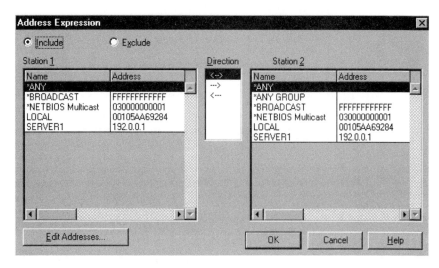

Figure 12.11   *Address Expression Dialog Box.*

Table 12.4 *Capture Filter Dialog Box Fields and Buttons*

Element	Description
Include	Includes the current address pair in the capture filter
Exclude	Excludes the current address pair from the capture filter
Station 1	Selects the first address of the pair. This can be the originating or the destination address, depending on the arrow you select in the Direction list.
Direction	Selects an arrow to indicate the direction of the traffic you want to include or exclude from the capture filter
Station 2	Selects the second address in the pair. This can be the originating or the destination address, depending on the arrow you select in the Direction list.
Edit Addresses	Modifies the current address database

In the Station 1 box, select the address for one of the target computers. In the Station 2 box, select the address of the other target computer. In the Direction box, select a direction as shown in Table 12.5.

Table 12.5 *Direction Box Fields and Buttons*

Element	Description
<-->	Use to monitor traffic passing in either direction between the addresses you selected
-->	Use to monitor only traffic passing from the address selected in the left pane to the address selected in the right pane
<--	Use to monitor only traffic passing from the address selected in the right pane to the address selected in the left pane

Now, choose OK to close the open dialog boxes. From the Capture menu, choose Start. Then, from the Capture menu, choose Stop at any time.

NETWORK CONDITIONS REPRODUCED

You must transmit frames onto the network when you want to reproduce network conditions. For example, you may do this to verify whether a diagnosis you made is correct. You must also transmit frames unto the network to generate an adequate amount of network activity. You might do this to simulate conditions you want to test. Before captured frames are transmitted onto the network, the destination addresses on these frames must be edited carefully. Otherwise, the retransmission of a large number of frames results in a substantial increase in the amount of network traffic.

EDITING FRAMES FOR RETRANSMISSION • As discussed earlier in this chapter, to edit frames for retransmission and to be able to complete this procedure, you need some captured data. From the SMS Administrator Console, follow these steps:

1. Open Sites Node and Expand Site Node.
2. Expand Tools Node.
3. Click on Network Monitor and right-click and Start Network Monitor.
4. From the Network Monitor Menu Choose Capture and Start Capture (F10).
5. Once Captured data is available, click Stop & View data (Shift & F11).

From the Capture menu, select Display Captured Data. The Frame Viewer window appears.

Now, from the Edit menu, clear Read Only. To avoid accidental transmission, the Transmit feature is disabled by default.

Display the frames you want to transmit and select a frame. In the Detail pane, expand the Ethernet or Token Ring entry until a Destination Address or Source Address entry appears and select this entry.

In the Hex pane, the section of characters that represent the address is highlighted. In this highlighted section, select any character. The character you select changes color to indicate that it can be edited. Now, edit the new address, and then choose OK to close the open dialog boxes.

SINGLE-FRAME NETWORK TRANSMISSION • After displaying a captured frame in the Frame Viewer window, retransmit the frame onto the network. You can transmit as many frames as you want. In addition, the same group of frames can be transmitted repeatedly, and you can specify how long a pause there should be between each transmission, also called a *cycle*. To analyze the effects of transmission, attempt to capture data from another computer on the LAN during transmission by performing the following steps:

1. Open the Frame Viewer window (described earlier in this chapter).
2. In the Summary pane of the Frame Viewer window, select the frame that you want to transmit.
3. From the Tools menu, choose Allow Transmit. The Select Transmit Network dialog box appears.
4. Select the network onto which you want to transmit the frame and choose OK.
5. From the Tools menu, choose Transmit Frame. Network Monitor transmits the frame onto the network.

TRANSMITTING FRAMES AND CAPTURE FILES • To repeatedly transmit a range of frames or a capture file onto the network, perform the following steps:

1. Open the Frame Viewer window (described earlier in this chapter).
2. In the Summary pane of the Frame Viewer window, display the frame(s) you want to send.
3. From the Tools menu, choose Allow Transmit. The Select Transmit Network dialog box appears.
4. Select the network onto which to transmit the frames and choose OK.
5. From the Tools menu, choose Transmit Capture. The Transmit Capture dialog box appears as shown in Figure 12.12. This dialog box has the fields shown in Table 12.6.
6. Specify the options you want and then choose OK.

DETECTING UNAUTHORIZED MONITORING

You can detect the users running Network Monitor on their computers. For instance, use this feature to identify possible violations in the company security policy or product licensing agreements.

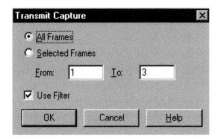

Figure 12.12 *Transmit Capture Dialog Box.*

Table 12.6 *Transmit Frames Dialog Box Fields and Buttons*

Element	Description
All Frames	Sends frames from the entire range of the capture file. You can send the entire range filtered or unfiltered.
Selected Frames	Specifies the range of frames to send. Specify a number for the first and for the last frame in the range.
Use Filter	Applies the current display filter to the frames and transmits only the frames that pass the filter

NETWORK MONITOR INSTALLATION DETECTION • To detect other installations of network monitor, follow these two steps using the SMS Administrator toolbar:

1. From Administrators Console, choose Expand Site Node.

2. From the Tools Node, expand and Start Network Monitor.

From the Tools menu, select Identify Network Monitor Users. A dialog box displays information about other installations of Network Monitor on your network, as shown in Figure 12.13. The Other Network Monitor Installations dialog box has the fields and buttons shown in Table 12.7. Now, to close the window and return to the Capture window, choose OK.

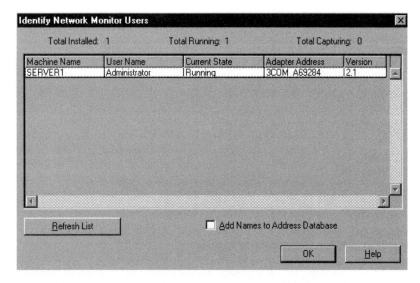

Figure 12.13 *Viewing Other Network Monitor Installations.*

In some instances, the architecture of your network may prevent one installation of Network Monitor from detecting another. For instance, if an installation is separated from yours by a router that does not forward multicasts, your installation will not be able to detect that installation.

Table 12.7 *Other Network Monitor Installations Dialog Box Fields and Buttons*

Element	Description
Machine Name	The name of the computer on which Network Monitor is installed
User Name	The user name of the user logged on to the computer specified by Machine Name
Current State	The state of Network Monitor on the remote computer: Driver Is Installed, Running, Capturing, or Transmitting
Adapter Address	The network adapter address of the remote computer
Version	The version number of Network Monitor on the remote computer
Add Names to Address Database	Adds names displayed in the dialog box to the default address database (DEFAULT.ADR)
Refresh List	Updates the statistics displayed in the Other Network Monitor Installations dialog box

MCSE 12.2 Generating and Tracking SMS Events

Using SMS Administrator, you can view SMS 2.0 events logged to a site database including events for any subsites. You can also use the Windows NT 4.0 Event Viewer to view SMS events logged to the Windows NT 4.0 event log.

SMS 2.0 queries on events that trigger an alert when an event occurs. For instance, you could have a query that searches for events with a value of four for WarningLevel. You could then specify that query in an alert. When the alert condition is met, the alert action is triggered. The alert can trigger a message, a command, or an SMS event. SMS also has other utilities and features to track and monitor the SMS system, such as:

- Detailed status for each Advertisements (job) to view the progress of each job
- Site status window in the Site Properties dialog box for each site to view the current status of a site
- SMS Service Manager to control and view the status of SMS services
- Trace logs for SMS services showing detailed actions of SMS services

The following sections describe ways to track the progress of SMS 2.0.

SMS Monitoring Features Use

SMS is made up components that are constantly running or waiting to perform their task. For each of the Systems Management Server components running at a site, you can see the status of that component, the events that are happening and have happened on your system, and whether they are warnings or errors. This information is invaluable for a systems administrator to understand the status of operations.

For each component, information is continually being updated and provided. This allows you to see problems not only at the main server, but also at the distribution points as software is distributed and at the clients as software is installed or other operations are performed. In this way you can follow a process through and be sure that it completes successfully.

Status information can also be filtered and forwarded to other servers in the hierarchy, allowing a summation of the state of the system to be created.

SMS STATUS VIEWING

SMS 2.0 status messages replace SMS 1.2 events. You can convert status messages to Windows NT events. SMS server service and thread components generate status messages when they carry out their tasks. A status message is a text message generated at a particular time by a particular component. Status messages are generated in two categories: flow-of-activity messages and exceptional messages. SMS stores all status messages in the SMS site database.

The SMS 2.0 Status Viewer resembles the Windows NT Event Viewer. With the Status Viewer, you can manipulate your view of status messages to help you extract information from the data and view the details for entire groups of messages at a glance. SMS groups status messages by task. For example, all the messages related to a site configuration change are grouped together.

STATUS SUMMARIES

Status summaries provide a quick overview of the health of your site. Site Status displays red, yellow, and green status health indicators. These indicators reflect the thresholds you specify. By using the SMS Administrator, you can view the status of events logged to your site and all sites beneath it. From the SMS Administrator Console, select and expand System Status Node as shown in Figure 12.14.

Figure 12.14   *Message Window.*

All status messages are displayed in the status viewer window. By default, the window displays the main attributes for each message. To control the way these messages are displayed, from the View menu, select all messages, Details, Filter, or Query info. To view details for a specific message, double-click the message. The message Detail dialog box appears as shown in Figure 12.15, and the attributes in Table 12.8 are displayed.

Depending on the type of message and the component that reported the message, the message may also display additional attributes. To view message details for the preceding or following event in the list, choose the Previous or Next buttons very similar to Windows NT Event Viewer. Choose close to return to the message window.

FLOW-OF-ACTIVITY MESSAGES

Components generate flow-of-activity messages to illustrate the tasks a component is carrying out. These messages:

- Educate the administrator about the tasks the component performs
- Facilitate the debugging of complex problems
- Facilitate the auditing of SMS activity
- Provide reports and summaries showing the overall health or progress of a specific SMS feature

Figure 12.15 *Status Message Details Dialog Box.*

Table 12.8 *Event Detail Dialog Box Attributes*

Attribute	Description
Date	The date the status message was generated
Time	The time the status message was generated (either Greenwich mean time or the time local to the computer running Status Message Viewer)
Site Code	The site code of the site where the message was generated
System	The name of the computer where the message was generated
Source	The source of the message (SMS server, SMS client, or SMS provider)
Component	The name of the SMS component that generated the message
Type	The message type
Severity	The Message severity
Message ID	The message ID
Process ID	The process ID of the process that generated the message
Thread ID	The name of the service or program that logged the event. For the SMS Executive service, Component may display the SMS Executive thread that logged the event.
Description	The message text
Properties	The message properties

EXCEPTIONAL MESSAGES

Components generate exceptional messages when they encounter a problem performing a task. These messages warn you about a problem that requires your attention.

You can also map Windows NT 4.0 events (such as low disk space or a security violation) to SNMP traps and forward these traps to other administrators—not just SMS administrators—to alert them of this event.

FINDING MESSAGES BY QUERIES

You can create or run queries to find status messages. In the following example, run a query to locate status messages from a specific site. From the SMS Administrator (Figure 12.16), proceed as follows:

1. Choose System Status Node and select Status Message Queries.
2. In the Queries window, choose Status Messages From a Specific Site.
3. Right-click on Query and Show Messages to run.

The Query Prompted dialog box appears as shown in Figure 12.17. Enter required criteria and Choose OK to continue running query for specified criteria and viewing messages.

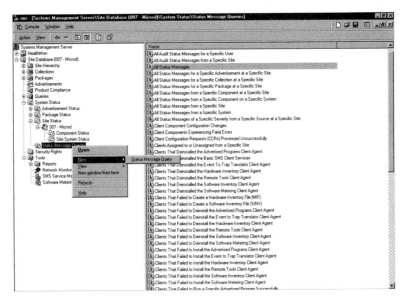

Figure 12.16 *SMS Administrator Site Database System Status Message Screen.*

Figure 12.17 *Query Prompted Dialog Box.*

OCCURRENCE OF A MESSAGE NOTIFICATION

SMS 2.0 allows you to view and generate alerts triggered when specific events occur based on predefined criteria. An alert can log an SMS message, execute a command, and send a message to a computer or user on the local network.

MCSE 12.3 Identifying Changes to a Site Server After SMS Installation

This section provides in-depth information on identifying changes to a site server after SMS installation, with a focus on directory services and directory service strategies. It is intended for networking groups planning to implement a Windows NT Server 4.0-based networking solution (after SMS installation) and those who may need help in designing and implementing directory services. The goal of this section is to explain the impact of Windows NT Server 4.0 on network infrastructure components such as DNS (domain name system) and how this will evolve in Windows 2000 (formerly Windows NT 5.0).

Types of Site Servers

As organizations gain more experience with SMS reliability and scalability, they are choosing to deploy Windows NT Server 4.0 as well as other site servers in mission-critical and enterprise situations. When planning an enterprise site server infrastructure deployment, administrators must consider current business and user requirements as well as anticipated future needs. Just as changes in business and user requirements are planned for during the design stages, changes in the network operating system and infrastructure should also be anticipated, as well as the different types of site servers available, such as:

- Domain controllers
- Nondomain controllers
- Secondary site servers

DOMAIN CONTROLLERS

Windows 2000 supports a mixed environment of Windows 2000 Active Directory domain controllers and Windows NT 4.0 domain controllers. Customers can migrate at their own pace based on business needs. Windows NT Workstation and Microsoft Windows 95 and 98 clients without Active Directory access software can log on to Active Directory domain controllers using Windows NT LAN Manager (NTLM) challenge/response authentication.

Backward compatibility allows businesses to migrate their domain controllers first and then migrate their clients, or they can migrate a combination of site servers and clients. The migration process does not require a mass migration to the new operating system version on site servers or clients. It is also unnecessary to take a complete domain offline to migrate domain controllers or clients. Individual domain controllers are unavailable only during their operating system update. This allows companies to migrate to Active Directory without interrupting their business.

SIMPLIFICATION OF DOMAIN MODELS • The Active Directory design allows simple migration of both centralized and decentralized Windows NT 4.0 domain models. The typical master or multiple master domain model can be migrated easily to an Active Directory tree or forest model.

The combination of the Active Directory and the improved security model allows users to reduce the number of domains in the enterprise. The primary reason organizations choose a master domain model is to allow local staff to administer local resource domains without granting these users administrative rights to user accounts in the master domain. This is useful for both the central information technology (IT) departments and local users. Central IT staff do not have to travel to remote locations or perform administrative operations over slow WAN links, and local users receive support more quickly from local support staff who tend to have a better understanding of the daily processes of their local users.

The origin of many multiple master domain environments can be found in the limitations of Windows NT 3.1 domain controllers. In the first release, Windows NT could not hold more than 10,000 objects in the database, which was insufficient for larger companies. Therefore, customers had to create additional accounts or master domains and establish trusts between these master domains. In the Active Directory, the scalability is sufficient to store up to 10 million objects in one domain, thereby reducing the need for additional domains.

The Windows NT 4.0 structure can be reestablished within a domain using an organizational unit (OU) hierarchy. Users can use the migration to the Active Directory as a means to reduce the number of domains and can thus simplify their network administration and their network structure.

SINGLE DOMAIN MODEL • The single domain model is the simplest domain architecture possible in a Windows NT 4.0 topology. In this architecture, there is simply one primary domain controller (PDC) that holds the master copy of the Security Account Manager (SAM) database. In addition, there may be one or more backup domain controllers and several member site servers present in the domain.

In this architecture, all user accounts, machine accounts, and resource definitions (such as printer queues and shares) draw security principal definitions from the PDC's SAM database. These accounts are granted rights based on Access Control Entries (ACEs) in the Access Control Lists (ACLs) on whatever resource is being shared or restricted. There can exist, by definition, only one copy of the SAM database that is modified at any given time, and the SAM database is owned by the PDC.

ACTIVE DIRECTORY PHYSICAL ARCHITECTURE • In the Windows 2000 Active Directory, a domain is a partition in the namespace. All domain controllers in the same domain contain the entire directory for the domain, and their databases are identical. Replicating objects always happens on the domain level. Domain controllers never replicate domain objects to domain controllers in different domains. This makes a domain both a naming context and a partition in the namespace.

THE SCHEMA OF DIRECTORY OBJECTS • The schema in the Active Directory defines what objects and properties can be created in the directory. A *forest* is a set of trees that share a common schema, configuration, and global catalog, with Kerberos trust among all members of the forest. When the Active Directory is installed on the first domain controller in a forest, the directory service creates a default schema. This schema includes all objects and properties required for the directory service to work, and it is replicated to all domain controllers that later join the forest.

Any directory service contains comprehensive information about users and objects in an organization. With the Active Directory, the fault tolerance created by the replication model and the extensibility of the database make the directory a great place to store information to be used by directory-aware applications. One example is a human resources (HR) application. The directory includes a great deal of information about users, such as their first and last names, their office numbers, their phone numbers, and perhaps their home addresses. While all this information is useful to a human resources application, additional information would need to be added, such as the employee's salary, social security number, tax withholding information, and health insurance information.

The Active Directory allows you to extend the schema to create new properties and classes for all the information you may want to add. New classes can be derived from existing classes and can inherit all properties from the previous classes. New properties can be created, and these properties can be added to classes. Properties in classes have *must* attributes or *may* attributes; that is, they are required or optional. Required properties (those with *must* attributes) are needed to obtain a value when a new object is created. These properties can be changed later, but they cannot be deleted. For example, a user object must contain a common name (cn), a *SamAccount Name* used for backward compatibility, and a password.

Optional properties (those with *may* attributes) can be added or changed at any time. These properties are not required for the directory service to work, but they hold additional information useful for system administration or for other users in the enterprise. Examples include phone numbers, office numbers, and a manager attribute.

For example, suppose you need to distinguish between employees and contractors who need network access. Derive a new user class, *AcmeUser*, specifically for full-time employees. You then determine that to support your HR application, you must add salary and social security number properties to the schema. Add the newly defined salary and social security properties to the AcmeUser class as *may* attributes. The security granularity of Windows 2000 allows you to grant read and write access to these properties to members of the HR department only. The individual user has read access to his or her data, although administrators do not have access to these attributes.

ACTIVE DIRECTORY REPLICATION • The Active Directory uses multimaster replication. The Active Directory does not distinguish between primary and backup domain controllers, where changes in the domain database can only be performed on one specific domain controller. Instead, it simply uses domain controllers (DCs), and all domain controllers are peers. Objects can be created or manipulated on any domain controller, and changes are then propagated to the remaining domain controllers.

> While this approach is conceptually simpler, it does require a means for transferring data among domain controllers and for reconciling contradictory settings among the different domain controllers.

Replication in the Active Directory is not based on time, but on Update Sequence Numbers (USNs). Each domain controller holds a table containing entries for its own USN and the USNs of its replication partners. During replication, the domain controller compares the last known USN of its replication partner saved in the table, with the current USN the replication partner provides. If there have been changes (that is, if the replication partner provides a higher USN), the data store requests all changes from the replication partner. This is known as *pull replication*. After receiving the data, the directory store sets the USN to the same value as that of the replication partner.

If properties on the same object are changed on different domain controllers, the domain controllers reconcile the data as follows:

- *By version number.* All properties carry a version number, and the Active Directory always uses the highest version. Although this is not always the correct solution, the use of an unequivocal algorithm ensures that reconciliation can be performed locally without negotiation with the replication partner. It also ensures that the same data are being used on all domain controllers.

- *By timestamp.* If the version numbers on the changed property are the same, the domain controller uses a timestamp to reconcile the data. The timestamp is created with the property and version number. The attribute with the latest timestamp is used. Domain controllers assume that time information is accurate and do not negotiate the time. Again, although this is not always the correct solution, the use of this algorithm ensures that domain controllers continue serving the clients rather than performing lengthy time negotiations.

- *By buffer size.* If both the version number and the timestamp are the same, the domain controller performs a binary memory copy operation and compares the buffer size. The highest buffer size wins. If the two buffers are equal, the attributes are binarily the same, and one can be discarded.

All reconciliation operations are logged, and administrators have the option of recovering and using the rejected values.

SITES AND DOMAINS • The *site* server concept has been used by various SMS applications to minimize replication traffic over slow WAN links. Unfortunately, the site server concepts used in different SMS applications do not match. Windows 2000 and the Active Directory introduce a new site server concept that is not optimized for the needs of a specific application, but uses the underlying IP network to determine locations where a good network connection is available. Eventually, all SMS-based applications will evolve to this site server concept.

An Active Directory site server is a combination of one or more IP subnets. The administrator can define these subnets and can add subnets to a site server. Sites support two features:

- They optimize replication traffic over slow WAN networks.
- They help clients to find domain controllers close to them.

Replication within a site server and between sites follows different topologies. Within a site server, a domain controller postpones notification of recent changes for a configurable interval. The default value is ten minutes. Unlike Microsoft Exchange, the Active Directory allows you to manipulate the replication topology within a site server. The directory store creates a default replication topology that consists of a bidirectional ring. You can change this topology and create another architecture—a star, for example. The Knowledge Consistency Checker (KCC) runs on all domain controllers, and checks that the topology is not broken and that no domain controller is excluded from the replication process. If the replication topology is broken, it is fixed automatically by the KCC.

Clients can use site server information to find domain controllers or resources close to them, which helps minimize network traffic over slow

WAN links. When a client starts a logon process, the first information a client receives from a domain controller is the client's site server membership, the domain controller's site server membership, and whether the domain controller is the closest to the client. If the domain controller is not the closest, the client can query for a domain controller in its own site server and can then communicate only with the closer domain controller.

> The client saves the site server information in the registry and can use it to talk to a close domain controller or to find close resources.

If a workstation is moved to a different location, the previous domain controller tells the client that it is no longer the closest domain controller and provides the new site server information to the client. The client can use the new site server information to query DNS for a closer domain controller.

GLOBAL CATALOG SERVERS • Another new concept in the Active Directory is the *global catalog* (GC). The global catalog holds all objects from all domains in the Windows 2000 directory and a subset of each object's properties. Internally, the global catalog implements the same hierarchy as the domain tree does. LDAP queries, however, usually return results in a flat record set or list. This allows the global catalog to be used as a repository that functions like a global address book, comparable to the Microsoft Exchange Global Address book. Global catalogs can be used for tree-wide searches. If all information can be found on a global catalog, no LDAP referrals to other domain controllers need to be created. It is a good idea to have at least one global catalog in each site server. By doing so, clients always have a local repository for search operations.

CONTIGUOUS AND DISJOINTED NAMESPACES • In an LDAP directory, the namespace can be organized in a contiguous or a disjointed namespace. In a contiguous namespace, the name of a child domain always contains the name of the parent domain. For example, if an Active Directory domain with the LDAP name *DC=Sales,DC=Microsoft,DC=com* is a child of *DC=Microsoft,DC=com*, a contiguous namespace was used. The name of the parent domain can always be constructed by removing the first part of the child domain name.

In a disjointed namespace, the names of the parent and child domains are not directly related. An example is the Active Directory domain *DC=MSN,DC=com*, which should be a child domain of *DC=Microsoft,*

DC=com. In this case, the child domain does not carry the name of the parent domain as part of its own name.

The use of a contiguous or a disjointed namespace affects LDAP search operations. In a contiguous namespace, a domain controller always creates referrals to the child domains. Using a disjointed namespace, however, terminates the search operation, and referrals are never created.

The use of both contiguous and disjointed namespaces within the same tree led to confusion about how search operations work in the tree. For that reason, the tree model was refined for the Active Directory, and the concept of trees and forests was introduced, which is explained next.

TREE METADATA • The tree metadata contains all information needed for a tree or a forest to work. The metadata is built of two containers: the *configuration* container and the *schema* container. Each container implements its own naming structure and, by doing this, its own replication topology. The configuration container is the information that glues together the trees in a forest. This information includes the available domains in the forest, the sites, and all domain controllers. Whenever a domain controller joins a domain, the configuration information must be updated and replicated.

NONDOMAIN CONTROLLERS

As Windows 2000 is presently in the beta stages, begin working with it as a member server (nondomain controller) in a Windows NT 4.0-based network environment. Upgrading a Windows NT Server 4.0 to Windows NT Server 2000 is a straightforward operation, and it easily interoperates as a member server in a Windows NT Server 4.0 network. This part of the chapter briefly detailed the evolutionary steps for planning a Windows NT Server 4.0 network that looks ahead to Windows 2000, but this should not discourage you from going ahead and installing Windows 2000 member site servers in the existing network environment. Start working with Windows 2000 in the role of a nondomain controller in your test areas and, after concluding your testing, in your existing network environments.

SECONDARY SITE SERVERS

A SMS secondary site server is a limited SMS installation. Secondary sites provide SMS connectivity with minimal administrative requirements. There are many advantages, in terms of maintenance and bandwidth, to having a SMS secondary site. SMS sends packages to a secondary site in a compressed format, and Maintenance Manager does not poll secondary site servers during every cycle, which reduces network traffic.

As discussed in earlier chapters, a SMS secondary site can be created only from a primary site or with SMS CDROM setup and there can be no child sites under a secondary site. A secondary site does not have a SQL Server database, and it usually does not have a local administrator. Although you can install SMS Administrator Utilities on the secondary site server, you must remove them before you can upgrade the secondary site.

SECONDARY SITE SERVER REQUIREMENTS • A secondary site server can be a Windows NT Server 4.0 domain controller or member server with an NTFS partition. A secondary site installation requires at least 55 MB of free disk space. After the installation, additional space is required to store packages sent to the site server. The parent primary site requires at least 55 MB of free disk space to prepare and process files sent to the secondary site during its creation or upgrade. More disk space is required when packages are distributed to that secondary site.

SECONDARY SITE SERVER SERVICES • Secondary sites use a number of SMS services, including Site Configuration Manager, SMS Executive, SMS Client Configuration Manager, and Inventory Agent. Installing the SMS client services on the secondary site server also installs the SMS Remote Tools Agent. Because secondary sites use the primary site SQL Server database maintained by the primary site's Hierarchy Manager service, this service is not installed on the secondary site server.

CREATING SECONDARY SITES • You can only create a secondary site from the parent primary site or by using the setup on the SMS CD while connecting to the primary site. During the installation process, files are copied from the primary site to the new secondary site server, SMS services are installed and started, and status reporting is returned to the primary site to update site configuration and complete installation jobs.

UPGRADING SECONDARY SITES • Normally, installing a service pack or a new version of SMS on a primary site automatically upgrades all secondary sites attached directly to it. This is the supported method of upgrading the sites, as it guarantees all sites are running the same version of SMS.

Although the automatic upgrade process is usually quick and efficient, a secondary site connected by a slow network link sometimes requires additional time to complete file transfers and to report. Upgrading multiple secondary sites concurrently may adversely impact network bandwidth. SMS

2.0 Service Pack 4 includes enhancements to the upgrade process that allow a selective upgrade of individual secondary sites.

MCSE 12.4 | Monitoring SMS Status Messages

SMS provides distribution services. It pinpoints the target clients, transfers files and instructions, and can monitor and configure status messages to determine whether or not an installation is successful. This also includes the monitoring and configuration of SMS site installation status messages and unwanted status messages

Viewing Advertisement Status Messages

Viewing the advertisement (job) status displays a detailed message about any individual advertisement (job). To view an advertisement (job) status, in the Advertisement (job) Properties dialog box, click Status as shown in Figure 12.18.

The Overall Status is determined by combining the sending and working status of the requests. Table 12.9 describes the Advertisement (job) Status.

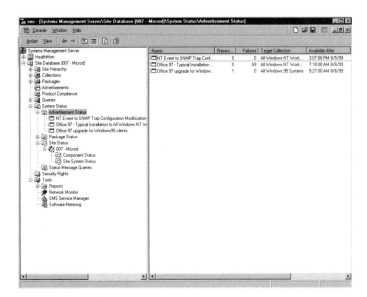

Figure 12.18 *Advertisement Status.*

Table 12.9 *Advertisement (Job) Status and Description of Each*

Advertisement Status	Description
Name	The name assigned to the advertisement when it was created
Received	The number of users and/or clients that received the advertisement
Failures	The number of users and/or clients that experienced an error processing the advertisement or its associated package or that attempted to run the advertised program but failed
Programs Started	The number of users and/or clients that started running the advertised program
Programs Errors	The number of users and/or clients that reported errors while running the advertised program
Program Success	The number of users and/or clients reporting that the advertisement ran successfully
Package	The name of the package being advertised
Program	The program type in the package being advertised
Target Collection	The collection that this advertisement was sent to
Available After	The time after which this advertisement is available to the target collection
Expires After	The time after which this advertisement is no longer available to the target collection
Advertisement ID	The ID number assigned to the advertisement when it was created

SENDING STATUS MESSAGES

Sending Status is sending the Advertisement (Job) Status data and instructions to a site. The Scheduler receives its status message information from the senders.

WORKING STATUS MESSAGES

Working Status indicates the working status of the job request at the target site. The working status is in a pending state until the package and instruction files are sent. The Despooler is responsible for returning status message information after carrying out the instructions it received. When the status message is received by the originating site, it is placed in the SMS database by the Inventory Data Loader. The SMS Administrator displays this status message by reading the database. The Scheduler uses this working status to update the overall job status and to retry the job if errors occurred.

CANCEL STATUS MESSAGES

When the job is canceled, the Cancel Status indicates the progress of the cancel command. This message displayed shows if the cancel command was received by the target site and whether it is active, complete, or has failed.

Viewing the Advertisement (Job) Status Messages

An organization that uses SMS can simultaneously advertise multiple programs in multiple target sites. All of the status messages generated by any component within the organization are collected by the status system, filtered, and processed to display meaningful information about each advertisement. You can either view the advertisement summary information, or you can view the status messages that produced the summary information as shown in Figure 12.19.

Monitoring and Configuring Unwanted "Access Denied" Messages in Workgroup-Based Networks

This section shows how to identify and resolve most common problems indicated by unwanted permissions status messages. These may state something like "Access has been denied" (hereafter referred to as an Access Denied

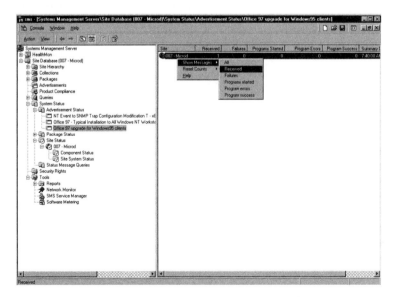

Figure 12.19 *Viewing Advertisement Summary Information.*

status message), or they may state that the user has only partial access, such as "You have only Read Access; changes will not be saved."

WORKGROUP NETWORKING

If you receive an Access Denied status message or similar message in a workgroup network, go to the computer with the share and examine the permissions on the share. Check to see if the share has permissions set to Read-Only or Full control. Also check to see if a password is required to access the share. This is the case if the administrator of a Windows 95 or 98 share specifies a password in the *Read-Only Password* or *Full Access Password* fields of the share's property dialog box.

SHARING FILES ON COMPUTERS IN A WINDOWS NT 4.0 WORKGROUP • Computers running Windows NT 4.0 have two capabilities in a workgroup that client computers running Windows 3.1, Windows for Workgroups 3.11, or Windows 95 or 98 do not. Computers running Windows NT 4.0 have the ability to specify specific users' access to a resource as well as the ability to specify users on the local file system.

FILE PERMISSIONS (WINDOWS NT 4.0 NTFS-PARTITIONS ONLY) AND SHARE PERMISSIONS • The *Directory Permissions* dialog box implies that the computer has an NTFS partition; it does not appear in FAT file system partitions. This allows the computer permissions underneath the share-permission level.

Everyone/Full Control is the file-level permission, and there is neither a user nor a group specified with *No Access*. Therefore, a fictitious user David would have all necessary permissions from the file system to read and write files from and to that share.

When a user attempts to connect to a remote resource that is on a Windows NT 4.0 computer, and the share is located on an NTFS file system, Windows NT 4.0 always uses the most restrictive of the share and file permissions to apply to that user. For example, assume there is a share called Documents on a computer running Windows NT 4.0, and a user named David wants to copy a file to this share, load (read) a file from that share into a word processor, and then save it with the same name after he makes changes to it.

If the Documents share has David/Read-Only permissions and file permissions are David/No Access, David's cumulative permissions are David/No Access. David will receive an *Access Denied* status message when he attempts to copy the file to the share or when he tries to access any files on that share.

If the Documents share has David /Read-Only permissions and file permissions are David Full Control, David's permissions resolve to David/Read-Only. David will receive an *Access Denied* status message when he attempts to copy the file to the share, but he can read and open files from that share. He will receive an *Access Denied* status message when he attempts to write changes to an exiting file with its current or a new name on that share.

If the Documents share has David/Full Control permissions and file permissions are David /Read-Only, David's resulting permissions are David/Read-Only for the existing files on that share. David can copy the file to the share, can read and open the Read-Only marked files from that share, but will receive an *Access Denied* status message when he attempts to write changes to those Read-Only files.

If the Documents share has David/Full Control permissions and the file permissions are David/Full Control, David's permissions are David/Full Control, and he can copy the file to the share and read, open, and write to all files on that share.

TROUBLESHOOTING UNWANTED ACCESS DENIED STATUS MESSAGES • The following are some things you can try when you receive Access Denied status messages:

- Check the share permissions to see if *Everyone* or only a particular user is specified.
- Try to connect to the share when you enable the local Guest account on the computer with the share.
- If both computers have the same user account, try resetting the passwords on both computers.
- In Windows NT Explorer, right-click on the file or directory you want to access, click Properties, click the Security tab, and click Permissions. Verify that there are no restrictions on the NTFS file system keeping clients from connecting or allowing clients fewer permissions than you want them to have. Windows NT 4.0 applies the most restrictive permission to the client when going from the share permission to the file permissions.
- Check to see if the user is specifically given permissions or if permissions are assigned to groups.
- Ensure that the user actually belongs to the groups with the proper permissions.
- Check to see if the Share or File System specifies a No Access permission to a group or user.

- Check to see if the resource is in the same domain as the user or if it is on the network in a domain with a trust relationship. Try to connect to the resource with a different user account.
- Check to see if someone with Administrator-level privileges to that resource can connect to it.

ACCESS DENIED STATUS MESSAGES FROM WITHIN APPLICATIONS • If an Access Denied status message appears while you are running an application (such as when you attempt to open a file in Microsoft Word from a shared directory), try using another application. If the same problem occurs, you can rule out the application as the problem. If you don't have another application, try to access the file you want to open from a command prompt and attempt to copy a file to your local drive as a test. If the copy works, the problem appears to be related to the particular application. At this point, it would be best to contact your systems administrator for a resolution to the problem.

If you are trying to save a file with the same name it had when you opened it and you receive an Access Denied status message, try saving the file with a different name. If that works, the original file has a Read-Only attribute assigned to it. If it does not work, however, you may not have write access to that share.

MCSE 12.5   Monitoring the Progress of SMS Functions

SMS allows you to monitor or track the progress of SMS functions. It provides you with the ability to monitor the progress of:

- Client installation
- Software distribution
- Inventory collection
- Remote control

Monitoring the Progress of Client Installation and Software Distribution

SMS pinpoints target clients; transfers files and instructions, and monitors whether client installations or software distributions have been successful. The process of distributing software or commands regarding the installation of client computers is described in the following sidebar, "The SMS Client Installation and Software Distribution Process."

Study Break

The SMS Client Installation and Software Distribution Process

SMS provides client installation and software distribution services at the site server, when the Advertisement (job) is distributed, and at the client.

At the site server:

1. The administrator creates a package.

2. The administrator creates Advertisement (job).

3. The administrator determines which server(s) are distribution points for the application.

The Advertisement (job) is distributed:

1. The Advertisement (job) is sent to destination sites with target client computers.

2. Packages are placed on software distribution servers in that site.

3. Advertisements include instruction files for clients and are sent to logon servers.

At the client:

1. The User logs on and advertisement pops up on user's desktop. The user selects to run available packages.

2. The client then connects to a distribution server and runs the package.

CREATING A PACKAGE

A package definition file is a specially formatted file describing a package and one or more programs that are created outside the SMS Administrator console. Use a package definition file as an alternative to creating a package in SMS. If you already have a package definition file, you simply import the file into a wizard, and SMS immediately creates the package and programs. SMS includes package definition files for commonly installed Microsoft applications with your SMS installation.

You can create a package in one of the following ways as shown in Figure 12.20:

• Import a package definition file using the Distribute Software wizard.
• Create Package from Definition wizard.

Figure 12.20 *Administrator's Console and Package Status Node.*

Package properties include the software name and version, the location of the package source directory, and group permissions for the distribution folder. Packages are typically used to distribute software to Systems Management Server clients. A package defines the files and instructions for distributing, installing, and running software.

SMS Administrator console, Package Status contains a status summarizer for each package distributed by SMS. Packages can be monitored from the System Status Node as shown in Figure 12.20.

DISTRIBUTION OF PACKAGE • When a package is received at a site, it is placed on software distribution servers by the Despooler. The Distribute Phase can be configured to overwrite the package at existing software distribution servers or place it on a new group of software distribution servers. The list displays the machine groups defined by the administrator and a group called <Default Servers>.

DEFAULT SOFTWARE DISTRIBUTION SERVERS • The <Default Servers> group is used when selected or when the Despooler cannot find any of the specified software distribution servers on which to place the package. This group, which initially contains only the site server, can be modified in the *Site Properties* dialog box by clicking *Servers*.

If any target computers are Novell NetWare clients, be sure to place a NetWare server in the <Default Servers> group.

If the target client computer cannot access the software distribution server, the user sees the command on the target client computer, but running the command will always fail. This might be due to incorrect account permissions or server type. A NetWare client, for example, cannot access a server running Windows NT Server 4.0.

Now, let's look at how to monitor the progress of the SMS inventory collection process. This information is to help you monitor and troubleshoot the client inventory collection scan and the inventory data flow, which starts at the client and ends on the primary site server's database.

HOW INVENTORY IS COLLECTED AND ADDED TO THE DATABASE

The Inventory Dataloader collects and updates the SMS database. The Inventory Dataloader then monitors and checks for Delta-MIF files in the `Site.srv\Dataload.box\Deltamifcol` directory that contain inventory collection data, advertisement (job) status, and event information.

HOW INVENTORY DATALOADER DETECTS MONITORS BAD .MIF FILES

When the Inventory Dataloader reads a .raw file or a .mif file, it monitors and checks the file for validity. If it fails, the file is placed in the `Site.srv\Dataload.box\Deltamif.col\Badmifs` directory. Isvmif files are also checked for an Architecture and Identification group. If those groups are missing, an error message is attached to the bottom of the .mif file and the file is placed in the `Badmifs` directory.

HOW INVENTORY DATALOADER UNIQUELY IDENTIFIES AND MONITORS EACH COMPUTER

The Inventory Dataloader monitors and searches the database for a matching computer to update. If it does not find a matching computer, it creates a new computer in the database. The Inventory Dataloader does not create a new record each time a computer's inventory is reported. Only the collected inventory data that has changed is stored in the database. This optimizes the size of the database. When a computer is updated, the old information is kept in the database to be viewed later in the SMS Administrator program.

GENERATING A RESYNC COMMAND

If the Inventory Dataloader cannot find the computer in the database and it receives only changes to a supposed existing computer, it generates a *resync* command requesting all inventory collection information for the computer. This can occur when a computer has been deleted from the SMS database, but SMS client software has not been removed from the client computer.

MAINTENANCE MANAGER • All logon servers in a site have a `Logon.srv` directory. When the Inventory Agent has finished its processing, it places its inventory collection data on the logon server.

The .raw files are placed in the `Logon.srv\Inventry.box` directory by the Inventory Agent that runs on Windows 3.x, Windows 95, Windows 98, and Windows NT 4.0 computers. Collected files are combined in the .raw files.

ISV is an acronym for Independent Software Vendors, who may design custom .mif files.

The Maintenance Manager running on the site server collects the inventory data from the `Logon.srv` directories. It then copies these files to the equivalent `Site.srv` directories.

INVENTORY COLLECTION PROCESSOR • After the inventory collection data is copied to the site server, the Inventory Collection Processor converts the .raw files or the .mif files into a useful format for the Inventory Dataloader. The Inventory Collection Processor performs two functions: it maintains inventory history files and produces Delta-MIF files.

MAINTAINING AND MONITORING INVENTORY HISTORY

History files are kept in the `Site.srv\Inventry.box\History` directory. A history file for each SMS client exists, and the file name matches its unique ID name, such as Abc000001.hms. NetWare servers, OS/2 clients, and Macintosh clients store their history in *.smh files. When the Inventory Collection Processor processes a .mif file or .raw file, it checks for a matching history file. If it finds a match, it compares the two files to determine the difference between the current information and the historical information. By maintaining and monitoring history files, the Inventory Collection Processor can reduce the amount of information passed to the Inventory Dataloader as well as that which is passed on to parent sites.

PRODUCING DELTA-MIF FILES

The Inventory Collection Processor turns the inventory data files (.raw, .mif) into a Delta-MIF file for the Inventory Dataloader to process. A Delta-MIF file is a .mif file with a binary header of SMS instructions attached to it. It generally contains only the changes in inventory collection data for a client. After the Inventory Collection Processor has finished converting the file to a Delta-MIF file, it places the finished file in the Inventory Dataloader's directory, `Site.srv\Dataload.box\Deltamif.col`.

If the information in the inventory collection data file matches the information in the history file, no Delta-MIF file is created. If no Delta-MIF files are created for a client for four days, a Delta-MIF file is created to update the WorkstationStatus for the client's inventory.

SMS uses history and Delta-MIF files to reduce the processing of the Inventory Dataloader as it adds the inventory collection data to the database. It also reduces the amount of inventory collection data to be passed up the site hierarchy to a parent site.

Monitoring the Progress of Remote Control

Once a client is located and permission granted, monitoring the progress of remote control begins. A variety of options and settings are available.

Some people have stated that certain third-party products are faster than SMS remote control monitoring. This has to do with the encryption phase. Currently, only SMS includes encryption, so only SMS remote viewing is secure. Speed can be enhanced using SMS by lowering resolution on the client computer and by forcing 16-color viewing. This lessens the amount of information going across the network. Speed is enhanced by default for Windows NT 4.0 remote control monitoring by sending changes only in compressed form. This is done by selecting "Install Accelerated Screen Transfer on Windows NT 4.0 Clients" in the Clients Options section of the Site Properties dialog box. Further, note that remote control monitoring is fastest over NetBEUI, and NetBIOS over TCP/IP is generally a bit faster than TCP/IP sockets.

If you are running SMS 2.0 with an older service pack, install the latest service pack before trying anything else. Be aware that two files related to remote control monitoring must be added manually to SMS Admin workstations that are not site servers If you have been considering an upgrade to SMS 2.0, do so first before looking for individual problems. Many of the changes required for Windows 95 and 98 remote control monitoring support that were fixed as *bugs* were incorporated into SMS 2.0, as well as changes needed to support new hardware and video drivers. For a successful remote control monitoring session, the server must be able to use the display information sent from the client, and the client must be able to use the keystroke information sent from the server.

MONITORING REMOTE CONTROL DISPLAY PROBLEMS

Once the client computer's remote control agent has been located and permissions have been granted, the remote agent hooks into the video driver graphic functions, encrypts them, and sends the graphics tables (raster information for Windows NT 4.0 computers, and Windows NT 3.51 computers not using Accelerated Screen Transfer) to the SMS Admin workstation. For the display to appear properly, the SMS Admin workstation video driver and card must be able to interpret and display the information they receive, including all drawing functions, colors, and font information. This is quite a challenge. Many display drivers and video cards are available. Further, graphical information requires a great deal of memory. Thus, the higher the resolution, and the greater the detail in the display, the more memory required to store the information. When this information is sent over a network in real time to display on another computer, a considerable amount of bandwidth can be used. Common display problems include font issues and display completeness or color mapping issues.

MONITORING PASSING KEYSTROKE INFORMATION PROBLEMS

Very few problems arise from passing keystrokes to the client computer. Basically, the keyboard drivers on the SMS Admin computer must be compatible with those on the client.

MCSE 12.6 Monitoring the SMS Database

The goal of this section is to show you how to configure SMS database maintenance tasks. It then describes procedures for basic database maintenance as well as troubleshooting inventory backlog problems.

Be very cautious when making changes to your SMS database, as errors can cause serious problems with an SMS system.

You must set your SQL Server to Single User Mode beforehand.

Configure SMS Database Maintenance Tasks

To keep an SMS Site Server and its interactions with SQL Server operating at peak efficiency, you need to perform periodic maintenance on the SMS database. This is especially important for central site databases that store large volumes of data.

Configure the SMS database maintenance tasks every three to five months, although the ideal interval depends on how often and how many inventories are being collected. Generally speaking, the more often you configure these tasks, the less time it will take to perform them.

DATABASE CONSISTENCY CHECKER COMMANDS

Before and after major database configurations and operations, always consider carrying out the following database consistency checker commands from *ISQL/w:*

- DBCC CHECKDB
- DBCC NEWALLOC
- DBCC CHECKCATALOG

The preceding commands help ensure that the configurations and operations go smoothly and that no damage occurs during the configuration and operation of the SMS database tasks. They are especially important in providing intact database backups. These commands assist in cleaning up unused allocations and can detect errors in the database.

STOP THE SERVER • Before you can configure any SMS database maintenance tasks, stop all SMS services. To stop the SMS services, stop the following services on the SMS Site Server in this order:

These queries can take a long time to complete on very large databases. System performance and the size of the **SMS database** determine the actual time required.

1. SMS Executive
2. SMS Site Configuration Manager
3. SMS Hierarchy Manager
4. All other SMS services running on the SMS Site Server

Close all utilities that make a connection to the SMS database, such as SMS Administrator, SMS Database Manager, and so on.

BACK UP THE DATABASE (OPTIONAL) • If the site has not been backed up recently, the next procedure is recommended though elective. To back up the database, complete the following steps:

1. Locally, at the SMS Site Server, run `Regedt32.exe`.
2. Highlight the SMS registry key, and choose Save Key from the Registry menu: \HKEY_LOCAL_MACHINE \SOFTWARE \Microsoft \SMS.
3. Use SQL Enterprise Manager to back up the SMS database and the master database. Click Tools, then click Database Backup/Restore.
4. Make a file backup of the \SMS directory structure on the SMS Site Server.

OBTAIN THE CURRENT DATABASE INFORMATION • You need the current database statistics for comparison purposes. To obtain the current statistics, in the ISQL/w window, type use smsdb, and press Enter. This selects the SMS database.

Now, in the ISQL/w window, type DBCC UPDATEUSAGE(0), and press ENTER. This resets the usage reporting so that sp_spaceused can correctly report the database size, unallocated space, data size, index size, and unused space. Typically, carry this out only after rebuilding the indexes.

 If you don't carry out **DBCC UPDATEUSAGE(0)** after rebuilding the indexes, sp_spaceused reports the numbers that existed before you rebuilt the indexes.

Next, in the ISQL/w window, type sp_spaceused, and press Enter. This displays the current database size, unallocated space, data size, index size, and unused space. Save the results for comparison. By analyzing the results, you can determine how frequently a specific site should be cleaned up. If the database size is reduced by less than 10%, you can probably do less frequent cleanups.

DELETE OLD INFORMATION • Use the SMS Administrator utility to delete information older than a number of days that fits your needs. To delete old information:

1. In SMS Administrator, with the Sites window active, click Edit.
2. Click Delete Special and then choose Machine History from menu.
3. Close the SMS Administrator utility.
4. In the ISQL/w window, type DBCC UPDATEUSAGE(0) and press Enter. This resets the usage reporting.
5. In the ISQL/w window, type sp_spaceused with the Systems Management Server database selected as default. Save results for comparison.

The amount of history information that can be deleted at one time is determined by the size of the transaction log on the SMS database. It is possible to delete too information at one time. Therefore, when deleting large amounts of history records, delete them in increments. For example, if you wanted to delete records older than 70 days, and you know that you have information for the last 370 days, begin by deleting machine history older than 350 days, 320 days, 290 days, 260 days, and so forth, until you reach the desired 70 days of history.

If you try to delete too much information at one time, you may receive a message in SMS Administrator stating that the query could not be completed. This means that the SQL transaction log did not have enough free space to process the deletion. You can either dump or expand the size of the transaction log. To dump the transaction log, perform these steps:

1. In SQL Enterprise Manager, right-click the SMS database.
2. Select Edit in the Edit Database window.
3. Under Transaction Log, select Truncate.
4. Click OK.

To expand the transaction log, perform the following steps:

1. In SQL Enterprise Manager, right-click the SMS database.
2. In the Edit Database window, select Edit.

3. Under Transaction Log, select Expand.
4. In the Size (MB) box, type the amount of additional space to allocate (not the total space). The default is the maximum space available on the selected device.
5. Click OK. The Edit Database window returns.
6. Click OK.

After you expand a transaction log, back up the master database.

DELETE INACTIVE MACHINES • Use the SMS Administrator to delete inactive machines. If inventory is reported regularly, you should also delete inactive machines from the database. To delete inactive machines, follow these steps:

1. In SMS Administrator, with the Sites window active, click Edit.
2. Click Delete Special and then select Machines With Last Activity from the menu.
3. Enter a date or time period.

Be careful not to enter a date or time period that is too recent. For example, if you only collect inventory every two weeks, you should delete systems that have been inactive for at least 60–75 days. If inventory is not reported regularly, this step should probably be skipped. If this is a central site to a huge client base and if you collect inventory every four or five days, then you should delete systems that have been inactive for 40 or more days. To finish, follow these steps:

1. Close the SMS Administrator utility.
2. In the ISQL/w window, type DBCC UPDATEUSAGE(0) and press Enter. This resets the usage reporting.
3. In the ISQL/w window, type sp_spaceused with the SMS database selected as default. Save the results for comparison.

DELETE DUPLICATE MACHINES • Use the SMS Database Manager to delete duplicate machines. Duplicate records occur if the SMS client is reinstalled on a system, and a new inventory record is generated in the SMS database. Since only one record in the database can be active for a specific machine, duplicates are eventually deleted as they age in the database. However, you can also view and delete duplicate machines by using the SMS Database Manager utility. To delete duplicate machines, follow these steps:

1. Open the SMS Database Manager utility and select Machines.
2. Select Display Duplicate Personal Computers.
3. Click Name and delete all but the most recent entry for each machine listed.

Alternatively, you can merge the duplicate computer history records to eliminate the duplication. To merge records, highlight the machine records and select Merge History For Selected PCs from the Edit menu. This deletes all the old inventory records and keeps only the newest machine record. If necessary, repeat these steps for the systems listed under NetCardID. Therefore, you now need to do the following:

1. Close the SMS Database Manager utility.
2. In the ISQL/w window, type DBCC UPDATEUSAGE(0) and press Enter. This resets the usage reporting.
3. In the ISQL/w window, type sp_spaceused with the SMS database selected as default. Save the results for comparison.

DELETE UNUSED RECORDS • This step actually purges the deleted records in SQL Server and reclaims space in the SMS database so that SQL Server can reuse it. This can take a long time, the length of which depends on how often the procedure is performed and how much space is going to be reclaimed. To delete the unused records, perform the following steps:

1. Open the SMS Database Manager utility and select Tools.
2. Select Delete Unused Common/Specific Records.
3. Close the SMS Database Manager utility.
4. In the ISQL/w window, type DBCC UPDATEUSAGE(0) and press Enter. This resets the usage reporting.
5. In the ISQL/w window, type sp_spaceused with the SMS database selected as default. Save the results for comparison.

REBUILD THE INDEXES (OPTIONAL) • If you removed many machines or records, you need to rebuild the indexes to eliminate the old index entries and thus reduce the index space used by the SMS database. You can skip this step if you didn't delete many machines or records from your site. Reducing the index size reduces paging. This helps to eliminate disk bottlenecks and decreases the disk space used by the SMS database and its backups. The amount of reduction depends on the number of records deleted since the last time the indexes were rebuilt and how fragmented those indexes have become. The reduction can be significant. For example, for one central site in use for several months, this procedure reduced the indexes by 60% and the total space used by the database went from 305 MB to 225 MB.

Use the `SQLMaint.exe` utility to rebuild the SQL indexes on the SMS database. This utility is supplied with SQL Server 7.0 and is located in the `\mssql\binn` directory. To rebuild the indexes:

1. Start a command prompt.
2. Go to \mssql\binn\ and type the following command:

```
SQLMAINT.EXE -S h1grsvr -D smsdb -RebldIdx 10 -Rpt
c:\dbmaint.rpt
```

In this command, h1grsvr is the name of the server that SQL is on, smsdb is the name of the SMS database on which all indexes for all tables will be rebuilt, 10 is the percentage of free space to be left in the indexes, and `c:\dbmaint.rpt` is the location for the log reporting results.

The procedure builds a table of all index information for the database, and then walks through rebuilding each index individually. For now, do this:

1. In the ISQL/w window, type DBCC UPDATEUSAGE(0) with the SMS database selected as the default. This resets the usage reporting.
2. In the ISQL/w window, type sp_spaceused with the SMS database selected as default. Save the results for comparison.

BACK UP THE DATABASE (OPTIONAL) • If all the maintenance tasks complete without errors, do a backup of the SMS system. Refer to the previous "Back up the Database (Optional)" section on page 448 for procedures.

RUN DATABASE CONSISTENCY CHECKER COMMANDS (OPTIONAL) • Before and after major database operations, consider carrying out these database consistency checker commands from ISQL/w:

- DBCC CHECKDB
- DBCC NEWALLOC
- DBCC CHECKCATALOG

RESTART THE SMS SERVICES • Restart the SMS services in the following order:

1. SMS Hierarchy Manager
2. SMS Site Configuration Manager
3. SMS Executive

Restart all other SMS services on the SMS Site Server.

RECOMMENDED OPTIONS FOR TEMPDB AND THE SMS DATABASE

The following discussion summarizes recommended options for the Tempdb and SMS databases. For example, use the SQL Enterprise Manager to change options as follows:

1. On the Manage menu, click Databases.
2. Double-click the database to edit and click the Options tab.
3. Double-click the database name in the Server Manager window.

> SQL Server 6.5 and SQL Server 7.0 provide several ways to change database options.

You can also change the database options by using the sp_dboption stored procedure.

TEMPDB DATABASE OPTIONS • Tempdb should be 10–20% of the SMS database size. Be sure Tempdb options are set as shown in Table 12.10.

Table 12.10 *Tempdb Database Options Settings*

Option	Enabled	Disabled
Select Info/Bulk Copy	x	
Truncate Log on Checkpoint	x	
Columns Null by Default		x
No CheckPoint on Recovery		x
Single User		x
DBO Use Only		x
Read Only		x

SMS DATABASE OPTIONS • To calculate the SMS size, determine the maximum number of clients and allow 40K per client, including clients from child sites. If there is custom Management Information Format (MIF) data, each client record size should be increased. For performance reasons, it may be advisable to place the SMS database and log devices on a different physical drive than the site directories. Be sure that the SMS database options are set as shown in Table 12.11.

Table 12.11 *SMS Database Options Settings*

Option	Enabled	Disabled
Truncate Log on Checkpoint	x	
Select Info/Bulk Copy		x
Columns Null by Default		x
No CheckPoint on Recovery		x
Single User		x
DBO Use Only		x
Read Only		x

TROUBLESHOOTING INVENTORY MIF BACKLOG PROBLEMS

The SMS Dataloader service is responsible for entering inventory data into the SMS database. At times, a backlog of inventory files can occur in the following directories:

```
\SMS\Site.srv\Dataloder.box\Deltamif.col
```

```
\SMS\Site.srv\Dataloder.box\Deltamif.col\Process
```

Although there can be many causes of this accumulation, a backlog normally occurs when data in the form of Management Information Format files comes in more quickly than it goes out. The fact that a backlog exists doesn't necessarily indicate a problem. It's not uncommon for SMS Site Server to receive a large number of inventory MIFs when users log on in the morning. This can become a problem if the SMS Site Server doesn't clear the backlog in a reasonable amount of time.

This part of the section contains information about tuning, maintaining, and troubleshooting the SMS Dataloader to prevent or resolve situations that result in backlogs of machine MIF files on the SMS Site Server. You should only need to use the tuning subsection when a site is first installed or if major changes to the SMS hierarchy occur. To keep your SMS site operating at peak efficiency, complete the steps outlined in the maintenance section regularly. If problems do occur, the troubleshooting section can help you isolate the problem and possibly correct it.

SYSTEM BACKUP • Before beginning any of the steps documented in this part of the section, perform a complete backup of the SMS site. This involves dumping (backing up) the SMS and Master databases, backing up the SMS directory structure, and backing up the following registry key:

```
HKEY_LOCAL_MACHINE

\SOFTWARE

\Microsoft

\SMS
```

THE DATALOADER SERVICE • The Dataloader service is part of the SMS Executive Service and maintains five threads to process the five different types of MIF files. This multithreaded approach permits the processing of more than one MIF file at a time, which provides faster processing of database information. The extension on the MIF file determines which kind of MIF it is and which thread processes it into the SMS database. Valid extensions are:

- `.mif`, which indicates a machine inventory MIF file
- `.emf`, which indicates an event MIF file
- `.jmf`, which indicates a job status MIF file.
- `.pmf`, which indicates a package location MIF file
- `.umf`, which indicates a user group MIF file

Understanding this five-threaded approach can assist you in analyzing problems with the functionality or performance of the Dataloader service. In addition, if a backlog occurs, the `\SMS\Logs\Datalodr.log` and the Windows NT 4.0 Application Event Log on both the SMS Site Server and SQL Server provide valuable information to help troubleshoot the problem. The SQL Server Error Log may contain other important information.

TROUBLESHOOTING THE BACKLOG

The SMS Dataloader service is responsible for processing the inventory; therefore, its log file is the primary source of information on how the service is functioning. Prior to checking any of the following items listed, examine the `Datalodr.log` file to see if the service is stopped, the machine MIF thread has stopped responding, or the performance is slower than usual.

When troubleshooting the `Datalodr.log` file, locate the entry that shows the following text:

```
"~There are already 1 machine MIF processing thread(s), the
last known thread ID = C7, won't start a new one
$$<SMS_INVENTORY_DATA_LOADER><Mon Feb 02 10:27:38
1998~><thread=DC>"
```

This log entry indicates that the machine MIF processing thread was busy at the time the service maintenance cycle occurred. This entry does not necessarily indicate a problem, but serves to identify the thread currently being used to process machine MIFs. Other entries can be used to identify the machine MIF thread. In this example, the thread ID is C7, and any log entries that contain the text <thread=C7> are related to machine MIFs.

Scan the `Datalodr.log` file for entries that occurred before the preceding sample entry. If none are found, look in the `Datalodr.log` file. It is important to determine if the thread has stopped responding, or if it is just taking a long time to process each machine MIF. If the Dataloader service has stopped, you may need to stop and restart the SMS Executive Service to see relevant entries in the `Datalodr.log` file.

The time/date stamp on each log entry makes it easy to see how long it's taking to process each machine. Be aware that SQL Server performance can vary greatly depending on system configuration and hardware.

When reading the Dataloader log, start at the line, "Processing a machine." This is where a thread of the Dataloader server is starting to process an MIF. The last entry logged when the Dataloader service has finished processing an MIF is "Finished processing current machine." Using these two lines, try to calculate the average time the Dataloader is spending on your MIFs. Typically, it should not spend more than 20–25 seconds on one MIF. Because the Dataloader is a multithreaded application, be sure to note the thread ID in the last column when reading the log.

If a SMS Site Server is taking longer to process MIF files than it used to, its SMS database most likely needs maintenance. In addition, check the SMS services, MIF size, inventory records, and client resynchronizations.

SMS SERVICES • Make sure the SMS Executive Service is running on the SMS Site Server. If the service is not behaving properly, use SMS Setup to reset the site. This reinstalls SMS services, including the SMS Executive, on the server. Reinstallation can correct some problems.

MIF SIZE • Check the `SMS\Site.srv\Dataloder.box\Deltamif.col` and the `SMS\Site.srv\Dataloder.box\Deltamif.col\Process` directories, and note the MIF size. Initial client inventory MIFs are usually 50K to 70K, while Delta MIFs (inventory changes only) are approximately 5K to 20K. These values can change if no ID MIFs are collected or extensive software inventory is performed. Use caution when collecting files during inventory as this can create MIFs with very large file sizes.

DUPLICATE INVENTORY RECORDS • Check the SMS database to see if you have any duplicate inventory records. Duplicate inventory can slow down the Dataloader. In addition, these extra records consume disk space on the database. To check for and eliminate duplicate records, perform these steps:

1. Open the SMS Database Manager utility and select Machines.
2. Select Display Duplicate Personal Computers. The duplicate inventoried records are listed by computer name or network card ID (NetCardID).
3. To merge records, highlight the machine records. From the Edit menu, select Merge History For Selected PCs. This deletes all old inventory records and keeps only the newest record.
4. Close SMS Database Manager utility.

Use the ISQL command line utility and the following query to identify multiple computers using the same SMS unique ID (SMSID):

```
SELECT smsid0, name0, count (*) FROM identification_spec

WHERE smsid0 IN

(SELECT smsid0 FROM identification_spec

GROUP BY smsid0 HAVING count (*)>1)

GROUP BY smsid0, name0 HAVING count (*) = 1 ORDER BY smsid0
```

Once certain systems have been identified as using the same SMSID, reinstall the SMS client on all but one of them. Be aware that even after you have reinstalled the SMS client with a new SMSID, this query continues to identify those systems as having the same SMSID.

You can damage the SMS database by writing to the SMSdatabase directly in ISQL.

CLIENT RESYNCHRONIZATION • Check the Windows NT 4.0 Event Log for a high number of client resynchronizations. Numerous resyncs can be caused by duplicate SMSIDs.

DBCC CHECKS • Carry out SQL DBCC CHECKDB and DBCC NEWALLOC on the SMS database in Single User Mode. This can correct some problems with the database, although in some cases you will need to take other steps to correct database problems. For syntax and usage information, refer to the platform software development kit.

SITE REPORTER • Check the SMS\Site.srv\Siterep.box directory to see if there are files present. If there are, and the site is a child primary site, ensure that site-to-site communication is functioning properly. Look in the appropriate sender log and check the addresses, Windows NT 4.0 Application Event Logs, and Outbox scheduling. If there are files present in the `Siterep.box`, move them into a temporary directory to see if the MIF processing improves.

CHILD SITE ATTACH • The following is relevant only if your Dataloader backlog is on a central site or a parent site with a currently attached child site. Normally, Dataloader monitors the `Deltamif.col` directory for a directory with the `*.upd` name. When it detects a `*.upd` directory (only when a child site attaches), it stops processing machine MIF files at the site and begins processing the files in the `*.upd` directory. During this time, in addition to processing the files in the `*.upd` directory, the Dataloader only processes status MIFs related to current jobs. In the meantime, all other inventory MIF files are backlogged.

USER GROUP MIFS • Check the `SMS\Site.srv\Dataloder.box\Deltamif.col` directory for .umf files. If there are several large .umf files, this can slow the processing of machine MIFs. If your network environment contains large numbers of user groups or a complicated trust matrix, you may want to change the default interval for user group enumeration using the `Setgug.exe` utility.

I/O ERRORS • If SQL devices and SMS directories are on the same drive or the drive is mirrored with a single disk controller, check for I/O disk errors reported in the SQL log file or the Performance Monitor. If disk I/O appears to be a bottleneck, you may need to move SQL devices to another physical disk drive, install a second controller, and so forth.

SQL TRACING • If you enable SQL tracing, you will be able to see the SQL statements that the Dataloader uses to read and write data to the SMS database. You can then use this detailed information to troubleshoot specific Dataloader service functions. To enable SQL tracing, go to the following registry key on the SMS Site Server:

```
HKEY_LOCAL_MACHINE
\SOFTWARE
\Microsoft
\SMS
\TRACING
```

First set the SQL enabled value to 1, and then stop and restart the SMS Executive Service.

note When you aren't troubleshooting, SQL tracing should be disabled (set to 0). Leaving it enabled causes the Dataloader to slow down slightly and the log to fill up more quickly.

SERVER PROCESS ID (SPID) PERFORMANCE • You can use SQLWHO and Performance Monitor to monitor the SQL Server process ID (SPID) performance. SQL Server assigns a SPID number to each new connection, and each number is globally unique.

■ Summary

You should come away from this chapter with an in-depth knowledge of the MCSE exam-specific components or functions of SMS monitoring and optimization needed to identify changes to a site server after installation. This also includes types of site servers and areas for change; monitoring SMS 2.0 status reporting and the progress of SMS functions; using SMS utilities to monitor SMS functions; and monitoring the SMS database.

The first part of the chapter discussed how Network Monitor works by monitoring the network's data stream.

The second part of the chapter showed how to view SMS 2.0 messages logged to a site database, including messages for subsites.

The third part of the chapter provided in-depth information on identifying changes to a site server after SMS installation, with a focus on directory services and directory service strategies. It was intended for networking groups planning to implement a Windows NT Server 4.0 networking solution (after SMS installation) and needing help in designing and implementing directory services.

The fourth part of the chapter showed how to monitor and configure SMS status messages. It pinpointed the target clients, transfers files and instructions, and showed how to monitor and configure status messages to determine whether an installation is successful.

The fifth part of the chapter showed how to monitor or track the progress of SMS functions. It provided information on how to monitor the progress of client installation, software distribution, inventory collection, and remote control.

The final part of this chapter discussed how to configure the SMS database maintenance tasks. The more often you configure these tasks, the less time it takes to perform them.

▲ CHAPTER REVIEW QUESTIONS

▲ True/False

1. *True or False? You do not need to capture network data to collect information about the functioning of a LAN.*

2. *True or False? You can use Network Monitor to view and filter network traffic through the use of a capture filter. A capture filter functions like a database query to single out all types of network traffic information.*

3. *True or False? Windows 2000 supports a mixed environment of Windows 2000 Active Directory domain controllers and Windows NT 4.0 domain controllers. Customers can migrate at their own pace, based on business needs. Windows NT Workstation and Microsoft Windows 95 and 98 clients without the Active Directory access software can log on to Active Directory domain controllers by using Windows NT LAN Manager (NTLM) challenge/response authentication.*

4. *True or False? As Windows 2000 is presently in the early beta stages, you should begin working with Windows 2000 as a member server (nondomain controller) in a Windows NT 4.0 network environment.*

5. *True or False? A SMS secondary site server is a limited SMS installation. Secondary sites provide SMS connectivity with minimal administrative requirements. There are many advantages, in terms of maintenance and bandwidth, to having a SMS secondary site. SMS sends packages to a secondary site in a compressed format, and Maintenance Manager does not poll secondary site servers during every cycle, which reduces network traffic.*

6. *True or False? SMS provides the distribution services. It pinpoints the target clients, transfers files and instructions, and can monitor and configure (track) status messages to determine whether an installation is successful. This also includes the monitoring and configuration of SMS site installation status messages and unwanted status messages.*

7. *True or False? SMS pinpoints the target clients; transfers files and instructions, and monitors the whether or not a client installation or software distribution has been successful.*

8. *True or False? Once the client has been located and permission granted, monitoring the progress of remote control begins. A variety of options and settings are available.*

9. *True or False? You should configure the SMS database maintenance tasks every three to five months, although the ideal interval depends on how often and how many inventories are being collected. Generally speaking, the more often you configure these tasks, the less time it will take to perform them.*

▲ Multiple Choice

10. *To capture data across more than one network from the SMS Administrator toolbar perform the following steps except:*
    A. Choose Open Window: Sites.
    B. Double-click the appropriate site to display SMS 2.0 domains.
    C. Double-click a domain to display the computers in that domain.
    D. Double-click an inventory to display computers in that inventory.
    E. Double-click the computer you want to use to capture data.

11. *In the Network Monitor Capture window, a graphical representation of the activity currently taking place on the network is called a:*
    A. SMS Directory
    B. Source Directory
    C. Remote chat Directory
    D. Remote launching of administrative tools Directory
    E. Graph

12. *In the Network Monitor Frame Viewer window, the frame's contents, including the protocols that were used to send it, is called:*
    A. Command Line
    B. Detail
    C. Configuration Command Line
    D. Display Icon in Program Group
    E. Run Minimized

13. *In the Capture Filter dialog box, what specifies the data patterns to capture?*

    A. Run Local Copy if Present

    B. Runs with UNC Name

    C. Requires Specific Drive Letter

    D. Pattern Matches

    E. Change Icon

14. *In the Capture Filter dialog box, what selects an arrow to indicate the direction of the traffic that you want to include or exclude from the capture filter?*

    A. Direction

    B. Details

    C. Schedules

    D. Status

    E. Job ID

15. *In the Transmit Frames dialog box, what sends frames multiple times?*

    A. Send Entire Range Multiple Times

    B. Comments

    C. Program Items

    D. ID

    E. Packages

16. *In the Other Network Monitor Installations dialog box, what adds names displayed in the dialog box to the default address database (DEFAULT.ADR)?*

    A. Name

    B. Comments

    C. Add Names to Address Database

    D. ID

    E. Packages

17. *In the Message Detail dialog box, what is the name of the service or program that logged the Message?*

    A. Name

    B. Comments

    C. Program Items

    D. Component

    E. Packages

18. *If an Message affects the processing of a Advertisement (job), what attribute specifies the job ID of the job that was affected?*

    A. Name

    B. Comments

    C. Program Items

    D. Advertisement ID

    E. Packages

▲ Open Ended

1. After displaying a captured frame in the Frame Viewer window, you can retransmit the frame onto the network. You can transmit as many frames as you want. In addition, the same group of frames can be transmitted repeatedly, and you can specify how long a pause there should be between each transmission (also called a cycle). To analyze the effects of transmission, name the steps used to capture data from another computer on the LAN during transmission.

2. Name the steps to transmit a range of frames or a capture file onto the network one or more times.

Trouble-shooting

Part 7 begins by taking you through SMS 2.0 Diagnostic and Help Desk utilities that allow direct monitoring and control of your inventoried computers. It examines the diagnostic options for viewing real time information about a client's environment, such as software and hardware configuration. Next, it looks at the diagnostic tools to solve SMS problems. This part then helps you resolve many common secondary site server creation, installation, and upgrade failures or problems. Furthermore, it explains why it's important to tune SQL Server for better performance with SMS.

Finally, this part provides an invaluable checklist of items to restore a SQL Server from scratch. It explains how Inventory data collected by SMS is valuable to the organization that collected it. It concludes by explaining how SMS allows you to use the Internet to perform a number of management tasks.

Diagnosing and Resolving SMS Problems

This chapter opens up Part 7, "Troubleshooting," by taking you through SMS 2.0 Diagnostic and Help Desk utilities that allow you to directly monitor and control your inventoried computers. The chapter shows you how to:

- Choose the appropriate diagnostic tool
- Diagnose and resolve installation problems in SMS site systems
- Diagnose and resolve installation problems with clients
- Diagnose and resolve problems with SMS features
- Diagnose and resolve problems with site-to-site communication

This chapter first examines the diagnostic options that allow you to view real time information about a client's environment such as software and hardware configuration. Next, you'll see how the Help Desk options provide remote access to clients. Finally, we cover requirements for remote troubleshooting, as well as requirements to remote control clients running Windows NT 4.0.

The second part of the chapter explains how to use the diagnostics and Help Desk features. It shows you how to take control of a client; how to remotely run a command at a client; how to remotely restart a client; how to transfer files to a client; and how to check a client's current hardware and software information.

This chapter also looks at the diagnostic tools that are available to solve SMS diagnostic problems:

- Network Monitor
- Dumpsend
- Tracer and SMSTrace
- MIFCheck
- WBEMTest
- Network Trace
- SMS Status Message Viewer
- MOFComp

This chapter helps you resolve many common secondary site server creation, installation, and upgrade failures or problems. You will examine and diagnose the system logs immediately following the failure and correct problems noted in these logs. This chapter further shows how you can use SMS Service Manager to increase log sizes.

Finally, the chapter explains why it's important to optimize SQL Server for better performance with SMS, and explains how to do it.

MCSE 13.1 Remote Troubleshooting

Reducing total cost of ownership requires centralized problem determination and resolution. SMS 2.0 includes utilities that enable you to directly control and monitor remote clients running Windows 95 and 98, Windows NT 3.51 and 4.0, or Windows 3.x operating systems, and utilities that allow diagnosis of network problems. SMS 2.0 also adds a preview of server health monitoring facilities to SMS. The following types of tools are available:

- HealthMon (server monitoring tools)
- Diagnostics options
- Help Desk utilities
- Requirements for remote troubleshooting
- Remote control on clients running Windows NT 4.0
- Network Monitor (network monitoring tools)

HealthMon

As discussed in Chapter 9, "Configuring, Auditing, and Controlling Network Clients with SMS," and Chapter 11, "SMS Network Installation and Configuration," a preview version of a server monitoring tool known as HealthMon is a new feature in SMS 2.0. It is designed to provide critical performance information on Windows NT Server 4.0 and BackOffice processes.

HealthMon uses information provided by Common Information Model (CIM), allowing administrators to set critical or warning thresholds. The console provides exception-based real-time status information grouped by system-level resources such as processor, memory, physical disk, and server work queues, and by BackOffice applications and processes such as SQL Server, Microsoft Exchange Server, and Windows NT Server 4.0's Internet Information Server services as shown in Figure 13.1.

CIM allows users to access information about objects in the management environment. Through CIM, applications can query for and make changes to static information in the CIM repository and dynamic information maintained by object providers.

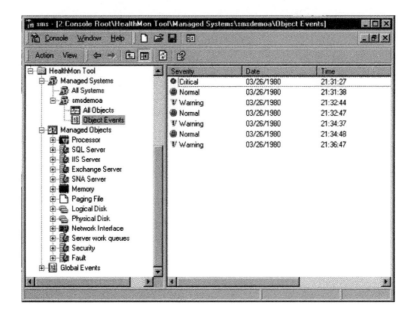

Figure 13.1 *HealthMon Root Console.*

A series of thresholds are provided by default, but the administrator can tune these policies based on network need. A value can also be set to indicate when the critical or warning event should be considered to be returned to normal.

> HealthMon is at preview quality in SMS 2.0, and should not be used in production environments.

Diagnostics Options

The Diagnostics options allow you to view real time information about a client's environment, such as software and hardware configuration. The options available for clients running Windows 3.1, Windows for Workgroups 3.11, and Windows 95 and 98 are as follows:

- CMOS settings
- Device drivers currently loaded
- DOS memory usage
- Interrupt vectors
- Ping tests
- ROM contents
- Windows-specific information such as Windows memory allocation, program modules loaded, and tasks in the task list

For clients running Windows NT 4.0, the Windows NT 4.0 Diagnostics feature is available. This feature provides information for the following:

- Devices
- DMA/Memory
- Drivers
- Hardware
- IRQ/Port status
- Network
- Operating system version
- Services

Remote Tools (Help Desk) Options

The Help Desk options provide remote access to clients. These options allow you to perform the following operations:

- Remote control
- Remote reboot
- Remote chat
- File transfer
- Remote execute

The Diagnostics and Help Desk utilities can be used on clients that are connected to the network locally, or are on a wide area network. SMS 2.0 supports all Windows NT 4.0 protocols, such as NetBIOS extended user interface (NetBEUI), NWLink (IPX), and TCP/IP. SMS can also perform help desk functions for a client on a remote network who is connected using RAS. Support is not available across an SNA link.

 For security purposes, the default setting for the Remote Tools (Help Desk) is disabled. Remote Tools (Help Desk) can be enabled by a user at the client.

REMOTE CONTROL

Using the Remote Control utility, administrators can view the display of a remote SMS 2.0 client. They can also take control of its keyboard and mouse.

REMOTE REBOOT

When administrators are providing support for a remote client, they may need to restart the client to test a change to a startup procedure, to load a new configuration, or to restart a client that has locked up due to a hardware or software malfunction. Using the Remote Reboot utility, administrators can restart the selected client.

REMOTE CHAT

Using the Remote Chat utility, administrators can communicate with a user at the selected client. When an administrator starts a chat session, Remote Chat windows appear on both the SMS 2.0 Administrator computer and the selected client. When either the administrator or the user at the client types text in the Remote Chat window, that text is displayed in the other computer's Remote Chat window.

FILE TRANSFER

Using the File Transfer utility, administrators can transfer files between the SMS-2.0 based console computer and the selected client. Now, let look at how Remote Execute works.

REMOTE EXECUTE

The Remote Execute utility enables administrators to run an application or batch file on a remote Windows-based client. When administrators use Remote Execute instead of Remote Control, the user does not see the command being executed, and the command may complete more quickly.

Administrators can also perform Windows 95 and 98 diagnostics via the Remote Tools utilities, and can remotely run Windows NT 4.0 administrative tools, such as User Manager.

REMOTE CONTROL SECURED • Remote Control is a powerful tool, and security is critical. Thus, this feature of SMS 2.0 is tightly integrated with operating system security, making it difficult to improperly use the tool.

Different administrators can be assigned different levels of remote administration over different groups of users. Logs are kept as to what actions administrators performed while a remote control session was active. Configuration is extensive, allowing exactly the level of security that a corporation requires, from the end user having no knowledge a remote control session is happening, to specific users never allowing remote control to take place, and everything in between.

REMOTE CONTROL VIEWED BY THE CLIENT • The user at the client can select the level of remote control allowed, although the administrator can restrict the changes the user can make to the remote control settings. Options include:

- Full remote control
- Limited remote control
- No remote control

If the user wants to allow limited remote control, the user is prompted to specify what operations a SMS 2.0 Administrator can perform. These operations are as follows:

- Exchange text messages (chat)
- Restart the client computer
- Run commands on the client computer
- Transfer files between the client computer and your computer
- View the client computer configuration information
- View the client video display and control the mouse and keyboard

Figure 13.2 *Remote Control Agent.*

Enabling full remote control allows all the remote access permissions previously described. In addition, the user can request for a pop-up window to ask permission each time remote control is requested and can specify which administrators may take over their desktop.

The user at the client can also control the way he or she is notified whenever you initiate a remote control session, as follows:

- Display an icon on the client desktop as a visual indicator of a remote control operation taking place

- Play a sound only when the remote control operation begins and when it ends

- Play a sound repeatedly every 15 seconds while the remote control session is in progress

When the client is running Remote Control Agent, a thumbnail image appears on the user's desktop, as shown in Figure 13.2. When no remote control session is taking place, the Windows title bar is gray. The user is alerted to an active remote control session when the title bar turns red. Double-clicking on the face of this window displays the Remote Control Status dialog box for WindowsNT 4.0 users shown in Figure 13.3 (Windows 95 and 98 users have a slightly different display).

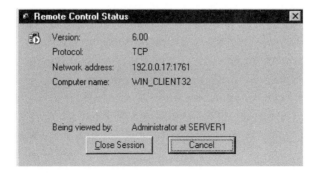

Figure 13.3 *Remote Control Status Dialog Box.*

Remote Troubleshooting Requirements

Before you can use the Diagnostics and Help Desk features on an SMS 2.0 client, the remote client must be part of the SMS 2.0 system.

Second, the appropriate SMS remote support software must be loaded on the client. This is installed by default when the client is added to SMS. SMS uses this software to view the display on a remote Windows-based client and to control its keyboard and mouse.

Third, both the SMS Administrator computer and the remote client must be running the same transport protocol (NetBEUI, TCP/IP, or IPX) and the two computers must be able to communicate using that same transport. If the client protocol is using a LANA number other than 0, the remote support terminate-and-stay-resident (TSR) software must be configured to use the correct LANA number (loaded protocol, or the default protocol).

Fourth, if the remote client runs Windows 3.1, or Windows for Workgroups 3.11 or higher, the client must have an 80386 processor or greater. Finally, at the remote client, a user must enable specific Help Desk options, such as Allow Remote Control and Allow Remote File Transfer.

Clients Running Windows NT 4.0 with Remote Control

The Remote Control (Help Desk) option has some additional requirements and features when used on clients running Windows NT 4.0 3.51 or higher. By default, to remotely control a client running Windows NT 4.0, the account being used to access the client must be a member of the client's Administrators local group. If this is not the case, when you request remote control, a dialog box appears in which you are prompted to enter an appropriate account name and password.

You can create your own list of user accounts to be used to remotely control a client. These accounts are referred to as permitted viewers and can be configured on a per site basis by opening the Sites window and selecting File: Properties. Next, choose Clients, and then Options.

To modify the list of permitted viewers for a particular client, you can edit the Windows NT 4.0 Registry.

If a client running Windows NT 4.0 has an installed video driver in the default list of supported video drivers for SMS 2.0, the transfer of screen data between the client and the administrator's computer is automatically accelerated during remote control. To access the list of supported video drivers do the following steps:

1. From the Administrator Console, open the Sites window.
2. Select Site Settings.
3. Choose Clients Agents and then Remote Tools Client Agent.

The access list of supported video drivers feature is only available for clients running Windows NT 4.0.

4. Double-click and go to Advanced Tab. (Here you can change Video Drivers and Network Settings.)

The default protocol on which clients listen during remote control is LANA0. To configure this option on a per site basis, open the Sites window, select File: Properties, choose Clients, and then choose Options. To modify this setting on a per-client basis, edit the Windows NT 4.0 Registry.

A user does not have to be logged on at the client for the client to be remotely controlled. The Permission Required option must, however, be disabled in the Help Desk Options dialog box on the client.

All access requests for remote control are logged automatically to the Windows NT 4.0 security event log on the client. Finally, you can remotely log on to and log off of, and lock and unlock, a Windows NT 4.0 client.

MCSE 13.2 Using Diagnostics and Help Desk Utilities

There are various tools available to aid an administrator in resolving user and network problems, as well as the types of tasks you can perform using the Diagnostics and Help Desk tools. The tools are listed in Table 13.1, together with the specific SMS 2.0 features you can use to achieve them.

You can view and control multiple clients from an SMS Administrator. You cannot, however, use more than one instance of an SMS Administrator to view or control the same client at the same time.

Table 13.1 *Diagnostics and Help Desk Tools Tasks and Associated SMS Features*

	Task	Feature
Taking control of a client	Use remote control to guide a user through a difficult task. A user can be watching the process and listening over the phone. While the remote control session is taking place, you have shared control over the desktop, keyboard, and mouse for the client.	Help Desk options (administrator and client) Remote Control options (administrator and client)
Remotely running a command at a clien	If you believe a client is experiencing problems due to a virus, and a virus scan program is installed on the client, run that program on the client. If it is not installed, use the File Transfer option to install the program on the client, and then run it remotely.	Remote Execute
Remotely restarting a client	Use Remote Reboot to restart a client.	Remote Reboot
Transferring files to a client	Use the file transfer feature for a quick way of downloading selected files to a client.	File Transfer
Checking a client's current hardware and software information	Use SMS to view hardware and software configuration parameters.	Diagnostics Windows NT 4.0 Diagnostics

REMOTELY ACCESSED CLIENT PREPARATION

For security reasons, SMS 2.0 remote access is disabled by default on a client. A user at the client must choose what level of remote help to allow.

SETTING UP A WINDOWS CLIENT FOR REMOTE ACCESS • During network descovery process SMS will arrange to tranfer remote access components to clients system. Clients must be properly setup at the administrator console as described earlier in the chapter. To make changes to a Windows client for remote access, at the clients Control Panel choose Remote Tools and then open to change options. The Help Desk Options dialog box is displayed as shown in Figure 13.4.

The dialog box allows the user at the client to control the degree to which the administrator is allowed to operate their computer, and whether or not they are notified whenever the administrator initiates an action. The dialog box has the fields and buttons shown in Table 13.2.

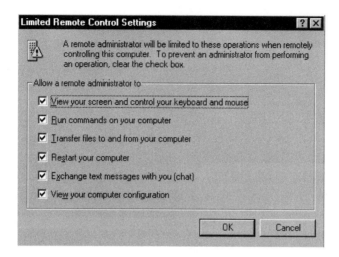

Figure 13.4   *Limited Remote Control Settings Dialog Box.*

On clients running Windows NT 4.0, the Remote Control feature is enabled automatically.

TAKING REMOTE CONTROL OF A CLIENT

To take remote control of a client, ensure that the Allow Remote Control Help Desk option is enabled at the client. In the SMS 2.0 Client program group or from the SMS menu, select the Remote Control icon to start the remote support software.

SMS 2.0 ADMINISTRATOR • From the SMS Administrator Console, perform the following steps as shown in Figure 13.5:

1. From the Administrator Console, open the Sites window.
2. Choose Collection and Expand Node.
3. Choose Client criteria from Collections.
4. Clients list will appear in right window.
5. Choose Correct Client then right-click to Start Remote Tools Client Agent.

For clients running the Windows NT 4.0 operating system, **Allow Remote Control Help Desk** option is started automatically.

Table 13.2 *Client Remote Tools Options Dialog Box (Fields and Buttons)*

Element	Description
View your screen and control your keyboard and mouse	Administrator can view your desktop and use the keyboard and mouse remotely. If you select this option, use the settings on the Notification tab to determine how you are notified when your computer is being controlled remotely. These settings do not apply to the other remote tasks.
Run commands on your computer	Administrator can run commands, such as a virus checker, on your computer.
Transfer files to and from your computer	Administrator can transfer files between your computer and the administrator computer. For example, if a corrupt or missing file is discovered, your administrator can transfer a replacement file to your computer or transfer a file from your computer to the administrator computer for troubleshooting purposes.
Restart your computer	Administrator can restart your computer. While your administrator is providing support, it may be necessary to restart your computer when testing a change to a startup procedure, when loading a new configuration, or when dealing with hardware or software malfunctions.
Exchange text messages with you (chat)	Administrator can communicate with you through a chat window on your desktop. Both of you can type text messages in the chat window and the messages are displayed on both screens.
View your computer configuration	Administrator can run diagnostic tools on your computer to learn about your computer configuration. The results can be used to solve hardware and other troubleshooting problems.

When you select Remote Tools, the SMS Administrator attempts to communicate with the Remote Agent running on the client. The Remote Tools window for the client appears as shown in Figure 13.6.

If the SMS Administrator succeeds, it checks for the remote troubleshooting features that the user has enabled. The buttons for the enabled features are activated and the buttons for disallowed features are grayed. When the session is established, the administrator will choose the remote control option as shown in Figure 13.7. SMS checks to verify if the user has granted permission to control the client. At the client, when a message is displayed

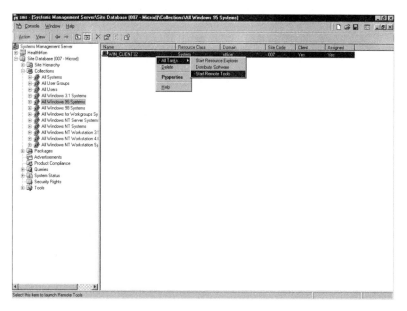

Figure 13.5   *SMS Site Database Collections.*

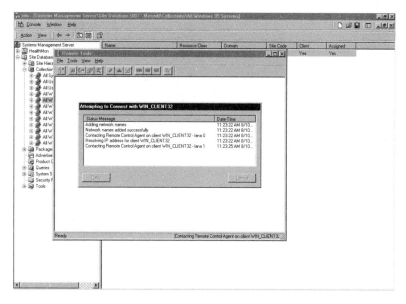

Figure 13.6   *Remote Tools Window Connecting to Client System.*

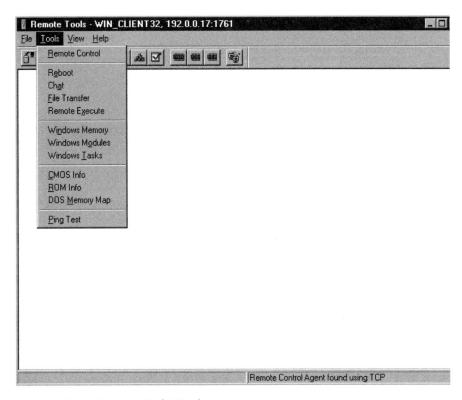

Figure 13.7 *Remote Tools Window.*

asking if the administrator can control the computer, choose Yes. SMS establishes a remote control session.

Once a Remote Session is made the client desktop will appear as shown in Figure 13.8. This window has a distinctive black and yellow border and displays the client's desktop. It shows all mouse and keyboard actions. The SMS Administrator computer has shared control with the client during the remote control session. If you move the mouse at the SMS Administrator computer, the mouse pointer moves on the remote client. If you or the user at the client enters text, it is displayed both at the client and in your view of the client's screen.

If you are remotely controlling a client and an MS-DOS window is displayed in the clients desktop window , mouse controls will not function if the MS-DOS window is maximized. Press Alt+Enter to reduce the size of the MS-DOS window and mouse control will return.

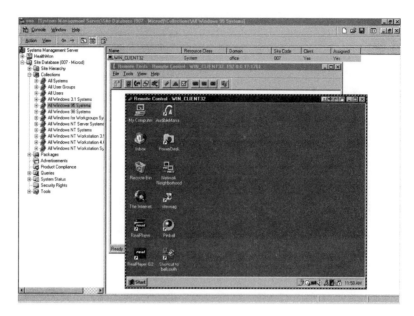

Figure 13.8   *Remote Session Window.*

REMOTE CONTROL SESSION CLOSER

A remote control session can be closed through the SMS 2.0 Administrator, or by the user at the client using the taskbar icon. At the SMS Administrator, close the window. You can also close the remote control session by selecting another Help Desk option. If you use the Task List to close the window, the SMS Administrator also closes.

At the client, in the Remote Control Agent program using the taskbar as seen earlier in Figure 13.3.

RUNNING A REMOTE COMMAND AT A CLIENT

The Remote Execute feature allows you to run an application on a remote client. If you run an MS-DOS application, an MS-DOS window opens to run the application.

Remote Tools is not supported on clients running only **MS-DOS**.

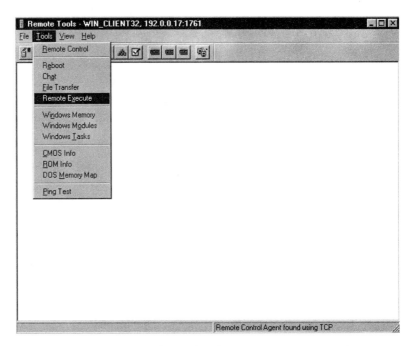

Figure 13.9 *Remote Tools Window (Remote Execute Option).*

To remotely run a command on a client, ensure that the Allow Remote Execute Help Desk option is enabled at the client. At the SMS Administrator, perform the following tasks :

1. From the Administrator Console, open the Sites window.
2. Choose Collection and Expand Node.
3. Choose Client criteria from Collections.
4. Clients list will appear in right window.
5. Choose Correct Client then right-click to start remote Tools Client Agent.

The Remote Tools window for the client appears, as shown in Figure 13.9. Under the Tools Menu, choose the execute. The Run Program at User's Workstation dialog box appears, as shown in Figure 13.10. In the Command Line box, type the command for the program you want to run, and choose OK.

RESTARTING A CLIENT REMOTELY

Using SMS 2.0 Administrator to restart a remote client with the Remote Reboot utility. You cannot use CTRL+ALT+DEL. By using CTRL+ALT+

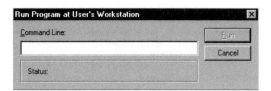

Figure 13.10 *Execute Program At Client Station.*

 The programs executed from the Run Program at User's Workstation dialog box must already be installed on the remote computer. The program or command must also be in the client's path; otherwise, you must specify the full path to the program on the client machine. For instance, if you wanted to run RUNME.BAT from the C:\MYDIR directory and C:\MYDIR was not in the client's path, you must specify C:\MYDIR \RUN ME.BAT in the Command Line box.

DEL, you open the Windows NT 4.0 Security window on your SMS Administrator computer.

To use the Remote Reboot utility to restart a remote client, ensure that the Allow Remote Reboot Help Desk option is enabled at the client. At the SMS Administrator, perform the following tasks shown in Figure 13.11:

1. From the Administrator Console, open the Sites window.
2. Choose Collection and Expand Node.
3. Choose Client criteria from Collections.
4. Clients list will appear in right window.
5. Choose Correct Client then right-click to start remote Tools Client Agent.

The Remote Tools window for the client appears, as shown in Figure 13.12. Under the Tools Menu, choose the reboot option. When prompted for confirmation to restart the client, choose Yes.

Once you restart a client, it becomes inaccessible through the remote troubleshooting utilities until the user logs on to the network and the logon script is reloaded. On clients running Windows 3.1, Windows for Workgroups, and Windows 95 and 98, the Remote Control Agent must also be started again to regain access.

On clients running Windows NT 4.0, no additional procedures are required on the client for you to be able to access the client using the remote troubleshooting utilities.

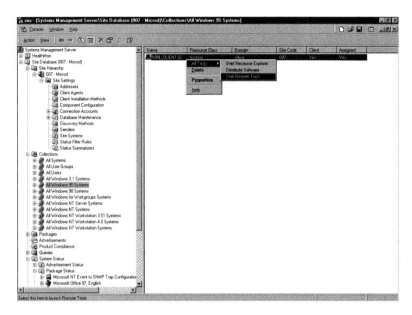

Figure 13.11 *Administrator Console.*

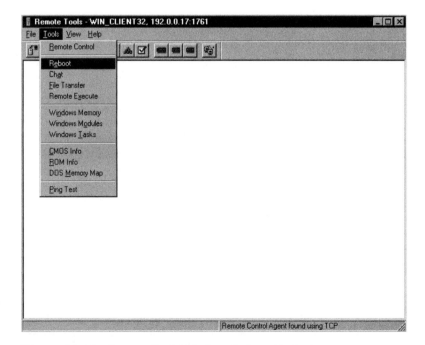

Figure 13.12 *Remote Tools Window (Reboot Option).*

TRANSFERRING FILES TO A CLIENT

Using the File Transfer option, you can transfer files between the SMS 2.0 Administrator computer and the selected client. To transfer files at the client, ensure that the Allow Remote File Transfer Help Desk option is enabled. At the SMS Administrator, perform the tasks:

1. From the Administrator Console, open the Sites window.
2. Choose Collection and Expand Node.
3. Choose Client criteria from Collections.
4. Clients list will appear in right window.
5. Choose Correct Client then right-click to start remote Tools Client Agent.

The Remote Tools window for the client appears, as shown in Figure 13.13. Under the Tools Menu, choose the File Transfer option as shown in Figure 13.14. The Local Files and Local lists display the files and directories on the SMS Administrator computer. The Remote Directories and Remote Files lists display the files and directories on the selected client.

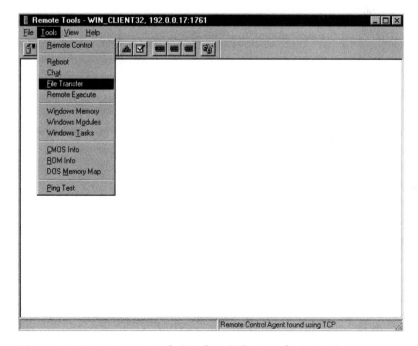

Figure 13.13 *Remote Tools Window (File Transfer Option).*

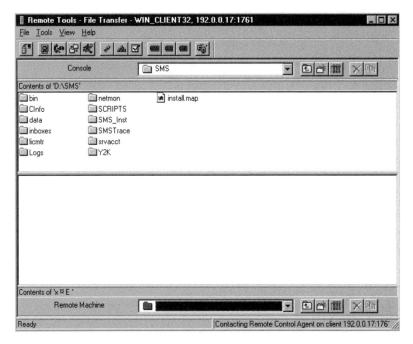

Figure 13.14 *File Transfer Window.*

Only local drives on the SMS Administrator and client computers are shown; network resources identified by drive letters are not displayed.

In the directory box for the computer for which you want to copy files, select the directory from which you want to copy files. The selected directory is displayed in the top pane of the window.

The Viewer is the selected directory on the SMS Administrator computer, and User is the selected directory on the client.

In the file list for the computer from which you want to copy the files, select the files to copy. You can select all files in the file list by choosing holding the shift key and selecting all files. To narrow the file list to display only files with specific extensions, you can set a file mask. The file mask feature enables you to narrow the file list to filenames or extensions. Also, the default file mask is *.*, which displays all files in the selected directory. And, the file masking feature enables you to use wild cards and to select multiple file extensions. For the computer to which you want to copy the files, select the directory in which you want them.

You can create directories on either the remote or local computer. To make a directory, choose the local or remote drive or directory where you want to create the new directory. Then, from the Local or Remote Directories list, select MAKE DIR.

To copy selected files drag files to the destination. A status line below the directory and file boxes displays the progress of the operation. To stop a copy operation, choose Cancel.

CLIENT'S HARDWARE AND SOFTWARE INFORMATION CHECKS

The Diagnostics property provides diagnostic utilities for clients running Windows 3.1, Windows for Workgroups 3.11, and Windows 95 and 98. For clients running Windows NT 4.0, you need to select the Windows NT 4.0 Diagnostics property to view diagnostics for these clients.

CLIENTS RUNNING DIAGNOSTICS

To view hardware and software diagnostic information for clients running Windows 3.1, Windows for Workgroups 3.11, and Windows 95 and 98, ensure that the appropriate Diagnostics options are enabled at the client. Now, at the SMS Administrator, perform the tasks shown in Figure 13.15:

1. From the Administrator Console, open the Sites window.
2. Choose Collection and Expand Node.
3. Choose Client criteria from Collections.
4. Clients list will appear in right window.
5. Choose Correct Client then right-click to start remote Tools Client Agent.

The Remote Tools window for the client appears, as shown in Figure 13.16. Under the Tools Menu, choose the File Transfer option.

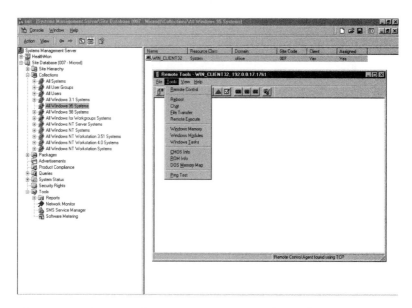

Figure 13.15 *SMS Administrator Remote Tools Window.*

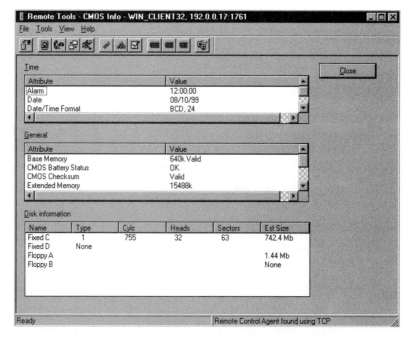

Figure 13.16 *Remote Tools Window (CMOS Option).*

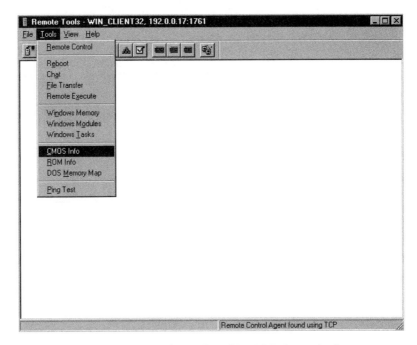

Figure 13.17   *Remote Tools Window (CMOS Information).*

The window displays information detected on the client for the selected option. Complementary Metal Oxide Semiconductor (CMOS) information is displayed in the example shown in Figure 13.17. SMS also provides additional Diagnostics options for Windows clients shown in Table 13.3.

Table 13.3 *SMS Diagnostics Options: Icons and Descriptions*

Icon	Description
CMOS Info	Displays the data stored in the client's CMOS memory. This data is used during startup to configure the computer properly. See Figure 13.17.
ROM Info	Provides detailed information about all installed ROM chips. See Figure 13.18.
Dos Memory	Lists the programs currently loaded in memory. See Figure 13.19.
Ping Test	Sends network packets between the SMS Administrator computer and the selected client and checks the accuracy of transmission. See Figure 13.20.

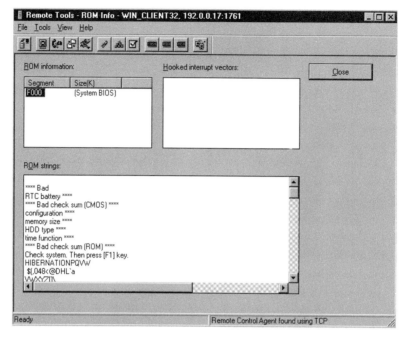

Figure 13.18 *Remote Tools Window (ROM Information).*

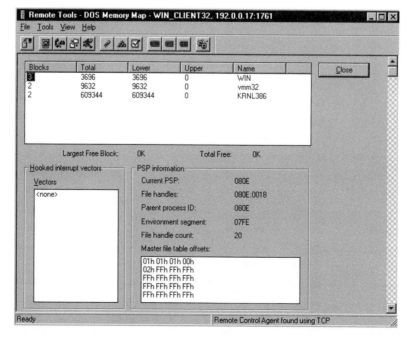

Figure 13.19 *Remote Tools Window (DOS Memory Map).*

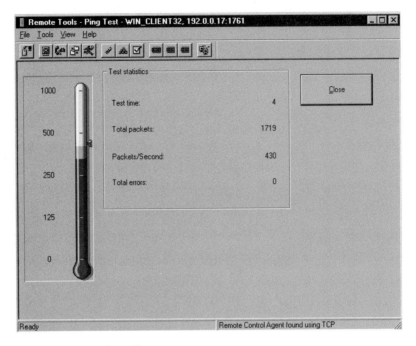

Figure 13.20 *Ping Test.*

SMS provides additonal detailed Diagnostics options to clients running Windows as shown in Table 13.4.

Table 13.4 *SMS Diagnostics Additional Options*

Icon	Description
Windows Memory	Provides information about memory and memory resources. See Figure 13.21.
Windows Modules	Provides information about active code modules. See Figure 13.22.
Windows Tasks	Provides information about programs in the Task List. See Figure 13.23.

CLIENTS DIAGNOSTICS FOR RUNNING THE WINDOWS NT 4.0 OPERATING SYSTEM

To view hardware and software diagnostic information for a Windows NT clients, perform the tasks from the SMS Administrator Console shown in Figure 13.24:

1. From the Administrator Console, open the Sites window.
2. Choose Collection and Expand Node.
3. Choose Client criteria from Collections.

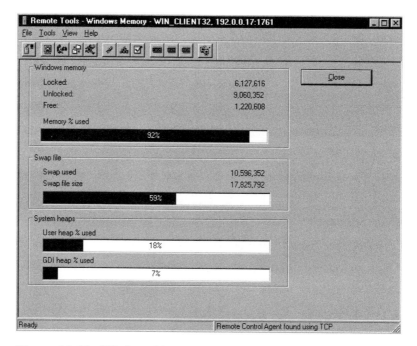

Figure 13.21   *Windows Memory.*

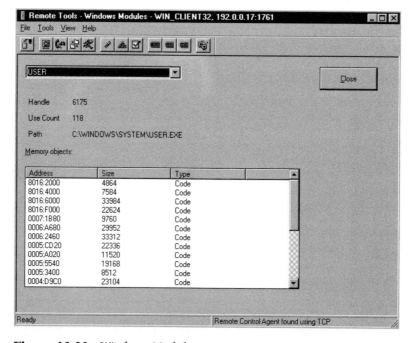

Figure 13.22   *Windows Modules.*

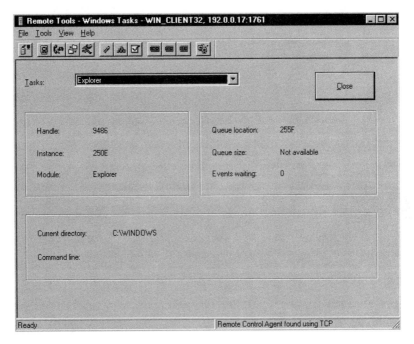

Figure 13.23   *Windows Tasks.*

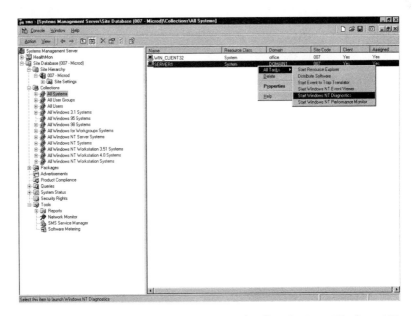

Figure 13.24   *SMS Administrator Console All Tasks Start Windows NT Diagnostics.*

Figure 13.25 *Windows NT Diagnostics (Network Analysis).*

4. Clients list will appear in right window.
5. Choose Correct Client then right-click to start Windows NT Diagnostics.

The appropriate dialog box appears with information that has been detected on the client. Network information is also displayed in the dialog box shown in Figure 13.25.

MCSE 13.3 Choosing the Appropriate Diagnostic Tool

The following diagnostic tools are available to solve SMS problems:

- Network Monitor
- Dumpsend
- Tracer and SMSTrace
- MIFCheck
- WBEMTest
- Network Trace
- MOFComp

Network Monitor

As previously discussed, Network Monitor is a traffic analyzer diagnostic tool that helps administrators find network problems. The SMS 2.0 Network Monitor allows the analyzing of network traffic and can pinpoint problems or potential bottlenecks. With Network Monitor, administrators can do the following:

- Capture frames on a remote computer and display capture statistics at specified intervals
- Capture frames (also called packets) directly from the network
- Display and filter captured frames
- Edit and transmit captured frames onto the network to test network resources or reproduce network problems

Network Monitor is entirely software-based. The only special hardware needed is a network card with an NDIS driver that supports promiscuous mode. Promiscuous mode enables the network adapter card to be directed by a device to pass on all frames passing over the network to the operating system. When administrators want to analyze traffic on a network segment, a capture agent (a program running on a computer attached to that segment) puts its network card into promiscuous mode. The agent makes a duplicate of frames that pass through that computer, stores the frames in a buffer, and sends the session summary statistics to the Network Monitor console locally or remotely. The summary statistics include graphs of total network utilization; statistics of frames, bytes, broadcasts, and multicasts per second; and statistics for individual computers.

Network Monitor provides a secure solution by announcing its presence on the network by sending a frame at regular intervals. This allows administrators to prevent unauthorized users from sniffing packets using this tool.

NEW EXPERTS AND MONITORS

Network Monitor in SMS 2.0 adds monitors and experts to make the administrator's task of analyzing collected network traffic much easier. Monitors look for particular patterns on the network and report problems as they happen. Monitors detect rogue Dynamic Host Configuration Protocol (DHCP) servers, duplicate IP addresses, and attempted Internet break-ins.

Experts interpret data after it has been collected to make it easier to find problem systems; for example, finding the top five talkers on a network or the top five error-generating systems as shown in Figure 13.26.

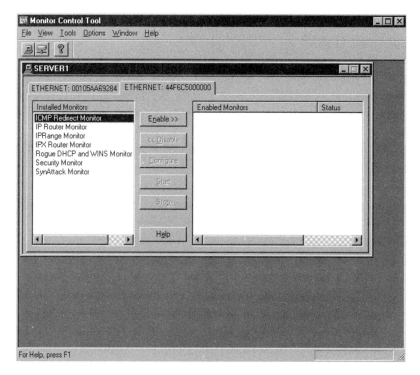

Figure 13.26 *Monitor Control Tool.*

Dumpsend

The DumpSend utility is accessed with the DUMPSEND command. It displays the binary SMS send request file in text format for review. It has the following syntax:

```
DUMPSEND [/P] [send request filename, *.SRS, *.SRQ]
```

These files reside in the \SMS\SITE.SRV\SENDER.BOX\REQUEST\<out box> directories and can have a *.SRQ (not processed yet) or *.SRS (processed, but not completed) extension.

A Sender monitors its associated outbox directory for the existence of a send request file. When this file is seen by the Sender, it parses the instructions and attempts to perform the requested operations. Some site-to-site communication problems can be resolved using DumpSend to determine the contents of these files.

A send request file is a variable length file composed of a series of records. This file contains, at a minimum, the INFO, STATUS, ADDRESS, and INSTRUCTION records.

DUMPSEND.EXE

Dumpsend.exe displays the contents of a send request (sendreq) file, which makes up the following records:

- *Send request data record:* gives information, such as the destination site, priority, job name, job ID, and outbox location
- *Cancel record:* shows whether the sendreq is canceled
- *Action code record:* includes retry, deleted, and so on
- *Address record (multiple records allowed):* includes all indecipherable encrypted names, as well as the gateway and destination addresses
- *Package file record:* the name of the package file
- *Instruction file record:* the name of the instruction file
- *Sender record:* includes information about the sender history, such as the status, time of last event, start time, the number of times a sender took this sendreq, and the size of the sendreq
- *Access record:* file access information
- *SSPS record:* includes information about the remote site installation. For instance:

```
Syntax: dumpsend <file_name>
```

Some record types are not parsed by DumpSend. The information in these record types is usually not needed for troubleshooting. See the sidebar, "Send Request Record Types," for more information.

Study Break

Send Request Record Types

The following is a list of the various Send Request record types and their structures listed in the order that DumpSend displays them:

Send Request RECORD (INFO, Record type 3)

- Priority: SMS Job priority as either 1 = high, 2 = medium, or 3 = low
- Dest Site: SMS Site code with a length of three characters
- Job name: SMS Job ID with a length of eight characters
- Job request: Unique send request ID with a length of seven characters
- Outbox: UNC path to outbox directory

Sender/Scheduler RECORD (STATUS, Record type 15)

- Sender status: Contains one of the following status flags:
  - SREQ_STATUS_NONE
  - SREQ_STATUS_STARTED
  - SREQ_STATUS_CONNECTING
  - SREQ_STATUS_SENDING
  - SREQ_STATUS_ERROR
  - SREQ_STATUS_INVALID
  - SREQ_STATUS_CANCELLED
  - SREQ_STATUS_SUSPENDED
  - SREQ_STATUS_OK
- First sender started at: Date/Time of first send attempt
- Sender started at: Date/Time of last send attempt
- Sender ended at: Date/Time when last send attempt stopped
- Sender gate heartbeat at: Date/Time interval for next attempt
- Scheduler to restart at: Date/Time of next send attempt
- Total bytes to send: Total bytes to send, including package file
- Bytes left to send: Total bytes left to send
- Sync point is: Total confirmed bytes sent and acknowledged
- File type is: 0 = Sender only, 1 = *.INS, 2 = *.PKG
- Number of connects: Number of connection attempts
- Sender ID: ID of sender working on send request

CANCEL RECORD (Record type 4)

Cancel Status: Indicates if Send Request has been canceled.

ACTION CODE RECORD (Record type 14)

Code: This code is set by the Sender after a send failure. The Scheduler service processes this code as follows: 0 = do nothing, 1 = retry, 2 = delete send request.

ADDRESS RECORD (Record type 5, multiple records allowed)

Address: Contains the destination \\<SMS Server>\SMS_SITE share and the encrypted account password to access this share.

PACKAGE FILE RECORD (Record type 7)

File: The universal naming convention (UNC) name of the package file to send. The package file contains a compressed copy of the original package to be sent to the despooler at the destination site.

INSTRUCTION FILE RECORD (Record type 8)

File: The UNC name of the instruction file to send. The instruction file contains the despooler instructions for the package. Other types of Sender records exist that DumpSend does not parse out at this time.

TRANSMISSION STATUS (Record type 1)

Contains such things as transmission status and errors between sites.

TRANSMISSION INFORMATION (Record type 2)

Transmission statistics.

CANCEL (Record type 4)

Cancel mode.

BOOTSTRAP (Record type 13)

Contains information necessary to start the bootstrap process for installing a secondary Systems Management Server Site.

SENDACTION (Record type 17)

Contains information specific to the individual types of Senders.

ROUTING (Record type 18)

Contains routing information.

Tracer and SMSTrace

SMS allows you to trace the actions performed by the SMS services. When tracing is enabled, each service makes log entries for actions it performs or errors it receives in a log file. The log files are ASCII text and can be viewed with a text editor. SMS also includes a Tracer utility that parses these log files and presents them in a clearer, more user-friendly manner than plain text viewing. Tracer allows interactive viewing of the SMS log files as the services

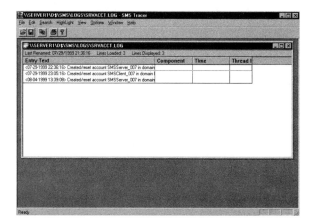

Figure 13.27 *SMS Tracer.*

are writing to them. There are currently two versions of this utility,
TRACER.EXE is a command line console-mode utility that reads changes
made to a text file in real time.

```
Usage: tracer <path to one of the SMS log files>--where
<path> is the path to one of the SMS log files.
```

SMSTRACE.EXE is the graphical user interface (GUI) multiple document interface (MDI) version of Tracer and is included in the
SITE.SRV\<arch> .BIN directory. SMSTRACE.EXE allows you to view SMS
log files and get real-time updates as lines are appended to the log files as
shown in Figure 13.27. You can use Smstrace.atd with SMSADDIN to add
SMSTRACE.EXE to the Tools menu of the SMS Administrator program.

**Smstrace.exe works only with the SMS 1.2 and 2.0 final releases, not ear-
lier versions due to DLL incompatibility.**

SMSTRACE.EXE also allows you to customize the display by selecting
options such as columns, filtering, and ignore new lines. You can Cut, Paste,
and Print from SMSTRACE. In addition, SMSTRACE.EXE allows viewing of
several log files simultaneously. To install SMSTRACE in the SMS Program
Group, perform these steps:

1. Open Windows Explorer to the Following Folder: <drive>\Program Files\SMS2.0 Supportability Files\Reskit\bin\intel.
2. Run SMStrace.exe.

SMS 2.0 log files for server components are stored in ...\SMS\LOGS directory. Client log files are stored in the <%windir%>\ms\sms\logs directory.

SMSTRACE: SEARCHING AND HIGHLIGHTING OF STRINGS

The Tracer utility has been updated with some news features. It now allows you to search for strings (Entry Text Column) and keywords. The following is available from the Search menu.

- Find string
- Find Next string (F3)
- Find Previous string (F4)

HIGHLIGHT AND ACTION • The Highlight toolbar option allows a text string to be entered. As new lines of log file are parsed by Smstrace, any line containing the search string will be displayed in an inverse font. The Highlight option also enables an optional action to be performed if the text string is located within the log file (For example, send a message to an administrator). The HighLight feature draws a black outline around a row containing the defined string. The last outlined row is the current selected row. The HighLight feature is also useful to facilitate reading the SMS Logs when looking for occurrences of a specific string. It's good for real-time monitoring, as well. For instance, only new, loaded lines are processed; you can not remove the outline from outlined rows; and to stop the outline process, you can set the string to an unexpected value.

The Action feature works with the HighLight string. It allows Smstrace to execute a command when the *HighLight* string is found. The action can be Enabled or Disabled.

MIFCheck

Mifcheck.exe is a MIF parser and syntax checker for use in verifying text MIFs before submitting them to the system. It reports syntax and semantic errors. It is designed to help independent software vendors (ISVs) who are writing MIFs for new components for the inventory agent to collect and report to the site server. For instance:

```
Syntax: mifcheck [/dump] <file>
```

In the example above, "/dump" dumps the parsed information to the console. If you run **MIFCHECK** without the /dump option, the MIF files are checked for syntax errors. Also, in the example "<file>" indicates a MIF text file.

CUSTOM MIF HAS INCORRECT FORMAT OR ILLEGAL VALUES FOR TIME

When using Mifcheck to validate a Custom MIF, you may receive an error message similar to, "Time has incorrect format or illegal values, on line number #, token 0." One example, for instance, is "Error in file `test.mif`," and "Time has incorrect format or illegal values, on line 12, token 0."

WORKAROUND • To avoid the preceding error, edit the Custom MIF and surround the Date/Time value with quotation marks, as in this example:

```
Start Component

Name = "Workstation Configuration"

Start Group

Name = "Installation Information"

ID = 1

Class = "Microsoft Corp.|Installation Information|1.0"

Start Attribute

Name = "Installation Date"

ID = 1

Type = Date

Storage = Specific

Value = "07/01/98 10:30:30"
```

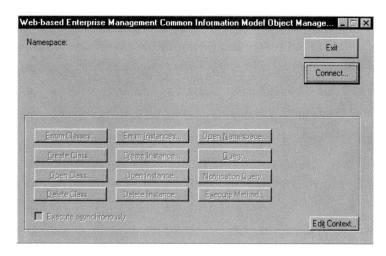

Figure 13.28 *WBEM TEST Window.*

WBEMTest

Microsoft Web Based Enterprise Management (WBEM) consist of two parts: the Core and the SDK. The Core is composed of components that become part of the operating system. These are the pieces required before an application can run. This installable bundle includes an application named WBE-MTest.exe as shown in Figure 13.28. Although WBEMTest can be run to see what it can do, WBEM can be better understood by using some of the SDK tools, such as CIM Studio. The core components are included by default on Windows 2000 and are an installable option in Windows 98. They are also shipped on Windows NT 4.0, SP4.

SDK is required for the Core to work. When the SDK install is started, if the core has not been previously installed, the SDK bundle will install the core. The SDK contains tools to browse the WBEM repository, extend its schema, and provides the documentation necessary to develop applications that will use WBEM.

SUBSCRIBING FOR DMI EVENTS AND NOTIFICATIONS

You can use the WBEMTEST application to subscribe for DMI events and notifications. To subscribe for events, select the Execute asynchronously check box, click on the Notification Query button, and enter the appropriate event subscription queries. For instance:

- This example shows how to subscribe for a DmiComponent Added notification:

```
Select * from __InstanceCreationEvent Where
TargetInstance is a "DmiComponent"
```

- This example shows how to subscribe for a DmiComponent Deleted notification:

```
Select * from __InstanceDeletionEvent Where
TargetInstance is a "DmiComponent"
```

- The following example shows how to subscribe for a DmiGroup Added/Deleted notification:

```
Select * from __ClassCreationEvent Where TargetClass
is a "DmiGroupRoot"

Select * from __ClassDeletionEvent Where TargetClass
is a "DmiGroupRoot"
```

- The last example shows how to subscribe for DMI extrinsic events:

```
Select * from DmiEvent
```

Network Trace

You can access Network Trace via site status, or you can select it from:

- Administrator Console
- Site Database (<name>)
- Site Hierarchy
- Site Systems

Select the site system in the right window and launch the Action menu. By default, this option discovers only information collected through server discovery, so the display may be quite basic. To make it more sophisticated, configure network discovery, which feeds network trace. To reach Network Discovery, select the following in order:

1. Systems Management Server
2. Site Database (<name>)
3. Site Hierarchy
4. Discovery Methods

In the Results window, click Network Discovery, and click Properties in the Action menu. The Network Discovery Properties dialog box displays General settings for network discovery.

By default, network discovery is enabled and configured to discover topology, clients, and client operating systems. However, network discovery does not run until you tell it to do so.

Before you trigger network discovery, investigate the following options: Subnets tab, Domains tab, SNMP tab, SNMP Devices tab, DHCP tab, and Schedule tab.

SUBNETS TAB

When you click on the Subnets tab, notice that by default network discovery is configured to discover resources on the local subnet. It will also add discover resources on any subnet on which a site system resides. You can further specify additional subnets.

DOMAINS TAB

When you click on the Domains tab, the dialog box displays domain settings for network discovery. Notice that by default network discovery is configured to discover resources in the local domain of the site server. You can also add new domains.

SNMP TAB

When you click on the SNMP tab, the dialog box displays SNMP settings for network discovery. Notice that by default network discovery is configured to discover resources within one hop if using SNMP in the public community. You can increase the hop count or add new community names.

SNMP DEVICES TAB

Notice that by default, network discovery is not configured to discover any devices other than routers or DHCP servers. This occurs when you click on the SNMP Devices tab.

DHCP TAB

When you click on the DHCP tab, the dialog box displays DHCP settings for network discovery. Notice that by default network discovery is not configured to discover resources by querying a DHCP server. If you have a DHCP Server, it is recommended that you use it to provide IP Addresses for discovery. Click the New Item button and type in the name or IP Address of your DHCP Server.

SCHEDULE TAB

Clicking on the Schedule tab, the dialog box displays schedule settings for network discovery. Notice that by default, network discovery is not configured to start. To configure a schedule for network discovery to complete, take the following steps.

1. Click the New Item button. The Schedule dialog box appears.
2. Under Time, verify the current date is configured and then set the time to five minutes past the current time.
3. Under Recurrence pattern, set the recurring interval to one day.
4. Click OK. The dialog box displays schedule settings for network discovery. Notice network discovery is scheduled to start in a few minutes.
5. Click OK.

You must wait a few minutes before returning to the Network Trace display. Discovery is designed to be nonintrusive, so it does take some time to complete. Check back on Network Trace later and you should see a more sophisticated display that includes a trace of your SMS site and information on the roles of the various site servers (there may be only one in your configuration). The more complicated your environment, the more sophisticated this display will be. When you check back, investigate the buttons at the top of the display. The three on the right allow you to ping devices and to poll for the correct functioning of components.

DYNAMIC HOST CONFIGURATION PROTOCOL SERVER RENEWAL REQUESTS

In a TCP/IP-based network, the DHCP server eliminates most of the effort associated with the configuration and management of the large number of static IP addresses computers use to communicate with one another. A DHCP server *leases* IP addresses to any DHCP client. Windows NT 4.0 DHCP clients request a lease renewal from a DHCP server at boot time, halfway through the default lease time of three days, and at 87.5% and 100% of the original lease interval if the original DHCP server is unavailable.

The network trace shown in Table 13.5, lists the packets that arise from a successful DHCP renewal request: a single directed request followed by a single acknowledgment (ACK).

Table 13.5 *Network Trace*

Frame	Time	Src MAC Address	Dst MAC Address	Protocol	Description
1	2.307	LAPTOP	LONDON	DHCP	Request (xid=7A074280)
2	2.378	LONDON	SERVER	DHCP	ACK (xid=7A074280)

MOFComp

The Managed Object Format (MOF) compiler (Comp) parses a file containing the following MOF statements and adds the classes and instances defined in the file to the Common Information Model Object Manager (CIMOM) repository listed in Table 13.6.

```
mofcomp

    [-check]
    [-N: <namespace path>]
    [-class:updateonly | -class:createonly]
    [-instance:updateonly | -instance:createonly]
    [-B:<filename>]
    [-WMI]
    [-P:<Password>]
    [-U:<UserName>]
    [-A:<Authority>]
    <MOF file>
```

RETURN VALUES

As its first operation, the MOFComp performs a syntax check on the MOF file. If it finds any errors, an error message is printed and the process is terminates. The values listed in Table 13.7 can be returned.

If the MOF file is parsed correctly, but an attempt is made to perform an operation that is forbidden by a command line switch, the compiler returns CIMOM error codes instead of any return codes listed in Table 13.7. For example, a CIMOM error is returned when the instance:updateonly switch is specified and the MOF file attempts to create an instance.

Table 13.6 *CIMOM Switches*

Switch	Description
Check	Requests that the compiler perform a syntax check only and print appropriate error messages. No other switch can be used with this switch, no connection to CIMOM is established, and no modifications to the repository are made.
N	Requests that the compiler load the MOF file into the specified namespace. The default namespace (Root\Default) is used unless this switch is used or a #pragma namespace ("namespace path") statement appears in the MOF file.
class:updateonly	Requests that the compiler not create any new classes, terminating if a class specified in the MOF file does not exist
class:createonly	Requests that the compiler not make any changes to existing classes, terminating if a class specified in the MOF file already exists
instance:updateonly	Requests that the compiler not create any new instances, terminating if an instance specified in the MOF file does not exist
instance:createonly	Requests that the compiler not make any changes to existing instances, terminating if an instance specified in the MOF file already exists
B	Requests that the compiler create a binary version of the MOF file without making any modifications to the repository
WMI	Requests that the compiler perform a WMI syntax check. The -B switch must be used with this switch
P	Specifies a password to use when logging on
U	Specifies the name of the user logging on
A	Specifies the authority (domain name) to use when logging on

Table 13.7 *MOFComp Return Values*

Return value	Description
0	MOFComp was successful
1	MOFComp could not connect with the CIMOM server, possibly due to a semantic error—such as an incompatibility with the existing repository—or an actual error—such as the failure of the CIMOM server to start
2	One or more command line switches were invalid
3	MOF syntax error

REMARKS

A file can be compiled with the following simple command line entries:

```
mofcomp <MOF filename>
```

When special processing is required, one or more of the switches can be used. All the switches are optional, and any combination is allowed. It does not make sense, however, to use some of the switches in combination with others. For example, to combine the -class:updateonly and -class:createonly switches results in the compiler not performing any action.

A MOF file that is using the Unicode character set contains a signature as the first two bytes of the file. This signature is U+FFFE or U+FEFF, depending on the byte ordering of the file.

When there are no errors in the parsing process, the MOFComp connects to the CIMOM server running on the local machine, unless the -check switch is specified. Classes and instances defined in the MOF file are added to the repository. When there is an error in updating the repository, no attempt is made to bring it back to the state it was in before the compiler began its processing.

Now, that we've examined the diagnostic tools that are available to solve SMS problems, let's examine how to diagnose and resolve installation problems in SMS site systems.

MCSE 13.4 Diagnosing and Resolving Installation Problems

You can resolve many common secondary site server creation, installation and upgrade problems by diagnosing system logs immediately following the failure and correcting problems noted in these logs. If you are planning to create or upgrade a number of secondary sites or if you expect the operations to take a long time due to slow links, you may want to increase the log size for the Hman.log and Scman.log files. You can use SMS Service Manager to increase log sizes.

Installation Problems Involving the Secondary Site Server

Secondary site server creation, installation, and upgrade processes initiate several jobs during the various installation and upgrade modes of operation.

These jobs run on a 12-hour time-out; if any job fails to respond appropriately within the time-out period, the site creation, installation, or upgrade will fail. At this point, although clients may continue to work properly at an existing secondary site, the site will probably be unusable within the SMS hierarchy.

TROUBLESHOOTING SITE SERVER PREINSTALL JOB FAILURES

You can troubleshoot *stuck* secondary site server creation, installation, or upgrade jobs just as you would any stuck job. Let's take a look at some of these problems.

PROBLEMS WITH SYSTEMS MANAGEMENT SERVER SERVICE ACCOUNTS • The best place to begin troubleshooting account problems is the `Lansend.log` file. For example, although a Win32 error = 1326 entry within the `Lansend.log` file translates to unknown user or bad password, LanSender continues to attempt the connection. The `Lansend.log` file also records errors to indicate a locked, disabled, or nonexistent account.

If an incorrect password is specified in the SMS Administrator program New Secondary Site configuration dialog box, and Windows NT Server 4.0 is configured to lock out accounts after repeated invalid logon attempts, a valid SMS service account may become locked. To resolve this problem, use the Windows NT Server 4.0 User Manager for Domains to unlock the account.

You must configure and select the account used by secondary site server SMS services carefully. If an invalid account is used, the target domain will deny access and the initial site Preinstall job will fail. You can test the selected account's capabilities by attempting a connection to the IPC$share on the target site using the desired account. If the connection fails, the site Preinstall job will also fail. The following paragraphs define account requirements and discuss methods to resolve problems with the service account.

PROBLEMS WITH HIERARCHIES THAT SPAN DOMAINS • If the secondary site server and the primary site server are in the same domain, use the same service account for both primary and secondary sites. Problems often occur, however, when primary and secondary sites are in different domains. If your hierarchy includes such sites, one of two conditions must be met. First of all, a duplicate SMS service account with the same username and password must exist in both domains. When you specify the username and password in the Site Properties dialog box, do not type primary site domain name\SMS service account. The secondary site domain will deny access to that account.

Enter the username from the secondary site domain for the SMS service account.

Second of all, correct trust relationships must exist between the domains to allow the primary site domain's SMS service account full administrative rights in the target domain. When you specify the username and password in the Site Properties dialog box, type domain\username from the primary site domain for the SMS service account, except when certain conditions are met in the following trust relationships.

If a *one-way trust* relationship exists where the target domain trusts the primary site domain, the administrator must create an identical SMS service account in the secondary site domain and add it to that domain's Domain Admins group. When you specify the username and password in the Site Properties dialog box, type the secondary site SMS service account without a domain prefix or with the secondary site domain prefix. SMS services at the primary site can use the primary site domain prefix for the SMS service account.

Now, if a *two-way trust* relationship exists between the two domains, the domain prefix is normally not required at either site. The exception would be if a duplicate SMS service account exists in the secondary site domain and the primary site domain prefix is not used, and if the secondary site server will detect the local domain's security token and deny access. This causes the site Preinstall job to fail. To resolve this conflict, delete the duplicate account in the secondary site domain or type the primary site domain prefix with the username when you specify the username and password in the Site Properties dialog box.

PROBLEMS WITH LANSENDER • Site Preinstall jobs will fail if notification is not received from the secondary site server that preinstallation of the secondary site has been completed, although the problem may be at the primary site. If the primary site's LanSender does not have sufficient sending capacity to transfer the Bootstrap job and related files to all secondary sites scheduled for installation or upgrade, jobs designated for some or all sites will fail.

You can start tracing these failures by selecting the secondary site server in the SMS Administrator program Sites window and clicking *Properties* on the *File* menu to display the current status:

```
Preinstall Job: Site Upgrade Initiated
```

For each site server that indicates this status, the primary site's Hman.log and Sched.log files show corresponding entries and Bootstrap jobs appear in the Jobs window. Send requests appear in the designated sender request directory $Sms\Site.srv\Sender.box\Requests\Lan_def a.xxx, or other sender subdirectories specified in the Installation Sender Type field of the SMS Administrator program New Secondary Site window.

The primary site's LanSender should then begin processing the send requests. However, if LanSender determines that no sending capacity is available, it will not look for send requests. No other jobs are capable of being processed, either. If you find such entries, you may be able to resolve the problem by verifying the sender registry settings on the primary site server. To do this, open the Registry Editor and locate the following parameter:

```
HKey_Local_Machine\Software\Microsoft\SMS\Components\

SMS_LAN_SENDER\MaximumConcurrentSendings
```

If the parameter value is set to zero or less than five (the default setting), modify the registry parameter value accordingly. Other problems with the initial Preinstall job may be related to not having an address for the secondary site. Hierarchy Manager should create the address, although problems with Site Configuration Manager may prevent this from occurring. Verify sender addresses for the secondary site(s) by doing the following:

- Select the parent primary site in the SMS Administrator program Sites window and click Properties on the File menu.
- Select Sender Addresses to display addresses in Current Properties as defined in the site control file. The secondary site sender address should appear in this list.
- Return to the Site Properties window, select Proposed Properties, and then select Sender Addresses again. If the sender address appears in this list, the address has not been written to the site control file. Stopping and restarting the primary site's Site Configuration Manager should update the site control file and the address should appear in Current Properties. At this point, the job should proceed normally.
- If the sender address does not appear in Current or Proposed properties, manually create the address.

LanSender should then find the send requests and transfer the Bootstrap jobs to the secondary sites.

 warning

The LanSender parameter accepts values in a range of 0 to 255. The value represents the number of threads the LanSender service will use, and thus affects the amount of memory and CPU time used by the service. If you plan to increase the setting above the default value, you may want to monitor CPU and memory usage to avoid overloading the server.

REMNANTS OF PREVIOUS INSTALLATIONS • It is possible for the remnants of another SMS installation to cause a problem in the secondary site server installation process. If the primary site's SMS Administrator program Jobs window shows Status Details for the job that indicate a Sending Status of Retrying, the directory you specified as the installation directory may already have files in it. You may see the following entries in the primary site's Lansend.log file:

```
<target directory> on <\\<target server> is not a SMS
directory and is not empty, we won't install to it.

Error from site bootstrap (8)

No need to disconnect
```

You may resolve the problem by removing existing SMS directories and files from the target server, and ensuring that any SMS services on the target site have been stopped and removed. This should allow the site Preinstall system job to proceed normally. Once the site Preinstall job is completed and the bootstrap service has been installed and started, processing usually continues through the successful completion of the installation or upgrade of the secondary site server.

TROUBLESHOOTING SITE SERVER INSTALL OR UPGRADE COMPLETION FAILURES

After the secondary site's Site Configuration Manager has installed the other services on the secondary site server, it should immediately report its status back to the parent. The following sections discuss why delays may occur.

PROBLEMS WITH LANSENDER • The secondary site's Site Configuration Manager creates a .ct2 file that initiates reporting to the primary site and records its actions in the Scman.log file as follows:

```
Created mini-job in (d:\sms\site.srv\schedule.box) to send
site control file

(\\EDITHWI6\SMS_SHRd\site.srv\sitecfg.box\00000000.ct2) to
parent site

DOM SMS_SITE_CONFIG_MANAGER 3/31/97 10:41:31 AM 8
```

The secondary site's Scheduler recognizes and processes the mini-job request and records its actions in the Sched.log file. The secondary site's

Despooler processes the mini-job instruction file created by the Scheduler and records its actions in the `Despoolr.log` file.

The secondary site's LanSender should then begin processing the send requests. If LanSender determines that no sending capacity is available, however, it will not look for send requests. If you find these entries in the logs, you might resolve the problem through the steps listed earlier in this section.

Once the secondary site's LanSender forwards the package to the parent primary site, the primary site's Despooler finds and decompresses the file, renames it with a .ct2 extension, and moves it to the $Sms\Site.srv\ Sitecfg.box directory.

The primary site's Hierarchy Manager then records the secondary site configuration data in the database and creates a `.ct1` file in the `$Sms\ Site.Srv\Sitecfg.box` directory. The primary site's Site Configuration Manager uses the `.ct1` file to update the `Sitectrl.ct0` site control file in the `$Sms\Site.srv\Sitecfg.box` directory. The following sections discuss errors that may occur during this process.

PROBLEMS WITH SITE CONFIGURATION MANAGER • If the primary site's Site Configuration Manager stops responding or is otherwise unable to process the `.ct1` file, the file remains in the `$Sms\Site.srv\Sitecfg.box` directory and the secondary site remains in the installation or upgrade completion mode, although it may be operational. To resolve these problems, go to the parent primary site and check for unprocessed `.ctx` files in the `$Sms\Site.srv\Sitecfg.box` directory. For instance:

- If you find `.ct2` files, look in the primary site's `Scman.log` file for related entries, including failure to connect to SQL Server.
- If you find `.ct1` files, look in the primary site's `Scman.log` file for entries related to site control file processing.

.CT2 FILE NOT RECEIVED BY THE PRIMARY SITE • If previous troubleshooting fails to isolate the problem and logs show normal processing capabilities on both the primary and secondary sites, you may be able to force a site configuration update and job completion by performing the following steps:

1. At the secondary site, copy the `$Secsite\Sitecfg.box\Sitectrl .ct0` file to a temporary location.
2. Move any other existing `.ctx` files in this directory to a temporary location.
3. Rename the original `.ct0` file to `00000000.ct2`.

The secondary site's Site Configuration Manager uses the `.ct2` file to re-create the `$Secsite\Site.srv\Sitecfg.box\Sitectrl.ct0` site control file. It then creates a corresponding `.ct2` file that is forwarded to the primary site by the secondary site's Scheduler, Despooler, and LanSender. At this point, you can use SMSTrace or a text editor to follow processing in the logs and identify the failure point. Once the primary site has received and processed the secondary site's `.ct2` file, the SMS Administrator program Sites window should list the secondary site as Active.

If the primary site is a child site to another parent primary site, Hierarchy Manager forwards a copy of the site control file to its parent site. This process continues upward through the site hierarchy to the central site.

USING PREINST/DELSITE TO REMOVE FAILED SECONDARY SITES

Secondary site server installation and upgrade jobs fail if the primary site does not receive system job status reports from the secondary site. If this occurs, you may have to delete and reinstall the failed site.

Clients that report to a deleted secondary site will be resynchronized when the site is reinstalled, which may temporarily increase network traffic and server load. Logon server UIDs must also be synchronized. In many cases, this may still be the quickest method to reestablish the secondary site.

You can remove failing secondary sites by selecting the site in the SMS Administrator Sites window and clicking *Delete*. The primary site's Hierarchy Manager then updates site configuration data and send a Deinstall job that removes all Systems Management Server files, directories, and services from the secondary site. If the computer is no longer physically accessible because it is off the network, the hardware has been replaced, or Windows NT Server 4.0 has been reinstalled, the Deinstall job will fail.

You can use the PREINST command to remove the failing secondary site without sending the Deinstall job. PREINST is an executable instance of Hierarchy Manager located in the `$Sms\Site.srv\X86.bin` directory. To display PREINST command options and syntax, perform these steps:

1. Open a command prompt window and change to the `$Sms\Site.srv\X86.bin` directory.
2. Type Preinst /? at the command prompt.

To remove a secondary site using PREINST, perform these steps:

1. At the primary site server, open a command prompt window and change to the `$Sms\Site.srv\X86.bin` directory.
2. Type the following command:

```
Preinst /Delsite: <secondary site code, primary site
code>
```

This command removes the secondary site from the SQL Server database and updates the primary site's site control file and other configuration data. Upon successful completion, the secondary site no longer appears in the SMS Administrator program Sites window.

Any SMS files, services, and registry entries remaining on the deleted secondary site server must be removed manually before you attempt to reinstall the secondary site.

We've examined how to diagnose and resolve installation problems in SMS site systems. Now let's look at how to optimize SQL Server for SMS.

MCSE 13.5 Optimizing SQL Server for SMS

It's important to tune SQL Server for better performance with SMS. Much of the internal operation of SQL Server is dynamically managed, and generally these rules do not need to be changed. When tuning SQL Server, however, you should be sure that the hardware is performing well and that the database performance does not degrade due to lack of hardware maintenance.

Undersized hardware, hardware or software configuration problems, or lack of database maintenance can cause system bottlenecks. Use `Perfmon .exe` to assist you in keeping the SMS database working smoothly.

NTFS or FAT?

SQL can run on a Windows NT 4.0 file system (NTFS) or File allocation table (FAT) file system. For SQL Server, read operations are slightly faster on NTFS, while write operations are faster on FAT. Because SQL spends most of its time reading from a SMS database, converting the file system to NTFS from FAT slightly improves performance and data reliability.

Setting up Automatic Maintenance

Consider using the SQL Maintenance Wizard accessed through SQL Enterprise Manager to set up automatic maintenance of the SMS database. The SQL Enterprise Manager does recommend manual configuration of automatic maintenance for databases larger than 400 MB. If the SMS database exceeds this limit, use the wizard cautiously. Browse through the choices presented by the wizard, and cancel without saving. Experiment with the wizard on a test server. Try running `SQLtrace.exe` as shown in Figure 13.29 with the logging option on while the wizard is running. This creates a record of the exact queries that the wizard runs. Later, you can study these logs to better understand which options the wizard is actually setting up.

Named Pipes Network Support

SMS requires Named Pipes network support to communicate with the SMS database. You can change SQL Server network support by running SQL

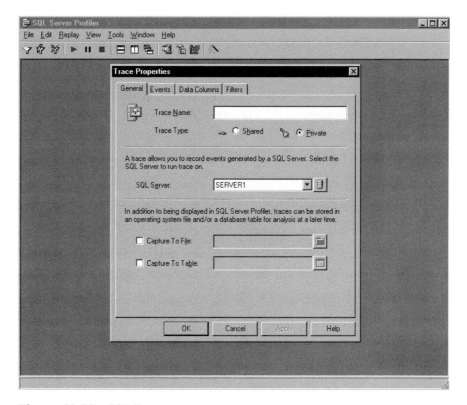

Figure 13.29 *SQL Trace.*

Server Setup, selecting the Change Network Support option, and then selecting Named Pipes as an installed network.

Recommended SQL Server Configuration Options

With SQL Server 6.5, and 7.0, you can change SQL Server configuration options by using the SQL Enterprise Manager user interface, as follows:

1. On the Server menu, click SQL Server Configure.
2. Click the Configuration tab.

The configuration options can also be changed by the sp_configure stored procedure.

SQL SERVER MEMORY

The amount of memory dedicated to SQL Server depends on the amount of physical RAM in the computer and the usage and performance requirements of SQL Server. Memory is designated in 2-K blocks. For example, for a dedicated SQL Server computer with 128 MB of RAM, you may want to set the memory to 64 MB of RAM (32,768 2-K blocks) for SQL Server. On a SQL Server and SMS Site Server with 128 MB of RAM, you may want to dedicate only 40 MB of RAM (20,480 2-K blocks) to SQL Server.

SQL SERVER OPEN OBJECTS

Set Open Objects to 5,000–7,000, depending on the size of your site and the size of the child sites below it. If Open Objects is set too low, you may see the following symptoms:

- Poor SMS or SQL Server performance
- A backlog of MIF files in the \Site.srv\Dataloder.box\Delta mif.col subdirectory
- Delays in such things as inventory, job status, MIF processing, or package distribution
- Errors indicating the server is out of open objects. These errors are in the \mssql\logs\error.log file on the SQL Server computer

The SQL Server default for open objects is 500, which is inadequate for even a small SMS site without child sites.

SQL SERVER USER CONNECTIONS

Each user connection takes 40 K of RAM. This value is determined by the amount of memory dedicated to the SQL Server computer and the number of concurrent connections required. If you set this value unnecessarily high, SQL Server will not have enough memory to operate normally. You should consider the following requirements when determining the correct value:

- Each SMS Primary Site Server communicating with a SQL Server computer requires at least ten connections; however, 20–30 connections are recommended in most cases.
- Each running instance of SMS Administrator requires at least one connection. It is best to configure approximately five connections for each instance.

TEMPDB IN RAM

Do not place Tempdb in RAM on a SQL Server running SMS. The memory is better used by SQL Server's cache.

 If you make any changes to these parameters, stop and restart the Microsoft SQL Server.

BACKUP AND RECOVERY

A regularly scheduled database dump, along with backup of the SMS registry and directory structure, is a mandatory part of a good backup and recovery procedure. Finally, let's take a look at how to tune SQL and SMS Server.

Tuning SMS and SQL Server

Before troubleshooting a backlog, verify that your system is properly tuned. This subsection provides basic guidelines for tuning SMS and SQL Server.

SERVICE RESPONSE SETTING

The Service Response Mode, or Site Speed, should never be set to Very Fast. A setting of Medium or Fast processes MIFs more quickly, because the Site Configuration Manager does not have to continually perform watchdog cycles. It also allows the Dataloader to run uninterrupted for a longer period of time. To check or change the Site Speed, click Site Properties, and then click Services.

SQL CONFIGURATION

Tempdb should be approximately 20% of the largest database on the SQL Server. Also make sure the database and its transaction log are not full. The transaction log should be 20% of the SMS database size.

 Increasing the SMS database size to an extremely large value can actually decrease SQL performance.

Use Performance Monitor to check the Cache Hit Ratio. Make sure the database is in cache (it should be above 99%), and is not paging out. If necessary, install additional RAM or dedicate more memory to SQL Server. Memory, Open Objects, and User Connections are important tuning parameters within SQL Server.

INVENTORY FREQUENCY

Turn down inventory frequency if necessary. For example, if six child sites with an average of 4,000 clients are inventoried daily, the SMS central site is forced to process 24,000 MIFs each day. This means that SMS and SQL Server must process 1 MIF every 3.6 seconds (24,000 MIFs /[24 hours*3,600 seconds/hour] = 1 MIF every 3.6 seconds). If the system is incapable of maintaining this load, reduce the inventory frequency to a manageable level.

■ Summary

You should come away from this chapter with an in-depth knowledge of the MCSE exam-specific components or functions of diagnosing and resolving SMS 2.0 problems. You should be able to do this with utilities that enable you to directly control and monitor remote clients running Windows 95 and 98, Windows NT 3.51 and 4.0, or Windows 3.x operating systems, and utilities that allow you to diagnose network problems. SMS 2.0 also adds a preview of server health monitoring tools to SMS. The first part of the chapter discussed the following types of available tools:

- Diagnostics options
- HealthMon (server monitoring tools)
- Help Desk utilities
- Network Monitor (network monitoring tools)
- Remote control on clients running Windows NT 4.0
- Requirements for remote troubleshooting

The second part of the chapter examined the various features available to aid an administrator in resolving user and network problems. It also examined the types of tasks you can perform using the Diagnostics and Help Desk tools.

The third part of the chapter looked at the diagnostic tools available to solve SMS diagnostic problems, such as:

- Network Monitor
- Dumpsend
- Tracer and SMSTrace
- MIFCheck
- WBEMTest
- Network Trace
- MOFComp

The fourth part of the chapter showed you how to resolve many common secondary site server creation, installation, and upgrade problems by diagnosing the system logs immediately following the failure and correcting problems noted in these logs. It showed you what to do if you are planning to create or upgrade a number of secondary sites or if you expect the operations to take a long time due to slow links.

Finally, the fifth part of the chapter explained why it's important to tune SQL Server for better performance with SMS. It explained that when tuning SQL Server, you should be sure that the hardware is performing well and that the database performance does not degrade due to lack of hardware maintenance.

▲ Chapter Review Questions

▲ True/False

1. *True or False? The access list of supported video drivers feature is only available for clients running Windows NT 4.0.*

2. *True or False? Although you can view and control multiple clients from an SMS Administrator, you cannot use more than one instance of an SMS Administrator to view or control the same client at the same time.*

3. *True or False? For clients running Windows NT 4.0, the remote access features are not automatically started.*

4. *True or False? MS-DOS Windows are not supported during a Remote Session.*

5. *True or False? For clients running Windows 3.11, Remote Control is unavailable.*

6. *True or False? Remote Execute is supported on clients running only MS-DOS.*

7. *True or False? With SMS's troubleshooting tools, you should be able to diagnose and resolve installation problems in SMS site systems involving distribution points.*

8. *True or False? With SMS's troubleshooting tools, you can't diagnose and resolve installation problems involving Hardware Problems.*

9. *True or False? With SMS's troubleshooting tools, you should be able to diagnose and resolve problems involving site-to-site communications.*

10. *True or False? Network Monitor is a traffic analyzer diagnostic tool that helps administrators find network problems. The SMS 2.0 Network Monitor allows the analysis of network traffic and can pinpoint problems or potential bottlenecks in realtime.*

11. *True or False? The DumpSend utility is accessed with the DUMPSEND command. It displays the binary SMS send request file in text format for review.*

12. *True or False? TRACER.EXE is a command line console-mode utility that reads changes made to a text file in real time.*

13. *True or False? SMSTRACE.EXE is a graphical user interface (GUI) multiple document interface (MDI) tool.*

14. *True or False? Mifcheck.exe is a MIF parser and syntax checker for use in verifying text MIFs before submitting them to the system. It reports syntax and semantic errors, and it is designed to help independent software vendors (ISVs) who are writing MIFs for new components for the inventory agent to collect and report to the site server.*

15. *True or False? Although WBEMTest can be run to see what it can do, WBEM can be better understood using some of the SDK tools such as CIM Studio. The core components are included by default on Windows 2000 and as an*

installable option in Windows 98. Additionally, they are shipped with Windows NT4.0, SP4.

16. *True or False? You can access Network Trace via Site Status.*

17. *True or False? The Managed Object Format (MOF) compiler (Comp) parses a file containing MOF statements and adds classes and instances defined in the file to the Common Information Model Object Manager (CIMOM) repository.*

18. *True or False? You can resolve many common secondary site server creation, installation, and upgrade problems by diagnosing the system logs immediately following the failure and correcting problems noted in these logs.*

19. *True or False? It's important to optimize SQL Server for SMS.*

▲ Multiple Choice

1. *The Help Desk options provide remote access to clients. These options allow you to perform the following operations except:*
   A. Remote control
   B. Remote reboot
   C. Remote chat
   D. File transfer
   E. Capture data

2. *If the user wants to allow limited remote control, the user is prompted to specify what operations a SMS 2.0 administrator can perform. These operations are as follows except:*
   A. Run SMS Directory
   B. Exchange text messages (chat).
   C. Restart the client computer
   D. Run commands on the client computer
   E. Transfer files between the client computer and your computer

3. *Network Monitor is a traffic analysis tool that helps administrators find network problems. The SMS 2.0 Network Monitor allows the analyzing of network traffic and can pinpoint problems or potential bottlenecks. With Network Monitor, administrators can do the following except:*
   A. Capture frames on a remote computer and display the capture statistics on the local computer at intervals that you specify

  B. Capture detail

  C. Capture frames (also called packets) directly from the network

  D. Display and filter captured frames

  E. Edit and transmit captured frames onto the network to test network resources or reproduce network problems

4. In the Remote Tools Options dialog box, what allows an administrator to remotely run Diagnostics on client computer?

  A. Run commands on your computer

  B. Transfer files to and from your computer

  C. View your computer configuration

  D. Restart your computer

  E. Change Remote Icons

▲ Open Ended

1. Reducing total cost of ownership requires centralized problem determination and resolution. SMS 2.0 includes utilities that enable you to directly control and monitor remote clients running Windows 95 and 98, Windows NT 3.51 and 4.0, or Windows 3.x operating systems, and utilities that allow you to diagnose network problems. SMS 2.0 also adds a preview of server health monitoring facilities to SMS. What are the available tools?

2. The Diagnostics options allow you to view real-time information about a client's environment, such as software and hardware configuration. What are the available options for clients running MS-DOS, Windows 3.1, Windows for Workgroups 3.11, and Windows 95 and 98?

Restoring SMS Sites

This chapter presents the automated process of regularly backing up and restoring all relevant SMS 2.0 data on both SMS site servers and SMS logon servers.

The first part of this chapter provides an invaluable checklist of items to restore a SQL Server from scratch. Unfortunately, database dumps alone are usually insufficient to reincarnate your system. You need additional pieces of information and files to do complete restorations.

The second part of the chapter explains how Inventory data collected by SMS is valuable to the organization that collected it. It would not be a simple task to recollect all this inventory data if it were lost. Therefore, it is recommended that you back up and restore this data on a regular basis. At first, this backing up and restoration of data seems to be a simple process. However, the data stored in the SQL Server database is only part of what is required to restore the SMS system to a known state after a failure occurs. Files on each SMS site

525

server's file system, the Windows NT Server 4.0 registry entries, and all SQL Server system and SMS databases must be backed up if the SMS system is to be completely restored.

The third part of the chapter explains how SMS allows you to use the Internet to perform a number of management tasks. You can, for instance, use the Internet to remotely manage Windows-based Web servers. You can also manage SMS sites across the Internet, create reports in HTML format for publication on the Internet (or your private intranet), and analyze frames from the Internet using Network Monitor.

MCSE 14.1   Restoring an SQL Server

Do you have a sound plan in case of complete loss of your database server? You should perform periodic database backups according to a rigorous schedule and keep backup media offsite or at least somewhere other than the same room as your SQL Server. Still, are you able to completely recover from these backups?

It's quite possible that after successfully restoring all databases you'll spend several days figuring out other missing bits and pieces, such as command files, SQL scripts, scheduled tasks, network shares, and so on. To avoid this and simplify your SQL Server recovery process, let's review some items so that you can create your own disaster recovery checklist.

Emergency Kit for Your SQL Server

It's a good idea to prepare an emergency kit in case you ever need to completely rebuild your SQL Server from the ground level. One way is to put all documentation and software needed in one box and store it in a secure location. It should contain:

- A list of key recovery people with their phone and pager numbers
- A SQL Server recovery manual, with all configuration options and settings (excluding passwords)
- Installation documentation and software for all custom-made applications on the SQL Server
- Instructions for locating the most recent backup tapes, which are stored separately
- Microsoft TechNet CD with NT and SQL Server service packs

- SQL Server installation manuals and CD including service packs
- Windows NT 4.0 installation manuals and CD including service packs[1]

With luck, you will never experience a loss of an SQL Server due to a theft, fire, or natural disasters. If you do, you will certainly appreciate having good recovery procedures. Upgrading NT to a new version or moving all databases to a bigger and faster server might turn out to be a disaster, too, unless you're prepared.

Hardware Know-How

Your recovery documentation should describe the hardware requirements for your SQL Server. In case the hardware is physically lost or destroyed, you will want to have detailed specification notes readily available to help you purchase or borrow a new server right away.

Add a section on minimal requirements for your server. It behooves you to know the absolute minimum configuration that could get you (or your client) up and running fast. Disk space is usually the most restrictive parameter. You can't load your databases onto a smaller storage system, but you can operate on a server with fewer processors or slower ones. Also bear in mind that a CD drive isn't an absolute necessity if you can access one across the network.

When you're documenting your hardware specification, make sure to include not only the total amount of disk space, but also information about disk partitioning and Remote Access Interactive Debugger (RAID) configuration. Although a replacement storage system doesn't have to be set up precisely the same way on the new server, disk partitions and names are very important. If your new server has different drive letters and partition sizes deviate from those on the original server, you will have to do extra work changing physical device locations and correcting any hard-coded references to drive letters. This manual work creates a potential for errors and slows down the recovery process. Ideally, you need a new server with partitions named and sized the same as the old one. In other words, be sure to document these details.

Strictly speaking, the amount of memory installed on SQL Server doesn't have to be the same as on the old machine. A server with less memory might still allow you to work, though it might be significantly slower.

---

1. Zanevsky, Andrew. "Prepare (Now) to Rebuild Your Server." *SQL Server Professional,* (March, 1998). Pinnacle Publishing, Inc., 1503 Johnson Ferry Road, Suite 100, Marietta, GA 30062. All rights reserved.

Service Packs and Versions

SQL Server 6.5, 7.0 and higher currently each have four service packs (SPs). The number of combinations and permutations of SQL server with Windows NT 4.0 and e-mail clients is a surprisingly large. If your site has numerous SQL servers, some of them might use older versions or don't have the most recent service packs applied. When you restore SQL Server, you will obviously want to use the same software as was installed on the lost server. Therefore, you need to keep track of what's installed where, perhaps in an easy-to-read table format.

Remember, service packs (SPs) are cumulative. If your server is up to SP3, all you need is SP3; you don't need to apply SP1 and SP2 first.

You might execute extended stored procedure `master..xp_msver` to obtain information about NT and SQL Server versions as well as the number of processors, processor type, and the total amount of memory. Unfortunately, it won't tell you which service packs have been applied in plain English, so you'll have to interpret the version number. The ERRORLOG file also contains SQL Server version information.

Another approach to restoring an SQL server is to piece together the NT version info from the Help/About dialog box and execute a SELECT @@version to get SQL Server version information. You still need to interpret output in the form of *Microsoft SQL Server 7.00 - 7.00.240 (Intel X86)* as SQL Server *7.0* with SP2. Have version numbers documented in your recovery manual.

Connectivity to E-mail

If your SQL Server is configured to send or receive e-mail messages, it can be difficult and time-consuming to duplicate the setup on a new server. Document all the steps you took to configure and activate your SQL Mail client and remember that you need a separate mail account to run SQL Mail. Make sure the name of the account appears in the recovery manual and that key people remember the password. The name and password are required during SQL Server installation.

Configuration and Setup Options during SQL Server Installation

Your recovery manual should include all setup and configuration choices you need to make during SQL Server installation. Let's look at the choices shown in the following sidebar, "Setup and Configuration Choices."

Study Break

Setup and Configuration Choices

The following describes the setup and configuration choices you need to make during SQL Server installation:

Master device size and physical path

Here, the Execute system stored procedure `master..sp_helpdevice` is used to obtain this information.

Character set and sort order

This is reported in the ERRORLOG file as IDs you can look up in the SQL Server setup documentation.

Network support

The default is Named Pipes protocol, but you might choose additional network support options; for instance, TCP/IP.

Server configuration options

Check your current settings by opening the Configuration dialog box. In SQL Enterprise Manager, go to Server|SQLServer| Configure and review Server Options. Click on the Parameters button to review startup parameters, use the Tape Support button to review tape support options, and finally, click on the Mail Login button to review the mail account.

Security options

Check your current settings by opening the Security Options dialog box. In SQL Enterprise Manager, go to Server|SQLServer| Configure, and then choose the Security Options tab.

Server configuration options

The easiest approach might be to document any deviation from the defaults. You've probably configured parameters such as memory, locks, open objects, user connections, and procedure cache to fit your needs. Every site might have its own setting for any configurable parameter, so it's a good idea to include the entire contents of the `master..sysconfigures` table in your recovery manual. Current settings can be obtained via the SQL Enterprise Manager, but you should use the system stored procedure `master..sp_configure`, as follows:

```
sp_configure 'show advanced options', 1
go
reconfigure with override
go
sp_configure
go
Licensing mode
```

This is per server or per client.

Name of user account used to start and run SQLExecutive and MSSQLServer services

If you're not sure about your current settings, open the Windows NT 4.0 Control Panel, then the Services applet, find MSSQLServer service, then review Startup Type and Log On As settings. If This Account option is used, you also need to document permissions of the specified account on the SQL Server machine and on the network. Use Windows NT 4.0 User Manager and User Manager for Domains applets to determine groups to which the account belongs and specific permissions that it has. Repeat this for SQLExecutive.

Databases and Devices

You might have learned by painful experience that just having a database dump file isn't enough to successfully restore it. First, you need to create a database of the same size or larger, with the same order, type, and size of data and log segments. And even if you create a database large enough to load the backup, you'll probably still end up with an error once you restore it. Information about segments is stored in system table `master..sysusages`. You might include it in your recovery documentation. You should also include output produced by system stored procedures `master..sp_helpdatabases`, `master..sp_helpdevices`, and `master..sp_helpservers` (in case there are any remote servers).

In addition to extracts from system tables, save the output of system stored procedure `master..sp_help_revdatabase` and include it as an appendix to your recovery manual. That way, you'll have both a hard copy and a text file of all the SQL commands needed to recreate each device, database, place data, and logs on the right segments. It will also show which database options are set. When you need to rebuild a server, the script generated by this procedure is a lifesaver. The only deficiency of this script is that it doesn't provide an option to build new databases FOR LOAD. You should manually modify all CREATE DATABASE and ALTER DATABASE commands to include the FOR LOAD option. This saves you several hours during recovery.

Passwords and Logins

You should consider making a complete backup of the `master..syslogins` table every day via `bcp`. It's much easier to allow updates on system tables and reload logins than to set them up manually. You should use a command similar to the following to make a backup:

```
exec master..xp_cmdshell

'bcp master..syslogins out

c:\temp\syslogins.bcp -c -Usa -P'
```

Use `xp_cmdshell` as part of a stored procedure, but also execute bcp directly. In this example, use C:\TEMP directory and an SQL Server set up with no password for sa. You have to substitute your own settings. Remember that the syslogins content is sensitive, and you should store it in a secure directory where only the DBA has access. It contains all user passwords in an encrypted form, but it takes only several hours to a couple of days to decrypt a password through a brute-force attack. When you need to reload syslogins, you can execute a script similar to the one shown in Listing 14.1.

The msdb Database

You can restore the msdb database from a backup just as you would any user database, and this is convenient when you need to restore all scheduled tasks. You might encounter a problem, however, if the server that you're rebuilding was upgraded through several SQL Server versions. In old versions, msdb used to be smaller—2 MB for data and 2 MB for transaction log. In SQL Server 7.0, it's 6 MB for data and 2 MB for log. When you upgraded an old server, msdb size increased. The problem is that an upgraded msdb has three segments: 2-MB data segment, 2-MB log segment, and a new 4-MB data segment added during the upgrade. If you restore a backup of this database into a freshly built msdb on a newly installed SQL Server, you will have data and log segment overlap. New servers have just two segments in msdb—6-MB data and 2-MB log.

Listing 14.1 *Reload syslogins Script*

```
exec master..sp_configure 'allow updates', 1
go
reconfigure with override
go
-- create a table with the same
-- structure as syslogins
select *
into    ##logins
from    master..syslogins
where   1=0

-- restore syslogins into a temporary table
exec    master..xp_cmdshell
  'bcp tempdb..##logins in
c:\temp\syslogins.bcp -c -Usa -P'

-- report logins that cannot be restored
select 'cannot setup login', a.name,
       'because suid is used by', b.name
from    ##logins a, master..syslogins b
where   a.suid = b.suid
and     a.name != b.name

-- restore syslogins
insert master..syslogins
select *
from    ##logins a
where   not exists (
    select *
    from    master..syslogins b
    where   b.suid = a.suid )
```

THE MSDB TABLES

In SQL Server 7.0, tables have been added to the msdb database to aid in maintaining backup information. The new tables are shown in Table 14.1.

SQL Server automatically maintains a complete online backup and restore history in the msdb database. This information includes who performed the backup, at what time, and on which devices or files it is stored.

Backup and restore events are recorded even if created with custom applications or third-party tools. A Visual Basic application that calls SQL-DMO objects to perform backup and restore operations causes the events to be logged in these tables. For instance, after each DUMP statement is exe-

Table 14.1 The New msdb Tables

Table Name	Description
sysbackupdetail	Specifies a summary of the devices used to backup (dump)
sysbackuphistory	Specifies a summary of each backup operation (dump)
sysrestoredetail	Specifies a summary of the devices used to restore (load)
sysrestorehistory	Specifies a summary of each restore operation (load)

cuted, a description of the dump is saved in sysbackuphistory and the dump device details are saved in sysbackupdetail as part of a single transaction.

After each LOAD statement is executed, a description of the restore is saved in sysrestorehistory and the device details are saved in sysrestoredetail. If for any reason the history cannot be written to msdb database, a message is written to the Windows NT 4.0 event log and to the SQL Server error log.

This is another instance of something you wouldn't expect during a database recovery, and it's a nasty issue that can get you if you're not careful. One possible solution to this problem is to drop the genuine msdb, then create a new database under the same name with a 2-MB data segment and a 2-MB log segment. You then need to alter it by adding another 4-MB data segment. This database might be used to load an old msdb dump.

Another way to handle the problem is to create a dummy database of 8-MB, load your msdb backup on it, and then copy the tables' contents directly from this database into the msdb created at installation. You'll need to copy tables MSwebtasks, MSWork, sysalerts, sysappname, syshistory, syshostname, sysnotifications, sysoperators, sysservermessages, systasks, and sysvolumelabel, and some of them might be empty. If you take this approach, don't forget to stop SQLExecutive service until you are finished.

If you have only a few scheduled tasks, you might decide to manually reschedule them in case of recovery. If you opt for this approach, remember that you need to preserve the list of tasks and their frequency, and also that you'll lose task execution history if you reschedule. Try to avoid msdb hassles by anticipating potential problems and carefully documenting the desired restore action for msdb in the recovery manual.

Objects Customization

You probably have your own system-stored procedures installed in the master database. Some DBAs even create their own tables or other objects in master. Ask yourself what happens to all these objects when you need to recover. Do you want to restore master from a backup? It's possible to avoid performing this task if you make certain preparations in advance.

First, don't create any custom-made tables in master. Limit your own objects there to system-stored procedures (since you have no other choice with them). If you need a special table, create a separate database for DBA purposes.

Second, keep a complete SQL script to recreate all your own system-stored procedures in master. Once you rebuild your SQL Server, execute the SQL script to restore your procedures.

SQL Server on the Outside

Most SQL Servers have a certain number of command files, data files, and executables stored outside of SQL Server databases. They might be used for DBA maintenance tasks, data loads, or different application purposes. You need to back up these files together with your database dumps. If you need to rebuild server on a new box, you'll want all your command and data files restored as well as databases.

Don't forget DLLs with your extended stored procedures. Back them up. They aren't a part of SQL Server databases and aren't protected from a loss. Keep the list of extended stored procedures, since you will need to reregister them once you restore the server.

Specific directories and shares on the SQL Server and the network might also be critical to your applications and scheduled jobs. Keep a list of those in the recovery document. Note permissions on these shares and directories (folders) that might be important for SQL Server.

If your SQL scripts or command files contain references to specific drive letters, document every such place in the recovery manual and keep it current. If you must restore to a server with different partitions and drive names, this will allow you to quickly find places that might need correction.

Even though SQL Server provides a good scheduling mechanism that is more flexible than the Schedule service on Windows NT 4.0, some installations use the NT scheduler or a third-party scheduling package. If you have any database-related tasks scheduled outside of SQL Server, be sure to include their descriptions and frequency in the recovery manual. To get the list of tasks scheduled on NT, simply execute the *at* command from the command prompt.

If you're lucky, you won't ever have to go through the recovery process. Still, you must have a plan in case anything destroys your SQL Server. It'll pay you back if you use it even once. Even if it only collects dust, you'll sleep better knowing you've got your bases covered.

MCSE 14.2   Restoring an SMS Site

Let's look at the problem of restoring an SMS site. Now, suppose an organization has three SMS site servers, one of which is acting as the SMS central site server. One of the primary site servers is located on the same local area network (LAN) as the central site server and the other is connected to the central site by a high-speed WAN connection. Each SMS primary site server has four SMS logon servers reporting to it.

An organization may not want to incur the expense and management problems associated with having a tape backup and restore unit for each SMS site server. The organization should take advantage of after-hours network availability to create a process that moves each SMS site server's backup information to one dedicated backup server containing a backup tape device. This strategy also offers the advantage of having two current copies of the backup, one on disk and one on tape.

An organization may also want to make complete known state backups and restoration of each SMS site server. To achieve this, an organization can stop all SMS services on all SMS site servers, back up the complete Windows NT Server 4.0 and SMS registry on each server, and dump all relevant SQL Server databases on each site server. By doing this, the organization creates a static SMS state and backs it up while in this mode. This ensures a stable state can be restored when required.

How does an organization specifically arrive at the solution to this problem? Let's take a look.

Problem Solution

The solution to the problem is presented here in a series of steps. The first task is to calculate the size of the central backup server. Do this by first calculating the total of each SMS site server's SMS file system. An organization may want to copy all files in the SMS file system, not just selected files. This is to ensure a synchronized state after restoring a backup. Second, add the sizes of each SMS and SQL Server database for each SMS site server. This includes the master, msdb, tempdb, and SMS databases. An organization may want to save the complete state of the system by backing up all relevant SQL Server databases. Finally, add the total size of the Windows NT Server 4.0 registry backup files from each SMS site server. All of the registry (not just selected parts) are backed up.

After you have calculated the disk space for the total current SMS system, determine the final amount of disk space required on the backup server.

As all files from the SMS file system are backed up, an estimated amount of space must be added, due to growth from SMS package distribution. This is because these packages are also backed up. The maximum size of each **SQL Server** database device must be used to ensure that an adequate amount of space is available on the backup server as the SMS inventory grows. The backup server will have multiple simultaneous network write operations performed during the backup process, so the backup server must be connected to the network by a high speed network adapter card and have a sufficient amount of system memory to perform adequately.

SITE SERVER BACKUP AND RESTORE

Backing up and restoring the site servers is a fairly complicated process. You must perform the following steps:

1. Schedule a regular backup task to run at 12:00 A.M. each morning. On the site servers, schedule this task by using the SQL Server Scheduler.
2. Stop all SMS services before starting the backup. This ensures that the state of the SMS site server is static before the backup is started.
3. Dump the master, msdb, tempdb, and SMS databases into one SQL Server backup device file, using Microsoft SQL Server Transact-SQL statements.
4. Dump the Windows NT Server 4.0 registry by using the REGBACK tool from the Windows NT Server 4.0 Resource Kit.
5. Copy the complete SMS file system, the SQL Server backup device file, and the Windows NT Server 4.0 registry files from the site server to the backup server, by using the ROBOCOPY tool from the Windows NT Server 4.0 Resource Kit.
6. Restart all SMS services.

BACKUP AND RESTORE DIRECTORIES CREATION

You should create two directories on each site server to store the SQL Server dump device and the Windows NT Server 4.0 registry backups. For convenience, place these directories in the site server's SMS root directory. For instance, you can use the following commands at a command prompt to create directories to store the SQL Server dump device and the Windows NT Server 4.0 registry backup:

```
md d:\sms\sql
```

```
md d:\sms\reg
```

ROBOCOPY AND REGBACK UTILITIES DISTRIBUTION

The simplest way to distribute the utilities ROBOCOPY and REGBACK is to use the Windows NT 4.0 Directory Replication system, which must be established to distribute the SMS logon scripts. Placing these two utilities into the Winnt\System32\Repl\Import\Scripts directory on the Windows NT Server 4.0 master Directory Replication server causes them to be replicated to all Windows NT Server 4.0 Directory Replication partners. It is assumed in this part of the chapter that all the SMS site servers are configured as Windows NT Server 4.0 Directory Replication partners.

SQL SERVER BACKUP AND RESTORE DUMP DEVICE CREATION

To create a SQL Server backup and restore dump device, first create a subdirectory under the main SMS directory to store the SQL Server backup dump device. This is so that files to be backed up are located in one directory structure. For instance, use the following command at a command prompt to create a directory:

```
md d:\sms\sql
```

Second, on the SQL Enterprise Manager application Tools menu, click Database Backup/Restore and create a backup device located in the directory you just created. For instance, create a backup device called SMSP, which will create a file named Smsp.dat in the Sms\Sql directory.

SQL SERVER STORED PROCEDURES: CREATION AND TESTING

The next step in the creation of the automated site server backup is to create four SQL Server stored procedures on each site server. These SQL Server stored procedures contain instructions to dump the SQL Server master, msdb, and tempdb databases and the SMS database. On the SQL Enterprise Manager application Tools menu, click SQL Query Tool. From the SQL Query Tool window, test the Transact-SQL statements you plan to use to dump the four databases before creating the SQL Server stored procedures.

For instance, use the following command, where SMSP is the name of the SQL Server dump device:

```
DUMP DATABASE

master TO SMSP VOLUME = 'SS0011' WITH NOUNLOAD,

STATS = 10, INIT, NOSKIP
```

The first DUMP command does an initialization of the dump device. This clears old backups from the device before starting the new dumps. This Transact-SQL statement must always be executed before the other statements, as shown by the following commands:

```
DUMP DATABASE msdb

TO SMSP VOLUME = 'SS0011' WITH NOUNLOAD,

STATS = 10, NOINIT,

NOSKIP DUMP DATABASE SMS TO SMSP VOLUME = 'SS0011'

WITH NOUNLOAD, STATS = 10,

NOINIT, NOSKIP DUMP DATABASE tempdb TO SMSP VOLUME = 'SS0011'

WITH NOUNLOAD, STATS = 10,

NOINIT, NOSKIP
```

The other three dump commands do not initialize the dump device.

After you have tested your Transact-SQL statements, create the SQL Server stored procedures to be used by the automated backup process. For instance, use the following commands:

```
create proc

Backup_tempdb

as
```

```
DUMP DATABASE tempdb TO SMSP VOLUME = 'SS0011' WITH NOUNLOAD,

STATS = 10, NOINIT, NOSKIP
```

The label `Backup_tempdb` is the name of the SQL Server stored procedure you created. Create stored procedures for each dump command for each database on each site server. After you have created all SQL Server stored procedures, check them for correctness by executing the following Transact-SQL statements:

```
sp_help
```

```
exec Backup_master
```

```
exec Backup_msdb
```

```
exec Backup_SMS
```

```
exec Backup_tempdb
```

The `sp_help` command displays your SQL Server stored procedures. The exec command runs your newly created SQL Server stored procedures.

WINDOWS NT SERVER 4.0 COMMAND PROCEDURES CREATION

Create two Windows NT Server 4.0 command procedures that are executed by each site server. The first Windows NT Server 4.0 command procedure stops all SMS services on the site server. The second does the following:

1. Delete old Windows NT Server 4.0 registry backup files from the Windows NT Server 4.0 registry backup directory. This task is performed because the REGBACK utility cannot overwrite existing backup files.
2. Back up the Windows NT Server 4.0 registry to the backup directory.
3. Copy the entire SMS directory file structure to the backup server.
4. Restart all the stopped SMS services on the site server.

Both of these Windows NT Server 4.0 command procedures are called from the SQL Server Scheduler and run in the context of the SQL Server Windows NT Server 4.0 service account. Also, Both Windows NT Server 4.0 command procedures must be stored on each site server in a well-known directory. For instance, you can place these procedures in the Windows NT Server 4.0 directory replication system. In this part of the chapter, these two Windows NT Server 4.0 command procedures are named `Smsp1.cmd` and `Smsp2.cmd`. They are stored in the Windows NT Server 4.0 Directory Replication system in the Winnt\System32\Repl \Import\Scripts directory and replicated to each site server:

FIRST WINDOWS NT SERVER 4.0 COMMAND PROCEDURE • The function of this Windows NT Server 4.0 command procedure is to stop all the SMS services running on the site server. An example is shown in Listing 14.2.

Listing 14.2 *Windows NT Server 4.0 Command Procedure*

```
REM  -----------------------------------------------------------
REM  SMS site server backup script section one.
REM  The site backup is done by the SQL Server Scheduler.
REM  See the SQL Server on each site server.
REM  -----------------------------------------------------------
REM  Stop all SMS site server services.
REM  -----------------------------------------------------------
NET  STOP   SMS_CLIENT_SERVICE
NET  STOP   SMS_EXECUTIVE
NET  STOP   SMS_SITE_COMPONENT_MANAGER
NET  STOP   SMS_SITE_BACKUP
NET  STOP   SMS_SQL_MONITOR
NET  STOP   SMS_LICENSE_SERVER
REM  -----------------------------------------------------------
REM  The SQL Server will now dump the SQL Server databases.
REM  -----------------------------------------------------------
```

SECOND WINDOWS NT SERVER 4.0 COMMAND PROCEDURE • This Windows NT Server 4.0 command procedure is called after the SQL Server databases have been dumped. It is more complicated than the first and is explained next.

The first command deletes any old Windows NT Server 4.0 registry backup files in the Windows NT Server 4.0 registry backup directory. This is because the REGBACK utility cannot overwrite old backup files. Furthermore, the /q option is used with the Windows NT Server 4.0 delete command to make it run in quiet mode. An example is shown in Listing 14.3.

Listing 14.3 *The Second Windows NT Server 4.0 Command Procedure*

```
REM  -----------------------------------------------------------
REM  SMS site server backup script.
REM  This is run after the SQL Server has dumped the databases.
REM  -----------------------------------------------------------
REM  Delete old backed up registry files and back up current.
REM  -----------------------------------------------------------
del      \\%computername%\sms_shrd\reg /q
```

The Windows NT Server 4.0 command procedure variable computer-name is used so that the Windows NT Server 4.0 command procedure can be generic.

The next command performs a fresh Windows NT Server 4.0 registry backup to the Windows NT Server 4.0 registry backup and recovery directory. Note that the SMS share is used rather than a hard-coded physical name, since the name may differ on different servers as shown by the following example:

```
%windir%\system32\repl\import\scripts\regback

\\%computername%\sms_shrd\reg
```

The next command performs a ROBOCOPY backup from the site server to the backup server. After the initial backup is made, subsequent backups only copy deltas to the backup server. This reduces the amount of time required for a regular backup and greatly reduces network traffic. The following ROBOCOPY switches are used to achieve this behavior:

- The /e option copies all subdirectories, including empty ones.
- The /purge option deletes destination files and directories that no longer exist at the source.
- The /r:10 and /w:10 options make sure that the copy times out if something goes wrong.

You should note that the Windows NT Server 4.0 command procedure variable computername is used to ensure that each backup from each site server is placed in a unique directory on the backup server. The following is an example:

```
REM -----------------------------------------------------------

REM Copy all SMS files to the backup

REM server SMSTEST.

REM -----------------------------------------------------------

%windir%\system32\repl\import\scripts\robocopy

\\%computername%\sms_shrd

\\smstest\smsdumps\%computername% /e /purge /r:10 /w:10
```

The next set of commands restarts all the stopped SMS services on the site server. An example is shown in Listing 14.4.

Listing 14.4 *Restarting All the Stopped SMS Services on the Site Server*

```
REM ---------------------------------------------------------
REM Start all SMS site server services.
REM ---------------------------------------------------------
NET START SMS_CLIENT_SERVICE
NET START SMS_EXECUTIVE
NET START SMS_SITE_COMPONENT_MANAGER
NET START SMS_SITE_BACKUP
NET START SMS_SQL_MONITOR
NET START SMS_LICENSE_SERVER
```

REGULAR BACKUP AND RESTORE SCHEDULE

Because the SQL Server Scheduler is used to perform the backup and restore on each site server, ensure that SQL Executive and MSSQLServer services are started using a valid Windows NT Server 4.0 domain service account that is a member of the Windows NT Server 4.0 Domain Admins global group. This is required since the SQL Server Scheduler must copy files from the site server to the backup server. By default, these two SQL Server services are started using the local Windows NT Server 4.0 system account, and this account does not have access rights to the backup server. Make these changes using the Services Control Panel.

On the SQL Enterprise Manager application Tools menu, click Task Scheduling. Open the Task Scheduling window to establish the required schedule, as shown in Figure 14.1.[2]

After you have established the task schedule, return to the New Task window and ensure that Type is set to Transact-SQL (TSQL). An example of this is shown in Figure 14.2. In the Command box, type your automated backup commands.

The Transact-SQL statement xp_cmdshell is used.

---

2. Microsoft Corporation. Copyright © 1998 Microsoft and/or its suppliers, One Microsoft Way, Redmond, Washington, 98052-6399. All rights reserved.

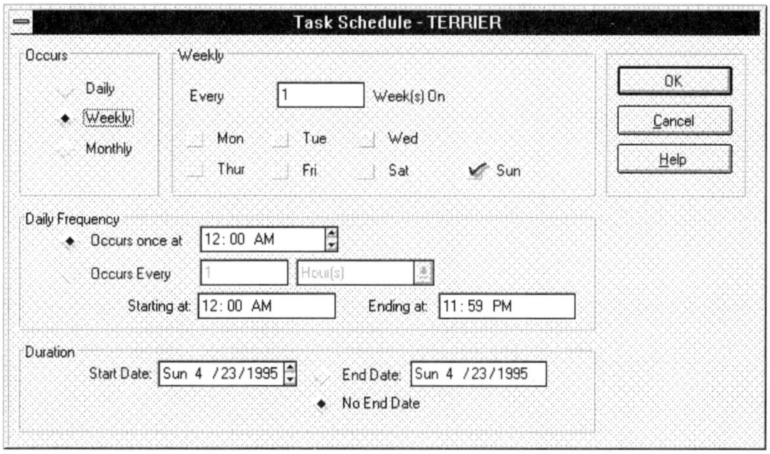

Figure 14.1 *Task Schedule Configuration.*

The Transact-SQL statement `xp_cmdshell` stored procedure allows Windows NT Server 4.0 commands to be called from within the Transact-SQL job. Also notice that the first Windows NT Server 4.0 command procedure is executed and the output from the procedure is placed in a log file located in the root directory of the system drive. This facilitates easier troubleshooting and creates a record of each backup run as shown in the following example:

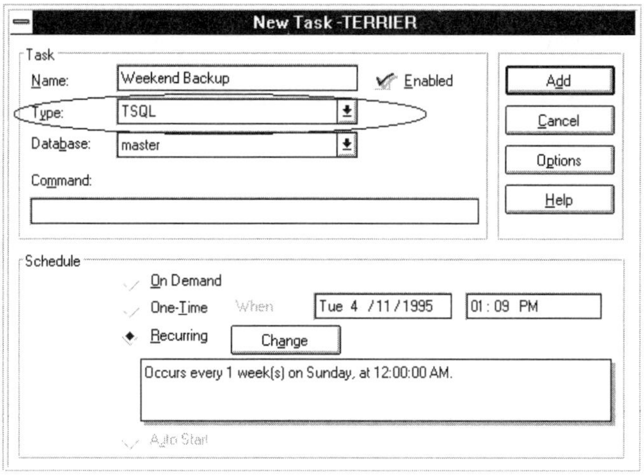

Figure 14.2 *Type of Scheduled Task.*

```
exec xp_cmdshell
"c:\winnt\system32\repl\import\scripts\smsp1.cmd >

c:\smsp1.log"
```

The next set of Transact-SQL statements executes the stored procedures you created earlier to dump the SQL Server databases:

```
exec Backup_master

exec Backup_msdb

exec Backup_SMS

exec Backup_tempdb
```

The second Windows NT Server 4.0 command procedure is now run, and the output from the procedure is placed in a log file located in the root directory of the system drive. This facilitates easier troubleshooting and creates a record of each backup run, as shown below:

```
exec xp_cmdshell
"c:\winnt\system32\repl\import\scripts\smsp2.cmd >

c:\smsp2.log"
```

OVERALL SITE SERVER BACKUP PROCESS

Figure 14.3 shows a flow chart of the major steps performed to back up a site server. Let's take a look.

LOGON SERVER BACKUP AND RESTORE

Unlike the site server backup procedure, you need only to create or restore one directory, the Windows NT Server 4.0 registry backup directory, on each SMS logon server. For convenience, restore this directory under the site server's SMS main directory. For instance, use the following command to restore a directory to store the Windows NT Server 4.0 registry backup:

```
md d:\sms\reg
```

ROBOCOPY AND REGBACK UTILITIES DISTRIBUTION • The simplest way to distribute these utilities is to use the Windows NT Server 4.0 Directory Replication system, which must be established to distribute the SMS logon scripts. For instance, placing the two utilities into the Winnt\System32\Repl

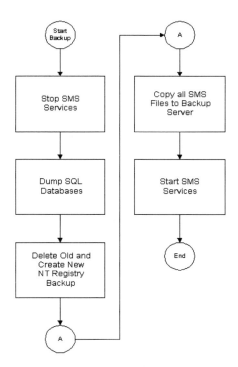

Figure 14.3 *Flow Chart of Site Server Backup Process.*

\Import\Scripts directory on the Windows NT Server 4.0 master Directory Replication server will cause them to be replicated to all Windows NT Server 4.0 Directory replication partners. It is assumed in this part of the chapter that all of the SMS logon servers are configured as Windows NT Server 4.0 Directory Replication partners.

RESTORING A WINDOWS NT SERVER 4.0 COMMAND PROCEDURE • You must create or restore one Windows NT Server 4.0 command procedure to be executed by each logon server. This Windows NT Server 4.0 command procedure will do the following:

1. Stop all SMS services on the logon server.
2. Delete old Windows NT Server 4.0 registry backup files from the Windows NT Server 4.0 registry backup directory. This task is performed because the REGBACK utility cannot overwrite existing backup files.
3. Back up the Windows NT Server 4.0 registry to the backup directory.
4. Copy the entire SMS directory file structure to the backup server.
5. Restart all the stopped SMS services on the logon server.

This Windows NT Server 4.0 command procedure is run by the Windows NT Server 4.0 Schedule service and runs in the context of the Windows NT Server 4.0 Schedule service. You must therefore ensure that the Schedule service is started on each logon server and that it is using a service account that is a member of the Windows NT Server 4.0 Domain Admins global group.

Store the Windows NT Server 4.0 command procedure on each logon server in a well-known directory. For instance, you can place it in the Windows NT Server 4.0 Directory Replication system. In this part of the chapter, this command procedure is named Sms1.cmd. It is stored in the Winnt\ System32\Repl\Import\Scripts directory of the Directory Replication system, and replicated to each logon server:

LOGON SERVER WINDOWS NT SERVER 4.0 COMMAND PROCEDURE • A first function of this Windows NT Server 4.0 command procedure is to stop all SMS services running on the logon server. The following is an example:

```
REM  ------------------------------------------------------------

REM SMS logon server backup script.

REM  ------------------------------------------------------------

REM Stop all SMS logon server services.

REM  ------------------------------------------------------------

NET STOP   SMS_CLIENT_SERVICE
NET STOP   SMS_EXECUTIVE
NET STOP   SMS_SITE_COMPONENT_MANAGER
```

The next command deletes any old Windows NT Server 4.0 registry backup files in the Windows NT Server 4.0 registry backup directory, because the REGBACK utility cannot overwrite old backup files. Furthermore, the /q option is used with the Windows NT Server 4.0 delete command to make it run in quiet mode, as shown by the following commands:

```
REM  ------------------------------------------------------------

REM Delete old backed up registry files and back up current.

REM  ------------------------------------------------------------

del     \\%computername%\sms_shrd\reg /q
```

The next command performs a fresh Windows NT Server 4.0 registry backup to the Windows NT Server 4.0 registry backup directory. The SMS

The Windows NT Server 4.0 command procedure variable computer-name is used so that the Windows NT Server 4.0 command procedure can be generic.

share is used rather than a hard-coded physical name, since the name may differ on different servers, as shown by the following commands:

```
%windir%\system32\repl\import\scripts\regback

\\%computername%\sms_shrd\reg
```

The next command performs a ROBOCOPY backup from the logon server to the backup server. After the initial backup is made, subsequent backups only copy deltas to the backup server. This reduces the amount of time required for a regular backup and greatly reduces network traffic. The following ROBOCOPY switches are used to achieve this behavior:

- The /e option copies all subdirectories, including empty ones.
- The /purge option deletes destination files and directories that no longer exist at the source.
- The /r:10 and /w:10 options make sure the copy times out if something goes wrong.

The following commands perform a ROBOCOPY backup from the logon server to the backup server:

```
REM ----------------------------------------------------------

REM Copy all SMS files to the backup

REM server SMSTEST.

REM ----------------------------------------------------------

%windir%\system32\repl\import\scripts\robocopy
\\%computername%\sms_shrd

\\smstest\smsdumps\%computername% /e /purge /r:10 /w:10
```

These commands restart stopped SMS services on the logon server:

```
REM ------------------------------------------------------------

REM Start all SMS logon server services.

REM ------------------------------------------------------------

NET START SMS_CLIENT_SERVICE
NET START SMS_EXECUTIVE
NET START SMS_SITE_COMPONENT_MANAGER
```

REGULAR BACKUP AND RESTORE OF A LOGON SERVER SCHEDULE • To perform a regular backup and restore on the SMS logon servers, use the Command Scheduler tool from the Windows NT Server 4.0 Resource Kit. This utility enables you to remotely schedule regular backups on each logon server. Schedule the following command on each SMS logon server:

```
c:\winnt\system32\repl\import\scripts\smsl.cmd > c:\smsl>log
```

This command will run the backup script and send the output to a log file in the root directory of the system drive as shown back in Figure 14.2.

TAPE BACKUP AND RESTORE

After all SMS site and logon servers have backed up their files to the backup server, create an automated process to back up the files to a specific tape device. You can use the Windows NT Server 4.0 Backup utility or many other third-party backup utilities to do this automatically and on a regular basis. An organization can create a regular tape backup to be performed after all SMS site and logon servers have completed their backups to the backup server. This process ensures that a complete SMS system backup history is maintained on tape.

LOGGING AND REPORTING

There are three ways to determine whether a backup has occurred as scheduled. First, look at the log files on each SMS system root directory. Each site server has two log files, and each logon server has one. Second, check the SQL Server Scheduler by using the SQL Enterprise Manager application and looking at the Task History window. Finally, check the Windows NT 4.0 Scheduler by using the Command Scheduler utility from the Windows NT Server 4.0 Resource Kit and connecting to each SMS logon server.

Accessibility to SMS for People with Disabilities

This sidebar provides information about the following features, products and services, which make Microsoft Windows, Windows NT 4.0, and SMS more accessible for people with disabilities:

- Hints for customizing Windows or Windows NT 4.0
- Products and services for people with disabilities
- Services for people who are deaf or hard of hearing
- Software documentation online, on audio cassette, floppy disk, or compact disc (CD)
- Third-party utilities to enhance accessibility

Accessibility features of Windows 95, 98, and Windows NT 4.0

Windows 95, 98, and Windows NT 4.0 include several accessibility features that provide users who are movement- or hearing-disabled with better access to their computers. These features enable you to change your display, mouse, and keyboard features, as well as to use sound to help you use Windows most effectively. For instance, if you have trouble using a mouse, you can use the MouseKeys feature that enables you to use the numeric keypad to move the mouse pointer. To find these features, double-click the Accessibility Options icon in Control Panel.

Windows or Windows NT 4.0 customization

There are many ways to customize Windows or Windows NT 4.0 to make your computer more accessible. Beginning with Windows 95, 98, and Windows NT 4.0, accessibility features are built in. These features are useful for individuals with difficulty typing or using a mouse, moderately impaired vision, or who are deaf or hard of hearing.

Many features that make Windows 95, 98, and Windows NT 4.0 more accessible can be added to earlier versions of Windows, Windows NT 4.0, and MS-DOS through Access Packs. You can download these files by modem, or you can order them on disks from Microsoft.

Use Control Panel and other built-in features to adjust the appearance and behavior of Windows or Windows NT 4.0 to suit varying vision and motor abilities. This includes adjusting colors and sizes, sound volume, and mouse and keyboard behavior.

Dvorak keyboard layouts make the most frequently typed characters on a keyboard more accessible if you have difficulty using the standard QWERTY layout. There are three Dvorak layouts: one if you are a two-handed user, one if you type with your left hand only, and one if you type with your right hand only. You do not need to purchase any special equipment to use these features. The specific features available, and whether they are built-in or must be obtained separately, depend on which operating system you are using.

Downloading or ordering files

You can obtain these files by downloading them via modem or ordering them on disks by phone. Specific information about downloading or ordering these files immediately follows this list of files. These files include:

- Access Packs and Dvorak keyboard layouts that provide additional features for versions of Windows or Windows NT 4.0 in which they are not already included
- Application Notes providing more complete documentation on ways to customize Windows and Windows NT 4.0
- Access Packs, Application Notes, and Alternative Keyboard Layouts by modem

If you have a modem, download files from these services:

- CompuServe®: type GO MSL
- GEnie™
- Microsoft Download Service (MSDL)
- Microsoft's Internet servers: ftp.microsoft.com, gopher.microsoft.com, in /softlib/mslfiles
- Microsoft's Web site on the Internet: http://www.microsoft.com
- MSN™: Microsoft Network online service

Assistive technology programs and trained evaluators referrals

For general information and recommendations on how computers can help specific needs, consult a trained evaluator. An assistive technology program in your area will provide referrals to available programs and services.

Using the Internet with SMS

SMS 2.0 allows you to use the Internet to perform a number of management tasks. You can, for example, use the Internet to remotely manage Windows-based Web servers. You can manage SMS sites across the Internet, create reports in HTML format for publication on the Internet (or your private intranet), and analyze frames from the Internet using Network Monitor. Table 14.2 lists the types of tasks you can perform, together with the specific SMS feature you can use to achieve them.

Web Server Management by SMS

SMS 2.0 allows you to manage Windows NT Server 4.0-based Web servers by taking inventory of a server's hardware and software, monitoring a server's activity (for instance, identifying how active a particular Internet-related protocol is on the server), and taking remote control of the server. Through remote control, you can reconfigure software at a server, start or stop a process, tune communications parameters, or adjust swap space—all from a remote location.

SMS can notify you when unsolicited conditions occur on a web server, such as a full disk, security breach, or a predetermined exceeded threshold. SMS uses SNMP within Windows NT 4.0 to do this by translating Windows NT 4.0 events into SNMP traps and instructing a Web server to forward

Table 14.2 *Types of Tasks to Perform with Specific SMS Features*

Task	Feature
Use SMS to manage Internet servers: Use SMS to monitor and remotely configure Windows NT Server 4.0 computers used as Web servers. Microsoft Internet Information Server (IIS) is available with Windows NT Server 3.51 or higher and provides the administrative features required for establishing Internet and intranet sites.	Remote troubleshooting (Help Desk and Diagnostics), Network Monitor, Event to Trap Translator
Transferring SMS data across the Internet: Use the Internet as a WAN connection across which you can collect hardware and software inventory data and distribute software to computers at remote SMS sites.	Collections, Packages and Advertisements
Publishing SMS management information on an intranet: Create reports from the information in the SMS database and distribute the reports so they can be viewed as Web pages on your corporate intranet site or on the Internet.	Crystal Info Reports
Analyzing traffic generated by Internet protocols: Use Network Monitor to analyze some of the main Internet protocols. You can also use the network analysis tools provided with SMS to find the top consumers and the distribution of traffic for each protocol on the network, including traffic from the Internet.	Network Monitor

SNMP trap alerts to one or more Internet addresses, including an SMS primary site server. When SMS receives an SNMP trap, it logs the condition into the database. You can then create a variety of SMS queries to retrieve and analyze this data. For instance, you can determine if user levels on web servers are too high or if response times are falling below an acceptable range.

SMS Transfers of Data Across the Internet

You can use the Internet as a WAN connection across which you can collect software and hardware inventory information, and distribute software to computers at remote SMS sites. For instance, you can use collected inventory information to determine which web servers need to be upgraded to the latest version of the web server software.

Transmission of data between computers on the Internet is potentially exposed to unauthorized access. SMS can use the Point-to-Point Tunneling Protocol (PPTP), with public-key encryption scheme, to secure the SMS data as it is exchanged from one SMS site to another. PPTP is a feature of Windows NT Server 4.0.

SMS Published Reports on the Web

Crystal Info Reports allows you to generate reports from information in an SMS database. After you create a report, you can save the report in HTML format for publication on a Web server. Crystal Reports can also save reports in other formats such as Microsoft Excel and Rich Text Format.

Using Network Monitor to Analyze Frames from the Internet

You can use Network Monitor to analyze many Internet protocols such as IP, HTTP, JAVA, SMTP, R_INTERNETSERVE, PPTP, and MP enhancement to PPP. You can also use the new analysis tools provided with SMS to find the top consumers and the distribution of traffic for each protocol on the network, including traffic from the Internet.

■ Summary

You should come away from this chapter with an in-depth knowledge of the MCSE exam-specific components or functions of how to restore an SQL Server, a site server, logon points, client access points, distribution points, and diagnose and resolve problems involving site-to-site communications. With that in mind, the first part of the chapter provides an invaluable checklist of items you need to rebuild a SQL Server from scratch. Unfortunately, database dumps alone are usually insufficient to reincarnate your system. You need additional pieces of information and files to perform a complete restoration.

The second part of the chapter examined the backup and restore procedures for SMS server sites and Logon servers and presented the following advantages:

- Automatic regular backup of all SMS site server file systems, the Windows NT Server 4.0 registry, and SQL Server and SMS site server databases
- Backups performed while the SMS system is shut down, which enables known state backups to be performed
- Centralized backup, which requires one backup server with one backup tape device
- Logging of all backup processes
- Only file deltas copied across the network, which reduces network load and reduces backup time
- Redundant backups stored on both disk and tape

Finally, the third part of this chapter discussed how SMS allows you to use the Internet to perform a number of management tasks. You can, for instance, use the Internet to remotely manage Windows-based Web servers. You can also analyze frames from the Internet by using Network Monitor, manage SMS sites across the Internet, or create reports in HTML and format them for publication on the Internet or your private intranet.

▲ CHAPTER REVIEW QUESTIONS

▲ True/False

1. *True or False? Another approach to restoring an SQL server is to piece together the NT version info from the Help/About dialog box and execute a SELECT @@version to get SQL Server version information. However, you still need to be able to interpret the output in the form of Microsoft SQL Server 7.00 - 7.0.240 (Intel X86) as SQL Server 7.0 with SP2. Have version numbers documented in your recovery manual.*

2. *True or False? As all files from the SMS file system are backed up, an estimated amount of space must be added, due to growth from SMS package distribution. This is because these packages are also backed up. The maximum size of each SQL Server database device must be used to ensure that an adequate amount of space is available on the backup server as the SMS inventory grows. The backup server will have multiple simultaneous network write operations performed during the backup process, so the backup server must be connected to the network by a high-speed network adapter card and have a sufficient amount of system memory to perform adequately.*

3. *True or False? CHARACTER SET AND SORT ORDER is reported in the ERRORLOG file as IDs you can look up in the SQL Server setup documentation. In other words, you can use SMS Trace to track and view the error log files.*

4. *True or False? You cannot restore the site msdb database from a backup just as you would any user database.*

5. *True or False? An organization may want to make complete known state backups and restoration of each SMS site server.*

6. *True or False? Suppose an organization has three SMS site servers, one of which is acting as the SMS central site server. One of the primary site servers is located on the same LAN as the central site server and the other is con-*

nected to the central site by a high-speed WAN connection. Each SMS primary site server has four SMS logon servers reporting to it. An organization may want to incur the expense and management problems associated with having a tape installation, backup, and restore unit for each SMS primary site server. The organization should take advantage of after-hours network availability to create a process that moves each SMS site server's installation and backup information to one dedicated backup server with a backup tape device. This strategy also offers the advantage of having two current copies of the backup, one on disk and one on tape.

7. *True or False? With SMS's troubleshooting capabilities, you can't restore logon points.*

8. *True or False? With SMS's troubleshooting capabilities, you can restore client access points.*

9. *True or False? With SMS's troubleshooting capabilities, you can't restore distribution points.*

▲ Multiple Choice

1. *Your recovery documentation should:*
   A. Describe the hardware requirements for your SQL Server.
   B. Describe the hardware requirements for your SMS Executive.
   C. Describe the hardware requirements for your Remote chat.
   D. Describe the hardware requirements for your File transfer.
   E. Describe the hardware requirements for your Capture data.

2. *SQL Server 6.5, 7.0, and higher currently each have:*
   A. Five service packs (SPs)
   B. Four (SPs)
   C. Three (SPs)
   D. Two (SPs)
   E. One (SPs)

3. *If your SQL Server is configured to send or receive e-mail messages:*
   A. It can be difficult and time consuming to capture frames on a remote computer and display the capture statistics on the local computer at intervals that you specify.
   B. It can be difficult and time consuming to CaptureDetail.

    C. It can be difficult and time consuming to duplicate the setup on a new server.

    D. It can be difficult and time consuming to display and filter captured frames.

    E. It can be difficult and time consuming to edit and transmit captured frames onto the network to test network resources or reproduce network problems.

4. *Your recovery manual should include all:*

    A. Local copy if present

    B. Runs with UNC name

    C. Remote control

    D. Setup and configuration choices you need to make during SQL Server installation

    E. Change icons

5. *You should create how many directories on each site server to store the SQL Server dump device and the Windows NT Server 4.0 registry backups?*

    A. None

    B. One

    C. Two

    D. Three

    E. Four

▲ Open Ended

1. It's a good idea to prepare an emergency kit in case you ever need to completely rebuild your SQL Server from the ground level. One way is to put all the needed documentation and software in one box and store it in a secure location. What should it contain?

2. What are the steps to back up and restore site servers?

▲ PART 1: OVERVIEW

▲ Chapter 1: What Is Systems Management Server?

True/False

1. True

2. False

3. True

4. False

5. False

6. True

7. True

8. True

Multiple Choice

1. B

2. D

3. E

4. B

5. A

6. C

▲ Chapter 2: Using SMS to Monitor an Enterprise

True/False

1. False

2. False

3. True

4. False

5. True

6. False

7. False

8. False

Multiple Choice

1. C

2. D

3. E

4. E

5. C

6. A

▲ PART 2: SITE PLANNING

▲ Chapter 3: SMS Site Design

True/False

1. False

2. True

3. False

4. False

5. True

6. True

7. False

8. True

Multiple Choice

1. E

2. B and/or E

3. C and/or E

4. B and/or E

5. B

6. B

7. B

▲ Chapter 4: SMS Site Hierarchy

True/False

1. False

2. True

3. False

4. True

5. True

6. True

7. True

8. False

9. False

Multiple Choice

1. A

2. D

3. D

4. A

5. C

6. C

7. E

8. B

9. E

▲ Chapter 5: SMS Security Strategy Plan

True/False

1. True

2. False

3. False

4. False

5. True

6. False

7. True

8. False

Multiple Choice

1. D

2. A, C, D

3. A, C, D

4. A

5. C

6. D

7. C

▲ Chapter 6: Interoperability and Upgrade Plan

True/False

1. False

2. True

3. False

4. True

5. True

6. True

7. False

Multiple Choice

1. A

2. B

3. A and/or E

4. A

5. C and/or E

6. C

▲ PART 3: INSTALLING AND CONFIGURING SMS SERVER

▲ Chapter 7: Establishing a Primary SMS Site

True/False

1. True

2. False

3. False

4. False

5. True

6. False

7. True

8. False

9. False

10. True

11. False

12. True

13. False

14. True

15. False

16. True

17. True

18. False

19. True

20. True

Multiple Choice

1. A and/or E

2. D

3. D

▲ Chapter 8: Configuring, Modifying, and Navigating an SMS Site

True/False

1. True

2. True

3. True

4. False

5. True

6. True

Multiple Choice

1. A

2. A

3. E

4. D

5. A

6. C

▲ PART 4: CONFIGURING AND MANAGING RESOURCES

▲ Chapter 9: Configuring, Auditing, and Controlling Network Clients with SMS

True/False

1. True

2. True

3. True

4. False

5. True

6. False

7. False

8. False

9. True

10. False

11. True

12. True

13. False

14. True

Multiple Choice

1. A

2. E

3. C

4. C

▲ Chapter 10: Managing the SMS System Model

True/False

1. False

2. False

3. True

4. True

5. True

6. False

7. True

8. False

9. True

10. False

Multiple Choice

1. B

2. C

3. D

4. B

▲ Part 5: Interoperability of an SMS Network

▲ Chapter 11: SMS Network Installation and Configuration

True/False

1. False

2. False

3. False

4. False

5. True

6. True

7. True

8. True

Multiple Choice

1. C

2. B

3. A or E

4. E

▲ Part 6: Monitoring and Optimization

▲ Chapter 12: Monitoring SMS

True/False

1. False

2. False

3. True

4. True

5. True

6. True

7. True

8. True

9. True

Multiple Choice

10. D

11. E

12. B

13. D

14. A

15. A

16. C

17. D

18. C

▲ PART 7: TROUBLESHOOTING

▲ Chapter 13: Diagnosing and Resolving SMS Problems

True/False

1. True

2. True

3. False

4. True

5. False

6. False

7. True

8. False

9. True

10. True

11. True

12. True

13. True

14. True

15. True

16. True

17. True

18. True

19. True

Multiple Choice

1. E

2. A

3. B

4. C

▲ Chapter 14: Restoring SMS Sites

True/False

1. True

2. True

3. True

4. False

5. True

6. False

7. False

8. True

9. False

Multiple Choice

1. A

2. B

3. C

4. D

5. C

Systems Management Server (SMS) has a unique set of terms to describe the roles of computers in the system and how they are structured within the management architecture. The following are some basic terms that are important to understand and that describe the roles played by computers in the SMS system.

Advertisements: The advertisement node is used to create or modify advertisements, which are simply the processes that tie collections, packages, and programs together assigning them to a particular schedule.

Client: The client is the computer from which a user tries to connect to a remote resource. This can be an MS Network Client for MS-DOS, a LAN Manager client, or a computer running Windows 3.1, Windows for Workgroups 3.11, Windows 95 and 98, or Windows NT 4.0 Workstation.

Collections: This node allows the creation and modification of collections. A collection is an arbitrary grouping of resources, such as machines and users, that is used to target software distribution and other tasks. The collection node can also be used to drive operations on resources in that collection, such as generating inventory information on a resource or diagnosing resource problems.

Create a Direct Membership Rule wizard: A wizard to help in the creation of collections.

Create a Package from a Definition wizard: A process that helps in the building of software packages to be distributed.

Delete Package/Program/Collection wizards: Three distinct wizards that not only delete critical software distribution processes, but also explain the ramifications deleting them has on specific users before completing the operation.

Distribution Server: This server is used as a distribution point when sending packages for clients to install or run. For Run Command on Workstation packages, the package is stored on the distribution server and made available to target clients. For Share Application on Server packages, the package is stored and shared on distribution servers. Clients connect to and run the network application from the distribution server. The system administrator has to send only one copy of the software (package) to each group of computers connected to a distribution server, thus reducing network traffic. A distribution server can be a Windows NT Server 4.0, a NetWare Server, a LAN Server, or a LAN Manager Server.

Domain: An SMS domain is a set of servers and client computers that have been grouped together. A domain is primarily used to organize servers and clients into manageable groups and provide logon validation, inventory collection, report generation, and package distribution. Within any one site there is always at least one domain, although each site can have multiple domains to meet your management requirements. Valid domains are Windows NT 4.0, NetWare, LAN Manager, and LAN Server.

Helper Server: To help ease the load on the site server, you can move some of the SMS components from the site server to a logon server running Windows NT Server 4.0. When you move these components to a logon server, it becomes a helper server, and continues to function as a logon server.

Inventory agent: Performs hardware inventory and moves data to the `Logon.srv\Inventry.box` directory on the logon server. Look for *.raw files for MS-DOS, Windows 3.x, Windows 95 and 98, and Windows NT 4.0 clients, and look for *.mif files for OS/2 and Macintosh clients.

Inventory Dataloader: Processes files in the directory `Site.srv\Dataload .box\Deltamif.col`, placing failed data in the `Site.srv\Data-load.box\ Deltamif\Badmifs` directory, forwarding it to a parent site, or updating the database.

Inventory Processor: Compares new and old inventory files from the `Site.srv\Inventry.box\History` directory and creates a difference file in the `Site.srv\Dataload.box\Deltamif.col` directory.

Logon (Instruction) Server: In SMS, a logon server is not necessarily the same as a domain controller. A logon server holds a copy of the client support files and information necessary for the client to obtain package instructions. It also provides a location for the client to deposit inventory information.

Logon Server: Logon servers support configuration, inventory collection, package installation, and network applications for the client computers in its domain. Any supported network server can act as a logon server. For example, a Novell NetWare server can act as a logon server for its existing client computers. Within a small SMS site, the site server will also likely function as the logon server, the distribution server, and the SQL Server.

Maintenance Manager: Moves inventory files to the `Site.srv\Inventory .box` directory on the site server.

Manage Distribution Points wizard: A wizard that allows the defining of staging points for software distribution.

Packages: This node allows the creation and modification of packages and also programs that are subcomponents of packages. A package defines the software to be distributed to a particular collection, including the location of the source files and the servers that will be the intermediary distribution points. A package is made up of one or more programs that define the command line the package uses to install the software on the target system.

Primary Site: A site that has a Microsoft SQL Server database is called a primary site. Primary sites create and own the database for all the computers in that site and in any sites below it in the hierarchy. A primary site can be managed by a local administrator. The primary site located at the top of the hierarchy is called the central site. An unlimited number of subsites can exist below a primary site.

Primary Site Server: A primary site has its own Microsoft SQL Server database in which to store the system, package, inventory, and status information for the primary site and the sites beneath it in the hierarchy. It also has administrative tools to directly manage all sites in the site hierarchy.

Queries: This node provides access to precanned queries as well as allows the creation of new queries. A query is a question that is asked of the inventory and is often used to create a collection. A typical query would check to find which machines can be upgraded to a new version of an operating system based on an inventory of their memory and disk space.

Reports: From this node in the interface, administrators can generate reports on any collected data.

Resource: A resource is something like a printer, fax machine, CD-ROM drive, or a directory on a remote computer to which a user attempts to connect. A resource may also be called a *share* because it can be shared out for clients to connect to.

Secondary Site: A site without a SQL Server database is called a secondary site. Secondary sites report information to the primary site directly above it in the hierarchy. Secondary sites do not install the SMS Administrator utility. Instead, a secondary site must be created, configured, and administered through one of the primary sites above it in the hierarchy. A secondary site cannot have sites beneath it.

Secondary Site Server: A secondary site does not have a SQL Server database to store its system, package, inventory, and status information. Instead, it forwards inventory and status information to its primary site for processing and storage. It also does not have administrative tools, since a secondary site must be administered through one of its parent sites.

Security Rights: This node allows the assignment of granular security rights. These can be specified on a per user, per target, and per operation basis.

Server or Host: The server or host is the computer that has the resource to which the user tries to connect. Before a computer can function as a server for clients to connect to, that computer must have a server component or service. Computers running Windows NT 4.0 Workstation or Windows NT Server 4.0 have the server service installed by default, but if you have a computer running Windows 95 and 98, you must manually add File and Printer Sharing for Microsoft Networks service in Control Panel Network.

Site: A site is a group of computers on the network. It includes a site server and at least one domain. Sites provide structure in the inventory database by matching the organization or the physical locations of all the LANs to their own SMS site.

Site Hierarchy: This node allows the administrator to see and manage all the sites in SMS hierarchy. This is a key area of functionality.

Site Reporter: Creates a minijob for the Scheduler if inventory files need to be forwarded to a parent site.

Site Server: Each site has at least one site server. A site server is a computer running Windows NT Server 4.0 that contains the SMS components needed to monitor and manage the site, its domains, and its computers. The site server also serves as a collection point for instructions and for inventory information.

SMS Database Connection wizard: A process that allows a quick connection to a different SMS hierarchy in a large environment.

Software Distribution wizard: A process that steps through all the functions required to define a package, create a program, target a collection through an advertisement and distribute software to users or machines.

SQL Server: Each primary site must have a SQL Server for Windows NT 4.0 installed. SMS uses Microsoft SQL Server to store the site database. SQL Server can be installed on the site server or on a separate server. While each site must have its own database, different sites can share the same SQL Server. However, it is more efficient for SQL Server to be on the same LAN as the sites using its databases.

System Status: This node provides detailed information on the status of SMS itself, including the status of system processes and software distribution advertisements. SMS 2.0 contains a sophisticated status engine to provide detailed information.

Windows NT Server 4.0 domain: With a Windows NT Server 4.0 domain, you can maintain machine and user accounts in a centralized location for easier administration and configuration. User and password information is maintained on the domain controller of the Windows NT Server 4.0 domain.

Workgroup: With workgroup networking, users and resources that are shared out are unique to that specific computer and are not common to other computers. The administrator of a particular computer must maintain users, shares, and permissions, instead of having a centralized location where users and resources are kept and maintained (such as a Windows NT Server 4.0 domain). Clients in this environment typically run Windows for Workgroups 3.11, Windows 95 and 98, or Windows NT 4.0 Workstation. The server typically runs Windows NT Server 4.0.

Y2K Products: This contains a list of software applications to be monitored for Year 2000 compliance and their compliance levels. Update or change this information by loading a new Year 2000 or Euro-compliance database.

INDEX